THE SCATHING EXPOSÉ OF HOW SOME THINGS
HAVE NEVER CHANGED IN AN ISOLATED COUNTY
—FROM 1850 U.S. HOMICIDE CAPITAL TO GOVERN-
MENT MACHINE 150 YEARS LATER:
Muckrakers, Gadflies, Whistleblowers, Blowhards, Grand-
standers, Drug Lords, Kingpins, Bosses, Fiefdoms, Cabals,
Cartels, and Trolls

What Others are Saying:

"*A must-read, firsthand account of trouble in paradise from a former mayor who spent years in the political trenches. Peterson offers a much-needed primer for keeping local government open and accountable. Buy two copies. One for you and one for your local representative.*"

–Dave Congalton, KVEC Radio Host

"*I didn't think anyone still had integrity, self-worth, and honesty. Debbie Peterson is the poster person for all of these.*"

–Gwinn & Jim McCandlish, retired teachers

"*Debbie Peterson is civic-minded and has pledged countless volunteer hours to work on city councils and other community service orgs. She is committed to positive change.*"

–Sharon Biddle, Publisher, The Real Estate Book

"*The Honorable Debbie Peterson's unwavering work fighting political corruption made her the best choice for voters.*"

–Stew Jenkins, Treasurer, Council of Elected Democrats, Past Harbor Commissioner, Attorney San Luis Obispo

"*Debbie's business was one of the outstanding success stories of the Glasgow University entrepreneurship program. She won national recognition and was sought after as a coach to start-up companies and as a speaker at conferences and business schools. She is a Star!*"

–Professor David Weir Former Dean of The Scottish Business School

"*Bringing the message of being a good citizen to more people is a noble task, indeed.*"

Valerie Cassity, Owner/Editor, Costa Creative Services

The HAPPIEST CORRUPTION

The HAPPIEST CORRUPTION

Sleaze, Lies, & Suicide in a California Beach Town

Debbie Peterson

For more information or to contact the author,
visit www.DebbiePeterson.com

Cover design: Carol Pearl

paperback ISBN: 979-8-9862195-0-9
hardcover ISBN: 979-8-9862195-1-6
ebook ISBN: 979-8-9862195-2-3

Printed in the United States of America

FREE TO READERS: As a thank you for reading this book, Debbie Peterson is granting you access to a seven-minute video, Profile of a Government Criminal, which will help readers understand the corrupt nature of government criminals. Please go to https://DebbiePeterson.com/books/#CriminalProfile to view or download it.

AUTHOR'S NOTE

As a citizen and public official, my training and nature have led me to be positive and proactive. I believe in the spirited discussion of ideas and policies.

My purpose for writing about my experiences in government, politics and public affairs is to turn on the lights—and keep them on— for the oblivious and the frightened by exposing the activities that may harm them. These activities often divert resources away from legitimate public works and services to the illegitimate gain of a few who have learned to channel public resources for their own benefit.

The facts described in my book are based on my own experience in public service and advocacy, my research in government and media sources, and the experiences that were related to me by others.

The opinions on matters of public interest and concern are my own.

DebbiePeterson.com
Info@DebbiePeterson.com

CONTENTS

FOREWORD

When the news broke that the FBI had charged a local cannabis mogul and deceased supervisor with bribery, the *LA Times* described the breaking story as, "a sordid account of how a wheeler and dealer in the state's nascent ill-regulated marijuana industry corrupted one of San Luis Obispo County's most powerful politicians, who was apparently brazen enough to write in a text message to his illicit benefactor that he deserved 'one giant French kiss wrapped in money.'" Local talk show host Dave Congalton had more to say:

> Ten years ago, we were the happiest town in the planet. In 2021, San Luis Obispo is now known as the town where it took 25 years to bring a guy to trial for the murder of a Cal Poly student. And now we're known as the county where a supervisor can be bought for $32,000.
>
> Even though Adam Hill is gone, and even though he is gone under tragic circumstances, he doesn't get a pass. Do you honestly believe, for example, that just this $32,000 is the only thing going on in this county? Do you believe it's the only time that Adam Hill ever did anything unethical?
>
> If you were a mayor or a city councilmember in Pismo Beach, Grover Beach, or San Luis Obispo, your hands are bloodied by all of this. You protected Adam Hill, you excused Adam Hill; you attacked anyone who dared criticize Adam Hill.

If you want an example of that, look what happened to the honorable Debbie Peterson when she raised allegations about cannabis money and dirty elected officials. [Mayor] Jeff Lee got all on her case and [Mayor Pro Tem] Mariam Shah said, "Oh I've never seen anything like this. I don't know what you're talking about." Of course, that's before the FBI showed up at Jeff Lee's house one morning. He's still not talking about that.

I've been trying to tell you that Adam Hill was a complicated guy, but he was also dishonest. He was not a very good person. I made a list of other people who tried to tell you the same thing. They've been ostracized because they dared to be critical of Supervisor Hill. They dared to hold him to a higher standard. And we told you so.

It's in the *Tribune* article. They asked Supervisor Dawn Ortiz Legg, "What do you think about the fact that your predecessor, your former boss, was soliciting bribes?" She spoke, "I have no comment." I'm sorry, Supervisor Ortiz Legg, really? You have no comment, you're not going to take this opportunity to condemn Adam Hill and say, 'you know what, we have our work cut out for us, we have to regain the faith of the voters because now we know a supervisor can be bought for $32,000?' Something, anything, supervisor, could have been said but instead we got a "no comment."

I suspect that sound you hear right now is the sound of several people picking up the phone and making sure they've got a really good attorney.

I don't think we should move on from this. I think we need to stop and examine who we are as a county right now. This investigation is a reminder of how important the FBI is. I want the FBI to keep digging and tell us more because sadly, I think there is more to tell.

920KVEC *The Dave Congalton Show* July 29, 2021

INTRODUCTION

This is true crime history written by an insider. I am the insider. This is my account of politicians, government officials, developers, contractors, and cannabis kings who operate a criminal machine that streams through every part of my small county, bankrolled by public funds, campaign donations, and pallet loads of cash generated by the most valuable crop in the nation.

My journey as a businesswoman from planning commission chair to city council to mayor in the friendly little beach town that I called "Kansas at the Beach" should be a happy memoire. Instead, it evolved into a sinister citizens-turned-spy suspense epic of bribery, extortion, dark money, and death.

Like my neighbors, for years I couldn't believe that the beaches, verdant crops, and wine-grape clad hills that Oprah called the 'happiest city in America' and locals call 'paradise' could be riddled with corruption. But as the mayor I heard whispered stories, sat around board room tables behind closed doors, and had access to people and facts that others do not.

When I ran for county supervisor for my district, I was able to connect the dots between dysfunctional boards, sexual harassment, whistleblowers, and millions of dollars missing from accounts. As the press and the public bought into and repeated the lies of the conmen, the cabal co-opted whole city councils, county departments, and businesses with threats and promises; both of which were delivered on.

A widely diverse group of sincere citizens from all walks of life previously unknown to one another with little in common except determination to bring integrity to their local government brought me

1

facts and figures corroborating an epidemic of crime as far reaching as Central America, Korea, Vietnam, and Russia. The informants coalesced to fight for honest governance, putting their jobs, their reputations, their businesses, and their families at risk of reprisal because they simply couldn't let this happen to their community. Together we uncovered the covert patterns and practices of the corrupt machine.

National statistics and press releases from the District Attorney and FBI matched the accounts I heard from the brave citizens—number one in the state and number two in the nation in real estate loan fraud in 2012, and in 2020 a spike in synthetic opioid deaths 55% above the state level according to the California Department of Public Health. The homicide capital of the country in 1850.

The book flows much the same as Dickens's *A Christmas Carol* if you substitute the word "corruption" for "Christmas." In the Dickens tale, three spirits reveal painful Corruptions Past, Corruptions Present, and Corruptions Yet to Come, all affecting the wellbeing of innocent and kindly townsfolk. In my county I became the unwelcome angel of truth; unwrapping the consequences of stealing from its people past, present, and future. The corruptions I discovered weave their way through all four parts of my story.

Part One, the first three chapters, is the history of how I came to love and respect the courageous whistleblowers, good citizens, and authorities who stood up to the callous Scrooge-on-steroids (or in our case, cocaine) cabal of good ol' boys, corrupt politicians, and drug dealers. It is the Corruption Present.

Part Two probes the win-lose debaucheries of the Corruption Present with revelations about three ghost districts, and a final chapter warning of buried secrets that may yet erupt.

Part Three is the tale of Corruptions Past. It is the past still alive with voter fraud (ghost voters), narcotics, organized crime, gambling, and zoning scams in three communities that are quite different from one another and a century apart, but all eerily alike, ruled by powerful criminal machines.

The city crime accounts are both heart-stopping and heart-warming. They gave me the insight I needed to understand how to clean up my community and restore honest government to the people. These histories illustrate how diversity of opinions, personalities, cultures, ethnicities, and gender, when unified, can lead to enlightenment. The spirit of integrity brought together women, minorities, businesspeople, ministers from every pulpit, political parties, state and federal justice systems, elected officials, and the courts to oust the bandits who were stealing from them.

The stories are hauntingly relevant today as we face off against crooked institutions and seek our paths as citizens in a government that is for the people, by the people, and of the people.

Part Four shines a light that portends the shadow of Corruptions Yet to Come if we fail to create road maps for a public well-served. Like Tiny Tim, the public can't thrive unless something changes. That something is the way that we the people manage our government.

Historical context creates a bridge to new ways of thinking about current political structures and culture. It delves into the three United Estates needed to support an ever larger and more complex political landscape. Our first three estates—the Legislative, Administrative, and Judicial Estates—are easily trampled in local government, and our fourth estate—the press and media—cannot stand alone as the watchdog of the people.

We need additional United Estates and a reformation of our roles and the roles of those who serve us, from our agency attorneys to our city managers. What are our roles? How do we restructure and reorganize our thinking and our institutions to better serve us?

It starts and ends with The People. We the people fulfill the promise of democracy when we acknowledge ourselves and our public servants as deliverers of the solemn task of governing **for** the people.

After reading this book:

+ You will be captivated by these true crime stories as you journey alongside determined citizens who work out how local government corruption happens, how to spot it, and how to fix it.

+ You will be inspired by the courage and tenacity of ordinary people who saved their communities and established good government.

+ You will know a government con when you see one and you will know why you know it.

+ You will have a historical perspective of how citizen heroes got things done and where you fit in to change our political present and future.

+ You will know how to beat city hall at its worst and how to be city hall at its best.

MOST IMPORTANTLY OF ALL, YOU WILL BE EQUIPPED TO MAKE SURE YOUR TOWN DOESN'T BECOME THE NEXT HAPPIEST CORRUPTION IN AMERICA.

"…as the physicians say of consumption, in the beginning of the illness it is easy to cure and difficult to recognize, but when it has not been recognized and treated in the beginning, it becomes easy to recognize and difficult to cure. So it happens in affairs of state, because when one recognizes from afar the evils that arise in a state (which is not given but to one who is prudent), they are soon healed; but when they are left to grow because they were not recognized, to the point that everyone recognizes them, there is no longer any remedy." Machiavelli

PART 1

CAN
IT
BE
TRUE?

'The Story Must be Told'
–Washington Post

CHAPTER 1 SUPERVISOR HILL IS DEAD

"**N**o one wants to read a true crime story unless someone dies," the talk show host counseled over a quick pre-broadcast lunch at a sidewalk table at the busy Shell Beach cafe.

Returning to my office, pausing for a moment in the parking lot to take in the warm sunshine, the sound of waves, the screech of a seagull, and the daily train whistle, I wondered, "Did County Supervisor Adam Hill really die, or did the FBI spirit him off to a new life somewhere? Or did someone, considering him now a liability, kill him?" In 2020 the local newspaper reported that County Supervisor Hill, 54, had died; the circumstances of his death being unclear.

A year later, the *LA Times* article "One Giant French Kiss Wrapped in Money" quoted court filings in which an unidentified official said, "Adam Hill… died of an overdose of cocaine and antidepressants," and went on to say, "Authorities ruled Hill's death a suicide. The supervisor had previously said he attempted suicide after federal agents served a search warrant at his government office in March, 2020." The FBI also raided Hill's Shell Beach home. The FBI had already raided Mayor Lee's home.

Can we trust the official ruling of suicide? This question has swirled through my head ever since. The incongruencies give me pause. Women, not men, are more likely to make unsuccessful suicide attempts with pills. Men usually do not use pills to commit suicide, and usually succeed when they attempt suicide. And what about the gun shot reported by neighbors in his eclectic artsy beach neighborhood when Hill failed in his first "suicide attempt" three months earlier? What about witness reports of a white van parked outside his rented cottage and the claim by an informant that he was there when Adam died?

It would have been so easy to lace Hill's cocaine with something more lethal. The supervisor was at the mercy of drug dealers—he had to feed his habit. It doesn't make sense that the FBI would have left their witness so exposed in a residential neighborhood. Homicide or witness protection seem more likely than suicide.

Nevertheless, Hill's vitriol has ended. I am relieved to be free of the war he waged against anyone who stood in the way of his illegal exploits; free of the character assassination by him and his cronies that convinced fellow democrats and councilmembers to shun me; free of some of the threat of personal or family retribution that has dogged me for nine years. Hill's reign caused irreparable damage in hundreds of other lives, and it will be years before the worst of the damage makes its way through the legal system, if it ever does.

But poor Adam was just a symptom of bigger, more insidious problems in San Luis Obispo (SLO) County.

The scenic and delightfully friendly SLO County is located on the famous California Highway One halfway between Los Angeles and San Francisco, and twice as far from the state Capitol in Sacramento. Two to three hundred miles of tedious stretches of uninhabited Highway 101 inland and hairpin turns and cliffs to the west rule out commuting to the big cities, but spell-bound tourists flock to the highways by the thousands. To the north, the county begins at the foot of the legendary Big Sur peninsula with its dangerous and beautifully rugged coastline, often blocked in recent years by massive rockslides.

Coastal mountain ranges form the eastern and western boundaries of the county, and detach the North County from the South County. The powerful Pacific surf and windswept beaches, backed by thick willows and marshes or towering sand dunes, for centuries prevented men and ships from coming ashore. Seven small cities are dotted along the highways on the coast and inland. The rest of the 3,300 square miles

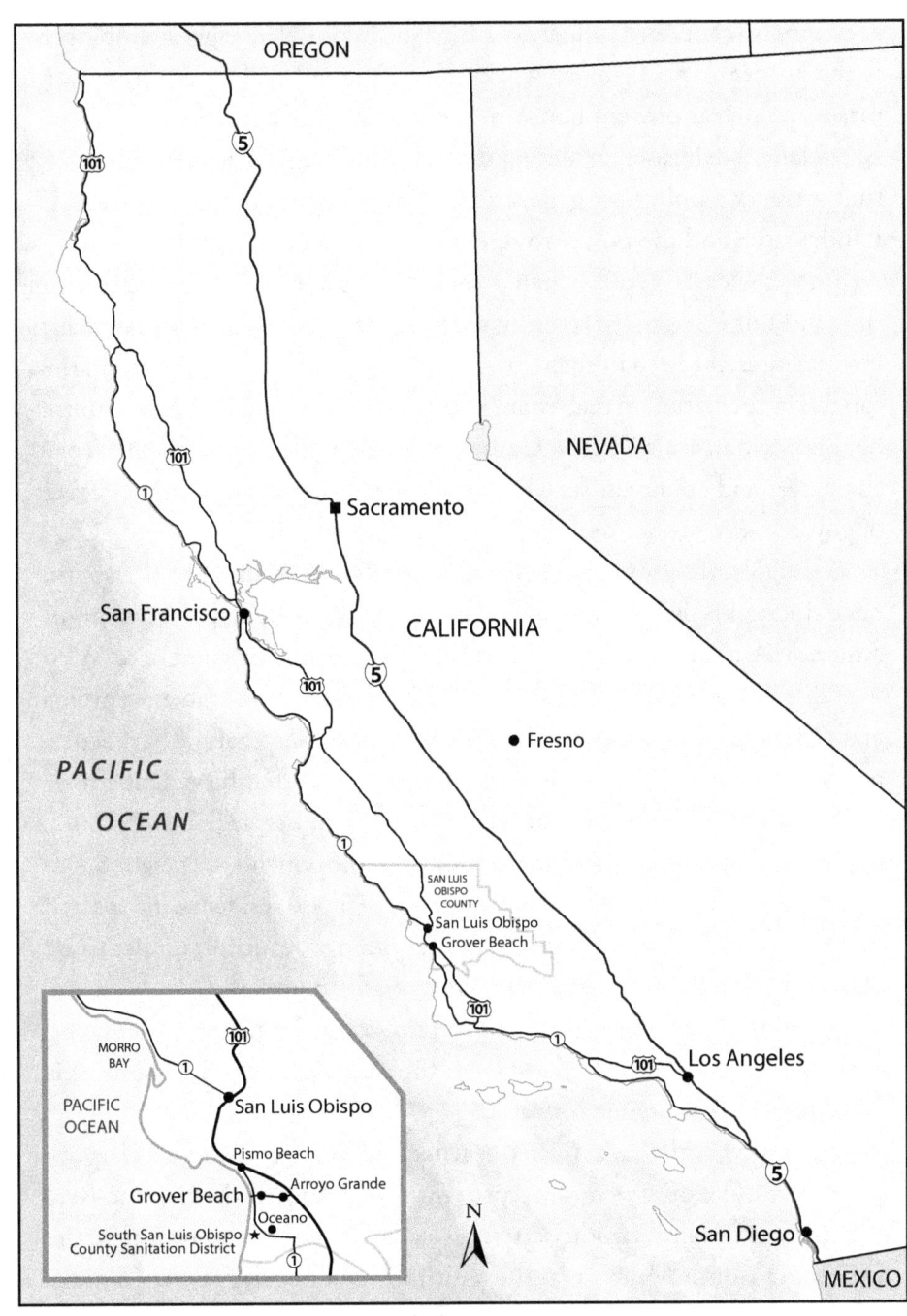

is mostly uninhabited, dedicated to agriculture and ranching.

There is scant hard industry or high-tech jobs. The biggest employer is the government. Primary workplaces include Cal Poly University, a prison, a nuclear power plant, vineyards, and other agricultural or tourism-related businesses, including the now quasi-legal marijuana industry that attracts a bold new generation of bootleggers and carpetbaggers. Land, water, and the power to operate them are at a premium.

Since the early 1900s, when a developer subdivided and sold lots in the sand dunes, to more recently when citizens, enticed by double digit interest rates, invested in sham loan schemes, the county has ranked in the top ten in the nation in real estate fraud. Thus, isolation and opportunity have made San Luis Obispo County an attractive hideout for unsavory characters and opportunists who know how to rip people off under cover of government service or showy civic engagement.

Oprah Winfrey, our famous neighbor a hundred miles to the south, once dubbed San Luis Obispo, the county seat, the happiest town in America. And indeed, the quality of life is exceptionally good here. Who wouldn't like being neighbors with humpback whales, adorable sea otters, giant elephant seals, and a climate that invites year-round barbecues, bonfires on the beach, and wine tasting in a place with little violent crime? Such distractions invite bookkeepers to quietly embezzle family fortunes, city councilmembers to siphon tax money to proponents, or neighbors to divert ground water. The kind and generous 275,000 residents, intoxicated by their good fortune to live in this easy-going, beautiful, undisturbed place, practically leave the bank vaults open for plunder.

When the cabal plots to co-opt water, power, land, government, and cannabis, and no one is looking from the outside, or on the inside, it is not long before everyone is fleeced.

It goes way back. Local retired teacher and history writer Jim Gregory recounts SLO County's notoriety; of murders along the El Camino Real (Highway 101) and famous criminals such as The James brothers, the Daltons, Joaquin Murieta, and even the Mafia bootlegger Al Capone. The county attracted these villains even as vigilante teams conducted frontier executions.

SLO County criminals today also make national news: a supervisor and mayor involved in bribery and sexual harassment, the cannabis king making those bribes, and a 25-year mystery surrounding the disappearance of Kristen Smart, a Cal Poly first-year student. *Your Own Backyard* documenting the Smart tragedy, had more than seven million downloads by April 2021, reaching number one in Apple's top 100 podcasts.

Gregory recounts that SLO County had the nation's highest homicide rate in the 1850s. "To put it in perspective, New Orleans, the deadliest city in America, had a rate of forty-three murders per 100,000 in 2016. In 1850, the only California County more murderous than New Orleans today was SLO county—four times more murderous—the equivalent of 176 murders per 100,000." Then, as now, it was the more trusting of the County's altruistic citizens who fell prey. The rest of the populace behaved much as they do now. Most were frightened, some indignant, some vastly irritated, and some amused. The population was small, but not as small as counted by the 1850 census that did not take place until 1851. Census counters found just 358 people—on the periphery—because no census-taker was willing to venture deep into the County to make a full count.

Gregory tells of notorious Joaquin Murieta, whose mother lived in San Luis Obispo. Despite his reputation as a horse thief at best, and the killer of dozens of mostly innocent citizens at worst, the townspeople of San Luis Obispo heartily welcomed Murieta with a parade and celebrations in local bars. Gregory surmises that townsfolk may have been afraid not to entertain him.

As San Luis Obispo was embracing Murieta, just over the Cuesta Grade in the North County, a posse was fixing to go after him, and eventually succeeded, according to most accounts. North County residents take a hard-nosed approach to malfeasance, while the cities south or west of the Cuesta Grade, and the mainstream local press, are more likely to shelter and fete the corrupt. That is, until July 2021, when the FBI announced bribery involving a supervisor in an "ongoing" investigation, and the District Attorney started pressing charges.

The North County has its share of little old ladies in the grocery store stacking their carts with casserole ingredients for church potlucks…with handguns in their purses. They are licensed to carry because they live in remote areas on acreage where first responders are stretched too thin over the vast county, and rattlesnakes, bears, mountain lions, and even human intruders necessitate autonomy and self-protection.

And I can tell you, they can shoot. If I were a rattlesnake, bear, lion, or thief, I would avoid those women. In 2016, the Sheriff's Posse invited me to attend a North County women-only gun training course. My father hunted, and my college boyfriend taught me to shoot a shotgun. I had a steady hand and impeccable aim but was a handgun amateur. I expected my classmates to be the same.

The other women were suspicious of me, a South County resident, but they put up with my presence by ignoring me. Sidelined, I was left to observe. During target practice, they ate cookies and sipped iced tea at picnic tables in the shade of ancient walnut trees, perfectly at home on the gun range. When their turn to shoot came up, each woman sashayed up to the line with all the nonchalance of the summer's day, knocking out bullseyes with the precision of a sharpshooter, and then sauntered back to the group to resume talk of grandchildren and good recipes, as if perfect aim was just an everyday occurrence.

Even so, no matter how many guns they possess, big or small, hired or otherwise, over the past two hundred years no one, whether vigilante, gun-toting or unarmed, has been able to deter highway robbery in SLO County, from outlaws robbing stagecoaches to public 'servants' stealing from and bullying or cajoling their constituents into submission.

The beautiful Salinas River in San Luis Obispo County flows mostly underground, as does far too much of the business of governance, converging in unseen channels beneath a verdant paradise.

'Beware the Demon'

I met Adam Hill in 2008. Until running for the office of county supervisor he had been a lecturer at Cal Poly, San Luis Obispo. His campaign was managed by a former mayor and councilmember (now fire chief). I was running for a seat on the city council.

One afternoon when walking precincts with Hill's campaign manager, I noticed he seemed rattled, so I asked how he was doing. He told me that he had just come from City Hall, which was in an uproar. His best friend, Mayor Shoals, had sexually harassed three employees. I noted that he did not say that the mayor was accused, he said the mayor had done it.

Over the course of the next few years the stories came out; a little here, a little there...whispered revelations that all three women had lost their jobs—had been told it would be best if they just left town—and one did. I heard that phrase another two times over the years to follow, "It would be best if you just left town," coming from the mayor and his best friend when dispatching with whistleblowers. The standard procedure with whistleblowers was to pay them off with large sums of money, secured by a silence clause, threats of character assassination, and a recommendation that they and their families leave town, and for good measure, the threat of exclusion from future jobs if they did not comply.

I now ask myself why I didn't act when the mayor's best friend told me that the mayor had sexually harassed three female city employees. The answer then and now has not changed. I would have known that it was a personnel matter in the hands of the city manager and that I would not have had access to the information. Furthermore, I was not yet a council person. Even if I had been, unless the women involved had brought it to me or the council or taken legal action, none of us could intervene in personnel matters.

Otherwise, it was a happy time. I had been on the planning commission for four years and the chairperson for two years. It had run smoothly, effectively, respectfully. Barack Obama was on the ballot, and I was proud to be a part of that moment in history when America elected an African American President. The mood was buoyant. The sun was shining on us. We thought racism was on its way out. Both Hill and I were elected.

Hill's campaign manager did very well in his relationship with Adam. He had loved being a volunteer firefighter in Grover Beach and often expressed his wish to someday be a fire chief. Hill lobbied for a new county position—County Emergency Medical Services Division Director—and his campaign manager, a phone systems salesperson with an economics degree, got the job.

I set out to be a representative of my community, finding solutions in a win-win partnership between the government and the public. It had seemed so simple to me—get dedicated people together to problem-solve with input from the public and produce creative, responsive solutions.

Most of all, I wanted to work with fellow councilmembers to best manage the people's business. I was deeply moved by the values expressed and protected in our state and national constitutions.

Pomposity

Katharine Graham, publisher of the *Washington Post*, in a note to reporters Bob Woodward and Carl Bernstein warned against an attitude that also affects newly-elected councilmembers. It follows soon after the elation of winning and the overwhelming realization that the thousands of people who voted for you have trusted you to work on their behalf.

When the Watergate scandal catapulted Woodward and Bernstein to instant journalistic stardom Graham wrote,

> *"You did some stories, and you did fine, that's our job. That's the business we're in, but ... don't start thinking too much of yourselves. Beware the demon pomposity."*

Woodward reflected on this in a 2018 interview with the *Business Insider*, "And, as we know, pomposity affects our business and the media, it affects politics, any institution. People get pompous and they start feeling they really are doing great work. And they blow it. I think it's one of the reasons people distrust the media. They see that kind of self-glow, the smugness, the self-satisfaction."

I was introduced to organizational culture as a communications student. Since then, tuning into organizational culture has become second nature to me. I caught myself adopting this culture of conceit shortly after being sworn in. As you quickly gain insider knowledge, it is easy to grow arrogant because you know more than everyone else and to think that therefore you know better than everyone else. The public is just a nuisance, or listening is a ritual we endure because, in the end, we know best.

John Stossel, long-time co-anchor of ABC's 20-20 called it out in his 2004 book *Give Me A Break*. Stossel quotes Author Thomas Sowell, who tags it the "Conceit of the Anointed." The thinking goes like this: "You are not to be trusted. We know better. The Conceit of the Anointed is so powerful that they insist on maintaining control even when they fail and fail again." Stossel admonishes, "It's not your [the politician's] money at risk. Problems will become your successor's problems. Elitism fosters arrogance and does not immunize against error."

I was fortunate to have friends who kept me honest. They welcomed conversations such as, "Do you really pledge allegiance to the values of our flag, or are we just performing a ritual; a requirement we don't think about? Do you say this stuff because you have to, but you don't really mean it?" I decided to mean it.

Councilmembers sit on numerous government boards, and as I served, I discerned the differences in how corporate, nonprofit, and government boards work. The main difference was that all government board business is subject to Sunshine Laws—all decisions and deliberation between the board majority must occur in public from the dais at publicly-noticed meetings. I was surprised that board members on county committees did not ask questions, did not appear to understand financials, and did not hold staff accountable.

Financials were difficult to understand. Board members did not wish to admit they did not understand (or had not read) staff reports, so did not seek clarification. Budget updates, if any, did not address over or under spending or other anomalies. For special districts, while the county auditor was the ex officio auditor, the auditor's office did not exercise oversight even though the districts use the county as their banker. The county auditors did not reconcile the figures provided by special districts or ensure that reporting was complete.

Outside accountants performing the annual audits were usually retained year after year and provided little feedback on the accounts themselves or on best accounting practices in the agencies.

It was explained to me that the auditors wanted to continue their long-term engagement with multiple government agencies and feared being blacklisted if they rocked the boat; a conflict of interest in itself. The boards relied on staff to tell them what to do in the same way they relied on the advice of the agency attorney. When staff, supplier, and attorney's contracts were never reviewed, and no questions were asked for decades at a time, it created an atmosphere conducive to deceit and sycophantic loyalty to public servants rather than loyalty to the public served.

I reasoned that San Luis Obispo County is a small remote California county and elected representatives do not have the experience, training, or opportunity to know their roles and responsibilities as board members. My assessment of lack of big-city sophistication in our isolated rural county was partly correct. The more sinister reasons are that a trained board is a board with oversight and malintended staff and elected officials do not find it in their best interests to have trained board members or to keep them fully informed. They groom candidates and appointees who are weak—who never show them up—patsies and staff they can manipulate to gain control of the board, and thereby control the day-to-day activities of the agency.

Put My Money Where My Mouth Is

My home, the unpretentious City of Grover Beach on California's legendary Highway One has a population of about 13,200 with a train station across from the beach. It has one of just two entrances to the only drive-on beach in the state with access to the dunes and free parking everywhere. I believed I should put my money where my mouth was by supporting the establishment of a vibrant beachfront business community envisioned by city residents in the 2004 Visioning Meetings in which I had participated. So, in 2011 I moved my real estate office to a unit near the beach and rented a condominium above the office.

One of our first actions as a real estate office in our new space was to recruit a nationally acclaimed local restaurant for the vacant unit next door. I had long advocated for outdoor seating and continued to push the city to make it happen. Now we have a reputation for some of the best restaurants in the county and outdoor seating for many of them.

I encountered Supervisor Hill occasionally at committee meetings where we both served on the same boards. I was impressed when he told me shortly after being elected that he was walking the streets, calling on local businesses, and getting to know the owners. Before long he had control of their campaign contributions. Large firms and developers reported that they dare not donate to Hill's opponents because Hill would harm them. This was not an unfounded fear.

About the time he would have started campaigning to keep his seat on the board of supervisors, Hill started sending late night nastygrams, which he copied liberally to the press, state authorities, and his social media trolls.

Adam Hill Targets Popular Senator

JUNE 17, 2011

Hill sent an email to our state senator, moderate Republican Sam Blakeslee, which was circulated widely in the press, lambasting the senator for "pandering to hate-mongers [sic]" because the Council of Labor and Business (COLAB) participated in one of the senator's fundraisers. Hill, a Democrat, accused COLAB of "hostile, secretive and frequently racist activities." To date, there is no evidence of any such activities, and elected Democrats and Republicans alike attended the organization's annual fundraisers. Hill defended his comments in the local press, conceding he should have been more tactful. Blakeslee, the respected statesman, responded, "I hope this situation will serve as a reminder that elected officials should never unfairly target or mischaracterize community groups for simply stating their differing views."

Blakeslee's professionally-delivered admonition was no surprise to me. I had come to respect him after attending a seminar he held with Bill Ostrander, an advocate for campaign finance reform [See Chapter 14]. Although from different parties, each presented a plan to improve transparency in government. In 2016, Sam Blakeslee had co-authored Proposition 54 with Charles Munger Jr. Californians voted for it by a two to one margin. Local, state, and federal governments have different laws that govern open government. Their bill improved public access to state lawmaking.

The Proposition:

+ Prohibits the California legislature from passing any bill unless it has been in print and published on the internet for at least 72 hours before the vote.

+ Requires the legislature to video record all its proceedings and post them on the internet within 24 hours.

+ Authorizes recording of legislative proceedings.

+ Prohibits the state from charging a fee for use of recordings.

My respect for Blakeslee grew as I noted that he spoke in opposition to our local nuclear power plant, even though that opposed his party's line. Although I hail from the party opposing his, I support nuclear power, so I wanted to understand his stance.

Blakeslee, published in numerous scientific journals, earned a Ph.D. from the University of California, Santa Barbara for his research in seismic scattering, micro-earthquake studies, and fault-zone attenuation. He explained to me that as the Richter Scale earthquake magnitude increases, the intensity of the shaking doesn't go up incrementally, but exponentially. As scientists discover more faults nearby, it becomes clear that the plant, designed in the 1960s, could not withstand the level of earthquake that scientists are predicting will hit this area at some point. I was further intrigued by his ingenuity and integrity when I learned that he had authored the "Dream Initiative" passed by 75% of the county's voters in 2000. The mandate of the initiative is that the lands on which the nuclear power plant stands would, upon decommissioning, never be developed, but be retained in perpetuity as habitat preservation, agriculture, and public use.

Blakeslee, a three-term state assemblyman before his term as senator, modeled leadership that produces good outcomes for those he represents. When leaders' first interest is their constituents' best interest; when they are intelligent, educated, creative, and reach across the aisle, letting conscience lead ahead of party preference, they bring good governance to a community.

Adam Hill Admits To Impersonating Opponent

JANUARY 6, 2012

The local daily newspaper printed a letter to the editor from Sheila Blake, one of Hill's supporters. Purporting to be his opponent in the District Three supervisorial race, Hill left a controversial voicemail for her, saying, "Hi Mrs. Blake, I read your letter in the Tribune, are you a communist, or a socialist, or both or maybe a Marxist, this is Ed Waage. Just wanted to let you know what I thought."

After denying for several days that he was the caller Hill finally admitted to making the call. Blake claimed to the press that it was a joke.

Adam Hill Attacks Independent Media

JANUARY 19, 2012

CalCoastNews owner Karen Velie, who had taken one of Hill's classes when he lectured at Cal Poly University, had carried the impersonation story. Hill attacked Velie for doing so. Velie published his remarks to her. "Mr. Hill … had this to say about the online publication *CalCoastNews*: 'I understand why *CalCoastNews* does what they do … [The site's Karen Velie] was a student of mine. And for a couple of years, I would talk to her, and I would hear her say things that I knew were fabrications or, you know, the axes being grinded for somebody who had some problem with whoever it was she was trying to write a story.'"

By this time Hill's supporters were beginning to question his suitability for office. My fellow councilmember Karen Bright asked if I would join her in telling Supervisor Hill that she couldn't continue support him if this kind of behavior continued. She wanted to meet at my office.

JANUARY 23, 2012

Email from Grover Beach Councilmember Karen Bright to Supervisor Adam Hill: *Time for a brief meeting?*

> *Debbie and I met with our core committee regarding the upcoming Grover Beach election. Debbie will seek the mayor seat and I will run to continue as a councilmember. During our discussion, the subject of your campaign was raised and concerns regarding recent events.*
>
> *We would like very much to talk with you. Debbie mentioned that you and she had previously discussed meeting, possibly we could do it all in one. Would you care to meet with us for a brief conversation …? Debbie has offered her office."*

When we met Hill was contrite, saying he had been going through a bad divorce and that's why he was not behaving well. He said he wouldn't want to do anything to embarrass "you girls" and promised he wouldn't do it again; but he seemed unable to stop.

Adam Hill Attempts to Destroy Online Publication

JUNE 2012

CalCoastNews covered employee reports of misappropriation of items intended for the homeless by Dee Torres, who was Hill's fiancé (unknown to Velie at the time). Velie received a call from Hill telling her she would have access to county government information denied/interrupted and he would destroy her and her publication if she did not stop reporting on the homeless services division of CAPSLO or its homeless services director Torres. Torres was later suspended and then resigned from the agency.

Hill then began contacting *CalCoastNews* advertisers, suggesting they stop advertising on the site. Posts began to appear on the site of the internet news aggregator, *Topix*, claiming that Velie was mentally ill, which Hill posted immediately when they appeared. When Velie sent a request to Hill asking him to cease and desist from interfering with her business through libel, Hill responded with "LOL!" Many of the harassing emails sent by Hill and others originated from County email IP addresses or were sent at the time Hill was seated at the dais during board of supervisor meetings.

Adam Hill Tries to Ban Talk Show Guest

JULY 16, 2012

Dave Congalton, popular daily talk show host on 920 KVEC Hometown Radio, was a one-time friend of Adam Hill. Over the next 11 years, Hill never let up on Congalton because he sometimes interviewed Velie on his show. Hill sent vicious emails to Velie and to the owners of KVEC suggesting they ban Velie. Hill also threatened to go after Congalton. Velie printed the email Hill sent to Congalton:

> *You need to take responsibility for promoting someone who has no ethics and gets paid to do hit pieces (yes, we have proof of this)…*

> *"Oh, my, my, after the file I just read about your beloved protégé (Karen Velie), I think you will be doing more than 'distancing' yourself. Probably you'll have to hold a press conference to apologize to the entire community. Wow.*

When *CalCoastNews* filed a request under the California Public Records Act to get a copy of the alleged "file," San Luis Obispo County Counsel Warren Jensen responded that the county did not have a file on *CalCoastNews* or its reporters, stating, in an email on July 6th, "He (Hill) did say that he may have referred to such a file in an email, but that any such remarks were not intended to be taken literally."

Years later, Velie's declaration filed with the SLO Superior Court detailed the extent of Hill's harassment. Her address had been posted on *Topix* in an article requesting that people go by her home to harass her, after which a threatening letter was taped to her door. Then a commercial alarm was placed under her porch that went off as she walked past it. A sheriff's deputy determined it was a crime and would be investigated, but a month later called to inform her that a higher up within the department instructed him to drop the case. The commander who issued the order was the uncle of a developer who was a close business associate of Adam Hill. Velie lost several advertisers and a photographer who Hill employed and then threatened that he would get no more jobs from Hill or the County if he continued to work with Velie.

Adam Hill Threatens Pismo Beach Council

OCTOBER 2, 2012

Hill's rampage in his own district extended to the Pismo Beach City Council where his (now defeated) opponent in the supervisor's race served. *CalCoastNews* reported that a developer had charged that a county agency abused their authority in order to promote Hill's re-election and their own political careers. Hill claimed that the agency was going to sue the City of Pismo Beach if the city did not pay for the defense of the county agency.

When the city declined to support the agency's defense, Hill sent a letter to a local newspaper claiming that the city was refusing to honor its indemnification contract with the agency, not paying bills to the agency for work on a planning application, and not paying redevelopment monies due to the local school district. Hill said, "As its representative to the county, Pismo's behavior is, quite frankly, embarrassing." It followed in later years that those who did not support Hill's positions found themselves out of a job when, in his role as a supervisor, Hill contacted their employers and peers asserting that they were an "embarrassment."

As Hill closed out the election year with one attack followed by another and another against the cities and people of his own district and county, it never occurred to me that I was on his radar. After all, I had endorsed him!

Just weeks before the November election, I got an email from Kevin Rice asking to meet with me. He stopped by my office with a $35 donation to my campaign. I had never met him, but I was always willing to meet with people.

Rice was a local activist whose interest was the SLO County Air Pollution Control District (APCD) and its attempts to shut down the county's drivable beach and off-roading in the dunes, and in open government. Councilmember Karen Bright's boyfriend was the campaign manager for her campaign for city council and helped with my campaign for mayor. When Rice later offered to assist in identifying the source of anonymous emails we were receiving, I emailed them to ask whether we should accept Rice's offer of help. They counseled, "Sure!" They both knew Rice.

Rice's input and the Council's position spurred me to research the controversy about vehicles in the dunes further and I came to support the position of my city council and that of Ed Waage, the Pismo Beach councilmember who represented his city on the APCD board. Waage, among his other qualifications, has a PhD in Physical Chemistry, and has also studied how material is transported in a plume. Waage has the positive bearing of a true statesman. No one on the APCD board was better qualified to review the reports we were receiving than Waage. I was finding that everyone I met who was maligned by Adam Hill was dedicated, kind, and sincere.

Rice shared more injurious behavior by Supervisor Hill. I was unaware of the extent of Hill's malevolence, including many of the incidents detailed earlier in this chapter. I was so disappointed by local Democrats that I didn't know if I could in good conscience stay in a party that I had believed to have the moral high ground but included so many who I knew to be playing the moral low ground. I called my friend and mentor, Stew Jenkins, who advised me to stick with them and keep going to meetings. I followed his advice. My friends and family will attest that I am not a drinker, so it is significant that the only way I could get through the central committee evening meetings was to have a glass of wine before going.

Rice was a night owl like me, and an avid researcher with years more experience observing local politics. We had a solid mutual even handed advisor in Stew Jenkins. Our friendship was cemented on the eve of election day. It being only the second election I had faced, I remained anxious the night before the election. Rice was also running—for a seat on the SLO City Council. I texted him to wish him good luck. He called later that evening, and I was relieved to have someone to talk to during those tense hours.

He encouraged me to read Francke's 400-page *Open Meetings in California* (the Brown Act) and the latest 900-page version of Robert's Rules of Order in preparation for my role as mayor. I read both cover to cover.

I noted that among my council colleagues that sometimes there was little regard for compliance with campaign laws. One councilmember and I attended the Homebuilders Association Candidate School, run by an old-school journalist; a respected character full of piss and vinegar with an infectious sense of humor. It was a captivating course packed with experts and a chance to meet others we would be serving alongside if elected. The Fair Political Practices Code requires campaign activities, including the course, to be paid out of campaign funds rather than candidates' personal funds. My colleague had forgotten to pay in advance and had to pay on the day of the event and had no access to campaign funds at that point, so decided to pay using personal funds.

No amount of pleading on my part could convince my fellow councilmember to handle it lawfully. I suggested three allowable options: the campaign manager who was in attendance could pay for it and be reimbursed for the expense, or I could pay for it and be reimbursed for the expense, or I could pay for it as a campaign donation. My colleague refused, brushing it off as unimportant.

At many times, my colleague had seemed quite principled. She often strongly proclaimed that she followed her conscience and wouldn't be swayed by her boyfriend's opinions, and I had learned from her stances. She had mused as to whether or not, when running for a non-partisan position, it was right to accept the endorsement and donations from political parties; the temptation being that it was easy money and support. She then went on to become the president of the South County Democrats with the attendant endorsements it brought in future campaigns.

First Directly Elected Female Mayor of Grover Beach

NOVEMBER 6, 2012

With 75% of the votes, I became the first directly elected female mayor of Grover Beach. Although it had appeared to me that Mayor Pro Tem Nicolls functioned as the former mayor's right arm, I was taken aback at my campaign party when, even as we were squinting at computer screens to confirm the election result, Nicolls sidled up to me and whispered in my ear, "Debbie, what do you want me to do?" I was shocked to be asked for orders but responded that I wanted him to do whatever he felt was right; that as a councilmember I did not believe his role was to take orders from the mayor but to vote independently.

Was he really that wrong-headed, or did he think he might be privy to useful information if he cozied up to me? Had he been sent? I had been warned that he had been dissing me with fellow Republicans and a council appointee, my former neighbor. Nicolls had a lot to be worried about. Under his chairmanship, the Sanitation District board teetered from investigation to investigation, claiming the whole time, "We have done nothing wrong," and flinging insults at or firing anyone who disagreed.

During the month between the election and my swearing in, I took stock of my accomplishments as a councilmember. I had encouraged city hall to be more approachable, to make government processes easier to understand, and to find ways to get constituents to speak up so that we could improve our service and be more responsive. The city manager responded by increasing staff training on how to be "customer" friendly. He repositioned staff based on their people skills. He moved the front desk to the front door, making it more accessible, and created a more open method of handling queries from drop-in constituents. This quickly created more positive outcomes.

As people were given a voice and listened to, the assumptions of malfeasance driven by lack of understanding of the process became fewer. People gained more understanding of why public decision-making is so painfully slow and were less frustrated. It also made the work of staff more pleasant when those skilled in dealing with the public were the ones out front and when there were fewer hostile encounters. In short, it more closely resembled that which is intended by our constitutions— government by the people and for the people, who are participating in the institutions that they have created. We are extremely fortunate in Grover Beach to have dedicated, conscientious employees who represent the best of small towns—conscientious, caring, and unpretentious.

As I progressed from planning commissioner to councilmember to mayor, I was spending more of my time working with others on open government and accountability. The more I sought to understand my role as an elected representative, determined to make government meetings and processes more accessible, the more resistance I met. I understand the resistance to open government. It demands vulnerability, courage, homework, and research. It is risky.

It is also the standard we and those who serve us must meet. As a result of my quest for clarity in presenting financials, city managers and the administrative director made improvements to the city budget, making it easier to understand and more transparent. By the time I left, the budgets were better detailed and slowly, councilmembers and the mayor began to ask one or two questions about the budget.

I had served on twelve committees. One of the four about which I had concerns is now thriving following the work of three dedicated and experienced female board members. We had all been CEOs and worked together on the board to tighten up accounting and reporting procedures. One resigned because of her concerns about shoddy nonprofit practices.

Another organization that was partly funded by the city did not want a city councilmember on the board. I suggested for two years running that given the size of the city's donation ($25,000) relative to the organization's income and mission we should have oversight with a seat on the board, even if as an ex officio member without the ability to vote. It took me two years to gain the support of the city manager and mayor for a city councilmember seat on the board. By then, in 2012, I was known for my quest for accountability both in financials and transparency. The council appointed me to the board.

Within two months of my arrival, the organization admitted it was bankrupt. The very emotional and leggy long-haired blonde chief executive had been placing invoices in a drawer for six months rather than paying them. Male members of the organization, apparently distracted by her seeming vulnerability and looks, did not exercise oversight. The CEO resigned, leaving the organization with no funds and $38,000 in outstanding bills. It combined with another agency with strong administrative organization and was able to partially continue its mission.

Nevertheless, two-thirds of the boards I served on were in good order and several were run in an inspired fashion, with highly engaged and professional CEOs who genuinely cared about their constituents and enthusiastically pursued best practices. Among the best run agencies was the San Luis Obispo County of Governments (SLOCOG), responsible for countywide infrastructure projects. The COG board was made up of the mayor of each city and the board of supervisors. An energetic and visionary former city planning director ran the COG, bringing inspiration and encouragement to the mayors with projects that would improve their cities. His staff reports were always thorough and detailed, never sugar-coating the challenges.

Getting Ready

I had a month in which to research and prepare to hit the ground running upon taking office. I watched archived committee meetings, read minutes and staff reports, met with supervisors and electeds from neighboring cities, and conversed with future board colleagues on the new agency boards on which I would serve. I asked myself, 'With just two years in office, how can I best advance the community's wellbeing?' For half a day my thoughts were paralyzed by the size of it all, but I went back to my philosophy of strengthening the positive and listed the city's strengths. That one action encouraged and energized me for the duration of my mayorship.

The most wonderful strength of Grover Beach is our main street beach access to the State Park; a 3,600-acre Off Highway Motor Vehicle Recreation Area (OHMVRA). Fifteen hundred acres are open to camping, day use, and off-highway vehicle (OHV) recreation, attracting up to two million visitors a year to our town for low-cost recreation, including the usual beach goers, surfers, kite surfers, anglers, boogie boarders, bird watchers, equestrians, dog walkers, beach walkers, golfers, diners, and hikers. Allowing vehicles on parts of the beach and into the dunes allows access to scenery that is otherwise inaccessible and also allows handicapped access. It allows anglers, surfers, and kayakers to unload gear close to the water. A large proportion of coastal camping opportunities in the State Park System are in our 6,200 campsites—the only place in California where you can camp directly in the beach sand. Our train station and compact 2.25 square miles enable us to be truly a car-free city. Nowhere is more than a mile from the beach.

I made my list of priorities—it was a lot to accomplish in two years. I decided to focus my energy on economic development, including the joint powers authority between State Parks, a developer, and the City to develop a beachfront hotel and conference center, optimizing train and tourism opportunities, and the fiber optic project that would bring higher speed and broader bandwidth to Grover Beach than exists even in San Francisco and Los Angeles. I set a date for a meeting of those who drive the tourism economic engine of our town—Friends of the Oceano Dunes, business organizations, State Parks, tourism agencies, chambers of commerce, the hotel and conference center marketing department, and our one other hotel to find ways to join together to strengthen local businesses, bring more visitors to town, and save money through coordinating our marketing when possible.

I called together the mayors to the north and south of my city to discuss how to work together to solve the problems of homelessness.

I attended the swearing-in of newly elected councilmembers in neighboring cities and the Oceano Community Services District, congratulating them during public comment and expressing eagerness to work together. That started us all off on the right foot for what would follow.

I met with the police chief and outlined my concerns about the sewer district. He made a point of telling me not to let go of it.

DECEMBER 2012

As the mayor-elect, one of my first actions was to reach out to Supervisor Hill. It was the first of three meetings we would have in his office, and one of many I had with supervisors over the years. The only supervisor who never reached out to me was the other supervisor in my own party, Bruce Gibson.

We talked about the problems I was seeing at the Sewer District. Hill affirmed that we could not let that continue. I also calmly and courteously told him, as we had discussed ten months before, that I could not continue to support him politically based on his unchanged behavior. I asked him to stop talking down State Parks; explaining that it hurt the whole county when he trash-talked the people who run one of its largest economic engines, who have been good partners to our town, and to his district, enhancing law enforcement, public safety, employment, and tourism.

He stroked his chin, saying he was growing a pacifying beard and would start going to the local Buddhist temple. It reads as if he was being facetious, but it seemed as though he meant it as a sort of mollification intended to convince people of his plan to change his behavior. It was a claim that he repeated often from the dais and to the press over the next few months. We agreed that regardless of political support, we would continue to work together to benefit our community.

CHAPTER 2 LOCAL GOVERNMENT 101 TO 911

Extortion

This is the hardest chapter to write. When I was mayor, it seemed to be the most fun I had had since I had launched and run my own manufacturing business in Scotland. Being mayor was a chance to really make a difference. And yet, as I now work to relay the events of those two years and the years that followed, I keep putting it off, not just because now it is painful, but also because there is so much information and getting the facts right is important to me. I can't tell it all. I wonder how many incidents I need to relay in order to demonstrate that the problem of corruption in my county is epidemic? It's not just cannabis, it's not just developers, it's not just politicians or criminals. It's like a tisane—a concoction of all of them that slowly oozes and spreads until every molecule is affected, and even if you strain out the debris, the permeation remains.

I began a five-year run of late nights and not enough sleep, bolstered by support from many super people. I loved every minute, even the tough ones. My ex-husband rented a room from me, and it was wonderful to have him living full-time with my son through his high school years. He and my son and I were always on the same page politically and they were helpful, keen listeners. When I asked their opinion as to what action I should take on choices that could impact them, that might put me or them in danger, they always told me to do what I thought was right no matter what the outcome might be.

Their support was practical. At night as I sat and worked, reading, researching, returning phone calls and emails, my son's dad would bring me dinner. My son inspired me. When I gave him and his friends rides home from high school, we talked about leadership and spiritual values. They went through difficult times together—a favorite teacher who was fired, the death of a sibling, the cancer diagnosis and ultimate death of a beloved teacher, and teachers who brilliantly inspired them with their enthusiasm, creativity, kindness, who still bring tears to my eyes as I recall the values they taught their students. One of those now-retired teachers, Jim Gregory, I quoted in the Introduction.

Having lived abroad for twenty years, I had returned to the States in part because I wasn't comfortable with the academic options in pre-college education in Great Britain. While I still desperately miss my dear friends there, I am glad for that decision. The Lucia Mar school district is filled with kind, caring teachers who inspired not only my son, but me as well, and prepare their students for constructive futures. They and the kids they graduate leave me heartfully encouraged about the next generation.

My son and his friends challenged and reminded me to seek the highest and best from those in office—I believe our local leaders should be positive role models. Talking with my son about my concerns about four hundred new oil wells proposed in the nearby Price Canyon and the possible effect on the water table, he spoke with the clarity of youth, "Mom, there's nothing clean about oil."

I was mesmerized by the tale his two best friends (one male, one female) told about their experience of the first Women's March in San Francisco. They're in their twenties now, but they've still got it. When the local paper asked, "Can't we just put all this behind us" in response to recent corruption charges, another great one-liner rolled out, "That's what enablers say."

But they weren't the only ones who stepped up for me. Other friends were willing to stay up late into the night talking through particularly difficult events or helping me to get to my dying mother when I was too exhausted to drive the three hours in the middle of the night. Others stepped up full time when a campaign manager became ill and had to resign, or knocked on doors to support my "Mitigate, Don't Litigate" position on the Dust Rule. I am not naming names, to protect them, but they know who they are, and I am so thankful for their friendship and support.

I could never have anticipated just how painful those two years would be. Just months into my mayorship, our city manager contracted an infection that took him away from work for months. Seven months into my term, on his way to work, my 24-year-old nephew was killed in a bizarre vehicle accident. Eight months later my mother died. And my 17-year-old son left for college three months before my term ended. The former mayor was scheming against me. He and members of the core group who had supported me, as well as the city council, were coalescing with County Supervisor Hill in what was to become a powerful cabal. It wasn't the first or only corruption in the county, but it was the nascence of Hill's organized control of the factions involved.

DECEMBER 6, 2012
Swearing-In and Council Committee Assignments

> *"I will support and defend the Constitution of the United States and the Constitution of the State of California **against all enemies**, foreign and **domestic**; I will bear true faith and allegiance to the Constitution of the United States and the Constitution of the State of California; I take this obligation freely, without any mental reservation or purpose of evasion; I will well and faithfully discharge the duties upon which I am about to enter." (State of California, Constitution)*

The previous mayor was a commanding presence, and I felt I could never live up to his ability to chair a meeting. It wasn't long before the hardships I faced with the council and the former mayor taught me that I could do it better. By contrast, I was able to manage dissension without losing my temper, without playing the sympathy card, and without justifying mistakes with the excuse of being a volunteer.

My first council meeting as mayor was on December 6, 2012. I agendized council committee assignments for this meeting, rather than waiting until January and having the city unrepresented until then. I wanted to serve on two committees that were new to me: the South San Luis Obispo County Sanitation District board (SSLOCSD) and the San Luis Obispo Air Pollution Control District (SLOAPCD). Although as mayor the positions were mine by law, the exiting council representatives would viciously attack my character and my credibility for years to follow for not ceding the role to them. In both cases, each previous representative contacted me numerous times, lobbying to retain their committee positions on the board, explaining that they liked being on the committees and had strong relationships with the chief executive and other board members. In both cases I felt that the representatives had become too cozy with the administrators and their cronies, Adam Hill and John Shoals, to serve the best interests of their constituents.

The APCD representative had served for five years. In addition to serving on the APCD board, she was the APCD representative on a subcommittee and travelled four times a year to meetings with the chief executive, the Air Pollution Control Officer (APCO). She adored him, gushing that everything was far too difficult for her to understand, but he was brilliant. I was the APCD alternate, and the council had appointed me to be the representative the previous year, but I could not serve due to a conflict with another committee.

These two positions pay a small stipend of $100 per meeting. The SSLOCSD met twice monthly, usually a rubber-stamping exercise that took about 15 minutes. Both agencies attracted so much controversy, lost so many lawsuits, or faced so many criminal charges that each has its own chapter later in the book.

DECEMBER 19, 2012
Supervisor Hill and businessman air concerns over homeless services center

Meanwhile, Hill continued his attacks on constituents. Local businesses proposed an alternative location to his preferred site for a much-needed homeless services center. A local businessman had the audacity to circulate a flyer expressing concerns about the impact the homeless center might have on a nearby business park. Hill emailed more than two dozen city leaders and people tied to the project, fuming,

> *"It's clear Bill Thoma is determined to defeat this project no matter what. He has shown himself to be selfish and dishonest when it comes to homelessness in our community,"* and accused Thoma of *"fear monger-ing;"* another phrase that would resurface to demean anyone disagreeing with him. The rest of his email would have a familiar ring also in future attempts to destroy his opponents. *"I have had quite enough of Mr. Thoma's passive-aggressive attitude and actions, and I have had enough of his dishonest dealing. If this project is to fail, and if the problem is to continue to exacerbate (as it will), the blame should fall squarely on the hunched shoulders of Bill Thoma."*

After the press admonished him, Hill penned the following viewpoint in *CalCoastNews*, apologizing for his behavior, concluding that he was only responding to other "venom and disrespect," although he seemed to be the only one who saw it.

> "The Tribune was right in strongly admonishing me for my over-the-top-attack on Bill Thoma, for which I apologize to Bill, his family and friends, and all those who have worked so hard to best address the crisis of homelessness in our community.
>
> I have too often, and to too many, expressed myself in a manner too offensive. There are no excuses I will hide behind, and my critics and adversaries also deserve my apology and my pledge to adopt a more civil and decent attitude when communicating on any issue.
>
> This holiday season allows me some time for reflection, and already doing so, I do understand the importance of not only better moderating my passions, but of embodying the sort of informed humility we all expect and deserve from our elected officials.
>
> There is much discussion these days in our culture of the

dismaying lack of civility, of the corrosive effects of hyper-partisanship and combative approaches to any and all disagreement. I am not sure we have made any tangible advances, but we must keep trying.

We must keep trying because the venom that consumes respect and dishonors differences courses through our own community in a variety of ways, and I have thoughtlessly engaged in it with my own spiteful retorts and have surrendered to the temptation to broadcast it when my anger has overcome my judgment.

While I have prided myself on candor, there is a point where that candor becomes an easy justification for behavior that is not acceptable from anyone, be it an elected official or an anonymous commenter.

So, I make a whole-hearted and community-wide apology and promise to live up to the moral ideals of a community that rightfully prides itself on friendliness and cooperation."

Hill went on to write about the homelessness crisis and overworked staff, and to lobby for the parcel of land upon which he wished the new homelessness center to be built.

Months later, the City of San Luis Obispo stepped in with help, and the location suggested by Thoma and the business community was approved by the SLO Council of Governments (SLOCOG)—almost unanimously. Hill slouched in his seat and refused to vote.

JANUARY 9, 2013
San Luis Obispo Council of Governments Board Meeting

My first committee meeting of the year was the board meeting of the San Luis Obispo Council of Governments. Hill was in line to be the chair of the important regional board. I was about to deliver on my word to Hill that I could not support his leadership. The local press was all over it.

SLOCOG Board Meeting 1/9/13

1:22:55-23:58 DEBBIE PETERSON

"This is my first time here, and so I would ask you all to bear with me on this. I understand that I have not earned the right with my colleagues here yet to say too much. Adam Hill has been a friend of mine and I do not have a political axe to grind with him. However, President Strong asked the public to be civil, polite, and respectful when they spoke, and my concern is that Vice Chair Hill has failed in that in several cases. He has asked our forgiveness in several cases. He continues to do that. He knows how I feel—I'm not comfortable with that standard. We need to be held to a higher standard and I would like to see someone in the post this year who is less contentious and more of a statesman."

JANUARY 10, 2013
SLOCOG chooses Frank Mecham as chairman over Adam Hill

The Tribune reported that while Hill was not present because he was "sick with the flu," SLOCOG chose a different board member to take his place as upcoming chairman of the board.

JANUARY 16-19, 2013
California League of Cities New Mayors and Councilmembers Conference

Most California cities are members of this league that lobbies on their behalf in Sacramento. Their conferences are a helpful resource for training and an opportunity to meet councilmembers from other areas.

Female councilmembers dreaded encountering Mayor Shoals at conferences because we all liked and respected his wife. At many events he arrived with a shapely consort on his arm, always in short, tight dresses. One former mayor recalls him introducing one buxom guest as his cousin. Thing is, he had a lot of cousins. Kissing cousins, the other mayor called them. That was one of the more genteel terms used by his colleagues.

I received a voicemail requesting a meeting from Supervisor Hill while I was attending the conference. I was fielding my real estate business during short breaks in the 16-hour days of sessions and was not able to get right back to Hill. He asked my council colleague, Karen Bright, also at the conference, to tell me he needed to talk to me right away. Then I received the following email from him:

JANUARY 16, 2013 EMAIL FROM ADAM HILL

Subject: Monday?

"Hi Debbie,

I'd like to meet with you Monday and can find any time that will work for you. I'd come to you but there are some items in my office—that I'd like to share with you. Please let me know as soon as possible.

Thanks!

Adam

I returned his call and agreed to meet him on Monday. I asked if the county building would be open on Martin Luther King Day. He said, "Oh, I will meet you outside the courthouse." There was nothing unusual about the suggestion. Often these kinds of informal meetings would start by meeting outside and then moving down the street to a restaurant or coffee spot.

JANUARY 21, 2013

As agreed, I met Supervisor Hill in front of the county building. I was aware of some of his incendiary emails involving others, but had no reason to be concerned for my safety. After agreeing to meet out front I was surprised that he didn't want to head down the street to a café. Then I was further surprised that he had to unlock the front door to get in to the county headquarters When he locked the door behind me, I looked around the foyer, usually occupied by security guards, staff, and members of the public headed to meetings or to the Clerk Recorders office. There was no one in sight. I reasoned that the supervisors' receptionist and Hill's assistant would be working if he was. We took the elevator to the fourth floor where the supervisors have their offices. Hill unlocked the door to the reception area. There was no one at reception. He locked the door behind me. He unlocked the door to the hallway leading to the supervisors' private offices and locked it behind him. He then unlocked the door to his own reception area. His assistant, who would normally be sitting there at her desk, was not in. He locked the door behind us. Finally, he unlocked his own office door—two rooms—and locked the door behind us. With every unlocked and locked door of the rabbit warren that was the domain of the supervisors, I became more uneasy. He ushered me into his back room where he had a table and a desk.

On the table were stacks of papers, several feet high. On the desk he had more piles of papers and a computer booted up, with files cued up on the computer monitor desktop. Two and a half months after the election, Hill's office was still several feet deep in files on his competitor (who he beat) and on his competitor's supporters. Hill was fixated on Kevin Rice, who had actively campaigned against him. He had file after file of the things he considered to be Rice's bad acts. I listened carefully but wasn't surprised by anything Hill told me because having accepted a donation from Rice, I had researched him carefully and questioned him on his activities. While I would not have operated as extremely as Rice did, I was impressed by Rice's willingness to own up to his actions, even those he may have later regretted. Certainly, none of it was illegal or even frightening. Hill wasn't telling me anything I didn't already know.

As I listened, I was thinking, "He has just locked me behind five doors. How do I get out of here?" and, "I have to keep him calm, so he doesn't act out." Seeing that I was not particularly concerned about Rice's activities, Hill became increasingly agitated, to the point that he finally burst out, "The Sheriff has given me a permit to carry a concealed weapon to protect myself from Rice!"

I thought about asking him where his gun was and immediately thought better of it. The last thing I wanted was for him, in his state, to break out a gun. I wondered, did he have it with him? Did he have it on his person? Was it in his briefcase? His desk? How could I get out of there?

He realized he had gone too far and said, "I'm not trying to scare you," to which I replied, "It's okay, Adam, you are not scaring me." Truth is, although I become very calm in such situations, which wound him up, I was embarrassed that I had allowed myself to be lured onto the fourth floor of an empty building with an agitated man who told me he had a gun. He must have realized that having gone too far, he needed to let me go. He unlocked all the doors and let me out. I was deeply unsettled and relayed the story to several friends, trying to come to terms with it.

On reflection, I realize that he was anxious to know whether I would oppose his chairmanship at the upcoming APCD meeting. He believed that Rice, who had campaigned against him, and Waage, who had run against him, were influencing my decision. A year earlier, when I had told Hill if his behavior continued that I wouldn't be able to support him, I had never met Rice, and didn't know Waage well. My values and my word were entirely my own.

FEBRUARY 2013
Appointing a New City Councilmember

About the time of the election, the other candidate for mayor, who was also a city councilmember, opened escrow on a new home in another town. One of the requirements for mayor or city councilmembers is that they must reside in the city.

Although she had moved out of town, my colleague reasoned that owning a small house that she used as her bookkeeping business would count as living in the city, thus allowing her to remain on the council. The city attorney reasoned otherwise: recorded loan documents conditioned her new home as her primary residence. She had a choice—commit loan fraud, commit fraud in office, or resign based on no longer living in the city she served. She resigned.

It had been only three months since the election. The local television station interviewed me about how we would fill the vacancy. My goal was to come as close as we could to an actual election where, not the council, but the people of Grover Beach would choose their new council person, because it was the people who had elected the councilmember who was resigning. I explained that I didn't think the council would support the $10,000 it would cost to run an election just two months after the last election because the city budget was still recovering from the economic downturn. In that event, I was recommending to the council that the next most transparent option would be to take applications and do the interviews in open session.

I think this really worried the city manager, who was still out on sick leave. Before long, both the chief of police and city attorney were trying to talk me out of it. One applicant dropped out before the council meeting, leaving twelve to interview in open session. The police chief called me days before the meeting to advise, "You know, Debbie, you don't have to open public comment after the interview process."

I conceded that I was aware of that, but still intended to do so. He suggested that people might say really awful things if we opened public comment. I said, "Well, if that's what they have to say, I guess we need to hear it."

On the night of the meeting, the city attorney tried again, "Debbie, we can shut down public comment on this." I replied, "Not when I'm mayor!"

It was exhausting to chair the meeting and to be fair on the timing and questioning of so many applicants, and then to deliberate on camera in front of the candidates and audience, but no one said anything awful during public comment. As the meeting progressed, I saw then, as I came to see often in the months that followed, the whole demeanor of the room change from tension and suspicion to appreciation, interest, and relaxation as the crowd realized they would be heard and respected, and they responded in kind. The next two times a councilmember resigned, in 2019 and 2020, the council followed the same protocol.

I had similar concerns from the top city executives when I said I wanted to hold a Brown Act workshop because most people don't understand the Sunshine Act. They suggested I not open public comment because then the activists might be difficult. I said, "Well, let's hear what they have to say. They have more experience of this than anyone."

Again, the tenor of the meeting changed from apprehensive to uplifting. Having begun my term by reaching out to other mayors, I continued that trend by inviting the councilmembers and mayors from neighboring cities to attend the workshop. I was touched that many of them came.

Water Presentation

Similarly, I thought we could make better decisions regarding our limited water supply if the council and city committees, as well as the community, had a background and understanding of the history and origins of our groundwater supply and the geology that affects the way it moves and collects. I asked our city engineer and state parks representatives to make the presentations. Again, the presentation was well attended by the public and leaders from neighboring cities. During the time I was mayor, Grover Beach residents used less water than any other city in the county.

Mayors Meetings

One of the things I found quite helpful was the monthly mayors' meeting. Each mayor took a turn at showcasing their town by hosting a lunch, where we also met with state and federal legislators. It was an opportunity to get to know the other mayors, to brag a little about our town, and to share our local concerns up the line. There was little, if any, chance that we would transgress the Brown Act because the seven of us rarely sat as a majority on any board. There was one meeting about which I later was embarrassed. One mayor, a lawyer by trade, aided by a presentation from her city's attorney, wanted to develop housing in the airport flight path. However, the Airport Land Use Commission made up of aeronautic specialists and professionals said it was too close to the airport to be safe. As a new mayor, I was not yet aware of the formal Mayors Committee that met only to recommend coastal commissioners and choose Airport Land Use commissioners.

The two attorneys—the mayor and city attorney—did not disclose that a meeting was coming up where we would be choosing one or two new Airport Land Use commissioners. The mayor launched into a whining rant about why it was all so unfair that they couldn't develop in the flight path and why we needed to choose a particular land use commissioner who would vote her way.

Later, I realized that this had been a Brown Act Violation in that even if we weren't making any decisions on that date, they were taking the opportunity of having us all together to plead their case in private. It didn't influence my vote, because I didn't remember who the mayor had wanted and simply chose the individuals I thought most competent, but I was disappointed in myself that I hadn't caught it. Even experienced councilmembers and mayors often miss Brown Act violations. In this case both the mayor and city attorney knew better. In the end, the mayor got her way when she and her council simply overruled the Airport Land Use Commission. This particular project is one of those being investigated by the FBI in their ongoing inquiries into corruption in the county.

"You have no idea, Debbie. No idea."

Local talk show host Dave Congalton suggested meeting for lunch one day. Once we were seated the first words out of his mouth were, "You have no idea, Debbie. No idea." He wanted to warn me that there would be tough days ahead if I continued to go up against Supervisor Hill. I was later to hear from Congalton that the falling out with Hill jeopardized his job and resulted in media gag orders regarding individuals Hill did not like.

Sure enough, it wasn't long before Hill closed ranks and took over the city council. That wasn't difficult. Three of the four other councilmembers worked for county public agencies, and the fourth needed to discredit me to divert attention from his role in the sewer district corruption.

Remember

Former mayors who remained active in service of the city after serving council terms urged me to remember those who came before us because they laid the groundwork for the progress of the city and should be honored. I realize now why that was important to them. The one thing Mayor Shoals almost never did was include anyone who had served before him, except the councilmember he referred to as his best friend. He seemed threatened by other past mayors. It's easy to see now. Of course he didn't like them. They had integrity. They knew too much. They could catch him out if he allowed them in.

MARCH 20, 2013

As a broker in Grover Beach, my Association of Realtors (whose office at the time was in my town) invited me to attend a COLAB fundraiser as one of the 40+/- Realtors who our association hosted, many of whom were Democrats like me. COLAB, the Coalition of Labor, Agriculture, and Business is a non-partisan but largely right-wing watchdog that hosts a popular and influential annual dinner.

I made sure they understood that I was accepting the invitation as a real estate broker, not as mayor, because the constant press rhetoric against county Republicans pushed me away from wanting anything to do with them. As a realtor I wanted to understand what was behind the divide between not just left and right on land use decisions, but between "townie" and "ag." What was behind the hard-hitting repartee? What was fueling it? Not only do I sometimes list and sell acreage in agricultural zoning, but I also have family farm roots and I have a solid regard for ag families and the risks they take year in and year out. I wanted to hear them out.

EMAIL TO: MAYOR PETERSON

From: SLO Sense

"SLOSense will be filming your secret fundraiser at the Madonna Inn, so be sure to smile for the cameras. Of course, you can hide behind sheets if you choose..."

I received an alarming email shortly after agreeing to attend in 2013. Supervisor Debbie Arnold, who I met when I heard she had received a similar email, explained that she suspected it was from Hill because she received the same email signed by him. I didn't understand that the reference to "sheets" was calling us Ku Klux Klan, which neither of us are! To this day I wonder how he knew I was attending, as it was at the invitation of a private business organization. Somehow, he had an inside line to the private guest list. As I drove in to park, it was unnerving to pass a tall man dressed all in black filming every car that entered, his face obscured.

I attended the COLAB dinners for the next two years. There were other Democrats at the dinner: Erik Howell, Pismo Beach City Councilmember; Dawn Legg (now Supervisor Ortiz-Legg), Candidate for State Assembly; and Don Stewart, Lucia Mar School Board member.

2014—WEASELISM

SATURDAY, JUNE 14, 2014

TEXT FROM ADAM HILL

When elections rolled around, Hill reached out to people and began to play the nice guy. Word was that his minders were giving him orders to be nice, and he kept himself in check for several months before elections. I received an email from Hill saying he wanted to meet at a local coffee shop to "bury the hatchet," to which I responded by saying I never had a hatchet and agreeing to meet on a set time and date. Hill then sent the following text:

> *"Hi Debbie, I was thinking it may be nicer if you came over to our house tomorrow eve (Father's Day) for a drink. Give you a chance to meet the family and take some pressure off the hatchet burying. We have some really good wine. What do you think?"*

Having once been locked in the county building by Hill, I would never again put myself in a situation where I could end up alone with him. I responded (truthfully) that I had only an hour between meetings on Father's Day and would be happy to reschedule the previously planned coffee shop meeting.

Weasel Words

As I struggled to reconcile the corruption detailed in the following chapters, I sought out my friend David, hoping he might be able to shed light on it. He had relocated to SLO from his successful law practice in Washington state, where he had also been in leadership of the Democrat party. Knowing that he would have the perspective and overview to give me a conclusive answer, I asked him, "Have I been wrong all my life in believing that most people are basically good or is this place really bad?"

He said "No, this place is really corrupt."

Then I asked, "How did it happen? How can we fix it?"

He said that the press euphemize corruption, just as we euphemize the dead, and that makes everything okay. For example, if someone behaves badly, instead of calling it immoral behavior, the press says, "He's from New Jersey," or use the phrase "Politics as usual;" the same as saying, "Don't speak ill of the dead," rather than speaking the truth.

These words give the impression that everything is fine when trying to avoid answering a question, telling the truth, or accepting blame. Theodore Roosevelt called it out in a speech in St. Louis, Missouri, on May 31, 1916:

"One of our defects as a nation is a tendency to use what have been called weasel words. When a weasel sucks eggs it sucks the meat out of the egg and leaves it an empty shell. If you use a weasel word after another there is nothing left of the other."

This allows us to rationalize; to explain flaws away and then look the other way. It is a way that we distance ourselves from something ugly to protect ourselves from having to confront it.

The most dangerous form of weasel words is the rationalization we do automatically when, rather than seeking to understand something that gives us cause to wonder, we make an excuse for it or assume a reason for it and then let it go. That's the spin with which we deceive ourselves. It's one thing to put a spin on a story. It's perilous when we start to believe the story we've spun.

"Weasel words" can also describe an ambiguous or vague term for an anonymous authority, such as "researchers believe" and "most people think" and are used to make arguments appear valid. I came across lots of weasel words. If the public were outraged, I heard, "We are all good people," translated: "Don't question what we do," or "Look the other way, folks." Voters brush off the immoral behavior of elected representatives by saying, "Business as usual;" i.e., "It's just how it is, so it is okay, and you can't do anything about it anyway." Or, "All is fair in love and war;" meaning "It's okay because of extenuating circumstances."

To stifle debate, boards would be told, "We all just need to get along;" i.e., "We all have to agree." The local favorite was the coercive "Collegiality" that deserves a paragraph all its own. Adam Hill coined this one and spread the blight everywhere. Collegiality is an organizational style that has merits. It also has its dark side as an unhealthy organizational form. It is about lateral control and power among peers, with emphasis on agreement as the highest order. It creates the superficial appearance of legislative harmony while imposing dictatorial control of voting. It is the byword of the corrupt political machine. It could be euphemized as consensus building, but it is the opposite because it is not based on deliberation but on monopoly of opinion.

Collegiality was epitomized and bragged about on our local boards. Members touted 'civility' rather than civil rights, and 'collegiality' rather than educated discourse, stressing the importance of agreeing (so long as you agree with them). Members of the political cabal publicly lauded their behavior, patting themselves on the back and declaring the virtue of all getting along; translation: "We all vote the same and if you don't, you're not part of the 'in' group and will be shunned." It feels embarrassingly adolescent, even pre-adolescent. "Collegiality" was going along to get along in order to get straight to the desired decision; thus avoiding spirited discourse. Collegiality was simulated camaraderie calculated to stifle diversity of viewpoints.

I received a well-intended piece of advice that narrowly fits in the category of weaselism, but so far off-base I could cry—from a past League of Women Voters president. It is a perfect example of the affliction in my county. "You just need to lower your standards."

What is my usefulness to my constituents if I lower my standards?

More Running

I decided to run for a second two-year mayoral term. Four months after I announced my candidacy, previous mayor Shoals announced he would run as well, and went on to claim that I, the incumbent, was running against HIM. My original plan had been to retire from local politics and to spend time writing. However, corruption was so rampant that I wasn't ready to quit working to change it.

On the ballot, for the first time ever, was the plan to finance and fix our streets created by the council during my term as mayor. There was a reason for the pot-holed streets. Over the years, as a little oil was sprinkled in our tire tracks in the sand dunes, the tracks began to look more like streets. As time went on, asphalt was layered onto the oiled sand and our tracks became roads without foundations. When the town incorporated in 1959, they didn't negotiate a large enough percentage of our property taxes to come back to us from the county to cover the cost of paving and maintaining our asphalt grid built upon the sand, and so we were stuck short on income and long on streets.

Our commercial district and businesses were gracious. They realized that fixing the streets would improve business. I knocked on every residential door explaining the history to voters and asking them to support the additional property taxes needed to repay a bond to finally repair and rebuild our streets. Grover Beach "Fix the Streets" Measure K-14 won by a narrow margin.

I was completing my term, at peace with having turned the sewer district around (see Chapter 4). I managed to achieve much that I am proud of, moving projects along more in two years than my predecessor had in 12 years. I had traveled with a busload of Grover Beach supporters to the Coastal Commission meeting in Santa Barbara to advocate for allowing an additional half-acre in the area next to the hotel for staging for the horseback riders who accessed the dunes from the area. The Coastal Commission wasn't having it, but they did approve our Local Coastal Plan, thus allowing us to move forward with our beachfront hotel and conference center. Supervisor Hill and former mayor Shoals promised to find an alternate location for the horseback riders. That never happened. I had also beat an appeal by the Friends of the Oceano Dunes who had been taunted into suing by two best-friend past mayors too fixated on their egos to de-escalate and negotiate in the best interest of the community.

"The ... District Attorney's Office is responsible for ensuring that public agencies ... comply with the open meeting requirements of the Ralph M. Brown Act."

-Michael S. Frye, SLO County Deputy District Attorney,
Public Integrity Unit

Candidate for District Attorney Dan Dow asked for my endorsement. I liked his commitment to victim support, particularly for women and children, and his commitment to go after human trafficking. I offered my endorsement conditioned on his promise to go after corruption in public office. He said he would create a Public Integrity Unit, recognizing that citizens have the right to expect that their elected and appointed officials, administrators, supervisors, and their immediate subordinates will carry out their duties in a lawful, ethical, and professional manner. I made sure that he had signs out throughout Grover Beach, whose voter base is majority Democrat. Dow, a Republican, won in Grover Beach despite the Democratic majority, and countywide.

In neighboring Arroyo Grande, in a nationally reported 6-week write-in campaign, Jim Hill narrowly beat 13-year incumbent Mayor Tony Ferrara. City businesses banded together, tired of Ferrara. But the cabal gained power under Supervisor Hill, who co-opted judges, staff, and businesses, and managed to discredit the good Mayor Jim Hill.

When Jim Hill beat him, Ferrara sold his home and moved to Palm Springs. Before long I began receiving calls from Ferrara's new neighbor, completely exasperated, not knowing where to turn. Having discovered that Ferrara had left the sewer district almost bankrupt here, he reported that in just a few years, under Ferrara's presidency the HOA reserves had dwindled to almost nothing.

Thumb on the Scale

I lost the mayoral election. My advisors had expected it would be close, but that I would win by a narrow margin and that I was in good shape with my campaign. For that reason, they threw their energy into the historic win of Jim Hill in Arroyo Grande. While they weren't looking, my opponent Shoals had his thumb on the scale, repeatedly violating the Political Reform act, filing his campaign financial disclosures days or weeks late, or not filing them at all, misleading all of us.

Hill had used the same ploy in his 2012 campaign managed by the best friend of Shoals. Hill failed to timely report fifteen payments of

$500 or more, totaling $68,058.73, for which he was fined $2,500. Hill paid the fine in 2015 using campaign funds.

In the seven days before the election, thousands of glossy Shoals mailers appeared; many more than his reported income could support. When the late final disclosures were finally filed, my friend Kevin Rice found that Shoals had committed fifty-two Fair Political Practice Commission (FPPC) violations in his campaign reports of the previous three months.

Rice filed a complaint with the FPPC asking them to enforce the law to protect against future violations, claiming that Shoals harmed the public, me, and the media who relied on truthful and accurate campaign finance reports, and by depriving us of timely and complete information about his contributions, influences, and lobbyists.

By signing his campaign statements, Shoals, acting as his own treasurer and sole signatory of his campaign disclosures, obligated himself to use "all reasonable diligence," signing under penalty of perjury that the information he provided was "to the best of his knowledge true and complete." Of the $20,712 in campaign funds that Shoals reported in 2014, over half was reported late. Five contribution reports were never filed until after the election, thus concealing one-third of his funding. Most of the late reports were donations from the former neighbor who in 2009 had rear-ended my car and left me with a broken ankle and whiplash injury that has made it impossible for me to sit at a desk ever since.

Shoals also failed to report three donations from local Democrat party political committees, filed incorrect addresses for donors, and made incomplete filings until five weeks before the election, thus making it appear that he had received no donations. When Shoals and I were interviewed by a *Tribune* panel they asked how much he had raised. His response was, "Not much, maybe $1,000." This was consistent with his sneaky reporting. I answered truthfully, "$10,000." By hiding a $7,229 glossy mailer expense just days before the election, Shoals gave the appearance all along that I was outraising him. Had he been truthful I would have campaigned differently.

An equivalent advertising campaign on my behalf, combined with knocking on every voter's door as I had always done, would have swayed the 170 voters (2.7 percent of registered voters) I needed to win; thus fulfilling my advisors' predictions.

By 2014, Shoals had been a councilmember or mayor for ten years. His were not the mistakes of an inexperienced candidate. He had served as the regional chair of the League of California Cities and had been required by the election code to complete up to six ethics courses. Shoals was the Government Affairs Executive for Pacific Gas & Electric at the time, representing the interest of PG&E's nuclear power plant at Diablo Canyon. The representation of the nuclear power plant in our community as its local government liaison mandates the highest level of integrity and trustworthiness.

He listed his PG&E colleague and campaign consultant's address as a box at the local UPS office. He would have known that Cory Black and his firm, Public Policy Solutions, Inc., also a fellow political party member, had his office in San Luis Obispo, not at a P.O. box at the UPS office in Arroyo Grande. These men would have or should have known that the law requires a physical address.

His campaign regularly placed signs illegally. Folks would complain privately when signs were placed in their yards without their knowledge or permission, but feared offending a potential mayor by taking the sign down, so they let it stand. On Friday nights after City Hall closed, signs appeared in high visibility commercial locations in violation of the city sign ordinance, thus maintaining the exposure for several days until the city could contact the campaign to remove the illegal signs.

What is Corruption?

Without a legal background, I found it difficult to describe the patterns of behavior I was uncovering. I observed, listened carefully, and researched meticulously to identify and stop the outflow of public funds to certain contractors and elected officials who were protected by staff and councilmembers fearing for their jobs, and unchallenged by business owners afraid for their businesses and reputations, all frightened for their families. Now I have the words for what I was seeing. The definitions are in Appendix 2 at the end of the book. Alongside each definition I offer an instance of corruption and the chapter where it comes up.

CHAPTER 3

TREPIDATION 2015–2020
Bribed: FBI Seeking Tips

"The vote of the People is not for sale."

JANUARY 2015

I had completed my plan to dedicate ten years to improving the city's image and industry; albeit I had hoped for another two years to rout the corruption I had found. But now I could begin phase four of my life as a writer. My supporters pointed out that while not in office I could take a more active role in bringing about the final overhaul of the Sewer District—the audit. Having wiled back his position as mayor and the representative on the sewer board, Shoals was in charge again. It would be an uphill battle.

Then, in March, friends thought I should run against Adam Hill in the 2016 supervisorial election. We agreed on two things. First, I would run to win, but probably couldn't, my objective being to keep my platform forefront; and second, in our district only a Democrat could beat Hill.

I launched my platform opposing Hill's role with developers and water rights:

THE VOTE OF THE PEOPLE IS NOT FOR SALE.
DEVELOPERS CANNOT BUY MY VOTE.

Wild Cherry Canyon will not be developed. The people of the county overwhelmingly voted in the Dream Initiative, ensuring that it would remain as conservation or agricultural land (a mandate Supervisor Hill was seeking to override).

1. Wild Cherry Canyon cannot be developed—ingress and egress is insufficient in the event of wildfire.

2. The Airport Land Use Commission says it is not safe to build homes next to the airport.

THE WATER OF OUR FARMERS IS NOT FOR SALE.

It must remain under local control for the benefit of our agriculture and residents.

It wasn't long before Hill was privately touting exactly the same platform as mine, despite his close association with PG&E executives and known associations with developers.

A week later, Dan Carpenter, a San Luis Obispo city councilmember and businessman, decided also to run for the seat. Initially, the mayor of Pismo Beach was also running, but stepped out of the race when Hill's goons began tailing her at pre-campaign events and threatening bad publicity against her children. Bob Shanbrom, one of my very fair-minded supporters and also a life-long progressive, organized a meeting with a member of the Democratic Central Committee, thinking that if we just talked, maybe we more independent Democrats could muster their understanding of our concerns about Hill. Although I worried that they would use it against me, I agreed to the meeting.

I shared with the central committee member my fear for my only son, who was starting university at 17, and teared up as I shared my fears that somehow Hill would exercise his standing as a former Cal Poly lecturer to harm my son; that his academic record or attendance might be tainted or worse, that he would be physically harmed. For good measure I also explained that I took solace in the fact that he worked for campus police—he even had a security clearance—and had shared with his supervisors and police officers that his mother was in politics and some of the issues that I was facing so they would be alerted to any problem with an awareness of the players and the possibilities so they could quickly come to his aid. She was sympathetic, and even agreed she had not been able to work in Hill's employ for long, but nothing changed. Hill remained their darling. I so often wonder why, when they could have a courteous, honest representative, they would choose one as mean-spirited as Hill.

Dan and I ran amicably against one another, supporting the democratic process that anyone may run and the people should choose. We agreed on most local issues, especially regarding Hill, but our campaigns were vastly different. He was the darling of the local Republicans and ran a 'Beat the Bully' campaign. His campaign was based on personal experience—his own, his family's and that of many others.

On one occasion, while at a ribbon cutting for a new affordable housing development seeing Carpenter chatting with a contractor, Adam told him not to talk to his donors because if he did, he would take him out to the parking lot and beat him up. Dan laughed. He wasn't laughing when his daughter became the subject of threats and degradation by Hill's online trolls. Humiliation and contempt for people they didn't know, people they never bothered to hear out, but who appeared to disagree with them, was a common theme for Adam and his collegiality acolytes.

In December 2015, veteran news broadcaster Dick Mason reported on a classic Hill tantrum. Hill had walked out of a supervisor's board meeting when the board was honoring the 50th anniversary of the agency where his fiancé had worked and left amidst alleged theft of donations meant for the homeless. Hill accused Mason of "bashing" him and targeted Mason's 25-year-old daughter via social media, asking why her father was going after him. He then contacted Mason's employer.

Adam's attacks and threats really hurt when family were targeted, or when supported and prolonged by the press over years, as in my case with the Dust Rule. The *Tribune* trotted out Hill's successful extortion of the city council at every election, painting me as a pariah disliked by my council. The democrats in power doubled down, telling voters I was "tea party" even though they well knew I was not.

I find being pilloried by a whisper campaign a curious thing. It started by someone who is cheating at every turn saying, "She's not very nice," (which I hope isn't true). Some people seemed to take a perverse delight in believing the gossip without knowing me or checking with those who did know me; enjoying the easy road of gossip, scorn, and being part of the "in" crowd or in the know. Even if true, since when has "not very nice" been worse than the instigator's illegal activities?

I was squeaky clean, and they couldn't find anything on me, so they made it up. I often joked that I had to read the troll blogs to find out who I was sleeping with so I would know how to vote. Councilmember Bright told people I was sleeping with Rice and that's why I supported the Dust Rule. When he asked her why she was spreading the lie she said, "Well, I just figured you were sleeping with her, because she's pretty."

Exchanges between members of the public and board members during meetings became so vicious that the League of Women Voters, who had for years done an outstanding job as sponsors and mediators of local political debates, decided they must adopt a civility campaign. I firmly advocate the practices the League put forth and I fervently adhere to the values of respect, professionalism, and civil speech in my political campaigns and when I speak from the dais, but I couldn't fully support the League's campaign.

The leaders set the tone of a meeting, and I believe that we should comport ourselves in a way that we feel meets the standard of role models for our children However, I don't believe we can legislate how elected representatives or citizens express themselves. Many times, I have been approached by members of private organizations, as well as city attorneys, councilmembers, city managers, and police chiefs seeking ways around hearing unpleasantness from members of the public. In so doing they thwart our constitutional first amendment freedom to speak our minds to our government. My approach has always been, "If people have something to say, then I want to hear it!" A private organization or institution can legitimately make rules that restrict free speech. Government agencies cannot. Requiring civility, however well-intentioned, is an impediment to the higher value of free speech.

Constituents by right, are allowed to be passionate, to be angry, even uncivil, and to express themselves; not necessarily as old white women, but as the diverse mix of ethnicities and backgrounds and personal styles they represent. The first amendment of both our federal and state constitutions and the courts have upheld free speech in government meetings. I fought and will continue to fight government 'decorum' requirements (a.k.a. censorship) that tell people what they can and cannot say and how they should say it.

Following the 2016 election, the stodgy SLO Democrat central committee was petitioned by a well-organized group of Bernie Sanders supporters; mostly younger democrats identifying as progressives requesting official recognition. I emailed fifty independent democrats who had supported my campaign for supervisor, encouraging them to support committee recognition for the newcomers. As a matter of principle, I believed it was the right thing to do.

The meeting was packed. Adam Hill and fellow Supervisor Bruce Gibson, who had for years been supported by the existing committee, jumped ship so quickly you couldn't see the splash and proceeded to take over the new group that inundated the old guard. A list of those who supported the inclusion of the new group was circulated at the meeting. All of my supporters' names were included, but not the name of the recruiter—mine. Not even the mayor of San Luis Obispo, the leader of the movement, ever told me how or why I had been excluded, despite the fact that I asked her more than once. I was also blocked from their Facebook page. I suspect it is because the operator of their campaigns was Nick Andre, an employee of Hill's campaign, and is now running a dispensary associated with confessed felon Helios "Bobby" Dayspring.

The primary election resulted in a run-off between Hill and Dan Carpenter. Dan, hailing from the larger city of San Luis Obispo, had the advantage even as a Republican, and split the vote. Between us, we took 59% of the vote. Had Dan not stepped into the race, we might have ousted Hill and forever changed much of what was to come. I was popular with independent Democrats and Republicans, and as I knew, only a Democrat could win in our district.

JULY 23, 2016

Adam Hill's planning commissioner invited me to his home to meet with him and Adam Hill because he was stepping down and felt I would be the best replacement. He and I didn't always agree on commission decisions, but we were always able to shed light on the issues for one another when we talked. I told him I thought it extremely unlikely that Hill would consider me for the position, but he felt that Hill would be open. The interview covered only one issue: Hill's insistence that he could not appoint me because I had written opinion pieces that had been printed in *CalCoastNews*. Hill said he could not appoint anyone to a county position who was friends with Karen Velie or Kevin Rice, an activist who sent opinion pieces to CalCoastNews. Hill further stated that by serving as a fellow board member of the SLO County ACLU with Karen Velie, it was clear that I was her friend. Hill said he would appoint me if I publicly renounced any friendship and business relationships with Karen Velie and Kevin Rice. I have never had a business relationship with either. I told him that regardless of my relationship with either Velie or Rice, I could not serve as a public representative in a post which conditioned my service on who I could and could not befriend. Hill seemed to really believe that the position was of such importance to me that I would allow him to control my actions. After two-and-a-half hours, when I realized we were just wasting our time, I stood up and said I could see that we were getting nowhere and I was sure we both had better things to do, thus ending the meeting. Hill appointed Dawn Ortiz-Legg to the position. When Hill died, the governor appointed Legg to fill his vacant supervisor seat.

AUGUST 30, 2016

The skulkery of Mayor Shoals caught up with him two years too late to keep things clean in Grover Beach. The California Fair Political Practices Commission (FPPC) had fined him $1,101 for Political Reform Act violations stemming from his 2014 mayoral campaign. If the FPPC had acted more quickly and forced a recall following their investigation and fine, how different might our city be now? Going back to when Adam Hill left Cal Poly, how different might the news reports coming out of SLO County be now if his employer had prosecuted him? Apparently, at work he chaired a charity for the homeless and there were questions as to his handling of the funds. Those are questions we can ask ourselves collectively as the story unfolds.

November 2016 General Election

When the June supervisor primary was narrowed down to two candidates, I realized I might still be able to keep corruption at bay as a city councilmember. I got more votes in my city than the two incumbents, Mariam Shah and Barbara Nicolls, who had both gotten into office two years before when no one else ran for city council seats.

Also on the ballot was Measure L-16. Cory Black of Public Policy Solutions, a close associate of both Hill and Shoals, was the campaign manager and treasurer:

> **Shall Grover Beach City Council adopt an Ordinance establishing an annual "Commercial Cannabis Tax" on marijuana businesses …? The Tax is estimated to generate one to two million dollars annually, will not sunset, and may be adjusted annually by CPI (Consumer Price Index).**

The following ballot "impartial analysis" of the measure was prepared by the office of the Grover Beach City Attorney:

The City Council of the City of Grover Beach has placed Measure L on the ..., ballot to ask ... voters to ... enact a tax on commercial cannabis businesses which ... establish in the City...The tax would apply to ... cannabis businesses, if ... allowed under State and local laws. The passage of the tax would not have any effect on legalization or land use regulation of cannabis activities in the City.

Measure L... would tax all cultivation and nurseries ... Dispensaries, manufacturing, testing, and other commercial cannabis activities ...

Revenue ... would go to the City's general fund ... to support ... municipal services ... including public safety, infrastructure improvements, parks and recreation, or other services.

I always struggle with the way these measures are couched. It is this kind of misleading information that usually changed when I challenged it from the dais. Measure L-16 appeared at the time the State was seeking to legalize cannabis use. It made sense for the city to chase up a tax, should the product be provided in the city.

The measure was not written, "do the voters wish" with a straightforward discussion of the pros and cons. It was rather, "the city council is asking you." When a measure is put forward by a city it should be written in a manner that is free of political spin and bias. An analysis is not impartial when the city attorney, employed by the council who are asking to public to vote "yes," has been directed by the council to write an "unbiased" analysis asking voters to approve the measure.

The "unbiased analysis" then goes on to state that the tax would have no effect on legalization or land use of cannabis activities in the city. That couldn't be more opposite to what happened. The legalization of cannabis in the city would cause the tax to take effect, and anticipation of income from cannabis taxes drove the creation of the measure. Staff, the attorney included, were at that time traveling the western United States seeking input on creating ordinances to permit cannabis and had already established a "zone" where cannabis businesses would be permitted.

Although it may have been the intent of the authors of the measure that it would be a mandate to bring cannabis businesses to town, the measure on its face was not such a mandate. It was a mandate to tax such businesses if they came to town. However, once the measure passed, the mayor and councilmembers let slip their intent by justifying decisions with the claim that the measure was a vote of the people to establish cannabis businesses in their city.

Once elected, I sent a friendly email to each councilmember and the mayor suggesting we meet for coffee so they could catch me up with what was happening on the council and what they felt was important. Mayor Shoals never responded; not surprising—it was a complaint I often heard. I had grown used to not hearing back from the mayor. Jeff Lee met me near his county office for coffee on his lunch break. I'm sure he went right back to Adam Hill with a report on all I said.

Barbara Nicolls said it was too near Christmas and she was far too busy to meet with me. Mariam Shah snipped that she didn't talk to anybody but the city manager and the mayor because it might be a Brown Act violation. For the next two years, when I raised a matter that she felt could subject the council to legal recourse, such as sexual harassment or corruption, I would experience a "Yeah, right" moment as she sniped, "Well, Debbie, I was right here. I don't know why you never spoke to me about this." More than once as a councilmember she had out and out called me a liar without fact-checking the allegation with me because, as she had previously said to me, she wouldn't talk to me.

I was surprised that as an attorney she didn't have a better grasp on the Brown Act, but it wasn't the first time I had come across an office holder/attorney who didn't seem to understand the Brown Act. Some years before I had called my then friend, Matt Guerrero, president of the Oceano Community Services District board, begging him not to take an action on his district board that would be a blatant violation of the Act. He ignored my entreaty, just as my former colleague had done with campaign expenses. As the cabal coalesced, the pattern of disregard for fair political practice and diversity of opinion began to emerge, punctuated by personal attacks on those who did not toe the collegiality line.

The city attorney did agree to meet with me. I like him. He's easy to talk to, interesting, same vintage as me, and from my home county. He was always accessible, even on weekends and evenings, and helpful when I had questions about my participation or what the FPPC might view as a conflict of interest. When I heard that he had worked for the City of Fresno before retiring, I asked what he knew of the "Fresno" story of the late eighties when suddenly a generation of politicians and developers went to jail (See Chapter 8).

He laughed and reminisced that it was his first experience as a young attorney. He said he used to see a black limousine with the tinted windows pull up to City Hall to take councilmembers to lunch. I forewarned him that I was a stickler for the Brown Act and believed that the city attorney's job was to protect the people from bad government by interpreting the law on their behalf. He chuckled again, saying there were two schools of thought on that, and it was oft discussed among attorneys at League of Cities conferences. I particularly liked that he was someone you could disagree with, agreeing to disagree, and continue to be friendly.

October 2016 "Me Too" Robocall

Hello, this is Debbie Peterson. When I was the mayor of Grover Beach, Supervisor Adam Hill locked me in county hall on a public holiday when no one else was in the building and told me he had a permit to carry a concealed gun. That's one of many reasons I ran against him in the District 3 supervisor race. Many others have had similar experiences with Supervisor Adam Hill. Most have been afraid to speak up, but more and more are doing so. Please consider this when you cast your vote for District 3 supervisor.

Paid for by me, Debbie Peterson. Not paid for or authorized by any candidate or candidate-controlled committee.

I wrestled with whether or not I should publicly share the incident in which Adam Hill had locked me in the courthouse and told me he had a gun. Would people believe me? Would the local paper beat me up? Didn't the people have a right to know how this guy operated before they cast their vote? I came down on the side of having a responsibility to say so. The local paper pilloried me as a liar in what they called an "investigation," interviewing Adam and his assistant, who started to cry when asked about the incident, and who was later awarded a generous sum by the county when she resigned. Although there is no official reason given for this assistant's resignation and generous payout, one of Hill's first assistants shared with me that she had resigned because she did not like the way Hill treated her.

Especially given my record for telling the truth, why anyone would think I would want to lie about something like this I can't imagine. I suspect that the newspaper regarded its relationship with Hill as more important than genuinely seeking the truth. I wasn't looking to lawyer up. I wasn't looking for money. I wasn't even still running against Hill at that point. I just thought people had a right to know and then, knowing, cast their vote. Several prominent people stood up for me; people with whom I had shared the experience. Unfortunately, all this happened a few months before the #MeToo movement, too early for me to benefit from a more enlightened hearing.

Those who make the law shouldn't break the law

This period of the city developing its cannabis regulations was remarkably interesting. Having been planning for months, staff jumped into action as soon as Measure L-16 passed to set up the ordinances that would legalize and regulate cannabis production and dispensaries in the city. We would be the first city in the county to allow cannabis businesses, and staff worked efficiently to draft what seemed to start out as good ordinances, but quickly deteriorated as Cory Black ran the cannabis agenda, signaling his wishes from the back of the council chambers. The ordinances were drafted such that regardless of background or adherence to the ordinance the decision as to whether or not to allow a cannabis business in town was entirely at the discretion of the city council.

From start to finish, campaign consultant Black, his company, Public Policy Solutions, or his employees ran the ballot measure. He brought in the specialists who oversaw the point system used to rate the many dispensary hopefuls applying for one of the four licenses, introduced the company that manages the tax collection and reporting, wrote the ordinances, recruited cannabis businesses, procured the real estate, represented permit applicants, funded the political campaigns of councilmembers and mayors, lurked at the back of the chambers at every council meeting backed by a motley crowd of supporters, invited council and staff to parties on his premises in the cannabis zone, owned numerous Cannabis LLC's, and set up public meetings to explain the ordinances. He then used the processes he put in place to get permits for his own businesses in the cannabis zone and those he represented.

It was easy to recognize the signature work of Black in at least three of the business proposals for cannabis dispensaries. At Easter, one of the applicants, Black's client, sponsored an Easter egg hunt and children's event at the local children's museum, the mayor pro tem appearing on local television to promote it. Meanwhile Black's client was evicting a beloved local youth dance school with a 20-year lease and four hundred students from a building he had purchased, and according to his June 2020 FBI confession, also bribing Supervisor Hill and Mayor Shoals.

When the proponent of new legislation is the major consultant, contractor, owner of businesses, administrator, political advisor, campaign manager, and committee to pass the ballot measure, red flags should be breaking out like the wildfires that have ripped across the state. There was no flagging.

Economic Impact

There was just one problem with the chosen Cannabis Zone. There were not enough industrial facilities to support existing businesses and bring in a huge new industry. The council refused to do an economic impact report. Previous city surveys revealed that a number of the business owners in the industrial area were from our city, thus locating their businesses in their city's industrial area. The area had been off the radar for decades. Because there were several large vacant lots it was assumed there were several vacant industrial units.

Having spent many years evaluating economic impacts as an owner, a real estate broker, and an advisor to manufacturing companies, I couldn't ethically participate in decisions affecting the industrial area without that information. I did my own economic impact report. It took a full two weeks to complete. I evaluated vacancy—almost zero—versus applications. I then looked at available space in the city suitably zoned for the applicants who were retail, manufacturing, commercial, visitor serving, medical, and agricultural. I evaluated the impacts of the tripling of rents and property values to existing businesses and jobs versus those proposed by the applicants. Once I tallied the results, I could see that what was best for the city as a whole would be to allow cannabis businesses to operate in the location zoned for the business activity, just as we do with all other businesses in the city; i.e., retail would be in retail zones, and medical in office zones, etc., with some allowed crossover and with the same additional oversight and legislation afforded the alcohol industry.

I had a measure of success when I took it to the council. The industrial area in which cannabis businesses were allowed was expanded, opening up space so some of the existing businesses could remain, but there was a lot of fancy footwork from the mayor when he chaired the council meetings, and it was clear that there were interests he had to protect.

Black, accompanied by men with briefcases chained to their wrists, was seen cruising the area in deluxe black SUVs with tinted windows offering same-day cash in gym bags if property owners would sell to them. A few old-timers nearing retirement did very well from it. Indeed, I heard that one retiring businessman did receive a satchel of cash as a deposit on his property. After stagnating for 30 years, prices tripled in our industrial area. Even as the jobs of existing industries and city heads of household were pushed out of town, councilmembers were parroting cannabis puffery about extensive job creation.

Business owners who were tenants were forced to move. Locals reported that Black told business owners not to worry about getting permits because he was the mayor's campaign manager and "had the mayor in his pocket." This is similar to the message that was also relayed to cannabis growers countywide by Supervisor Hill. Stories came from multiple sources of a Russian investor and another investor who claimed to own five Burger King franchises in Russia and a rapper who wanted to invest. Real estate brokers relayed that Shoals asked clients for $15,000 to smooth the way forward for an application for a cannabis business permit. Brokers said that the system of bribes to Adam Hill was so sophisticated that there was a code to indicate how much had to go to Hill, using times as code, such as, "that would be a 4:00 meeting" to indicate that $4,000 was the required extortion. Developers had to pony up before getting into escrow on a land purchase deal.

What I hadn't thought about because I was thinking about the best possible zoning for the city, not about myself or my property, was that it would bring a dispensary across the street from me. Its history makes me uneasy. It wasn't just the cocaine trafficking conviction of one of the dispensary applicants' husbands and his friendship with the mayor and Cannabis business principles reporting that the two of them were doing coke at a local restaurant and at parties, or the registration of a Cory Black business at their home.

It wasn't even just their promise to "clean up the neighborhood" by regularly picking up trash, which I found offensive because I lived across the street and there was almost no trash in the neighborhood (I have never seen them pick up trash and it has never been recorded on my security cameras). It wasn't even just their dishonest reporting of no residential property near the dispensary (mine and others were just two doors to a block away) that was never acknowledged, amended, or even voiced despite my communication with the city manager and planning commission about this pertinent omission. It wasn't just their close association with the California League of Cities with three principals or their spouses employed there, or the fact that the developer of our beach front lodge and conference center purchased the building, or that the ownership of the business had changed, seemingly without the required permit review. It is the combination of all of these things and the secrecy around them and that Black reportedly had an office around the corner, which caused me to be uneasy living just three doors away.

Background reports are required of all dispensary applicants. When it came time to choose the four dispensaries that would be granted licenses, over a hundred cannabis supporters came to make public comments at council meetings. The scoring system was convoluted. Staff did their own scoring, possibly overseen by the committee of Shoals and Lee who had assigned themselves to watch over the city cannabis measure. A consulting firm hand-picked by Black did its own scoring, and then it all went to the council, with each councilmember doing his or her own scoring. All the while, Black smirked from the back of the council chambers, unseen on the cameras, but clearly seen by the council. Mayor pro tem Lee, when things went sideways, would get a worried look on his face and lean in to the mayor for guidance.

Sometimes meetings would stop abruptly, and the mayor would rush down the hall, followed by Black, into the city office to meet behind closed doors before resuming or adjourning the council meeting. The few local applicants who stood out as being more professional than the others, or more kind-hearted, with a genuine wish to serve those with medical needs were not granted dispensary licenses. None of the dispensaries were awarded to Grover Beach applicants, even though they were experienced and competent, were on the short-list, and had clean background reports. In the end, the scores were ignored, or twisted by the mayor with credible "reasons" such as choosing those that promised him that they could be up and running the quickest. The FBI have now reported that in September 2017 applicants Helios Dayspring and a business partner offered Mayor Shoals $100,000 for permits for two dispensaries. Being offered a large bribe didn't stop the mayor from voting in favor of Dayspring's dispensary. The many others who had invested millions in property purchases, business and building plans and consultants, and attorneys, lost it all.

Jeff Lee, Adam Hill, Helios Dayspring, John Shoals

Out of four, two succeeded in opening "quickly" within nine months. Three years later, one is still not open. Twice the mayor returned to the dais sweating profusely. I felt for him, wondering if he had a medical condition. I didn't know then that sweating is quite common following a cocaine hit. Other things happened in the back of the chambers and in the reception area and hallway. One cannabis hopeful reported that another bragged about giving councilmembers envelopes with money in them, some of it reported as campaign donations, some not. The bragger then opened a briefcase to reveal envelopes with money in them and copies of the actual campaign filings reporting part of the money he had handed over.

The only businesses chosen to operate dispensaries had principals or closely related parties with prior felony convictions. You would have thought, as did locals, that a felony conviction would disqualify them, but the council majority amended draft ordinances to leave all decisions to the discretion of the council, provided the offender was "suitably rehabilitated to run a business in the City." Resident comments against the industry were met with one or more of the councilmembers responding piously, "The people voted to have it in our town, so it is our duty."

What's the big deal about a felony? A felony isn't just a speeding ticket. It's not even just a misdemeanor. It's serious. What were the felonies? They are public record. Of those I can recall they were rape of a minor (his sister), cocaine trafficking, engaging with a prostitute, and receiving stolen goods. In July 2021, the FBI published a release noting that dispensary owner Helios Dayspring had confessed to attempting to bribe the mayor but his county businesses remain open because he put everything in his girlfriend's name. On October 7, 2021, the press

TREPIDATION 2015-2020 | 69

reported that planning permission has been withdrawn for one of his dispensaries in the city of San Luis Obispo.

Another of the approved dispensaries removed the principal on the day the dispensary application was to come before the council. The third that is up and running also had an ownership change. But no bother; Black had made sure the ordinance was written in such a way that his clients could do that and the City would approve it.

I want honest businesspeople of character in my town. Many people who spoke during public comment at our council meetings depend on cannabis to help with incorrigible medical conditions such as multiple sclerosis, cancer, autism, or chronic pain. At one meeting, my doctor came in unannounced with two studies showing the importance of cannabis as an alternative pain medication to opioids, explaining that you can't overdose on cannabis. It's too easy to overdose on opioids, and legalizing cannabis as an effective, alternative pain reliever would save lives.

But it hasn't worked out this way in SLO County. The rate of opioid-related deaths in SLO County in 2020 was double the number in 2019; 55% higher than the state rate. According to data from the California Public Health Department, SLO County has 20.5 vs. 13.1 deaths per 100,000 people statewide. The Centers for Disease Control and Prevention National Center for Health Statistics reports that figures have risen 29% nationally, attributed to pandemic-association hardships; not nearly the rate at which SLO County deaths have increased.

The comparison between 200% (doubling) in SLO County over the same time period and a 28% increase nationally is striking. There is no reason to believe that the pandemic in SLO County accounts for the near doubling in rates. Several deaths have come from the legitimate use for relief from temporary pain using medications provided by "friends" that have been laced with fentanyl.

That leads to the question of why suddenly are there more dangerous drugs on the street? Press releases in 2020 and 2021 from the FBI asking for tips on corruption in the cannabis industry and in our county provide a clue. Many cannabis dealers are known on the street to have a wider product selection than just cannabis, and continue their illicit business alongside their now legalized businesses. As local governments in SLO County followed my city's lead, more felonies were overlooked, and the cannabis purveyors were invited to town, bringing their full product range and associated business with them.

A product people need for medical conditions must be safe, of consistent potency, and contaminant-free. With the histories of the parties chosen to operate dispensaries in my county, there is no reason to trust that they will take any care in ensuring the best interests of their customers.

Black owns several LLCs, all at the same address as his 'Yes on L' and of the Shoals campaigns. Black has also opened a cannabis distribution business in my city's cannabis zone. He was the brains behind the meetings the city organized to talk with residents about the cannabis industry. At the February 21, 2017 city council meeting during council communications, Mayor Shoals waved a glossy flyer identified as the work of Black, inviting people to come to a presentation on cannabis, but when I asked who was sponsoring it, he feigned uncertainty. Black kept a low profile in public meetings, his fingers in not just cannabis pots but also water and electricity in several counties.

As concessions to the environment and public safety concerns, cannabis businesses were required by ordinance, regulation, or resolution to take several actions. They were to hook up to sewers, install rooftop solar panels, reapply for permits in the event of a change of ownership, and to hook up security cameras connected to the police department. At the time of writing, in 2021, these legal requirements have slipped or have been unfulfilled. The mayor crows about $1.5m income from the cannabis industry, but none of it appears to have been spent on the promised infrastructure or oversight. The public, whose fears were appeased by these measures, are none the wiser. Those who make the law are breaking the laws they make.

In closed session, and sometimes even in open session, I grew used to the petulant whines or defiant demands my colleagues made of the City

Attorney, asking, "Is she right?" when I opposed an action, they chose to take on the grounds that it was an ethical or Brown Act violation.

On every occasion, the city attorney would concede, "Well, yes, technically, she is correct," or, "If you want to be strictly on the side of the law, yes," or, "She is suggesting the legally conservative course of action." Sometimes the attorney would have to look it up and think a bit. Sometimes the answer was just, "Yes, she's right." The public loved it because it was always in their favor, as it should be! Collectively, they own the institution!

Cannabis Plant

In 2018, although it was kept from me for several months, I discovered that Mayor Shoals, who had been "laid off" from his PG&E job, had been employed as a County of Santa Barbara planning supervisor. Santa Barbara County is the county just south of SLO County, and the county in which Shoals started his career as a planner for the City of Santa Maria. He was the perfect plant for the cannabis machine, having set up the Grover Beach cannabis infrastructure. He had an excellent position from which to consult with those seeking planning permissions.

A jolly hail-fellow-well-met who could produce excellent proposals for civic projects, he had a network of contacts throughout San Luis Obispo County and northern Santa Barbara County. His resume included planning positions in the cities of Atascadero, San Luis Obispo, Santa Maria, two development firms, and PG&E, as well as the longest—from 2002—2018 as a councilmember and mayor in Grover Beach.

MAY 25, 2017
I received an unexpected phone call

The developer of our long-awaited hotel and conference center needed a mayor to go with him to China to raise funds that he would then use for the conference center. He told me that Mayor Shoals couldn't do it because it was a conflict of interest. I told him that if it was illegal for Shoals, it would probably be illegal for me, but that I would look into it. The hotel and conference center project is the work of a public-private Joint Powers Authority including the City of Grover Beach, California State Parks, and Pacifica, a private developer.

I reported the conversation to the city manager, who squirmed and fidgeted and made no response. Weeks later, when the mayor violated sewer district bylaws by unilaterally canceling a board meeting and didn't show up to a fire district board meeting, I asked the city manager if the mayor was in China and got the same fidgets, squirms, and lack of response. In meetings with the city manager every other week, questions about the mayor's participation in certain activities or ownership of certain properties would be evaded, and updates on the cannabis industry were withheld.

In this case Chinese internet photos surfaced of Shoals with Pacifica Hotels speaking in six Chinese cities, including Beijing and Shanghai promoting the EB-5 visa program that provided visas to wealthy foreigners to emigrate to the United States in exchange for investments in a U.S. project. Public questions surfaced about the secrecy of the trip and the land use development vote Shoals cast a week after the tour ended, on June 5th, Resolution 17-28, a One-Year Time Extension for Development Application for Pacifica's Grover Beach Lodge and Conference Center Project.

Although Shoals was portrayed as traveling in his official capacity as mayor, no record of city council approval of the trip could be found, nor did the mayor disclose the trip prior to voting to approve the time extension.

A public records request showed that Shoals had a 10 year multiple entry visa applied for by the City of Grover Beach for the trip. Stating that the mayor was covering the cost himself, the City provided a guarantee to the Chinese government that the mayor had sufficient funds to cover travel and accommodation while in China and would cause no expense to the Chinese government. This ten-year giveaway by the City extends eight years past his final day as mayor. I don't know if any funds were raised or not, but I do know that as of 2022 there is no hotel or conference center.

JUNE 26, 2017

My political enemies made sure that their lackeys and anyone they could influence was informed that I was the enemy of cannabis. My beef wasn't with cannabis; it was with corruption. On two occasions, cannabis insiders exclaimed that Black was really scared of me. I found it hard to believe that a little blonde lady would scare these guys. Really? But bullies scare easily. What wasn't so funny was that Black made sure the cannabis boss knew I was getting in the way, and I'm told the boss regularly made disparaging comments about me.

Once I began to go after the sewer district corruption, friends begged me to get a gun and get trained in how to shoot because, "Debbie, what would someone do to protect their wealth if you are threatening it?" I never took country roads alone, especially not at night, because I was warned that a vehicle "accident" was more likely than being shot. I didn't go anywhere at the same time on the same day of the week. I never said whether I was in town or out of town. I never said what I was doing or where I was going. I never discussed family members or where family members lived, despite regular inquiries by the mayor and mayor pro tem.

Except I often did one thing the same day and time—I got together with a friend. Neither of us ever stopped to think that since she lived near someone under investigation by Knudson that may not be wise, but I never expected trouble in broad daylight at lunch time on our main street en route to see my friend. When it occurred my first thought was, "I was warned that this might happen." You would think a BMW all-wheel-drive SUV would be pretty safe, but the worst injuries often happen at the slowest speeds, because your body takes the impact rather than the vehicle. In 2017, you would not expect to find a 2009 SUV sandwiched between two even older SUVs. But I was.

While stopped at a light, my SUV was rammed from behind by a Jeep going about thirty-five miles an hour that propelled my vehicle into a 4x4. Both of the other drivers were alone. When the burly guy jumped out of the Jeep asking if I was okay, I did not open my car door. He looked like a bouncer. Even bigger was the driver in the car my car was pushed into. He looked like a body builder. Both appeared to be in their late thirties or early forties. I did not get out of my vehicle until they had both finished talking to the police. Following my whiplash injury of 2009, when my neighbor had rear-ended me, the injury was consequential. I still feel the effects of the eleven herniated disks caused by the accidents.

Three members of the cannabis community and other professionals unknown to one another later told me they believed it was no accident: it was a hit. Following the chain of command, I reported it to the city manager, the police chief's superior. He said, defensively, "Well, if you think that, you should report it to the chief of police."

I missed six council meetings because I could not sit in a chair for more than fifteen minutes or negotiate the step onto the podium. The city clerk was gracious, suggesting a footstool for under the dais, but even that did not provide enough relief to attend a meeting of several hours' length.

If I didn't return to meetings within four months, the council could legally appoint a replacement. Earlier in the year, before my accident, the council voted to allow health insurance as a councilmember benefit, but while I was recovering the council withdrew health insurance for councilmembers. So, I went back. It was a struggle to do it for many months.

Back on the council, committee assignments for the year 2018 followed the usual pattern. Councilmembers had their favorites, vying for chairmanships. This time I beat them at their own game. I put in my usual request, offering to sit on most committees, knowing they would allow me none where I could make a difference. It worked well for me not to have committee assignments, because then I had more time to pursue other council concerns. Every time a colleague made a grab for a committee assignment, I graciously conceded until I had none.

Having kept me from any important committees, they were looking very self-satisfied. I saw it dawn on the mayor as he started to read the list of new council assignments. They had been outsmarted and it was too late to do anything about it. He tried to make the appearance of balancing committee assignments by giving me two committees that never met, and I accepted. His frustration was palpable. The others had not figured it out—they were doing all the work. I was looking pretty smug, too, having had the last laugh.

FEBRUARY 4, 2018
Adam Hill Tells Local Businessman to "F-Off"

In January 2018, once again the board of supervisors voted not to install Adam Hill as the board chair because of allegations of bullying and a lack of decorum. Mark Burnes, a Hill supporter sent a viewpoint to the *Tribune* calling out a local conservative. He included one sentence agreeing that Hill's antics and attitude were disappointing. The letter appeared in the Sunday edition.

On Sunday just after 8:30 a.m. before Burnes had even seen the letter, Hill messaged Burnes. The full content of their exchange follows.

> **Adam** Thanks but no thanks for your stupid letter. When you have walked in my shoes, when you taken the hate I have taken—and then been as effective as I've been, mark, [sic] then you can take shots at me. Now? Fuck off. All talk, no balls.

> **SUN 12:15PM**

> **Mark** Actually, Adam, I walked in those shoes for 8 years on the Pismo Beach Planning Commission, where, I was every bit as effective in my role as you've been in yours. (A role that also gave my a prominent voice in the community that I used to help you get elected twice). I was also attacked by those who did not agree with the way I voted. Many of those attacks were ad hominem, and in Strawman Fallacy, by people who did everything they could to assassinate my character, and destroy my business. Unlike you, I

never lashed out at them. I've always believed as a Public Official, we need to hold ourselves to a higher standard and conduct ourselves accordingly. E.g. my responses to my detractors were always civil and based on fact. (Thus my issue with Andrea, which was actually the subject of my letter). As to the letter: out of five paragraphs, there is one sentence about you. That sentence was neither disparaging or disrespectful. It was a simple disagreement. How you managed to take that as an attack that warranted that response is beyond me. I can tell you this, Adam, that you as a member of the SLOCBOS, would address anyone, particularly one of your constituents, in that manner is unconscionable. It's not too dissimilar from the thick-skinned manner in which Donald Trump attacks those who disagree with or are critical of him. You complain about the "hate that [you] have taken" yet you dish out hate—look in the mirror, Adam. The audaciousness of your response to me and others who disagree with you and your continued vitriol against other members of the Board is a clear indication that you are no longer fit to serve.

Mark Actually, Adam, now that I think about it; I was a great deal more effective in my role than you've been in yours, as I always chose to function within the boundaries of decorum, and, whenever possible, diffused dissensions and tensions, as opposed to exacerbating them as you have, and as you continue to do.

Adam I'm sure you were as great as you think you were, Mark. Which only shows how little you know about what I've done or who I am.

Mark A little Strawman Fallacy of your own, eh, Adam? I never said "great," I used the same term you did: "effective."

Adam Whatever please your ego, Mark. Fine by me. And please go ask the eleven companies out by the airport that I worked with to keep here. Or the HotHouse downtown that I helped start and got the funding for. Or the $1.5 million I got to purchase the Pismo

Preserve. Or the grants I secured for five different low-income housing projects Tell me if you want names and contacts because your knowledge of me and my work is very underfed. I haven't even seen you in years and you don't show up in our data base as a supporter (it goes back 8 years) but I'm sure you are as important as you say I am bad.

Mark Gaslighting will get you nowhere with me.

Adam Not even sure how that is a response.

Mark Then you probably don't know what it is—google it

Adam No, I know what it is but I made it clear to you that you have no idea what I have accomplished and offered to have to confirm it for your edification You seem quite comfortable with your accomplishments and legacy and I don't dispute them, I don't know anything about them. I also have not seen you in quite a while nor heard about you so I don't make any judgments about your character

Mark You're wrong, Adam. You've done some great things for the county, and I am quite clear on that. But the vitriolic manner in which you conduct yourself these days is unacceptable. That you would attack me, and others, as you do, who disagree with you, is unacceptable. It's megalomaniacal. Regardless what you've done, who the hell do you think you are treating people this way???

Adam What way? Be specific as to your injury I will gladly apologize for hurting your feelings and still maintain you have no idea what I do or who I am.

Mark "Thanks but no thanks for your stupid letter. When you have walked in my shoes, when you taken the hate I have taken—and then been as effective as I've been, mark, then you can take shots at me. Now? Fuck off. All talk, no balls"—you think it's OK for you to address one of your constituents this way?

Adam According to you, you are a personal friend and supporter If you were a stranger no I wouldn't say that to you You want or both ways

Mark You didn't hurt my feelings—you demonstrated a quality that is unacceptable for an elected offical—it's Turmmp'ile

Mark Sorry—Trump-like

Adam Please. I'll let you have your self aggrandizing morally superior stance.

Mark I'm tired of you attacking the other Supes too—there is a more dignified manner in which a person in that position should proceed—and again, Adam, gaslighting does not have an effect on me

Adam You be well, Mark, you don't know what's going on but seem to care about politeness over substance

Mark Adam, as a citizen of the SLO County 3rd District, I have the right to address my elected representative to the county. I have a First Amendment right to make my views public without reprisal, and without being attacked by that representative. A little contrition will get you a lot further than being vitriolic.

Adam I've attacked you?

Mark Yes. Your response to my letter about Andrea in which you bragged about your accomplishments, then told me to "fuck off" and that I was "all talk, no balls." Don't misunderstand that for by thinking you've insulted me or hurt my feelings, you didn't You don't have that capacity. To reiterate: what you did was demonstrate that you're unfit to serve on the Board. I expect decorum form my elected representatives...

Adam If you feel hurt, I am sorry. I don't agree with anything you've said and you are welcome to bang the drum against me all you'd like.

Mark LOL! Did you see what I said? You DID NOT HURT MY FEELINGS! You're outside the bounds of decorum as I see it, and you can count on me banging the drum against you in 2020 ... or sooner.

Adam You have a great opinion of yourself and I don't want to interfere with that, Mark. Go for it.

Mark Not really, Adam, But my opinion of you has sure gone south—even further so as a result of this unpleasant conversation ...

Adam You have not actually ever attempted to sit down with me You've judge me in a harsh way without even attempting to speak with me, which for a friend and supporter, seems a shabby way to act

Mark You have got to be kidding???? You started this conversation first thing this morning by telling me to "fuck off" and that I'm "all talk, no balls" and now you say that I have been "harsh" and treated YOU shabbily??? Brother, you need help ...

Adam Thanks for your compassion, I will note it next time you go public attacking me without even talking to me.

Mark *[You missed a call from Adam. Sunday 2:09pm Call Back]*

Adam I moved recently to Shell Beach and now that I know you are the most important person here and everywhere, please let know how I can chip in for your local Decorum lectures

Mark Gorw up ...

Mark GROW UP

Adam As soon as you show me how I need your help, Mark

7:29AM [Monday]

Adam Mark, after a few emails from people based on your letter, I want to sincerely apologize to you, and wish you well.

On Tuesday Burnes responded by attending the board of supervisors' meeting on February 6, 2018 to read some of Hill's comments and to ask the board to remove Hill from the board or to censure him. Hill was not in attendance, having called in sick. The board agreed to draft a code of decorum. Finding that the only means of removing Hill from the board would be a recall, Burnes began to speak publicly of a recall.

As he had done so many times in the past, Hill apologized, promising to seek help and rehabilitation. While expressing skepticism, Burnes agreed to hold off on a recall campaign to give Hill a chance to make good on his promise.

AUGUST 2018

Meanwhile, reports of a scandal involving Mayor Pro Tem Lee began to emerge. An investigation into the Integrated Waste Management Authority (See Chapter 5), over which he had presided for three years, was being obstructed. Lee, as president of the board, was a stooge for Hill. Requests for credit card receipts to document $500,000 of employee expenditure on the agency credit card were unavailable.

Turns out the files were at Lee's house. He had put the files in his pickup truck and taken them home. That had a familiar ring to it. I remembered another occasion when he had suggested he would use his truck to "rescue" the sewer district files at administrator Wallace's house in the dark of night (Chapter 4).

In 2018, when Shoals termed out again his Pro-Tem, Jeff Lee ran for mayor. At the eleventh hour I joined the race, concerned that Lee's election or ability to take office would be prevented by the outcome of the IWMA investigation. His opponent for the mayor's seat had never won any of the offices she had run for over the years. If Lee was removed, I was worried about her capacity for the position. I had 18% more of the votes when incumbent Lee and I ran for a city council position in 2016, but I knew I could not beat him this time. He had an 18-month head start and over $30,000 from cannabis interests. I ran to be sure his opponent could not win either, and was willing and able to assume the seat again if needed.

On the morning of the last day to sign up to run, it was confirmed that Lee's opponent was indeed running. I was out of town. I contacted the city clerk asking if I could complete the paperwork from somewhere else. She wasn't sure and wanted to contact county and state authorities and the city attorney.

By noon when I still had not received an answer, I gently reminded her that by not responding they were obstructing my right to participate in the democratic process. That got things moving. By 1:00 p.m. I had an answer—it had been done before in the county, so yes, I could do it if I completed all the necessary paperwork and had it notarized and had it to the clerk with the required thirty signatures before 5 p.m. I got to work on the forms and the campaign statements. I texted, emailed, and called supporters asking them to go and bring friends in the next three hours to sign the petition supporting my candidacy. We did it, and I was on the ballot. Lee survived to win the election. The IWMA has not fared as well.

2019

The council was the most toxic job environment I have encountered in my 50-year working life. It was like the mean girls in junior high school. Many times, after a council meeting, I would be approached by a member of the public who, having observed how nasty councilmembers were to me, would ask me, "But you are professional, fair, reasonable, kind. Why are they so awful to you?" I often made a new friend after explaining that the council didn't like that I refused to go along to get along, no matter how professionally and pleasantly I did so.

I wrestled with resigning for months. Quitting would be a first for me. However, the atmosphere was so debased that I couldn't legitimize it by continuing.

The mayor and mayor pro tem had appointed themselves (illegally and without council approval or Brown Act compliance) as a committee to oversee the cannabis applications, but never reported back to the council, as most committees do. Staff reports, devised to further the will of the mayor and his minions, went beyond the usual spin, supporting a certain course of action to outright lies of omission and commission. They almost never included information regarding similar activities in other communities or historical background to provide context. They avoided economic impact research, looking only at the promise of huge income in the case of cannabis business. Staff reports and council meetings were like a kaleidoscope—a fascinating seemingly stable image, but every time you turned it it changed and you could never understand what had happened, how it had been before, what it meant, and in any event; if you turned it, it would change again.

Campaign donations to councilmembers hid that the donors were, in fact, applicants for City cannabis permits. Campaign launches were attended by three councilmembers and the mayor at Cory Black's business premises. Oversight promised to the community in the ordinances created by the council and its back-room advisor Black never materialized or were removed from draft ordinances, such as the requirement for security systems that would dovetail with the police system, and tax software that would tie in with city hall software. The advice of paid consultants was ignored. Numbers were skewed. Public records requests were ignored.

The police chief provided updates on a social media site for neighbors. On average, 75% of the police calls were for dangerous activity related to the transient population (i.e. needles, loitering, trespassing, assault, theft, damage, threats, aggressive behavior). When applications for transient services came up and neighbors protested, the city manager and police wrote staff reports saying there were no problems.

It was so invasive, so pervasive, that I couldn't outpace their moves, nor could I ignore them.

By voting on items as they came up, I was sanctioning a process that I knew to be rigged. I wrestled with the decision to "let down" the people who had elected me to stand up for them. I was beating my head against a brick wall as deep and wide as the Great Wall of China. Finally, I just couldn't do it anymore. In retrospect, it was the right decision, even for the community, that now colloquially refers to it as the day I "dropped the mic."

The two minutes it took to read my resignation speech from the dais on February 22, 2019, were the hardest two minutes of my life.

I wrote to state and national publications pleading with them to take an interest:

> For nearly 20 years residents have complained of pay-to-play schemes operating at city and county level in our geographically isolated San Luis Obispo County. The county seat, the college town of San Luis Obispo, was dubbed by Oprah in 2011 as "The Happiest Town in America."[1]
>
> In 2013, while mayor, I recruited renowned criminal investigator Carl Knudson to investigate our bankrupt sewer district following depletion of the $11m reserve funds (https://www.slocounty. ca.gov/Departments/District-Attorney/Forms-Documents/ Press-Releases/2017/John-Lee-Wallace.aspx). Knudson tendered a 400-page report but was limited in his research by the remit and limited funds provided by the sewer district. The DA relayed to me that there was much more there, but his team sought only the low-hanging fruit, charging the sewer district chief executive with multiple felony and misdemeanor conflicts of interest.
>
> Concerned residents keep trying to bring attention to the problem, even personally funding Knudson, to investigate suspected malfeasance. Knudson has just completed several reports of malfeasance at the county's Integrated Waste Management Authority (IWMA), now under investigation by the District Attorney Dan Dow.
>
> Knudson, a former IRS special agent (http://www.knudsoninvestigations.com/our-solutions.html) and former Price Waterhouse Director, is the most competent and highly regarded fraud investigator in the country. In the early 1990s he masterminded the investigation of the largest known narcotics money laundering

---

1. http://www.oprah.com/own-oprahshow/happiest-city-in-america-san-luis-obispo-video.

organization in U.S. history, coordinating the IRS, DEA, FBI, and U.S. Customs Service personnel nationwide with the Los Angeles United States Attorney's Office. It revealed that over $1 billion in U.S. currency had been laundered for the infamous "Medellin" Colombian Cartel.

Knudson's findings in San Luis Obispo County, although on a much smaller scale, are only scratching the surface. The informed, concerned residents, working on their own time with their own funds, have been unable to keep up with the rapid expansion and success of raids on the public purse by political bosses and the staff and contractors they control. Their elaborate web extends to water, cannabis, development, and public contracts; in fact, anything that can generate income for the players and their sycophants.

Dear Mayor Lee and Members of the City Council,

After much soul-searching I have decided to submit my resignation, effective after this evening's council meeting, because I can no longer in good conscience associate myself with the council.

I want to thank the voters of Grover Beach for electing me to serve them for over ten years as their councilmember and mayor. Thanks also to our dedicated city employees who have been a delight to work with.

Much good has been accomplished by the council over the past few years.

During my tenure criminals were ferreted out from public roles, pockmarked streets are being repaired, and our city has balanced its budget with greater transparency. While I was a member of the sewer district board, facing the depletion of over $11m of reserves, we restructured the organization. This ultimately led to the investigation and conflict-of-interest conviction of the former chief executive.

The DA is still investigating alleged extensive misappropriation of funds at the Integrated Waste Management Authority. Yet, the council continues to appoint people to the sewer district and waste management authority boards who have supported those who have been convicted or accused of fiddling, cheating, and double dealing at both public agencies.

Finally, while I support the legalization of cannabis and the benefits of bringing the industry to Grover Beach, I cannot support those on the council, who with their political consultant, crafted a pay-to-play insider game. Many members of the community and the cannabis industry report that some dispensary applicants paid councilmembers and their consultant to get their licenses approved. In the end, applicants with clean backgrounds were pushed out of town while those with felony convictions were granted licenses.

I cannot betray the trust of those who elected me by looking the other way to avoid rocking the boat. Doing so, just to get along, is complicit and would make me as guilty as those who commit the evil, or those who choose to wear a blindfold. Every councilmember's first duty is to the people to take bold action when there is no other viable option.

Yours faithfully,

Debbie Peterson

Councilmember Mariam Shah's sanctimonious response to *KSBY*, our local TV news station, was curious. She said she had,

> "never seen ANY evidence to substantiate ANY of Ms. Peterson's claims. She knows that she can talk to me, the city attorney, the police chief, the city manager .... Instead of reaching out to us or providing actual evidence of ANY wrongdoing, she chose to abandon her office. A true public servant works to fix problems carefully, respectfully, methodically. Her resignation and all of her actions surrounding it show that she is the opposite of that."

Contrary to her claim that I could talk to her any time, Shah knew I couldn't talk to her because she refused to speak to me! She was in no position to maintain that I had not reached out to the city attorney, the police chief, or the city manager or provided evidence to them because she was not a party to those conversations, nor was there any reason that she should have been. Two years later Shah resigned from the city council, during the time frame that the FBI was investigating the actions of the council. Mayor Lee "categorically" denied all because,

> "it's … false … this is an issue …with no substance in reality, no basis in actual proof, nothing that would lend credence to what she was actually saying, … I've been fully above board and fully compliant with the FPC regulations and …, I have never hid money or received money inappropriately… I don't know why she feels necessary to come forward at this point."
>
> City Manager Matt Bronson said, "The allegations made by Ms. Peterson against Mayor Lee and former Mayor Shoals are unfounded and have not been corroborated with any evidence presented to the City at this time."

As to whether or not my comments were unfounded, they were very well founded and recently confirmed by DA and FBI press releases, charges, and confessions. I said,

> "… I am representing people better by saying …, it's time to take a look at these things … I can't continue to participate, …I want you to know why."

Assistant DA Eric Dobroth, when asked if the SLO County DA's office was investigating my claims, said, "While this office has been made aware of the public statement of Councilmember Debbie Peterson, it is the general policy of the District Attorney's Office Public Integrity Unit to not confirm the existence of an investigation or otherwise comment about an ongoing investigation."

After resigning, on the advice of worried friends I installed cameras everywhere and left town for weeks and months at a time. I couldn't even walk my dog because while I could disguise myself, I couldn't disguise my dog.

I am grateful to the DA's office for living up to its promise to investigate government corruption; albeit, not as aggressively as I would like.

I received then, and still receive, more feedback from my town on this matter than any other—hundreds of calls, texts, emails, and hugs thanking me for telling the truth about what was going on. Over two years later I am still being thanked; although now I much more often hear, "Debbie was right" or "Debbie told us about this!"

With the backing and participation of local citizens, I had successfully routed illegal or potentially compromised practices for fifteen years, leading to the resignation of two complicit attorneys, the prosecution of a self-dealing administrator, and more transparent practices of county agencies.

The corruption had always been there, but it had coalesced under Hill. When I resigned, their power was so absolute and their coffers so rich with cannabis donations that I didn't stand a chance. Hill polarized the council and mobilized each of them in his favor. All the pieces were in place to transfer the control of a happy little town to a wanna-be cannabis gangster and his comrades.

Things that would bring immediate legal action and public outcry in other counties do not even raise an eyebrow in SLO County. It's hard to contemplate in most communities that a councilmember and former mayor could recount multiple reports of a "hit" causing serious injury, and rather than acting, the city manager would get pissy and the council would reverse council medical insurance coverage.

Isolation

Looking back at the time Hill locked me in the County building on a public holiday and told me he had a gun, at best what he did was strong-arm me. He got away with it because he could do it unobserved by anyone but me. The question of crime and why it appeared that no one was doing anything haunted me and others. Our frustration was palpable. Sometimes the intensity of the fight wears us out, and we step aside, exhausted by the frustration; sometimes we must step out to recuperate. But usually, those of us who see it find a renewed energy to keep fighting.

The *Tribune* infuriates a sizable portion of the community. They almost never researched or reported on the projects of the right or even far left movements. They reported fairly on my resignation, so why didn't they print this FBI release six months later? *CalCoastNews* was the only local news outlet to report on the following podcast.

FBI seeks tips on corruption in the marijuana industry

AUGUST 15, 2019

> **Regino Chavez:** We've seen in some states the price go as high as $500,000 for a license to sell marijuana. So, we see people willing to pay large amounts of money to get into the industry.

> **Mollie Halpern:** As an increasing number of states change their marijuana legislation, the FBI is seeing a public corruption threat emerge in the expanding cannabis industry. States require licenses to grow and sell the drug—opening the possibility for public officials to become susceptible to bribes in exchange for those licenses.

> The corruption is more prevalent in western states where the licensing is decentralized—the level of corruption can span from the highest to the lowest level of public officials.

> As recreational marijuana becomes more widespread, Intelligence Analyst David Kirschner says states should expect the corruption problem to increase.

Halpern ended the podcast with a plea to listeners who "suspect a dispensary is operating with an illegally obtained license, or suspect public corruption in the marijuana industry, contact your local FBI field office."

I continue to be stunned by what credible sources tell me. In a February, 2020 conversation with Morgan, a principal in the cannabis industry, I was told, "One day I helped count $20 million in cash. It took a whole day."

Astounded, I asked, "Where on earth do you store that amount of money safely?"

The answer was, "Costa Rica."

I asked, "How do you get it safely to Costa Rica?"

The response was, "Remember, I told you he has a boat in Mexico and a plane? He uses his boat and plane."

I then said, "How do you keep it safe in Costa Rica?"

The answer was, "It is deposited into a bank there."

Not long after, I asked a DA if he had any idea of how many lives Adam Hill has harmed irreparably; hundreds across the county who will never be the same? His voice was sad, as was mine. He confirmed that, yes, he did.

MARCH 11, 2020

Thirteen months after I resigned, and a year after the FBI asked for tips on public corruption and illegally obtained cannabis licenses, the FBI searched Hill's home, his office at the county government center, and a third, undisclosed location. The San Joaquin Sun reported on October 6, 2020 that the third location was Dayspring's home.

The county administrator was quoted by the *Tribune* as saying there was no danger to the public. Perhaps there was no immediate physical danger, but any time the U.S. District Court's Central California Division issues a warrant signed by a federal judge that is executed a at 7:10 a.m. in three locations, there is good reason to believe that the public's wellbeing is at risk.

Soon after the FBI left Hill's home, Hill made what was reported as a first suicide attempt.

MAY 15, 2020

CalCoastNews reported that the FBI was actively interviewing several people countywide, including the other four county supervisors.

JUNE 2020

Once they made their raids, the FBI moved quickly, getting a confession out of Dayspring just three months after their raids.

AUGUST 6, 2020

Two months after Dayspring's confession and on the day the board of supervisors announced it would hear his assistant's claim of sexual harassment, Hill was found dead in his home.

AUGUST 13, 2020
SLO County supervisor accused of sexual misconduct

A week later the county board of supervisors settled Hill's assistant's sexual harassment claim.

Meanwhile, as government white collar crime proliferates, SLO County remains a safe place to live. Homicides are rare, and the FBI 2020 Uniform Crime Report, analyzed by *Wallstreet 24/7*, reports that SLO metro areas have the lowest car theft rates in the state, and that other property crime is also much lower than the state figure.

PART 2

The Devil is in the District

CHAPTER 4 SEWER TOUR
Overcharged and Underserved

"**D**ebbie, the web will be deeper and wider than you can imagine, and you probably won't be able to take it down," warned renowned government fraud investigator Carl Knudson.

Knudson did not know me well, but like all good forensic accountants he is astute, and he knows human nature. Perhaps Knudson had figured out that telling me I could not do something was the best way to make it happen. I had just given him two overflowing file boxes and megabytes of emailed evidence of malfeasance involving two mayors, a vice mayor, the chief administrator and engineer, and the attorney of our tri-city sewer district—a microcosmic sample of an epidemic of countywide corruption going back years before Adam Hill came on the scene. Knudson had just given me a mission—fix it.

If tallied over 15 years, over $50 million dollars have gone astray in just this one of dozens of special districts, the South SLO County Sanitation District (SSLOCSD). The tally includes $10 million in depleted reserves, $25 million in burgeoning quotes, reworking $10 million of failed projects, and $15 million of legal fees and fines. Multiply that over a hundred agencies and districts countywide and it becomes easy to understand why we can't fund critical infrastructure or affordable housing. These costs keep increasing, and greater and greater resources are needed from the public—the never-ending source of funds—to address sewer plant safety and depleted ground water. I wanted to know how they did it.

John Oliver, the British-American political commentator and comedian in his HBO series *Last Week Tonight*, dubbed special districts "Ghost Districts" because they are mostly hidden. His brilliant expose has eight million views on YouTube at John Oliver—Special "Ghost" Districts.

The more I learned, the more I came to see the sewer district as a best example of worst government practices. California Health and Safety Statutes appoint the presiding officer of each city as the city's sewer board member. The Statutes dictate that in the event the presiding officer is unable to serve, an alternate is to be selected by the city council. Therefore, the board is made up of the presiding officers of the three communities it serves. That was not how it played out with the directors from Oceano and Grover Beach. For over twenty years, both communities (except when Jim Hill was President) often strayed from the legal mandate that the presiding officer is the sewer board member. In each of the 10 years of his mayorship, Shoals insisted that he and he alone was responsible for appointing the representative and alternate. This cavalier approach to the law portended future, more serious breaches of duty.

In 2008, when I was first elected to the city council, the sewer board members were Jim Hill, Tony Ferrara, and Bill Nicolls. Jim Hill is an engineer with a law degree and accounting training who works in a senior safety role at the nearby PG&E nuclear power plant. The soft-spoken Jim Hill served on the dysfunctional Oceano Community Services District (OCSD) board from 2004 to 2011. Equally as tall and good looking as the substantial presiding officers in neighboring cities, with a penchant for diligent preparation for meetings, Hill was quickly appointed the Oceano CSD board president, gaining him a seat on the South SLO County Sanitation District board. Hill was the OCSD President for five terms between 2005 and 2011, and duly served on the sewer board each of those years. Jim Hill followed the rules. He says that three former Grover Beach mayors, who had also served on the sewer district before him between 2003 and 2006, told him that meetings were short and efficient, and it seemed that everything ran well.

OCSD President Jim Hill's first sewer board meeting included a pay increase for the sewer district administrator, John Wallace and his firm. Jim (I will call him this to avoid confusion with Supervisor Hill) brought a high standard of corporate expertise and professionalism to the board. He found that neither the administrator's nor the engineer's performance had been reviewed before instituting previous pay raises, and only one board member, Tony Ferrara, the mayor of Arroyo Grande, had any consistent long-term experience with either.

Jim set about reviewing Wallace's contract as part of his research for the meeting. Concerned because Wallace, the administrator, was passing work to his engineering firm, The Wallace Group, Jim asked for a copy of the engineering services contract with the Wallace Group. There was none, so he asked the board to go out to bid for engineering services. The board refused, so Jim asked the board to create two contracts—one for Wallace, the administrator, and one for his company as the sewer plant engineers. The board again refused.

Jim observed that Ferrara and Wallace were buddies. Whether this dates back to before arriving in Arroyo Grande when both were employed by Los Angeles County is unknown, but certainly by 2005 Jim and employees recall that Ferrara and Wallace often talked enthusiastically about the vacations they took together on Wallace's private plane in Florida, where Wallace grew up and went to college. Researching online, I came across a reference to Tony Ferrara as a retired sheriff detective employed by Los Angeles County and a reference to his 1986 retirement. Ferrara moved to Arroyo Grande and was elected to the city council in 1998.

Contractor Wallace was a former engineer with the Los Angeles County Flood Control District. In an interview with the Economic Vitality Corporation, Wallace said he relocated to take a job with San Luis Obispo County in 1979 because he wanted to raise his sons there. He said he later realized he could be doing the work the county was doing with his own firm, so he left to form The Wallace Group.

In 2002, Ferrara was elected mayor of Arroyo Grande, serving unopposed until 2014. Ferrara served continuously on the sewer board, more often than not as the chair, until he was unseated in the historic, nationally reported six-week write-in campaign by the same Oceano Community Services District's Jim Hill, who had moved from Oceano to Arroyo Grande and been asked to run for mayor by the town's business community.

From 2002, accounts began to emerge that the Arroyo Grande planning department would suggest to applicants that using the Wallace Group on projects was advisable. From 2005, Shoals, Nicolls, and Ferrara held an iron grip on the sewer district along with the district administrator and engineer, John Wallace, Wallace's engineering firm, The Wallace Group, and the District's attorney, Mike Seitz.

Mayor Tony Ferrara was an imposing figure with an ego as big as his resume, claiming he:

- Retired from a 42-year career in law enforcement and emergency management training and planning at county and state level

- Was a principal partner in Arroyo Consulting Group, founded in 2006, specializing in Energy Contingency Planning

- Served in the Army Reserves for 12 years as a military police officer and helicopter pilot

- Had a bachelor's degree in Business Administration from the University of Redlands and

- A master's degree in Public Admin from the University of Southern California, and is a

- Lifetime member of Phi Kappa Phi Scholastic Honor Society.

If his ego and resume were big, his office was bigger. SLO County mayors are non-executive mayors, and while the other presiding officers Ferrara served with had not so much as a shared desk in their city halls, Ferrara set himself up with an impressive office/boardroom on the second floor of a newly constructed city hall, with a huge view window and balcony overlooking Arroyo Grande Creek.

The 47 years in law enforcement must have begun in his mother's womb. Born in 1945, graduating from college in 1966 and retiring in 1986 per Transparent California's report, adds up to 20 years, providing he went on to get his master's degree while working in law enforcement. It is hard to credit his claim of 47 years in law enforcement unless you count from his undergraduate graduation through his retirement and every year he was mayor until 2013. Ferrara also held an appointment as Chief of State Agency Training and Support for the California Specialized Training Institute in the Governor's Office of Emergency Services. Given his pedigree as chair of a state emergency services board, and Wallace's pedigree and engineering experience with several counties and his own engineering company, it is hard to fathom what came next. How did a teeny-weeny sewer plant with such luminaries on the board fail so overwhelmingly in 2010?

The third member of the board in 2008 was not Grover Beach Mayor Shoals, as mandated by California Statutes. Shoals was the self-appointed alternate. Mayor Shoals was a close friend of Arroyo Grande Mayor Ferrara. Having worked in planning departments in three local towns, and for two SLO infrastructure design companies, he had been professionally associated with Wallace for decades by the time he was elected. When Shoals strutted into the room, he took up space. An architecture/planning graduate and basketball star at Cal Poly, San Luis Obispo, he looked more like football had been his sport. Like Ferrara, Shoals started up a couple of corporations and a consulting company that he would crank up whenever he was in one of his between-jobs phases.

Mayor Shoals decreed that Mayor Pro Tem Nicolls would serve on the sewer board. From 2008 until 2020, except for the two years when I was the mayor (2012-2014), either Nicolls, his wife Barbara, or Shoals served as the District representative from Grover Beach. By 2008, Wallace and the plant attorney had worked at the plant for thirty years after the near bankruptcy of the District in the early 1980s. Paul Karp, a much-loved former Arroyo Grande Public Works Director, was hired to go in and turn the place around. Karp did so successfully, turning it over to Wallace in 1988 with a very competent superintendent, John Ellison. Ellison ran a ship-shape operation. He and his team of seven operators and a lab technician added $500,000 a year to the reserves, building up a fund of $11 million.

Ellison retired in 2000 to form his own company with funding from Wallace. They had what has been described as a painful falling out in 2009, and there became two companies with the same name. Ellison has gone on to build a successful nationwide business.

But not to worry about Ellison retiring. The plant was served by an engineering firm (The Wallace Group), administrator (John Wallace), and attorney (Mike Seitz) who served at least twenty similar districts. Wallace or his group installed, designed, managed, or owned much of the public, housing subdivision, and commercial water and sewer infrastructure in SLO County and counties to the north and south. The board and alternates included a planner, an engineer, and a governor-appointed statewide emergency expert. The little plant protecting 38,000 residents had revenues of $3 million a year and its $11 million reserves to cover a $7 million quote to upgrade to a state-of-the-art plant with streamlined operations, a safety back-up plan for every process and piece of equipment, and improved services in the years to come, as well as a good relationship with the water quality control board.

Nicolls was immensely proud of his role and was appointed chairman in 2009. He quickly became part of the inner circle. He had equally as much ego as Ferrara and Shoals but lacked their stature and polish. He was a retired insurance investigator from Oakland, and boasted of his status as a Marine, having served in the reserves. Nicolls fitted the 'good ol' boy' stereotype with his butch haircut and husky build. There was no mistaking that he was on assignment if he strolled into your office or summoned you to a meeting. Taller men, even lawmen, felt they were being threatened when Nicolls came calling. His forceful humorless approach left no room for any response but that which he was pursuing.

Board in Charge of Millions and Ten Years of Losses

Together, Ferrara, Shoals, and Nicolls presided over a decade that decimated the reserves of the sewer plant. About the time Shoals first became involved with the District he formed two LLC's. Ferrara formed a consulting company in 2006. In 2007, when councilmember Steve Lieberman was appointed mayor, Shoals served on the sewer board. For the first time in over 22 years, the annual operating budget showed a deficit—a big deficit—of $500,000 on income of less than $3 million, as shown in the chart below in a screenshot from the Sewer District 2010/2011 budget. Every year the District had $500,000 surplus to deposit to its reserve accounts. This year the District showed a loss of $500,000, a gap of a million dollars from previous years.

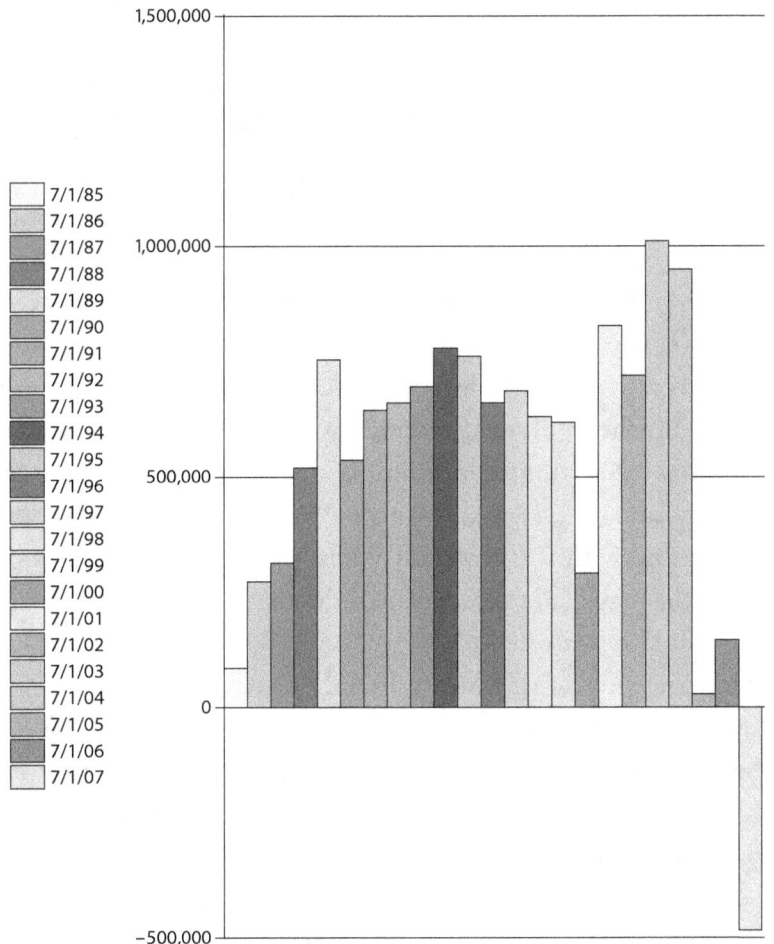

The chart above is taken from the SSLOCSD Bylaws approved March 2, 2011, p.6; Fiscal Year Budget 2010-2011, Exhibit A, p. 97

By 2008, District reserves had fallen to $8 million. My friend, former Mayor Peter Keith, asked me to serve on the sewer district board because he was hearing that there were problems there.

I had bad news for my friend. The mayor would be making that decision and, as I believed at the time, there was nothing as a councilmember that I could do about it. I had no reason not to believe that the staff reports, and the assertions of the mayor were correct—that the mayor was in charge of who served on the sewer board.

Other concerns began to surface in 2009. Surfers were getting sick after being in the water and started testing the water quality at the sewer outflow and other locations along our 19-mile stretch of beach. In addition to being ocean activists, they were savvy businesspeople and scientists with strong observation and analytical skills. The Surfriders began an aggressive campaign calling out the management practices at the sewer plant by speaking during public comment periods at local city council and community service district meetings.

I surmised that Mayor Shoals was making a shrewd political move. He was clever enough to distance himself from the plummeting reserves. If he served on the sewer board, he would be held accountable for doing nothing about the outflow of reserves, which would affect his political and even his consulting reputation. But if he called out the issue of budgets exceeding the $3 million income by 100%, he would jeopardize his relationship with the powerful Wallace Group. So, Shoals worked the ego of the mayor pro tem, putting him in the hot seat, knowing his pro tem would be flattered to be part of the good ol' boys club, would do his bidding and would be loyal to the club at all costs.

Mayor Pro Tem Nicolls made it his business to stand in the way of any threat to the club. When State Parks representatives asked to meet with him about Wallace, he brought Wallace. When a businessman chose not to use Wallace to engineer his sewer system, Nicolls called on the businessman. When whistleblowers contacted Nicolls about problems with Wallace, Nicolls told him. In other cities in the county, the pro-tempore position is rotated. The simple role of the mayor pro-tempore, as described in California code, is to stand in as the city spokesperson or meeting chair if the mayor is unavailable. Not so in Grover Beach under the Shoals regime. Nicolls relished, and seldom received, positions of leadership anywhere else. His relational approach was not well-liked. Identifying as a Marine, he had an outdated understanding of military leadership and saw the mayor as the general and himself, the mayor pro tem, as the one to do the mayor's bidding. Nicolls was like the perfect Alexa. Say, "Alexa, do 'X,'" and Nicolls did 'X'—aggressively.

The District had hired a top-notch microbiologist lab technician, Devina Douglas, a winner of the statewide title of Laboratory Person of the Year from the California Water Environment Association. Surfriders continued their assault on bad sewer district practices. My friend the former mayor did not let up, either. He continued to assert that something needed to be done, and even one of my employees was angry that I was not doing more. The dream team's favorite little enterprise agency was showing signs of wear. Wallace continued to assert that the SSLOCSD was his favorite sewer plant, that he was undercharging, and that he was saving the District so much money.

In 2010, technician Douglas objected when the work of the licensed operators was taken over by Wallace Group staff who, like Wallace, were not licensed to run a sewer plant. The Wallace Group accumulated and charged for in-house tasks while maintaining the same employment numbers at the plant. As the costs soared, plant performance plummeted. More money, more staff, more Wallace Group did not equate to more quality. The District was overcharged and underserved.

The more the Wallace Group intervened the faster the plant and its reserves failed, so the board appointed Wallace as treasurer. Chairmen Mayor Ferrara, Mayor Pro Tem Nicolls, and new OCSD President (now judge) Matt Guerrero began to (illegally) sign for payments from the reserves dedicated for capital improvements to pay salaries (operating costs). The legally mandated reporting to the County Auditor ceased. The water quality readings of water discharged from the plant nose-dived. The Regional Water Quality Control Board became increasingly angry, frustrated, and worried as their requests for "redundancy"—the new plant—were promised but not delivered year after year.

Information about how badly the plant was performing was obscured. Chair Nicolls, in council committee reports at council meetings, either had nothing to report or made glowing reports. The SSLOCSD website contained scant information, and the meetings were audio tape recorded by Wallace and destroyed after 30 days, but not video recorded. Wallace prepared the minutes. Public records requests were obstructed, and there was little public interest because it was not as if anyone wanted to visit a sewer plant.

DECEMBER 19 AND 20, 2010
THE SPILL

The repeated warnings from Surfrider presidents Brad Snook and Jeff Pienak were borne out in December 2010. A large spill of still-contested magnitude occurred when stormwater flooded the plant. As floodwaters rose, staff attempted to turn on three pumps, all of which failed, shorting out the electrical system and causing the over-taxed plant to spill sewage into surrounding neighborhoods and the sea. Maintenance holes bubbled sewage through the streets, garlanding the willows in the ancient lagoon with toilet paper.

How was it that the mayor of Arroyo Grande as a board member at the sewer district and chair of a statewide emergency advisory committee could not manage an emergency in a small sewer plant? How was it that an engineer/administrator with decades of experience and a firm of fifty employees could not manage a small sewer plant? Charged with preserving public health and safety, why did Wallace and his firm not ensure that the plant had backup after backup, as even any mediocre engineer and engineering firm would have done? Given Wallace's fees, the sewer plant should have had state-of-the-art systems with multiple working backups. Instead, they had nothing but problems. The Regional Water Control Authority stepped in, levying a fine of $1.4 million.

The organizational culture of the District was as septic as the spill waters that engulfed it. Technician Devina Douglas and Plant Operator Scott Mascolo, thinking that Nicolls, as a church member, would be "a good guy," reported to him as outlined in the employee handbook, their concerns about what was going on with Wallace. Nicolls reported them to Wallace and they were bought off, but not before being accused of having an affair and anger management issues.

What was the "anger" issue? It was the righteous anger that most honest employees would have and should have. An employee was using the sewer district shop to run his street sweeping business, apparently with Wallace's blessing. The shop was needed for sewer plant projects. When the whistleblower lost his temper because he was unable to do District work in the shop because he would be in the way of the employee who was running his personal business there, the whistleblower was reported to the sheriff, accused of a violent outburst. Although I was on the board by the time the case was settled with the third whistleblower out of a workforce numbering nine, while sure there was a payout, I was never to know where the funds came from, whether directly from the district or the insurance company, or how much. I know that the administrator had either let the insurance lapse or it had been denied—this was never cleared up, either.

The Regional Water Quality Control Board (RWQCB) had been hammering the plant for years to develop backup systems. They had been ignored by Wallace and his board. The spill set in motion a 12-hour hearing by the RWQCB, more press and media reports, and denials by the sewer board of any wrongdoing. The agency lawyers did what all good criminal attorneys do—deny wrongdoing and smear and belittle the accusers.

Open government does not look like this; nor, for that matter, does best practice in any industry. Mature, responsible companies, governments, good engineers, and scientists admit mistakes and learn from them. They reward and honor honest employees who seek the best for their customers, who look for cost savings, and who want equipment to function well.

The transcript below provides an example of how council committee assignments for the position on the sewer board were carried out year after year.

JANUARY 3, 2011
Grover Beach City Council Meeting Appointments to Various Boards, Commissions, and Committees

Councilmembers Molnar, Peterson, Bright, and Nicolls indicated they would like to be appointed to the SSLOCSD.

> **Mayor Pro Tem Bill Nicolls** *"…Sanitation District, which I would like to keep."*

> **Councilwoman Molnar**: *"I was gonna say you could give it to me. It's a fair trade."*

> **Councilwoman Bright:** *"I was liking the look of that one. Really all I have is APCD."*

> **Mayor Shoals:** *"Bill sounds like he would like to remain in that capacity."*

> **Mayor Pro Tem Nicolls:** *"There's a lot of things going on there; we've got going over the last couple of years, and I have really enjoyed working with John Wallace and Tony. I do enjoy it. We have the CSD representative Jim Hill, Tony Ferrara, and myself."*

> **Councilwoman Bright:** *"I can't make the daytime meetings. If I am not going to get the sanitation district because Bill's going to be snippy about it, then I'd like to be the alternate, please."*

> **Mayor Shoals:** *"I've already penciled you in as the alternate."* (NOTE the choice should have been the council's, NOT the mayor's)

At this council meeting and those that followed it could have all changed. Had we been accurately informed, the three-woman council majority would have overruled the mayor. We would have replaced Nicolls, whose autocratic leadership style was creating a cacophony of public dismay as he covered for the misdeeds of sewer District Administrator Wallace and Mayor Ferrara.

This Shoals/Nicolls shuffle repeated every year with lengthy staff reports made up of health and safety codes and references to past practices. In 2012 and 2013, the mayor asserted that the bylaws called for the mayor to make the appointment to the sewer district. There's only one problem: there are no bylaws. The governing documents are California Health and Safety Code and our State Constitution. I know for sure because I asked the city manager, city attorney, and even the city finance officer for the bylaws. None exist. In 2014, Shoals appointed Nicolls's wife when Nicolls was termed out. Nicolls had announced that his wife would run for office and do his bidding. She jealously warded off attempts by the public to recover their lost funds, even while admitting in a council meeting that she had "a vested interest" in being the SSLOCSD representative.

Local press kept it coming, covering the stories of the whistleblowers which were later corroborated by the 2015 malfeasance audit by Knudson Associates.

JANUARY 26, 2011

"See no evil, smell no evil - Is a South County sanitation district corking whistleblowers?"

This was the question posed by the *San Luis Obispo New Times* headline. Two conscientious employees claimed retaliation, lawyered up, and went to the press. The district denied firing anyone and countersued one of the employees. The whistleblowers' colleagues refused to testify against them, despite their fear of becoming victims themselves. A third was off on leave. At issue was rigged water sample testing, private use of public property, and various conflicts of interest between the district administrator/engineer and the district.

Neither Wallace nor the district's attorney, Michael Seitz, would comment on the cases; perhaps because they did, indeed, have a conflict or two. The attorney's wife was employed as the human resources director by Wallace, who administered the plant; an insider ostensibly representing the employees against Wallace while married to the attorney protecting District Administrator Wallace's interest against the employees. They dropped their countersuit against the whistleblowers and settled with all three.

FEBRUARY 25, 2011

The district placed a puff piece in the local paper in response to a notice of violation filed by the state Water Resources Control Board, saying they had complied in every respect. Have you noticed a pattern here? Wallace never seemed to do the right thing until backed into a corner by a legal authority.

MARCH 2011
Two Oceano leaders suddenly resign

Meanwhile, as trouble was brewing in Oceano at the sewer plant, it was also brewing at the Oceano Community Services District (OCSD). Jim Hill, board member of each board, resigned. As the President of the OCSD, he had tried to right decades of wrongs at the sewer plant. While the two agencies, the Oceano Community Services District and the South SLO County Sanitation District, are different, they are inexorably linked. The sewer plant is in Oceano and an Oceano board member serves on the sewer board. The mystery of disappearing funds has never been solved, at least not publicly. No doubt some former board members and employees know the answers. At the time, as a new councilmember I was not aware of what was happening at the OCSD. Like so many members of the public, I figured it was just political in-fighting. The District's new director, (now judge) Matt Guerrero, said he didn't know what to think, except that the board had to figure out how to move forward and couldn't continue to be bogged down. Part of his 'de-bogging' was done by hiring his aunt as the bookkeeper.

MARCH 30, 2011
Show me the money

San Luis Obispo New Times staff reporter Robert A. McDonald detailed the issues so colorfully that I have extracted parts of his article in the following paragraphs.

Thousands of dollars may be missing from Oceano accounts, and no one seems to know what to do.

What do you call it when thousands of dollars go missing from the coffers of a local government? Embezzlement? A crime? Simply a case of sloppy bookkeeping? Magic?

In the case of Oceano, a small, unincorporated town south of Grover Beach and Arroyo Grande, it is a question that will likely never be answered. In what might be a surprise to those unfamiliar with the kooky world of Oceano politics, both the district's leadership and the San Luis Obispo County District Attorney's Office aren't expressing any interest in the mystery of what happened to thousands of dollars of taxpayer money.

MONEY MYSTERY

The Oceano Board of Directors wants to put its troubled financial past behind them.

Bi-monthly CSD meetings are ... lively.

The directors constantly snipe at each other, while one steadily whispers into the microphone when another speaks. One director persistently accuses the directors of plotting against her.

There is one thing all the directors seem to agree on: the district's finances are deeply troubled, and no one knows exactly what is going on with the money. The Oceano Community Services District has been trying to deal with the mystery of its finances for years, and its books are an accountant's worst nightmare.

The books have not had a complete audit for the last three years, and district insiders say it's unlikely anyone will be able to figure out what was going on financially during that time.

Only recently has the money situation begun to be ironed out; a rough overview of the district's recent finances—the first in years—happened in February.

Considering the district's loose hold on the millions of dollars it has rustling around, the December 2009 discovery that someone may have been writing district checks without the board of directors realizing it didn't surprise locals.

In August 2010, officials discovered $368,000 in district funds tucked away in previously unknown accounts. The directors ordered a forensic audit—a specialized inventory of financial information to be used in legal proceedings—to examine a three-month period of 2008.

Results of the sample were revealed in August 2010, and they were dramatic: The partial audit found that, of 438 financial transactions examined, 134 were thought "questionable." This intrigued the District Attorney's Office, which, according to Oceano leaders, wanted to see more financial information.

Then, something odd happened. For six months, the board did little. Members repeatedly turned down proposals for another, more thorough audit.

Oceano officials discovered the money coming into the district through fees in those three months didn't equal the money being deposited. At any one time in that period, $10,000 to $60,000 seemed to be missing from the district's coffers, said the officials.

Could someone have embezzled money from the district?

"Someone got away with something," said Christy Proctor, an Oceano resident. "The sheriff doesn't care. The district attorney doesn't care. Somebody stole our money, and no one gives a damn."

APRIL 2011
Grand Jury releases damning report on Sanitation District

While no one was looking at the state of Oceano Community Services District finances, the 2010-2011 Grand Jury was looking at the sewer district, following up on citizen complaints and press reports. The Grand Jury noted multiple lawsuits, high employee turnover, losses of $1-2 million a year, equipment failure, a major spill, a potential $1.4 million water board fine, and conflicts of interest.

To allay public concern, the board commissioned an investigation, hiring Richard Thomas of Thomas Consulting, a friend of long-time District director, Arroyo Grande Mayor Ferrara. Insider Thomas found no conflict of interest.

The Grand Jury criticized the practice of having Wallace, the plant administrator, assign contracts to his engineering firm, The Wallace Group, who then assigned themselves the project management contract to oversee their own work, all without going out to bid. Wallace the administrator also served as the engineer, district finance officer, and treasurer with no written agreements between him and the District for his services in any of these other capacities. The Grand Jury found this a conflict of interest and called for an audit.

The board closed ranks, denying any wrongdoing, as they had when the whistleblowers went to the media, claiming they corrected everything before the report was even released. Facing increasing public outcry, Mayors Shoals and Ferrara invited Wallace to provide a report to their respective councils.

JUNE 14, 2011
Arroyo Grande City Council Meeting

Mayor Ferrara and Councilmembers Tony Costello and Caren Ray Russom (now mayor) said the Grand Jury report was "written colloquially, with unprofessional finger-pointing." Ray rambled on about a conversation she had with a friend who is a supervisor who told her

"*Fantastic* meeting! ... Just *fantastic*. Why don't I have my weasels call your weasels."

that the Grand Jury reports were not law. (Ray had been a planning commission appointee and subsequently the council appointee when Councilmember Ed Arnold resigned after being jailed on charges of assault and possession of child pornography.)

The council threesome assured constituents that the sewer plant was "working just fine." These assertions were based on the investigation by Thomas, Mayor Ferrara's friend and former colleague. The Grand Jury had found this investigation to be "inept" and the conclusions that the plant was running satisfactorily "not substantiated." The Arroyo Grande City Council later hired the "independent" Steve Bowman, owner of the Sintec Group, a crony of Ferrara's friend Thomas, to "investigate" new allegations of misconduct in the City of Arroyo Grande. Ray concluded by saying of the Arroyo Grande City Council and the SSLOCSD board, "I am sure we are all good people." Read on to decide if that is true.[2]

OCTOBER 21, 2011
Sewer District County Audit

At the bidding of the Grand Jury, the County auditor performed an audit that was slightly more extensive than the usual annual audit and made findings that could be implemented, saying there was no real problem. As they say in Britain, "They would say that, wouldn't they." As the ex officio auditor, the auditor's office had a conflict, auditing an agency that their office should have been tracking all along. The County Auditor's Office protested that they didn't have the time or the resources to audit the sewer district in greater depth. As Americans would say, "Yeah, right."

2. For a Weasel Words Glossary go to www.DebbiePeterson.com

As the ex-officio auditor of the District, a better approach would have been to ask the board of supervisors to fund a more thorough look at the District whose budget they approved with nary a question year after year after year. But that might have prompted the Board to wonder about the dozens of other special districts under their auspices or caused a deeper dive into the auditor's obligation.

Although the Grand Jury findings were voluminous, they did not extend to the auditor's office, where they might have found that the auditor could have exercised better oversight or suggested that the board of supervisors should better monitor the agencies whose budgets they approved.

Near the end of my council term, I had a request from a constituent to meet with him to discuss water banking. He was alarmed that once it was suggested, the board of supervisors considered it and then suddenly just dropped the matter. I was not at all familiar with the topic, so deferred to Robert Mires, the councilmember (and an attorney) who served on the Water Regional Advisory Committee. Mires was not interested in taking the matter further. However, I did learn a thing or two. The constituent described to me an unsettling occurrence with Mayor Pro Tem Nicolls who reportedly was calling on applicants seeking planning permission in Arroyo Grande, the city just to the South of Grover Beach. Nicolls's message was that they must use Wallace to install sewer systems or else.

The constituent I was meeting had hoped to develop a large parcel in Arroyo Grande. He found a much less expensive contractor. Although taller and equally as intimidating, the businessman reports that Nicolls's demeanor left him feeling threatened. While Nicolls was unquestionably working on Wallace's behalf, I have been unable to document even a trace of money to Nicolls.

The developer's project was not approved. I wonder how many other applicants who found other contractors were not approved. That information becomes harder and harder to verify now because under Ray Russom, all staff who would have known have been removed.

By 2012, shortly after the County's audit, the county auditor's records showed $6 million in sewer plant funds; $3 million more than the actual bank balance. Neither I nor the public knew until two sewer plant employees showed up at the county auditor's office on another matter and found the discrepancy. Even though the Sewer District covers territory overseen by two of the five supervisors, for decades figures went unchecked, and budgets were, and continue to be, rubber-stamped, brought to the board of supervisors on the consent agenda rather than the regular agenda. Consent agenda items are considered routine business and very seldom come up for public scrutiny or board comment. There is no expectation of discussion, and blanket approval usually is granted.

Special districts, such as the sewer plant, must also report to the State, but that seems to garner no real oversight by state auditors. There appears to be no cross-checking between agencies, and what should be layers of accountability in reality is none at all. It is actually worse than none at all, because with state financial data submitted online, board of supervisor budget approvals, and a county ex-officio auditor, there is an appearance that someone is paying attention. A whole lot of people were not paying attention, and it looks as if they still are not paying attention. Even as the District's reserves slipped to the point of bankruptcy, there was never any discussion by the board of supervisors, only consent.

AUGUST 15, 2012
Superior Court of the State of California COUNTY OF SACRAMENTO
Office of the Attorney General, Kamala Harris

The District Board decided to sue the state Water Board for levying the $1.4 million fine for the 2010 spill and wanted the papers related to the State's defense. The papers had not been released due to possible criminal charges. Despite Attorney General (now Vice President) Harris's ruling not to release the papers to the sewer plant board, they continued their suit. Although I joined the board just four months after Harris's ruling, that was never disclosed to me by the board or the plant attorney.

SEPTEMBER 7, 2012

When no settlement could be reached with the sewer district board, the Regional Water Quality Control Board held a public hearing. The water board reported that public furor erupted again regarding the 2010 spill that had affected more homes than any other spill since the state had started collecting information in its database in 2007.

The water board said there was no applicable defense for the event, caused by overdue preventative maintenance and improper operator procedures—the very problems identified by the whistleblowers. The penalties were increased because the District failed to report the backups into private residences that had been caused by the spill, instead blaming the homeowners.

Before I was elected mayor, I met with Matt Guerrero, the President of the Oceano Community Services District. He was angry about what was going on at the sewer plant. A SLO County superior court public defender, he had been on the board since the resignation of Jim Hill. He was adamant that the board should order a forensic audit as he said had been done at the OCSD.

I dedicated several weeks to researching the issues at the sewer district.

I read over two hundred pages of reports, noting recommendations that remained unaddressed. There was no shortage of investigations. I reviewed the "independent" investigator's report, the Grand Jury report, the Grand Jury-commissioned county audit, and got earfuls from Nicolls and Wallace. The first thing I asked for prior to taking my seat on the board was the budgets for the SSLOCSD. I also requested the audits, and the administrator's, engineer's, and counsel's contracts.

I would finally be in a position, as mayor, to make good on the promise I had made to my friend four years earlier—to investigate malfeasance at the sewer plant. I was horrified by what I found. I was even more horrified by what I couldn't find.

Sitting Chair Nicolls arranged a meeting with me, and another, and another, and another. He had a lot to tell me but provided no information. He reminded me repeatedly that Wallace was "the nicest person I would ever meet."

The first meeting was at Nicolls's home. He had summoned me to lecture me on the reasons he should remain as the council representative to the sewer district. He was, in effect, asking me to break the law. I had no authority to make that appointment. State code appoints the mayor as the representative, or if the mayor is unwilling or unable to serve, enlists the council to appoint an alternate. I listened and did not commit. I asked for his file for the period he served on the sewer plant board. Once before I had succeeded Nicolls as a board member, and he had turned over meticulous and thorough files of the agency meetings. I expected the same again. He said he didn't have them and that, "the city has the files." Not so. Neither the city clerk, the city manager, nor the city attorney had a file on the agency or its meetings.

NOVEMBER 21, 2012

I was working at my desk in my real estate office when, just after 11 a.m., I received a call from Wallace. He wanted me to meet him to tour the sewer plant. I had toured the plant a few months earlier with other elected officials, so I felt no urgency to do so again. I refused his offer to show me around. I felt uneasy about meeting with him alone at a sparsely staffed plant.

We chatted a while, and he answered a few questions after which I asked again for the accounts and budgets for the past five years. Almost whispering, in a drawn-out drawl, Wallace said, "Ohhhhh, that would be very difficult."

When I had asked previously, he commented dismissively that I could see them at the plant or get them from the bookkeeper or on the website. The bookkeeper said he didn't have them. They were not on the website, either.

Our call ended at about 11:25 a.m. Still unnerved by the phone call, I left the office to go to a chamber of commerce luncheon, arriving five minutes early. Nicolls was already there. He made a beeline for me as soon as I entered and confirmed my trepidation, accusing: "I hear you've been speaking to John Wallace." I believe he intended to intimidate me.

I was shocked that a simple phone conversation with the requests that any good director-to-be would make would prompt the CEO of a large engineering firm with so many contracts to immediately call the chair of a small sewer district, one of many he managed, to tell him about a run-of-the-mill phone call. I asked Nicolls for the files again. He gloated, "Oh, I've destroyed them."

While I was mayor-elect there were three SSLOCSD board meetings. Wallace and Nicolls met with me at a local coffee shop before each upcoming board meeting until I was seated to indoctrinate me as to the correct behavior for a District board member. At each meeting I requested the financials and budget for the District. On one occasion, Wallace asked me a question in his long, slow, quiet drawl in a "sincere" sycophantic tone, "Debbie, what can we do to make you happy?"

It was so foreign to me to be asked such a question in such a way that I didn't recognize it for what it was until someone else reported having the same experience with him and I realized that had been my opening to do a deal.

I told him I wanted the budgets and the audited accounts. Wallace said again, quietly, slowly, thoughtfully, "That would be very difficult." I slammed my hand down on the table in the coffee shop where we met and (for the first and last time, to date) roared, "I WILL NOT SERVE ON A BOARD WHERE I CANNOT SEE THE FINANCIALS!" That got their attention, but, after looking around to see who heard me, they recovered quickly enough to double down and tag team me.

They advised me that would be "very expensive" for me, as there were several hundred pages, and I would have to pay for copies at 10 cents a page. Still angry, I suggested that Wallace with his large consulting fees could cover the cost for a director because my $300 council stipend didn't stretch to those expenses, but the $80,000 a month he charged the sewer district might make it affordable for him to cover it. I suggested that otherwise, he might wish to email the budget and financials to me.

Finally, on December 4, 2012, two days before my swearing in, I received the budgets by email from Wallace's secretary at his San Luis Obispo Office (a city twelve miles north of the SSLOCSD), dubbed by sewer district staff, "San District North."

The red flags raised in the two hundred pages of investigations were reinforced by the budgets I had finally received. I still had not received the audited accounts, so I couldn't compare accounts from one year to the next to see trends. I then recalled that special districts have to report to the County. I emailed the county auditor, who sent the audited accounts within the hour, surprised that I hadn't been able to get them from the sewer district. I took the PDF files I received and converted them to Excel spreadsheet files to make year-over-year comparisons.

I couldn't deny the figures however much I just wanted everything to be okay. Several times I woke up in the middle of the night and thought, "No, it can't be true, not in this beautiful place." After wrestling with it for a while, I would force myself back to the numbers. The numbers didn't lie. Every time I went through that exercise I felt the same sense of conviction that I must address the information I was finding. I wondered about Wallace. There's nothing online of his background prior to coming here. Who was he? What was the quality of his work? Why did he leave LA County or Florida?

I followed the procedure I had used as a management consultant, putting on my manufacturing hat to analyze past years of accounts, taking into consideration the concerns of the Grand Jury, listing the items that that the board had not implemented. I created a presentation highlighting the red flags. I concluded that the administrator/engineer was overpaid to underperform.

About this time, I received an anonymous hand-written letter from someone saying they were a Grand Jury member advising me I was on the right trail.

I asked every attorney I could trust if they could recommend a forensic accountant/auditor with no ties to the County. There were no recommendations. I then began asking trusted friends from out of town the same question. One friend said, "I think I might be able to help you." He worked with a young woman whose father was an investigator. My friend asked his colleague if I might call her father, and she supplied his cell phone number.

That is how I met Carl Knudson. Knudson's website identifies him thus: "Knudson & Associates specialize in Forensic Accounting and Private Investigations. Led by Carl R. Knudson, former IRS special agent, former "Big 5 Accounting Firm" Director, and successful forensic accountant, Knudson & Associates specializes in White Collar Crime and Criminal Defense." Researching further, I concluded that Knudson is the leading government fraud investigator in the United States. Concerned citizens told me that according to staff, several office computers had been removed or wiped clean. Given the number of other red flags I was encountering, the bad press, the attitude of the board, and exorbitant legal fees, I wanted to preserve audit trails. I was encouraged to see that Knudson & Associates specializes in electronic discovery and hoped his firm could pull as much as possible from the remaining computers.

Knudson and I had a long phone conversation. Like many good forensic accountants, he had an unobtrusive, quiet approach that completely belied his accomplishments and drive.

He asked to meet with me. We met in my office. I was predisposed to like him because Knudson is the name of my great grandfather and talking with him, I was struck by his resemblance to my father's own quiet and studious father. However, his resume suggests a level of activity that is far from quiet. Knudson has over 40 years of fraud investigative experience at the highest level of government as an IRS Special Agent at the Office of Naval Intelligence and CIA in the Criminal Investigation Division. He has investigated tax evasion, money laundering, drug trafficking, and organized crime syndicates. Two books mention his involvement, *Washed in Gold* and *Dark Alliance*, which was also made into a movie chronicling the cases.

I explained that the District was cash poor, and I would have difficulty getting support for an expensive audit. Knudson suggested ways to keep his costs at a minimum and was later true to his promise, delivering comprehensive multi-agency reports with detailed audits, suggestions for improvement, and preventative measures charging significantly less than the rates charged by other local government consultants in SLO County. He later said that with a larger budget and broader remit there was much more graft he could have documented.

Then I began to hear the stories, and they were nearly the same every time despite different situations and different informants unknown to one another. I discovered the many ways used to divert taxpayer funds. The fraudsters have formulas—mining deep pockets or lesser-known agencies—and they stick with what works. As Knudson warned, there would be many more crimes than I could imagine. I am still discovering that to be true.

Sewer Talk

The week after I had been sworn in, unsure as to the seriousness of the spill and fine at the District, I contacted the Regional Water Quality Control Board to ask, "How bad was the flood on a scale of 1 to 10? As a board member, how concerned do I need to be? How do I put it in context with similar agencies statewide?"

I called, explaining that I was the new mayor and would be sitting on the board and needed help getting my bearings. I blew through twelve minutes and as many people and departments before I got through to the staff member assigned. Like me, she was new to the job. The city council's representative, Mayor Pro Tem Nicolls, indicated that all was well except for a silly report from the Grand Jury that the board was disputing, so on the face of it I had no reason for concern, so had not read the full deposition of the 2010 spill and had not attended the 12-hour hearing earlier in the year.

We had a candid conversation which I very much appreciated. As an engineer, she explained the mechanical problems at the plant. In addition to getting an opinion other than that of the District officials, who had run the plant into the ground, I wanted to plead with the Water Board for leniency on behalf of the customers who were not the guilty parties, but who would have to pay more for services because of the agency's mismanagement and graft in addition to the $1.4 million fine. My goal was to buy just a little time so we could turn things around without incurring more fines, which were just taking people's money from one public source and giving to another, but would result in inflated costs to communities already struggling with the high cost of living in California beach towns. She said it was Wallace who should pay the fine. All well and good, but also typical of government agencies' tendency to shift responsibility and never fully address or work in tandem to solve a problem on behalf of the people they are sworn to serve.

She observed that plant employees were frightened and had nowhere to turn. Employees worried about not being able to comply with the legal standards required to retain their licenses to operate the plant and ensure their employment. I said I understood that staff would feel compromised at work because Wallace "owned" the plant. She had explained that there was no go-between to advocate for staff. In most industries there would be a separation of roles with an administrator, human relations director, Chief Finance Officer, and engineer, and any one of these would or could advocate for employees. When Wallace did everything and only a very part-time board with patchy experience and abilities was responsible to oversee him, it was difficult for employees. There was no alternative 'go to' person for them, made all the more difficult because the head of the Wallace Group Human Resources was Sharon Seitz, the wife of Mike Seitz, Counsel for the District, who was assisting Wallace in pursuing the whistleblowers.

We talked for over an hour, and over the next year I received a couple of other calls when she had reached her wits end with frustration with Wallace. No number of warnings or inspections had been able to induce the board or its administrator to fulfill their promise to update the plant and create back-up plans for what is a critical public health service.

Over the five-year course of the lawsuit against the RWQCB, the

District spent upwards of $400,000 a year on legal fees. When I sat on the board, they were openly admitting that they were stalling to allow statutes of limitation to pass. The Wallace Group made out because, although the guilty party, they billed the District for time spent preparing for court appearances. The ratepayers paid many times over. They paid for the defense of the firm that was responsible for the infraction—twice the cost of the fine—and they paid the $1.1 million fine. Now, twenty-two years later, they will pay six times the original amount needed to create redundancy at the plant because all of their reserves were gone. The price for redundancy is at the time of writing $44 million, when the original cost had been more than covered by the $11 million in reserves, almost all of which made its way into the pockets of the District administrator, his firm, and government attorneys as one agency sued another: SSLOCSD vs. RWQCB, while a third government agency, the Attorney General's office, was entrained to rule on a dispute on lawsuits lodged with the fourth government agency; the courts.

Having toured the plant and spoken with the RWQCB, I had no trouble grasping the workings of the plant, but it took me years to understand how the finances worked because they were so convoluted. The board violated its own statutes, so much so that they did not release the 2010 accounts for three years as the board fought with the accountant who had noted in the accounts that the sewer district was violating their own statutes.

The plant was straightforward, like the manufacturing business I had launched and the many I consulted for: one thing goes in, something different comes out. As a management consultant, I also considered company culture and the finances arising from and supporting the process. The sanitation district was much smaller than companies I had helped restructure as a management consultant. We needed new legal counsel, a new administrator, a new engineer, a forensic audit, and initial professional advice as to how best to structure the plant management. I interviewed several engineers recommended by others in the community who I trusted. One in particular turned out to have been the man who spent five years turning the District around in the eighties and installed

John Wallace. He said he was alarmed by what he saw going on and was keen to go back in and sort it out again. He was well respected by the board, and in particular by Mayor Ferrara.

Even by 2012, I saw Wallace as just one bad apple, or just one of a small basket of bad apples. I didn't see that the fleecing of the Five Cities was only a small part of a plethora of criminal activity in the county.

DECEMBER 19, 2012
SSLOCSD Board Meeting

Over the course of the next three meetings, Ferrara and the attorney blocked my request to agendize a conversation about the structure and management of the District. First it was ignored, then when I asked for a second time in public, it was acknowledged but not agendized. Then the attorney told me that Ferrara determined that the board would meet in closed session because I was seeking a forensic audit which implied that I was making accusations against the administrator.

When I denied that I was making legal accusations, the chair determined that the agenda item was a personnel matter and the board would have to meet in closed session. When I denied that I would be discussing personnel issues, the attorney summoned me to his board room to set me straight. I held my ground, making sure to follow every requirement for getting it agendized and recording it all in email correspondence with the parties involved. Finally, they had no choice but to follow through on their public promise to put it on the open agenda.

FEBRUARY 6, 2013
SSLOCSD Board Meeting—Flags and Video

I was ready for my red flags presentation. I photocopied my year-over-year comparisons of the accounts and my list of forty red flags, putting them out on the edge of the dais at the beginning of my report for the press and public to pick up so they could read along. The board could not object, because it is a requirement of the Brown Act that the public gets the same information as the board. There were over a hundred people in the room, from Surfriders to my colleagues on the council, along with my supporters, angry ratepayers, and the media. The large public outpouring served to hold the board to account, but what saved the day was the arrival at the last minute of my friend Kevin Rice with his video camera. There would be a permanent record of the issues and the board response. It would take another three years before ratepayers would be able to convince the board majority to videotape the meetings.

My red flags report is at www.DebbiePeterson.com (live video of report), and in Appendix 3.

Wallace announced his retirement at the next meeting by scheduling a light agenda with cookies and punch. There were about twenty-five in attendance.

It took just six weeks to turn the District around, but it took nine months and $15,000 to get back the District files that Wallace had stored at his company's headquarters. Newly elected Councilmember Jeff Lee proposed to me that he would use his pickup truck to get all the files at Wallace's offices and home on the night the board accepted his resignation. I offered that to the board, but they refused.

People tell you what they are going to do, and they develop a modus operandi and terminology for their actions. If you listen carefully, you begin to discern who is working with whom and recognize who is pulling the strings as you come to know their speaking and writing styles and how they operate. In this case, it was the actions and the terminology that came back to me five years later when an agency Jeff Lee chaired was facing investigation by Carl Knudson, and later, the district attorney. Picking up agency files in his pickup truck was exactly what Jeff Lee did as the Adam Hill patsy and president of another organization seriously lacking in oversight, the IWMA (Chapter 5). It didn't occur to me that the purpose of picking up the boxes was not for the protection of the District, but for the protection of Wallace. Hill subverted Lee much earlier than I had realized.

I had been privy to the financial difficulties Lee was facing, and he and his wife had come to me for advice on their situation. To help, I regularly ordered from a part-time business they were running. I strongly encouraged Lee to run for office, as he was someone everybody seemed to immediately like and had solid engineering training that would be an asset on the council and on various committees with the public works projects at hand. He seemed like an honest guy. He had been a partner in a landscaping architectural business and had just secured a temporary position with the County to manage a flooding study. He was reticent to add more to his plate. As it turns out, running for office was his insurance. The County moved him into a permanent position in the public works department when he completed the project. It wouldn't have taken long for him, as a County employee, to realize that he had to stay on the right side of Supervisor Hill. On several occasions I was confused by his take on things and talked with him as a friend, never really coming to understand. That's because he was talking out of two sides of his mouth. He very effectively became a mole in my camp before finally publicly jumping ship.

APRIL 2013
SSLOCSD Board Meeting

Paul Karp, the consultant brought in to reorganize the sewer district, shared that he had a crack team of engineers who would assist him in turning the plant around again. It turns out that the plant, which was designed to use a biological process, was being run using a mishmash of biological, mechanical, and chemical processes, resulting in mediocre performance, high chemical costs, and poor discharge statistics.

It had been heart wrenching to sit at the dais at the twice-monthly meetings, because plant staff in the audience would catch my eye, silently pleading with me to do something. Shortly after I joined the board, the beleaguered superintendent, brought back after he retired, finally got his long-due and well-deserved retirement. It was a joyful moment when the new team presented a straightforward, simple 20-minute presentation as to why the plant process wasn't working, how it should be working, and how they were correcting it. Having set up and run a manufacturing company and consulted for many more, the transformation was so profound that it moved me to tears.

At around the same time activist Julie Tacker warned me that the board had violated the Brown Act by hiring and determining the pay of Mr. Karp in closed session. I was embarrassed and worried. I asked her to explain, and said the sewer plant's attorney hadn't advised the board on that. I then went to the city attorney who confirmed, yes, she was right. I asked the board to correct it by bringing it back on the agenda in open session. Thanks to Tacker, it was a practice that I was able to challenge time and again, and soon agency attorneys countywide ceased the opaque practice, thus allowing the public to weigh in on the employment and salaries of agency executives before boards approved their contracts.

MAY 2013

The reorganized SSLOCSD team of engineers and newly hired supervisor, John Clemons, presented the budget for the next fiscal year. I immediately liked Clemons because he was unfazed by the question I asked about every government employee hired during my watch—had the agency background-checked the applicants?

The budget was an improvement the past six-year run of annual losses of $1,000,000, but was still $250,000 in the red. When the chair asked for a motion to pass the budget, I said I would not pass an unbalanced budget.

Not one to avoid the elephant in the room, Clemons asked to speak from the audience, saying, "You would have the $250,000 you need to balance this year's budget if you got out of litigation."

Chair Ferrara didn't take that on board; rather, he asked staff to sharpen their pencils. Staff came back a month later with a balanced budget.

A year later, Clemons had the plant running within its budget, at HALF the annual cost of running the plant over the previous decade. Water quality statistics were the best they had been since the year 2000. The regional water quality control board was happy with the sanitation results they were seeing. There were no more violations. Staff were happy and empowered.

The turnaround was everything I had hoped for with one exception: an in-depth organization-wide audit. Mayor Ferrara and Attorney Seitz used the same tactics as before to avoid agendizing the matter. I had a phone call from Attorney Seitz telling me that it would have to be a closed session item because I was threatening a lawsuit. I said, "Absolutely not!"

I was asking for something that an organization should do every five years or so—a full operating audit of equipment, processes, and costs.

I explained ways in which operating audits could be helpful, and that they had been so for me in my own businesses. Guerrero had called for a forensic audit. I, a businessperson, wanted something different. But Guererro (now Judge Guererro) lost interest in what he had angrily raised prior to becoming the board chair. So I asked for the audit in public in a board meeting. It was on the record. The board weaseled out of it with the old, 'let us not go over the past. Let us look to the future.' ("Don't look over there, folks!")

At the board meeting, I explained that an operational audit is simply best practice; especially in an enterprise agency run as a business. Backed into a corner, they agreed to put it on the agenda. Then, while I was on vacation, the board changed the date it would be heard to the meeting that I would miss and voted it down. I was beat on the audit but had achieved a functional agency moving forward with a good company culture and a positive bottom line; $1 million better than the previous year, with the reserves building again. The District was performing as it had when Superintendent Ellison ran it.

Along the way there was a tragedy. The brilliant young engineer was cycling home from a board meeting one summer evening and a car hit her, running over her neck. She is now permanently in a wheelchair but continues her excellent work for government agencies. Years later I awoke in the middle of the night in tears. As others have, I had thought of myself as Wallace's worst enemy. We were wrong. His worst enemy was the brilliant young engineer who could take a plant he had mismanaged for over a decade and turn it around in six weeks, and, like other good government engineers, could explain it in terms that everyday people could understand.

Pony Up or No Permit

In his audit Knudson reported on some of the anomalies discovered at the sewer plant.

> The new plant superintendent met with the State Parks specialist in 2014 and reviewed the discharge application submitted to him. He visited the station and issued a discharge permit. He could not understand why the District had refused to issue the permit when everything seemed to be in order. Even though State Parks had no permit from 2009 on, they continued to dump at the station with no apparent protest from the District.
>
> At about the same time, in 2013-2014, the sanitation district superintendent met with Yo Banana Boys and issued a discharge permit as well and could find no reason why the discharge permit was not approved by the District in 2009.
>
> The State Parks specialist had been contacted by John Wallace, acting as the District Administrator, and a group of District people during July 2009. Wallace advised her…they were going to be shut down and fined for violations related to chemicals or high readings of chemicals at their dump station.
>
> The State Parks specialist asked Wallace for proof of the violations or reports showing that the violation came from her dump site. Wallace or one of the other people, she believed it was Bill Lindahl, showed her a report that allegedly documented the violation. When she looked at the report, it had a date of 2006, three years earlier, she told Wallace that this report was three years old and wanted to see something that was current that showed that it was their dump station that had caused the problem.

A District person introduced as Heather Billing, who was also with Wallace, explained that there was Formaldehyde detected ... and they were certain that it came from the State Parks dumpsite. At that time there was no report shown to the specialist to support that claim, either. She requested a copy of the 2006 report, but it was not provided.

Wallace, at that meeting, said that the problem could be easily fixed by his firm, The Wallace Group, and handed her one of his calling cards for the Wallace Group. Wallace told her that his firm could draw up new engineering plans for their discharge site for a cost of $300,000. The specialist recalled telling Wallace that she didn't need his firm to do the plans since they had their own group of engineers who could do the plans without any additional cost. Ms. Bellman recalled at that meeting she felt that Wallace was threatening to close down the dumpsite if she didn't use his firm to fix dumpsite issues that had something to do with violations. This was very upsetting to her.

She also noticed the SSLOCSD logo on Billing's calling card, which made her believe that Billing was an employee of the District, but she also noticed that the email address for Billing was for the Wallace Group. The specialist believed that the other people who had accompanied Wallace also worked for the District.

The former Chief Plant Operator recalled that Wallace had calling cards made up for his employees with the District logo and the cost of the cards was paid by the District. The specialist recalled other meetings with people whom she thought were District employees but, as she later learned, all worked for the Wallace Group.

After all the meetings and providing additional information, she was getting the run around about getting the permit. She finally got tired of all the delays and called Bill Nicolls, who she knew, in 2010. She arranged to meet with Mr. Nicolls at the offices of her boss, Superintendent Andy Zilke, where they planned to tell Mr. Nicolls about the improper business proposal made by John Wallace. On the day of the meeting, she walked into the meeting room and immediately saw that Bill Nicolls had brought John Wallace with him.

She was surprised and shocked that Nicolls had brought Wallace to the meeting, because they wanted to discuss this sensitive issue without Wallace. Ms. Bellman recalled that Wallace had a smirk on his face when she noticed that he was in the room. She and her boss decided not to bring up the issue with Nicolls about Wallace's attempt to shake them down for $300,000, but kept the conversation about getting the discharge permit. At the end of the meeting, Wallace made a gesture to her and said with a smirk on his face, "We're going to get you that permit."

After the meeting, she and her boss decided not to press any further on the permit because they were "weirded out" by Nicolls and Wallace and they definitely were not going to pay $300,000 to Wallace.

She had subsequent conversations with Billing about the status of the application and was told that it was still being considered. Billing eventually told her that they found out that the source of the formaldehyde was not from their dump station, but from a taxidermist in a town several miles away.

In 2012, the specialist asked Wallace about the status of the Discharge Permit Application, and he stated to her that they were still working on it.

When Knudson interviewed Nicolls about the 2010 meeting with the State Parks specialist and her boss, Nicolls replied that he didn't recall such a meeting, but recently had a nice chat with the specialist.

It makes me sad to read Knudson's interview with the State Parks concessionaire, Yo Banana Boy, who also needed a permit from Wallace. The state had continued to provide a dumpsite to campers, but their concessionaire dared not do so.

The private mobile dump operator, approved by State Parks to service recreational vehicles on the beach, first spoke with Wallace in the fall of 2008. They received initial approval from Wallace in December. At one of the meetings with John Wallace, Wallace wanted his firm (Wallace Group) to draw up the building and site plans for the project. The owner drew up his own plans.

Kraus subsequently got a Land Use approval from SLO County and obtained building permits (approved by both Wallace & OCSD) from the County Building Dept. They received the signed Use Permit from the District dated January 19, 2009.

They did not start construction of their dump-station until they had the Use Permit in hand. They started building their dump station and completed it in February 2009. It was first used the weekend of President's Day in 2009. Then, after less than one month, John Wallace closed their dump station down ... without giving any "real" reason. He just said more sample tests needed to be done.

The owner said he had complied with every request given to him by Wallace or the OCSD. They gave numerous samples, without receiving any completed results or explanation for the continued closure of his dump station.

Over the next two years, Kraus tried through many phone conversations and emails with John Wallace and other Wallace Group employees (they kept giving him a new contact person) to get their dump station re-opened, stating their case and the importance of the dump station to their business success. Unfortunately, they never heard anything else further from Wallace, and their dump station remained closed.

The owner met with the new plant superintendent in October 2013 about opening the dump station. After their meeting, the superintendent authorized the re-opening of the private dump station in November 2013. They have been doing the required self-sampling and have not had any problems with OCSD or the District.

Things I could change

By the time committee assignments rolled around again for 2014, I had achieved as much as I was able to at the sewer district. I realized that I would not be able to get an audit with the current board. I asked the council to appoint Councilmember Glenn Marshall as the alternate so I could focus on things I *could* change.

AUGUST 15, 2014

A news release from Carolyn Berg, president of the San Luis Obispo branch of the American Society of Civil Engineers, awarded John L. Wallace, president and founder of Wallace Group, the 2014 Lifetime Achievement Award in Civil Engineering for his "resourcefulness, innovation, long-term dedication to civil engineering, and community engagement."

The release described the Wallace Group as a San Luis Obispo-based, multi-disciplinary professional services firm offering engineering, planning, landscape architecture, public administration, surveying, and construction management services, founded by Wallace in 1984, with more than 60 staff serving both public and private clients.

SEPTEMBER 2014

As I was campaigning for a second term for mayor, the superintendent of the District asked to meet with me. Over lunch, he explained that he simply could not keep to himself the information he had come across in his 18 months as superintendent. He explained that the offenses of the engineer/administrator whose retirement I had hastened were much greater than we knew. He unloaded in almost a stream of consciousness as I took notes.

> —Wallace sued contractors often and was often sued himself for not awarding lowest bid. Clemons explained that Wallace designed, engineered, managed, built, redesigned, reengineered, and administrated, then when things went wrong, as they inevitably did, Wallace charged to prepare court briefs and made more money from his bad project management, taking up ten times the usual time to complete a project.

> —The Wallace Group was still billing to review work of a subcontractor that had installed a $1.6 million centrifuge for two years after certifying that the project was complete.

—Two years before that, the same contractor had installed a chlorinator. The Wallace Group was the administrator and engineer of the District, awarding contracts to itself, and also was the engineer that designed the chlorinator as well as the project manager overseeing and managing themselves as the engineer. The Wallace group had not installed the chlorinator on the level—it leaned. In most cases, the project manager would be on the hook for an incorrect installation. In this case, the Wallace Group as their own project manager just continued to bill for work on the equipment. For two years following the installation, the Wallace Group continued work on the chlorinator, never correcting the problem.

—The specifications for the backup diesel pump were set out by Wallace. The pump arrived and did not meet the required specifications. Wallace shipped it back to the manufacturer three times for corrections. This went on for years. Upon its final return it still was not up to the task. Wallace then told the staff he could get a bargain rate from another company to repair the pump. The staff told Wallace, "NO, NO and NO!!! it will not do the job!! In an emergency it would stop running without notice."

Wallace, against the staff's adamant pleas, said, "Too bad, we are accepting it as is."

It stopped running in 2010 when, in desperation, waist-deep in sewer flow, staff tried to quell the floodwaters and overflow at the plant.

Clemons said it sat in the shop and staff later stored it near the headworks, where he assumed it still sat; an expensive and useless piece of equipment.

—Part of the cause of the 2010 flood was that although three of the four headworks pumps operating the plant were working, the pumps could not have handled the flood even if the electrical system hadn't failed. The pumps were insufficient. Wallace used 40hp pumps when the plant needed 60hp pumps. Wallace, when his budget ran out, bought used pumps and had them tested at the Lopez Lake facility where he was also on the board; an entirely different County operation unrelated to the sewer district.

—CoGen was another piece of equipment that never worked. The board touted it to convert sewage to gas to power the plant. The manufacturer had declared bankruptcy. The Wallace Group designed and redesigned it. The agency paid Counsel $400,000 to prosecute the CoGen supplier (an amount equal to the annual District payroll, twelve percent of the District's $3 million annual income). On top of that, the agency borrowed $400,000 for the equipment. The agency had to repay the loan.

The Wallace Group had received Engineering and Service contracts and re-engineering fees of $500,000. These expenditures totaled $1.3 million of the ratepayers' money gone with nothing to show for it. Clemons believed that the board should have sued the Wallace Group because it was the project manager. What bothered him more was that even if it had worked properly, over twenty years the CoGen would have cost $2 million. Even at the lowest price it would never have recovered its cost. But the Wallace Group got rich. The lawyers got rich. The board should have paid for it via the LAIF (the Long-Term Investment Fund), which had about $8 million in it, but instead took out a loan to pay the engineers (Wallace) first. The lawsuit recovered $55,000 for the District, but not $400,000 in legal fees or the $400,000 loan.

—Wallace took three years to build chlorine chambers that should have taken two months.

—From 2004, Wallace, the administrator and engineer, was also the treasurer. He was responsible for reporting plant figures to the County, but the County did not have a correct figure for the LAIF fund—the equipment replacement fund, funded solely by connection fees and by ordinance exclusively for long-term use equipment and projects. It was illegal for the board to transfer connection fees into the operating fund or to use these funds for operating costs. Nevertheless, the board was using connection fees to meet payroll.

—The Wallace Group had been billing $50,000-80,000 a month, which, by the time we talked, was down to $1,000-2,000 a month, and attorney Mike Seitz had gone from $9,000-18,000 a month to only $1,000 and $4,000 a month in 2014. Given the huge costs of each, Clemons just could not think that the board would not have seen all this and realized something was wrong, but continued with revenues of $3.1 million a year to pass $6 million budgets.

—The Wallace Group as engineers billed $800,000 a year. For $200,000, the District could have hired a full-time engineer, or four engineers at the price it paid the Wallace Group.

—Not only was there a conflict of interest; Wallace exploited the conflict. He did not control and minimize the transactions of the District. He controlled and extended, reengineered, built in 12-month obsolescence, and then started all over again, and again, and again, obscuring his information by sidestepping questions, denying information requests, and speaking in circles, hypnotizing, and confusing questioners until they gave up looking for answers, and by not carrying forward account balances from one year to the next or doing year-over-year comparisons.

—There is more that went out to Wallace than previously thought. He did not just sprinkle his charges through various accounts; he also used other companies he owned to do the work. He traded District equipment to outside private interests.

—Wallace conducted personal business and/or allowed staff or professional colleagues to carry out personal business using District equipment and premises. He allowed one staff member to live on site. He allowed another to operate a street sweeping business out of the District shop, he made equipment trades with a farm in Huasna, and he had electrical work done by a sometime-employee, sometime electrical contractor.

—Wallace claimed that the District had only one spill in 25 years, but there had been several notices of violation and a 160,000-gallon sewage flow a few years before.

—He did not disclose to the board that insurance had lapsed in the midst of three whistleblower lawsuits.

—The budget at the County that was approved by the board of supervisors was incomplete because it did not include payroll that was being paid out of a separate account.

—Apparently, at some point Mayor Ferrara's wife, an engineer, had also worked for the District or had been employed by The Wallace Group.

It went on, and on, and on. Some of it I had some awareness of. Most of it I did not or had not perceived with the clarity that Clemons acquired from working at the plant every day.

What I heard from Superintendent Clemons haunted me. I felt ethically compelled to act, but what to do? As it went around and around in my head over the next few days, I came to understand that Clemons was telling me because he wanted me to do something. I asked to meet with him again and asked if he wanted me to act. I told him it would get ugly; uglier than he could imagine. A retired marine and former minister, he said he was not worried. He knew that he was doing his job well and they could not get him if he just continued to do that, and that he would always be able to find work because he was one of the best in the business. I demurred, saying, I thought they might be able to get him.

I made a Public Records Request (for a public records request template go to www.DebbiePeterson.com) to the County Auditor, who requested a meeting to discuss what I needed. I was looking for the ledgers and bank account statements. I had asked Kevin Rice to help with the complicated request. He is known, even by attorneys, as being the best in the County in preparing public records requests. The Auditor seemed worried and included one of the executive auditors in the meeting. When he asked why we wanted these items, I began to tell him some of our findings. The deputy auditor's eyes grew wide, and she gasped. They very efficiently and helpfully provided everything we asked for. Not long after, the auditor resigned and moved out of town.

When not on the council in 2015 and 2016, I had more time to rally groups of people to petition the District for an audit. Finally, the SSLOCSD board, after months of badgering by the public, appointed a citizens panel to hire an investigator. Guererro, during a board meeting, called all of us who were on the committee or advocating for an audit racists because Tacker, of native American ancestry, said that sometime OCSD representative Lucey, also part native-American, was "off the reservation." The people Guerrero were publicly accusing are some of the least racist people I know. The accusations stopped when I hung in my office an old photo of family members and my grandmother, who appear to be light skinned African Americans. That indicated that they were watching me. I also began sharing that I had attended a junior high school that was predominantly African American to support the Fresno desegregation effort in the 1970s.

It is curious that Guerrero would have approved those he called racist to sit on a selection panel. The panel had two applicants and recommended Knudson, who the board accepted and hired. It is a testament to Knudson's credentials that the District's attorney of 28 years resigned, claiming a conflict of interest after ten years of claiming there was no conflict of interest.

JANUARY 2016
Operational Audit Expected to Explain Diminishment of Public Funds

Knudson had completed his report, but the board planned not to release it. My supporters were adamant that I put out a press release about the Forensic Audit before other interests twisted the information. The release is excerpted below:

Former Mayor's actions unravel agency mismanagement

Grover Beach—Former Grover Beach Mayor Debbie Peterson wants the South San Luis Obispo County Sanitation District Board to release the forensic audit staff received last week, rather than discuss it in closed session. Peterson maintains that such a report should not be reviewed and possibly edited in closed session by a board that steadfastly resisted the investigation until forced into it by public pressure. She is calling on residents to attend the Board meeting to petition the Board to release the unedited report at once.

The report is the culmination of a three-year effort initiated by Peterson and several members of the public seeking an in-depth audit of the South San Luis Obispo County Sanitation District. If the report is released, the public may finally learn why the District's $11 million reserves shrank to the point of bankruptcy by 2013.

"Based on the red flags apparent over 12 years, I expect the report to reveal activity that will require review by the District Attorney. The public, the employees, the whistleblowers, the neighborhood, and I have paid a very high price over these past years. We deserve to see the report and we need our elected representatives to learn from it how to govern more responsibly going forward," Peterson declared.

"My concern is this is not an isolated incident. In the interests of transparency and accountability to the citizens of this county, and perhaps

further afield, it is critical that all agencies 'served' by these parties be investigated in light of this information to be sure the agencies are fiscally healthy and transparent. The public and their representatives must become aware of the practices to guard against and ensure ratepayers recover misused funds so they can carry out the health and safety mission of their sanitation district."

JANUARY 14, 2016
SSLOCSD Past Management Practices—Knudson Report

The following list comes from the Executive Summary of SSLOCSD Past Management Practices in Appendix 4. This condensed list validates much of what Superintendent Clemons shared with me in 2014.

KNUDSON'S FINDINGS BY THE NUMBER:

1. Wallace Group monthly billings grew from 81 hours ($3,600) in 1999 to 600+ hours ($70,000) in 2010
2. Major Projects went from seven in 2003 to twenty-eight in 2011
3. Wallace Group employees charging time: seven in 1999 and over twenty-eight in 2010
4. The Wallace Group, per its website, was providing administration and engineering services to ten other county government agencies at the same time
5. Wallace Group billed $90/hr. for work done by District employees who were paid $20-$44/hr.
6. The Wallace Group was charging for the chlorine contact chamber but not showing their involvement in reports
7. Files contained no documentation of Wallace Group billings for major projects, making it virtually impossible to audit the payments
8. Confidential SSLOCSD personnel files and agency records were stored at the Wallace Group office

9. As a SSLOCSD co-defendant in three civil actions brought by whistleblowers, Wallace used the Wallace Group HR department to provide services in defense of the allegations made by SSLOSCD employees, thereby using rate payer funds to defend himself as an outside contractor against the interest of SSLOCSD employees

10. The SSLOCSD attorney's wife was the Wallace Group HR Director. The attorney said she worked for Wallace for eight months. Wallace said it was "2-3 years"

11. Wallace used his position as District Administrator to obtain work for the Wallace Group from government agencies and local businesses seeking permits from the sewer district

12. Wallace Group employees had SSLOCSD business cards, leading the public to believe they were District employees when they were Wallace Group employees

13. Some District records are in the possession of the former District Attorney's law offices

14. Hundreds of thousands of dollars were paid by the District to Seitz and Wallace to "consult" or defend themselves, rewarding them for their incompetence

15. There was no board contractual record of the work or the payouts to the Wallace Group

16. Twenty-five years of institutional weakness included lack of performance standards and accountability

17. Hours billed, staff, and project numbers suggest that 50% of the Wallace Group employees worked for the SSLOCSD. Knudson said, "One wonders how they found the hours in a day to serve the other ten County government agencies at the same time."

Go to www.DebbiePeterson.com for the full report

We should have known that Superintendent Clemons would not survive this turn of events. The pressure began to mount for him to quit. I was so upset and frustrated that I called Knudson and asked to meet with him. He said, "Sure, come now."

I drove for hours, and when I got there and told him the story, he laughed. He said, "Oh, that's wonderful! They are setting themselves up to be in real trouble in court. This will make him rich."

The board had hired a new administrator, apparently with the sole purpose of getting rid of Clemons. The administrator never relocated his home or family because he "didn't like the smell" of the sewer district. To avoid the smell, he ordered a trailer as his office that he sited away from the actual works. The sewer plant is next door to the State Park, and while most of us would chuckle, he was scared away when a family of four racoons took up residence under his trailer.

Several times we heard on the down low that the administrator had been unemployed or on leave for quite some time because of nasty tactics against staff. Many of his former subordinates sent us written testimony of unbelievably cruel treatment. During his short stay, he dispatched with Clemons and then, following public protest about his dreadful people skills, quit with full pay and health insurance for his whole family for the duration of his lifetime after just 18 months of employment with the District.

I was right. It got very ugly. But Clemons was right, too. Although it took a year and he had to go out of County to find work, Clemons is working two jobs now because his work speaks for itself, and his services are in high demand.

Are You Sitting Down? 2016–2018

"Wallace should pay the fine."

-Ratepayers, RWQCB

JANUARY 2017

I was sitting in my car in the grocery store parking lot, just getting ready to drive back to my office, when a call came in from Mark London. "Are you sitting down, Debbie?"

He read me the paragraph in the scoop led by Karen Velie in *CalCoastNews*.

> "The San Luis Obispo County District Attorney's office has filed felony conflict of interest charges against 73-year-old John Wallace, the former administrator of the South San Luis Obispo County Sanitation District."

Later that day, I had to speak to the DA on another matter. A representative from the district attorney's office brought up the Wallace matter, asking me not to be disappointed, explaining that there was a lot more they could go after with Wallace, but they were going for the charge easiest to prosecute, which was conflict of interest. He said that a judge would reject even the many conflict-of-interest violations they found due to those violations occurring too long ago. Judges determine statutes of limitation, and they apply to conflict-of-interest charges. Crimes against the people by those charged with protecting the public trust should never time out. Surely, the loss of millions of dollars makes it sufficiently in the public interest to extend the statutes of limitation to protect the public from opportunistic officials.

JANUARY 10, 2018
Wallace Case Moved to Santa Maria After Guerrero Appointed Judge

Just weeks after Matt Guerrero was appointed judge, the SLO County bench unanimously ordered Wallace's case to be moved to Santa Barbara.

Although the order contained no individual judge's signature and made no mention of Guererro, it is possible that Guerrero could have been called as a witness in Wallace's case. As board president, Guerrero had signed bank orders to move funds from the District's Long Term Investment Fund (LAIF) to make payroll; a practice forbidden by District ordinance, and while on the board Guerrero verbally condemned several people seeking an audit of the District.

MARCH 6, 2018

On the second day of his preliminary hearing for felony conflict-of-interest, Wallace plea bargained for misdemeanors, allowing him to keep his engineering license and his membership in the American Society of Civil Engineers. Wallace had a very profitable business model. The target market? Unsupervised special (ghost) districts, such as sewer districts, that no one really wanted to know about. As late as 2021 this is still becoming known.

Julie Tacker defends the public interest in a *CalCoastNews* "Opinion" excerpted below.

MARCH 27, 2018
Fleeced residents deserve restitution from John Wallace

OPINION by JULIE TACKER

In 2011, the SLO County Grand Jury found conflicts of interest with John Wallace wearing two hats as district administrator at the South San Luis Obispo County Sanitation District and District engineer as CEO of the Wallace Group, his private engineering and consulting firm.

The District board of directors, then chaired by Bill Nicolls of Grover Beach, vehemently disagreed with seven of the fifteen findings and five of the seven recommendations in the Grand Jury report. The sanitation district board responded repeatedly by citing a similar 1993 Grand Jury investigation that did not find conflicts of interest with Wallace's dual role as San Simeon Community Services District general manager and his engineering firm.

The 2011-12 Grand Jury found the District's *"reasoning flawed because the San Simeon CSD is not comparable in size or budget to this district. Moreover, a Grand Jury report does not establish a precedent or case law; each Grand Jury report stands on its own findings and recommendations."* San Simeon CSD serves a population of just five hundred and their hotel visitors, while the sanitation district serves 37,000 people.

It took several years and several changes in the District board of directors to commission the 2015 Knudson Report, an independent investigation into the contracts and resulting work done by Wallace and/or his firm.

The sanitation district invested $100,000 into the investigation, fully expecting conflicts would be found, and—they were. The results were turned over to the SLO County District Attorney's office and charges were filed against Wallace for not only his conflicts at the sanitation district, but also at Avila Beach Community Services District, where he also maintained the same cozy dual relationship.

In early 2017, felony and misdemeanor charges were filed against Wallace. Wallace went through three attorneys over one year, ending up with a high-powered attorney specializing in white collar crimes. A change in venue, while welcomed, ended up too close for comfort—right next door in Santa Maria where the judge in the case has old ties to Wallace.

A March 5 preliminary hearing was held before Judge Timothy Staffel. In 1992, Judge Staffel was elected as Santa Barbara County Fourth District Supervisor and represented the Santa Maria and Lompoc Valleys from 1993-1998.

He also served on the California Coastal Commission from 1995-1998. In June of 1998, Governor Wilson appointed him to the Santa Barbara County Superior Court.

Wallace has worked in both San Luis Obispo and Santa Barbara Counties for many years. Staffel, as county supervisor, likely had projects engineered by Wallace's firm before him for approval. The record reflects Staffel, as a coastal commissioner, voted and/or influenced projects brought to the commission by Wallace.

These projects include SLO County's 1998 iteration of the Los Osos wastewater project and a 1996 San Simeon CSD pipeline project.

Local news reports indicate that during the preliminary hearing, Judge Staffel appeared irritated with the SLO County District Attorney's case citing statutes of limitation and suggested these were civil matters. Staffel also asserted the victims were not seeking monetary restitution.

It is unclear whether the districts were ever asked if they wanted restitution. Doesn't it go without saying? Public funds should be returned to the ratepayers. Old ties to Wallace may have prevented this question from ever being posed to the sanitation district or Avila Beach CSD boards of directors.

The current Avila Beach CSD general manager is Brad Hagemann, who is a former employee of the Wallace Group. Hagemann worked much of his career at the Central Coast Regional Water Quality Control Board alongside Gerhardt Hubner. Until recently, Hubner served as the sanitation district administrator.

While the Avila Beach CSD was under Wallace's representation, the water board and the CSD were among the parties in the $23 million UNOCAL beach clean-up. Furthermore, since August, the sanitation district has been under the interim administration of "technical consultants" Rick Sweet, formerly an engineer with the city of Santa Maria, and Paul Karp, who has worked with many government agencies throughout Santa Barbara and San Luis Obispo Counties; both have openly said they are "friends" of Wallace.

How likely were any of these advisors to recommend to their respective boards they seek restitution?

On March 6, Wallace pleaded guilty to two misdemeanors and offered up a pittance as restitution to the two districts, barely $60,000 to be split between the two, with the majority of the money going to Avila Beach CSD.

It is the sanitation district that has been fleeced the most.

The biggest public payout and windfall for Wallace was the sewage spill of 2010 into the neighborhoods of Oceano around the sewage plant. Years earlier, his firm designed improvements to the sewer plant that may have prevented or reduced the severity of a spill. When the flood waters swamped the sewer plant site and the sewage spill resulted, he capitalized on the situation by hiring his firm to engineer the fixes, compile the data, and present "expert testimony" in his defense before the water board.

The sanitation district funded hundreds of thousands of dollars' worth of work as his private paralegals. These monies were paid to Wallace's engineering firm to create the administrative record for the water board hearing in September 2012, in an effort to defend the District from punitive damages and damage to Wallace's own reputation. He was able to convince the sanitation board of directors to fight the $1.1 million fine rather than settle or concede (early on there was a settlement offer on the table of less than $400,000).

After enduring tremendous public pressure for the costs associated with the "litigation business," it was the 2015 sanitation district board of directors that dropped the lawsuits. This board included Arroyo Grande Mayor Jim Hill, Grover Beach Mayor Shoals, and the tag-team flip-flop duo from Oceano CSD, Mary Lucey and Matt Guerrero.

Earlier boards spent over $1 million defending (most of this money went to the Wallace Group) and simply paid the $1.1 million fine.

Today, the sanitation district is faced with the question of whether to pursue monetary restitution through the civil court. Complicating matters is its newest board make-up including the representative from Grover Beach and its Vice Chair Barbara Nicolls; she is the wife of Bill Nicolls, the same Nicolls who signed the response to the Grand Jury in 2011. She should not only recuse herself but should be replaced as the city's representative on the sanitation district board.

On behalf of the ratepayers, both Avila Beach CSD and South San Luis Obispo County Sanitation District should be made whole. Citizens in these districts need to let their representatives know they want their money back.

Letting Wallace walk away with years of double-dipping constitutes a gift of public funds and it's unacceptable.

The penalties were steep, but the Water Board, from the outset, said they would return half the penalty to the agency for environmental improvements. The board paid the $1.1 million penalty in 2018, having negotiated a $300,000 reduction from the original $1.4m. When the District received the $550,000 environmental funds, Shoals spun it as winning an award with no mention that it had come at a cost of $550,000, not counting several millions paid to attorneys and The Wallace Group.

Payback

Meanwhile, over in Arroyo Grande, Ferrara retained loyal supporters who staged a witch hunt against Mayor Jim Hill, attempting to oust him from his sewer district seat and to discredit him in the 2018 mayoral race. The councilmember who had denied wrongdoing at the sewer district castigated the new mayor. Hill had supported economic development by advocating with a lessor to approve a grocery store run by beloved local grocers who live in the city. The space remained open for months and has since changed ownership yet again.

But why go after Jim Hill? Surely it wasn't just political maneuvering, because in opposing local redevelopment they were harming the community. Did they fear that a Sanitation District investigation might turn the floodlights on the Oceano Community Services District and embarrass them again, or worse? Discrediting opponents would deflect attention from their misfeasance.

As long as the old mayor of Arroyo Grande and Wallace cronies held office they could keep everything secret. But now an auditor was investigating the Wallace era, the old mayor was out, the attorney had quit, and their cover was getting a little thin.

They all had something to gain if Mayor Jim Hill went down. They all had more to lose if he did not. Others who had once denounced Wallace changed camps and teamed up. Mary Lucey and Patty Welsh, known for loving a good bust-up, and for public cannabis habits, became a tag team to go after Mayor Jim Hill. Attendees overheard Welsh sniggering about doing dope deals in the council chambers during council meetings. Lucey had a habit that so startled even a couple of 19-year-olds (before the state legalized cannabis) that they asked me about it, genuinely shocked when at an OCSD board meeting Lucey called for a cannabis break and then toked up outside the Sheriff's department before returning to the dais.

When Lucey and Welsh showed up during public comment in an Arroyo Grande council meeting claiming that the mayor had violated the

Brown Act, the council launched a $100,000 investigation that uncovered nothing more than that he had called his wife when he was out of town asking her to look up his city email password for him. While she could look it up for him, she could not have used it because she is legally blind and can't read a computer screen. The irony is that this "investigation" came at the same price tag as the extensive Knudson Report that led to criminal prosecution.

The modus operandi of the cabal was to find the weakness of someone they needed to bring on board, and then work it. Addicts are good targets, and addiction is a common factor in political corruption. It wouldn't be difficult to co-opt Lucey and Welsh. All they needed was a marijuana source.

The Mayor Got the Memo

Back in Grover Beach, I asked the city attorney to take a look at how the council made the appointment to the sewer district, explaining that we appeared to be doing it wrong. He agreed. I gave him a heads up that if the practice continued, I would be challenging it from the dais. For the first time in over a decade, we got it right. The mayor was the council representative, and the council appointed the alternate.

In the 2018 election, Ferrara's appointee and friend Caren Ray won the mayoral seat, but not without controversy. Patty Welsh, the accuser in the Mayor Jim Hill witch hunt, often at Russom Ray's side in campaign photos, sneaked out of a council meeting while the police force attended an agenda item in the council chambers, and with an unidentified accomplice threw brown paint bombs at eleven of Hill's election signs, damaging city and Hill family property. Did someone on the council tip her off that the police department would all be at the council meeting? Under probation for earlier vandalism, the courts convicted Welsh of felony vandalism, and for misdemeanor vandalism on a separate matter.

By then the Arroyo Grande chickens—the council's preoccupation with beating down the mayor, and failure to address economic development—had really come home to roost. The inflated budget left by former Mayor Ferrara coupled with the effects of online trading decimated retail sales, causing both sales tax and thereby the city's income to plummet. The city council voted themselves pay increases and laid off staff as big box stores and franchise restaurants closed their doors. Ferrara left empty coffers in every agency he controlled. But at least the SSLOCSD, number three of four agencies about which I had concerns, was functioning well.

CHAPTER 5 THE AIR POLLUTION TROLL DISTRICT (APCD) Weakness Manipulated

"Weakness properly manipulated
can be a powerful tool."
inspired by *Star Wars: The Last Jedi* (2017)

The fourth agency I had begun to wonder about while a city councilmember was the SLO Air Pollution Control District (APCD). Adam Hill was not publicly involved with either of the sewer districts covered in the previous chapter, although both were in his supervisorial district. However, he was mightily involved in the APCD, even though the area affected was not in his district.

I knew from the outset that this would be the most difficult battle of my life, and that I might (politically) die on this hill. The *LA Times* later quoted me as saying so. I felt compelled to represent the wishes of the citizens of Grover Beach and to address the skewed information the District was putting out. With my arrival on the APCD, the Board was split 50/50.

The inability to make progress with this agency stems from the way it was set up. It is a rare agency that overrides our careful American checks and balances. The Air Pollution Control Officer APCO has sole authority. The board can fire him but cannot override his decisions. There is an appeal committee appointed by the APCO, which answers to him.

The urgency that had informed this unique setup came to life for me when knocking on doors in the tiny town of Avila Beach seeking votes in my run against Supervisor Hill. A retired respiratory therapist, likely an octogenarian, invited me to sit with him in the living room of his '20s beach bungalow. We sat and talked against a backdrop of the Pacific Ocean, sparkling with whitecaps. As we talked, a white heron hunted for frogs in the vacant field next door. Tears streaming down his face, he told me how devastating it was in the 1970s on bad smog days in Los Angeles, when his hospital would receive dying children that he couldn't save. Air Pollution Control Officers needed this kind of clout at the time, but it evolved in our county into the perfect retirement for the former County department head.

The APCD was an offshoot of the county, as were several other agencies. Shortly after Wallace left the county to start his own engineering company, several County department managers suggested that their departments should spin off as independent agencies, with them at the helm, touting it to the board of supervisors as a money-saving measure. In true government style, no one has yet evaluated whether their money-saving argument proved accurate. I once suggested that the board review it. There was stunned silence. But what is true is that these managers, by leaving the county and becoming CEOs of their own agencies, held their positions for 20 years with less accountability, higher pay, and better retirements than they would have had if they had stayed as county department heads. The APCD and IWMA even had their own buildings. The worst part of it is that now both the APCD and the IWMA, along with three state agencies, are using taxpayer money to fight one another in court. It is much less likely that this would have occurred had these tasks continued as county entities.

Air pollution control districts create rules requiring polluters that they can classify as articles, equipment, machines, or contrivances to buy a permit and renew it annually. In addition, the polluters must pay fees to the APCD for oversight and administration, and meet air quality standards determined by the APCO (Air Pollution Control Officer). Failure to achieve these standards can result in fees of up to $1,000 a day.

NOVEMBER 7, 2011
Grover Beach City Council Meeting

The mayor and mayor pro tem advised the council that they had been meeting with Pismo Beach Councilmember and APCD representative Ed Waage about a serious matter. The APCD was proposing a dust rule that would fine the local State Park for particulate blowing into new subdivisions built downwind of the 19-mile stretch of beach and dunes, a third of which allows vehicles.

Waage, with his knowledge of plume transport—the study of how airborne matter spreads—had reviewed the studies presented supporting the Rule and found several glaring problems. There were biases and omissions that would change the conclusions of the reports. I was inclined to support the APCD because ecologically I did not like the idea of vehicles in the dunes.

The mayor and mayor pro tem were firm with Councilmember Bright, the APCD representative, in an unprecedented manner providing clear direction to her to vote against Rule 1001, 'The Dust Rule'. The mayor insisted twice in the meeting and read into the minutes of the meeting that council representative Bright was to vote against the upcoming Dust Rule and was to share the council's position in the APCD board meeting. The mayor then asked me to attend the APCD meeting as the alternate to be sure Councilmember Bright represented the city's position.

This is a clear example of the dangers of councilmembers who are appointed to represent their constituents on county boards becoming too cozy with the agency staff. The councilmember appointed to a board is there to protect not the interests of the CEO she oversees, or even her colleagues on that board, but the colleagues and constituents who appointed and elected her to protect their interests. It is not her job to be a friend to the agency head or to be their buddy. Her job as a board member is to oversee the CEO and to represent her council and constituents. To do otherwise is to betray them all.

In the case of the sewer district, the buddy system was maintained to protect and defend erroneous, if not criminal, activity. While in this case it was not criminal per se, it was complicit misplaced loyalty to her department head and political party that betrayed her council and her city.

NOVEMBER 11, 2011
Air Pollution Control District Board Meeting

I attended as the mayor requested. Bright was the swing vote. She did not vote against the Dust Rule. She did not present the council's position. She abstained, saying the council directed her to vote one way, but her conscience directed otherwise. By abstaining, she allowed board approval of the Dust Rule. Had she followed council direction, the rule would have failed. From my position in the audience of a darkened auditorium where the only lights were the stage-lit dais, I was unable to participate in the proceedings as they unfolded because Bright made her decision after the opportunity for public comment, when I would have been able to remind her of the council's direction, had I known. When Bright, trembling and tearful, reported back to the council, I felt for her. Looking back, I realize that the APCO and Supervisors Hill and Gibson were putting pressure on her.

NOVEMBER 14, 2012
APCD board meeting

Hill staged a rant about the superintendent of state parks, who I knew to be a straight shooter—honest, knowledgeable, and exceptionally good at his job.

> "This is nonsense ... we're getting played by a wily bureaucrat who shows up ... with a gun on his belt and tells us he wants to be our partner and then joins a lawsuit against us. I would recommend that you ... meet with county counsel to brief them... OHV is continuing to force our hand, which is a far greater priority than ensuring access to recreation... if OHV and the county and APCD don't make progress, then that forces us as property owners to make a decision [to close La

Grande]... they've denied the science from the beginning in the same way the fossil fuel industry denies climate change ... they don't want to take responsibility and they don't want to change or pay for anything... so they challenge and dilute the science... this is NOT the only court case that I foresee, ... so I hope you... meet with county counsel so the board of supervisors can meet in closed session in the future..."

Note the reference in the last line to meeting in closed session. Hill made numerous mentions of legal action in order to set it up for a closed session discussion which would exclude the public and his target, State Parks.

FRIDAY, NOVEMBER 16, 2012

Hill sent a nastygram version of his board meeting rant to the "wily bureaucrat's" boss. He wrote convincingly enough that while the State Parks team would have known he was talking nonsense, their higher ups would not have known. Nor would they have known that neither the board of supervisors nor the APCD agreed to or had authorized the email. Hill was writing of his own accord under color of authority, using his official title and email address, creating the appearance of a communication sanctioned by both the supervisors and the APCD. Reviewing his ccs it was easy to see which colleagues were in cahoots— SLO City Mayor Marx and Supervisor Gibson, whose ego and sexual proclivities weren't any more respectable than Hill's but were disguised by a veneer of supercilious intellectualism and high falutin' grandiose language, akin to the professor on the television sitcom Gilligan's Island. Anyone who dared to disagree with the misfeasance of Hill, Gibson, and Marx was bound to find that someone contacted their boss, and if a business, their advertisers, attempting to destabilize their target's reputation, employment, and finances.

From: ahill@co.slo.ca.us [mailto:ahill@co.slo.ca.us] Sent: Friday, November 16, 2012, 9:50 AM To: lallen@co.slo.ca.us Cc: Jenkins, Phil; Robertson, Aaron; Beland, Janelle; Larry Allen (lallen_apcd@co.slo.ca.us); hmiller@co.slo.ca.us; bgibson@co.slo.ca.us; Jan Marx; Raymond A. Biering; rneal@co.slo.ca.us Subject: Re: Regarding letter dated Oct. 23, 2012

I would like to make some salient points, and I have also included Secretary Laird, Senator-elect Monning, and the governor's chief of staff in this email (they are Bcc'd as I only have their personal email addresses):

1. The current position of the OHV division of State Parks, which now includes suing our county's Air District, is embarrassing and wholly undermines the Brown administration's work on air pollution and other important environmental issues. It is my contention that OHV Chief Phil Jenkins has treated SLO County with contempt and has spoken and acted in utterly misleading and dishonest ways.

2. This position will have the effect of forcing SLO County's hand. All along we have tried to balance the interests of the OHV recreation area with the health concerns of our residents. We believed we could mitigate the dust and keep the recreation area open. But now we will likely be advised by our counsel that State Parks' actions have left us entirely vulnerable to a slew of legitimate lawsuits from our citizens. This will inevitably necessitate SLO County having to fence off and patrol the Le Grande tract, thereby significantly reducing the recreation area.

3. The embrace of scientific denialism by State Parks is incredibly disconcerting in that it only worsens already bad relations between state agencies and local governments, and because it is redolent of the worst kind of special interest politics. Perhaps Mr. Jenkins would be better suited working for the Koch Brothers or ExxonMobil.

In closing, I am hoping that we can arrange a meeting as soon as possible before this escalates further. Please circulate this to General Jackson [Head of California State Parks OHV division] as well.

Sincerely,

ADAM HILL District Three Supervisor San Luis Obispo County 1055 Monterrey, Rm D430 San Luis Obispo, CA 93408 (805)781-5450 (805)781-1350

JANUARY 15, 2013

Coastal Commission

The California Coastal Commission meets monthly in cities throughout the state, and met in January 2013 in Pismo Beach, the next city north of Grover Beach. As the new mayor, I pondered how best to support the Grover Beach hotel and conference center. I decided it would be best to advocate for peace in the dunes. I had the good fortune of meeting Diana Perez at the Coastal Commission meeting. Perez was vice chair of the Oceano Dunes State Vehicle Recreation Area Commission, a school board member, and administrator at a local city college. We shared the goal of peace in the dunes. We agreed to work to bring the county and state together to reconsider previous negotiations for the state to purchase land they currently use for the State Vehicle Recreation Area.

Back in 1905, a dodgy real estate developer bought some sand dunes from the state and "subdivided" them. Over the years, as owners realized they could never build on shifting sand, many quit paying property taxes on their lots. Some of the lots remain in private ownership or were sold, and many fell into the hands of the county, which repossessed the "lots" when owners defaulted on property tax payments. The county had accepted ownership of the streets and now also owns some of the lots. It is the proceeds of this scam, the streets and repossessed lots, that are the property that the county. The few private owners and the county allow State Parks to traverse this property for its Off Highway Vehicle Riding Area.

In the early 2000s, the state and county came close to negotiating a state purchase of the county property until they discovered a title error that shut down negotiations.

As a real estate broker, it made sense to me to clean up the 600-acre mess of leasing paper lots to the park, which had been willing to purchase the county-owned lots and bring much of the "subdivision" back under state ownership.

The governor had appointed a personable retired general to lead the OHV division. After a year on the job, General Jackson proposed that his second in command, Colonel Chris Conlin, take over. I had great respect for both of them and their leadership styles. They were efficient, hardworking, and dedicated to their jobs, as were their subordinates with whom I had the pleasure of working. The role of State Parks as they operated their 19-mile stretch of beach was to be the peacekeepers—to ensure that everyone had the opportunity to recreate in their preferred fashion peacefully and safely.

General Jackson surprised me with a belly laugh when I expressed my wish for peace in the dunes. Now I know why the general laughed! He knew a lot about war, and he knew there would be no peace in this politically impossible task; even though the agencies could solve it if they so wished.

Senior Engineering Geologist, California Geological Survey

The affable California Geological Survey Senior Engineering Geologist Will Harris asked to meet with me. His office was a picnic table in a clearing in the coastal willows under the pine trees outside the State Parks ranger station. No one manages more dune complexes than our State Parks, and Harris is one of the country's leading dune experts. As a contributor to the 2010 dust study that was the basis for the Dust Rule, he explained to me the flaws in the study. He and Waage were the best and most experienced science minds in dunes and plumes involved with the APCD. After going over the dust study with them, I agreed that it had glaring errors.

The problem for the park, one that any local could have told you, was that you cannot stop the wind and the waves, which is why, over an 18,000-year span, this incredible dune complex has developed. That is why the county had zoned the area in the path of the prevailing northwest winds 'industrial' and why no one lived on it until the county rezoned it, launching a calamity of three residential golf-course communities housing mostly seniors and retirees who would later agitate to have trees (aka wind and sound blocks) removed to enhance their ocean views.

Not one to miss an opportunity, Supervisor Hill wooed these folks, presenting as the knight in shining armor; the one who would save them from the evil rednecks from out of town who were riding their 4x4s, kicking up dangerous sand and causing deadly downwind sand plumes. Riding in the dunes is not an inexpensive sport, and economic impact studies and surveys noted that many participants were not the stereotypical rednecks, but professionals with significant income camping at the state park with large family groups.

State Parks leaders knew they could not eradicate the particulate that the wind entrains. And for that they would pay dearly. The APCO and Hill told the residents who built their homes on the dunes in the plume that OSHA (Occupational Safety and Health Administration) found that silicone, which they claimed was the main component of the particulate blowing at them, is deadly; even co-opting the county health officer to say so. That scared the residents, especially on windy days. They seemed to believe with all their hearts that removing the vehicles would save them. Sadly, for those who suffered health problems in that environment, the only safe move was not to remove vehicles in the dunes but to move out of the dunes because the level of sand stirred up by high winds can cause issues for sensitive individuals even without particulate. Sadder still, the fear of ill health overrode their executive brains, thus causing them to litigate, not mitigate.

Early on, General Jackson advised the mayor of Pismo Beach and me in confidence that our particulate problem had piqued the interest of the world-renowned San Diego-based Scripps Institute, which was keen to study the particulate blowing to the golf course developments. We began to hear murmurings that they were discovering that the particulate wasn't composed of silicone but saltwater and crustaceans, and that it wasn't coming from the sand on the dunes, but from the spray atop the huge waves as they crashed onto our shoreline. The power of vehicles to move sand is a mere grain of sand by comparison to the gargantuan Pacific and the 19-mile shoreline of wind and waves.

My friend, former Grover Beach Mayor Peter Keith, was the long-standing business representative of the Technical Review Team (TRT) set up by State Parks to make sure there was balance between the activities of off highway vehicle enthusiasts and the environment. He explained to me that when he came to SLO County in the 1970s, people could ride in the dunes, the largest intact coastal dune ecosystem on earth according to the Nature Conservancy, for the entire length of the beach.

In the 1980s, State Parks and the leader of the Sierra Club crafted the state legislation creating the 3,490-acre State Vehicle Recreation Area in the 15,000-acre dune complex to protect the environment and the rights of off highway vehicle enthusiasts to recreate. The state allows vehicles in only 12-1500 naturally unvegetated acres, fencing some of it to protect snowy plover nesting sites. Oddly enough, the OHVs seem to have a positive influence on the plover populace—we now have the highest western snowy plover fledgling rate in the country. Since 1993, State Parks' efforts have increased the nests from 16 to 172 in 2011. The OHVs drive off hawks and foxes, the plovers' natural predators. In addition, the Park has carefully planted and tended 650 acres of native vegetation. Vegetation is the only proven impediment to particulate creation and entrainment, and the Park now has twenty percent more vegetation than at any other time in the past one hundred years.

The APCD is fee and grant funded and with their cash cow, Duke Energy in Morro Bay, closing, they admitted to needing to replace that deep pocket and had begun imposing fees upon wineries for their environmental footprint. Next, despite their own studies rating dirt roads as the highest generator of particulate in our agricultural county, the APCD finagled its way into the pockets of the highest earning State Park in California's Parks system.

My family taught me to like our neighbors to the west, the State Park. My father had always wanted to be a forest ranger, but couldn't afford to study in Denver, the only college offering the degree at the time. As a child, I spent weekends with my family camping there, clamming on the beach, and going to ranger talks.

As a councilmember I got to know Grover Beach old-timers and became aware of how important State Parks is to our local economy. Around 60% of our residents live in rented housing. They are the gas station attendants and tow truck drivers who rescue you when you get stuck on the beach. My city hosts the vehicle entrance to the State Park. A few rangers manage the miles of camping and recreation; a veritable city requiring sewer, water, fire, and emergency services. State Parks staff are the miracle workers who manage a changing population of up to 10,000 people, all sharing the same space, and except for vehicle accidents, without incident.

As mayor, I was the council representative to the joint powers authority working together with State Parks and a private developer to establish a beachfront lodge and conference center on the site. While at the state level getting movement on anything was next to impossible, I found the State Parks folks and their local staff to be straightforward and easy to work with.

JANUARY 2013
APCD South County Community Monitoring Project

Without alerting or inviting the board, the APCD rolled out its new air quality zone map ranking air quality in the South County. In my town the air quality is good, protected by an expanse of wet sand and vegetated back dunes and hills to the north that block the highest of the prevailing northwest winds. Moving south, the hill-effect protection diminishes, the dunes get bigger, and the air quality worsens.

The zone map and the concerns that we hear at APCD meetings from residents who live in the new developments caused me to wonder, "Why is the air worse at one golf course development than the other two?" I started researching and wrote my findings in a white paper, the West Mesa Dust Report. This is available at www.DebbiePeterson.com.

As I studied the Specific Plan, the Environmental Impact Report (EIR), and APCD and State Parks publications, visited the golf resort construction site, and pored over Google Earth maps, it began to emerge. Simple observation of the geography and conditions—topography, development, orientation, and vegetation—on repeated site visits were the most informative. As an APCD board member, I was concerned about reports I was receiving that someone was cutting down trees near the development where the air quality was worst. One thing that stood out was that all but one of the many long-time residents who I asked if the air quality was a problem for them said "not at all," but would shake their heads in disbelief at the thought of anyone living in the path of the blowing sand. I also queried several doctors who treated patients from the area. They were unable to confirm that there were any higher incidences of issues related to blowing sand there than anywhere else in the county, although one old-timer told me that the Chumash name for the area was 'The Valley of the Sick.'

JANUARY 23, 2013
APCD Board Meeting: Hill Promises Not to Send any More Letters on the Board's Behalf Without Board Agreement

Even some of those who voted with Hill were unhappy about the nastygram he sent to state authorities implicitly on their behalf. Hill was next in line to chair the APCD board, but his actions put his leadership in question. When it came time for the vote, the supervisors' chambers were standing room only, filled mostly with citizens opposing Hill's appointment as chair, and a few supporting him.

For the second time that month, I did not support a board choosing Hill as chair. After he locked me in the courthouse in an effort to ensure my support while telling me he had a gun, I was all the more certain that Hill was not made of the right stuff.

Hill's fellow directors did not elect him to the committee chair position. Later in the agenda, the APCO was proud to report that the APCD gets very few complaints. "What a crock!" or less genteel expressions along those lines was what I heard when I asked business owners if they ever complained to the APCO, because they certainly complained to me! Businesses with dealings with the agency said that they didn't dare complain because there was no recourse but through the courts. The APCO is all powerful and can shut them down at a moment's notice or fine them out of existence. They wouldn't dream of complaining. Instead, they befriend the agency as much as they can to safeguard themselves and their businesses and complain to elected representatives.

I did a Red Flags Analysis of the APCD to focus my thinking. Apart from their need to continually find deep pockets to fund the agency, the red flags at the APCD were mostly related to the practices and culture of the organization:

- Staff reports do not provide information as to how issues are addressed by nearby or similar agencies (consistency in governance).

- Staff reports do not provide alternative solutions, only staff's recommendations.

- Counsel is too cozy with staff, working for the interest of the APCO and not for the public or the board.

- Reports are filed without correcting errors, so errors become fact.

- As time passes no one remembers the board deliberation.

- APCO has too much power. Answers to no one. No legitimate appeal process. The public is afraid to question anything because of his unchecked power to fine.

- Response to questions is defensive as opposed to informative or considered.

- Excessive litigation.

- Culture—"YOU MUST NOT QUESTION THE APCO!"

- Resistance to supplying information. Resistance or refusal to correct errors.

- Response to questions: baffle with science, talk in circles, techno-speak, say don't have the information on hand, if disagree, say it's incorrect and pick out a technicality to deny, speak in an authoritative (dismissive) manner, offer assurances that of course they do everything fairly, and everything is OK because nobody ever complains.

- Frequent spelling, clerical, accuracy errors in reports.

- Derisive attitude toward board members.

- APCO goes out on his own, publishing editorial viewpoints, press releases, and presentations before presenting to or without notifying the board.

- Only meet every other month, so consistent oversight is impossible.

- Constant whining or blaming someone else for lack of forward progress: "Oh we've spent SOOOOO much time on this that there's not enough time to do our jobs." Or "THEY aren't responding." Or "THEY aren't cooperating."

- Cannot complete work.

- Not enforcing mitigations they put in place. Not collecting required information from pollution sources.

- Failed to include particulate from dunes and dirt roads in industrial areas in Environmental Impact Reports.

- Deselecting facts that do not support their position and selecting those that do.

The APCD was one of three agencies that I notified of errors in their organizational charts. They were honest in their representations as to how it worked in their organizations, but at fault. None included 'The People,' who belong at the top. Many showed the attorney under the control of the CEO. That is incorrect. The attorney is hired by and under the authority of the board. All corrected their charts, if not their practices.

MAY 6, 2013
Grover Beach City Council Meeting (at 53 minutes)

Supervisor Hill attended council meetings from time to time. On this occasion, Hill "officially" welcomed the new city councilmember, a county employee, saying he had already personally congratulated him and went on to say that if we had one more county employee on the council we would have "a troika" (and a council majority!). He also reminded everyone to contact him if they needed funding for city and community events.

The new councilmember thanked Supervisor Hill for his support for the community and said Hill was doing an excellent job.

1:00:05 Councilmember Bright asked Hill to comment on the sale of the La Grande tract. While denying that discussions of a sale would be conditioned on State Parks' cooperation with the Dust Rule, he repeated four times that the rule would have to be sorted out before he could consider a sale. Not that it was his decision alone; he was one of five votes on the board of supervisors.

> "My personal position is that we have an issue we have to take care of that we are obligated to take care of with the air pollution that affects the people on the mesa. I think there was a fair amount of closure with the recent court case in terms of the Dust Rule and the authority to move forward with that. I've had a conversation with the [state] Secretary of Natural Resources, and we feel that this provides an opportunity to address the matter which, I should point out, as far as we're concerned is completely separate of anything to do with the sale of the La Grande Tract.
>
> My main concern is that we address the particle pollution, we mitigate the dust and work together with State Parks. If State Parks were to come to us once again we would entertain it, but I would say at this point I wouldn't feel this is something I would want to entertain unless I feel the efforts to address the particle pollution were underway.
>
> Should State Parks decide it wants to once again negotiate with the county, that would be something that would be possible. My sense of it

at least is we want to show we can work together on the dust mitigation first and foremost to get that underway and then anything else that might come up we'll be happy to entertain.

Essentially separate, but that would be the order of things from my perspective. That's the most important. And then we'll see what else is on the table."

Meeting Prep

I emailed budget questions to the APCO in preparation for the next board meeting. I was seeking clarity on numbers and comments, responding to questions raised by the public, and following up on board direction and correction of errors. I asked why there was no allowance for litigation in the budget and when the board would be informed of the amount spent on litigation for the current year. I asked for details of who was paying for Dust Rule parts, repairs, and monitors and whether these would be included as part of the fees to State Parks, or in addition. I asked about a comment indicating that budgets would be achieved by using reserves and not contributing to reserves. I asked about settlements, interest increases, and contingencies. I asked for the criteria used to make budget adjustments and why revisions to language in a report were not consistent throughout the report. My question about revisions to language in a report raised a weasel word answer that illustrates many of the red flags I had noted.

Question: Shouldn't language revisions be consistent in the report? There are numerous incidences in the report where the same wording is used in the same context, but not revised. [The board had directed the APCO to make these changes and he had not done so.]

Answer: *As discussed in the introduction and conclusion sections of the addendum, the original statements in the intro/conclusions for the main report regarding Mesa2 PM levels ("no evidence of improvement,* *but rather it may be/appears to be increasing") are still warranted. Whether we say this in the executive summary and conclusion of the main report, or simply leave it as "no evidence of improvement", is just a matter of emphasis and was only changed to reflect the preference of a few Board members. It's more conservative to simply leave it as "no evidence of improvement", but this language does not exclude the possibility/probability of deterioration. If you read the entire report and addendum [I had done so], you'll see that there's no evidence of PM improvement but there are several indicators of deterioration at Mesa 2; however, the evidence for deterioration (upward trend) is not as strong as the evidence for decreasing trends in countywide ozone and North County PM. So, the question is, how do we reflect this in the report conclusions? Originally, we stated that, for Mesa 2 PM, there's "no evidence of improvement; in fact, the situation may worsen" and that levels there "appear to be increasing". The data shows that statement is still correct, but we've revised it to give more emphasis to the uncertainty of the deterioration, leaving it simply as "no evidence of improvement." The underlying data remains the same, so changes to the rest of the report are not warranted.*

Finally, I asked if reporting errors by an APCD contractor that had led to higher fees for projects in my city had been corrected. Supervisor Hill's public response to the questions I posed following my review of the board packet is below.

MAY 28, 2013

Supervisor Gibson called Councilmember Bright asking her to remove me from the APCD board. Supervisor Hill emailed Councilmember Bright saying, "This nonsense needs to stop. Your mayor is doing harm to an important public health agency, seeking to paralyze it. Please let me kow if her actions represent Grover Beach's city council.

MAY 29, 2013
APCD Board Meeting

3:47:49: Adam Hill—"Larry, we have seen a continuing rather um zealous pursuit of information regarding the dunes uh for quite a while, especially from some board members. I wonder if we're keeping track of the staff time that is being spent on this. How much I mean are we doing overtime, how is this impacting our budget, how is this impacting the other work that the district has to do? I'm wondering if we had some information on that."

Hill then launched into the following statement.

"I think the board at some time needs to consider that this is an ongoing pursuit by Mr. Waage and Miss Peterson at a great expense to the taxpayers following up on things that I'm not really sure unless we want to hire outside consultants perhaps a research scientist that can um review uh Mr. Waage's pursuits, and I guess uh a legal consultant that Miss Peterson could follow up on and they could bear the cost of it. Because it just seems excessive. I mean a hundred staff hours to continue to answer questions that have been addressed repeatedly and again on research scientists from previous studies seems to be squandering public resources. The questions I heard just on the last item from Miss Peterson essentially questioning the effectiveness of our counsel, who is very well regarded as a public agency attorney and considered one of the best litigators in our county, and we're having these kind questions of despite the fact that he won the most recent case and has won most of the cases that have come before him are continuing to have to put staff on the spot to explain again and again and again as if the answers will change because they don't like the answers. I don't think that that's the best use of our public resources. I think that this is a um an ill-advised continuation of politicizing of the dunes issue that's completely unnecessary, completely unproductive, and would be best left to the District staff and the State Parks staff and not become this constant ongoing battle. I think we are seeing enormous amounts of staff time being put in with no great public interested being served."

History of the APCD on the Mesa

The genesis of the Dust Rule dates to the 1990s, when APCO Larry Allen failed to include several critical factors in the Mesa particulate problem when reporting on the air quality impacts of a third golf course resort community; factors that he and his agency had documented previously: the air is bad on the Mesa. In the Specific Plan, and the Environmental Impact Report (EIR), Allen failed to include the most significant contributors to this bad air: dust from the sand roads in the industrial zone and the sandy soils of the farms on the Mesa. The zoning change from Industrial to Recreational leapfrogged what would usually be several intermediary zonings in terms of quality-of-life residential locations.

Allen acknowledged that data showed that the air was bad, would be worse during construction, and would continue to get worse after construction because of increased traffic. To put it simply, the air *was* bad, the air *is* bad, and the *air will always be bad*. To address worsening air quality, Allen and the County of SLO put in place over a hundred mitigations to manage air quality. These mitigations were specific to development of the area with the worst air quality, and SLOAPCD assigned itself responsibility to monitor eighteen of these mitigations. A public records request provided the written confirmation of what was in plain sight. Over the 20-year construction period, the APCD was neither monitoring nor enforcing any of the standard mitigation measures that it had assigned to itself to control construction site air pollution.

Other factors are proven to influence air quality: traffic generated by the tripled population, increased agriculture, construction, and removal of 1,000 acres of trees that had historically functioned as wind blocks.

Early settlers had reservations about moving to a treeless area offering no shade, no shelter from the strong persistent winds, no protection for crops, and no wood to build homes. Their salvation, rows of trees, was fulfilled by James F. Goodwin the "tree missionary", who sold and donated thousands of eucalyptus seedlings that grew into the ancient windblocks we still see along our coastline.

MAY 2013

Colonel Chris Conlin, Deputy Director ODSVRA, advised that Scripps Institute had formally contracted with State Parks to conduct a study of the particulate. Conlin led the first surge into Iraq and established governance there. I enjoyed working with a leader who demonstrated such integrity. Unfortunately, he could establish a democracy in a war zone but could not win the APCD battle.

MAY 29, 2013

The APCD Board introduced the first reading of amendments to Rule 503, which set the permitting fees for the Dust Rule. The second reading was to follow in July, prior to implementation of the Rule.

JUNE 2013

Grover Beach United, a local business group, invited me to their meeting to update them on our hotel and conference center. I did so, explaining my wish to re-open discussions with the County regarding State Parks' purchase of the La Grande Tract to consolidate the ownership of the area, and my concerns about the Dust Rule. Their greatest concern was that the APCD was trying to shut down the dunes. The members wished to circulate a petition to repeal the Dust Rule. Wanting to be sure that the information in the petition was accurate, I offered to draft the wording they wanted. The "Mitigate don't Litigate" petition was launched on paper and online at http://www.ipetitions.com/petition/repeal-the-dust-rule. Volunteers walked the streets of Grover Beach collecting signatures. There was widespread support. Only two days of petition gathering by a handful of individuals netted 410 online signatures and 108 hand-gathered signatures.

I supported the petition for two reasons. The first was market research. I wanted to confirm that the strong community support for riding in the dunes that had first come to my attention when I ran for city council in 2008 was still strong before sticking my neck out at the next APCD meeting and asking the board to reconsider the Dust Rule. Second, I hoped that if public response was strong enough, that the Board might be willing to reconsider their position based on community response and discuss whether a rule would successfully mitigate particulate blowing onto the Mesa.

This meeting would be the last chance for board consideration before Rule 302 went into effect. This timing was critical, because as of July 31st the APCD would require that State Parks apply for a permit, setting a statewide precedent that air districts could require land with minimal improvements—parks and agriculture—to permit their land uses using APCD rules. More permitting by an additional government agency would be crippling to California's two largest economic engines, tourism and agriculture, and a significant overreach of the intent of APCD legislation. Agencies statewide have successfully addressed these issues with mutually agreed upon memoranda of understanding rather than unilateral rulemaking.

The Petition

As part of the dune creation process on high wind days dust blows onto the Nipomo Mesa from the beach. The San Luis Obispo Air Pollution Control District (SLO APCD) has tasked the landowner of the dunes, California State Parks' Oceano Dunes State Vehicle Recreation Area (ODSVRA), with the job of determining and implementing the best way to mitigate the blowing sand. SLO APCD is doing so on the premise that their Phase II Study says that vehicles on the beach are causing the dust to blow onto the Mesa.

The California Geological Survey, and other technical experts, including environmental and air quality professionals, extensively reviewed the Phase II Study and its appendices. From these reviews, as well as from subsequent analyses of available and acquired data, it was determined that the Phase II conclusion attributing elevated concentrations of particulate matter on the Mesa to off-highway vehicle recreation at Oceano Dunes SVRA was not supported by the data presented in the Phase II document.

The SLO APCD has created a rule (The Dust Rule) that fines State Parks $1,000 a day when the wind blows up excessive dust, $920 a year for a permit to operate, $4,080 a year to monitor each air monitor (22 have been installed) and $40,160 a year for an existing APCD monitor. The purpose of these charges is to fund the SLO APCD for monitoring the work of the ODSVRA.

NO OTHER Air Pollution Control District in California has a State Vehicle Recreation Area that is required to have APCD permits or is fined for the wind blowing or for monitoring, even though most other areas have worse air quality and larger SVRA acreage. The Dust Rule is not in keeping with standard practice.

The net result is that one state agency is requiring another to carry out and fund work and mitigation and then charging them again to monitor their work and then fining them if they don't get the desired result.

Taxpayers are funding two state agencies and their lawyers, paying two to three times for the same work. These funds would be far better spent to research and solve the problem.

What sense does it make to 1) Require that State Parks pay for and carry out the necessary research to mitigate the dust;

2) Require that State Parks pay for the necessary equipment, 3) Then fine them when the wind blows and; 4) Charge them for the APCD to monitor their work when State Parks are WILLING and the MOST ABLE agency to actually address the problem; and then 5) Charge them for a permit to operate their Park which is already permitted by the legislature?

The majority of the board members who imposed the Dust Rule NEVER EVEN TOOK A TOUR OF THE AREA before voting.

The APCD Board promised to look at alternate points of view following the Phase II study and never did so.

As of July 31st, 2013, the power to revoke the permit for vehicles on the beach lays solely in the hands of one individual, the SLO Air Pollution Control Officer (APCO). No other institution, including the APCD board has authority over the Control Officer's decision to revoke the permit.

For these reasons, those signing below request that the APCD board repeal the Dust Rule.

Hill showed up at the next city council meeting.

JULY 15, 2013
Grover Beach City Council Meeting Public Comment

1:42:11 SUPERVISOR ADAM HILL

"Um, I think that we're; the issue that was presented tonight has become a huge and unnecessary distraction from what we should all be focusing on and what our council should be doing. Um, I think that you know I think, I'm probably in the best place to assure people both as a member of the board of supervisors and as the second member representing this community on the Air Pollution Control District that **there is absolutely no threat to the recreation area, the riding area of the dunes. That is not true. We have never had a discussion at the board. We have never had a discussion at the APCD board about closing the recreation area. That has never been discussed in any discussion we have had about the particulate matter pollution on the dunes. And so, what's going on is that there's a lot of fear and anxiety being spread to merchants and to residents and to visitors that's unnecessary because there is no threat there. The Dust Rule does not pose a threat. The Air Pollution Control District itself does not pose a threat; the county does not pose a threat. When I first ran for this office, I met with all the existing councilmembers then and many of the residents and assured them that I supported the recreation area that hasn't changed publicly or privately. It has not changed in my role on any level in the county. And so, I just, I would like to offer you a chance to basically just say, you know 'We don't really need to focus on this; there's not a threat.'** [See 'Weasel Words'.][FACT CHECK—APCO Allen's short online bio says only this, "I'm the Executive Director of the agency and have worked in the air quality regulatory field for over 30 years. Much of my professional focus has been on promoting smart growth and transportation options to reduce air pollution and climate impacts caused by vehicle use."]

I've provided all of you and I'll hand it out, I'll leave it here for anybody here some factual corrections to some of the statements have been made, but I think this is a good chance to hopefully diplomatically say, you know what this is not the issue that it's being made out to be. Let's see if Larry and Dave can talk again. Let's um you know this is false. We don't need to have it. I would love to see you focus on all the other things as **I continue to work with your city on the equestrian staging area for the Lodge.** [Nothing ever materialized.] These are the important things that I enjoy helping you on and I love to hear what your input is on a variety of issues in the county as well. I like serving with each of you, but I just think this is an opportunity now for us just to say you know **this is not really what's going on. Let's put it aside.** Let's focus on what matters and let's not cause more anxiety in our residents and our businesspeople."

JULY 24, 2013
APCD Board Meeting

Faced with over five hundred petitions against the Dust Rule and knowing they did not have the majority to pass it, the six outnumbered members and their alternates staged a "no show" two days before the meeting, during which time Supervisors Gibson and Hill called and emailed the Grover Beach Council seeking my removal from the APCD board.

With the meeting canceled it was impossible for the public to present the 'Repeal the Dust Rule' petition and for Rule 302 to get final board approval. They had made it impossible for State Parks not to apply for a permit. Despite the absence of a board-approved permitting fee, State Parks submitted the permit application in a showing of good faith never returned by their adversaries, the APCD, or its APCO. The APCO issued a permit to State Parks on August 31, 2013, in the absence of the Rule defining the fees. (See definition Collusion and Nonfeasance—p. 58.) Hill emailed city councilmembers with his excuse for boycotting the meeting and made a few other choice remarks.

c/o Donna at City Hall

From: Adam Hill Sent: Friday, July 26, 2013, 10:49 AM Subject: from Adam

Councilmembers,

There has been another cycle of misinformation, so a quick correction is in order.

My absence at the APCD meeting was precipitated by the illness of my fiancé's 11-year-old daughter (Sage). This occurred Monday morning while she was at camp and her mother (Dee) was in DC.

On Wednesday morning at 8 a.m., Kevin P Rice was parked outside my house. He then followed me as I took Sage to the doctor. After that, he followed me as I dropped another daughter off at day camp. Then he followed me as I met for coffee with AG City Councilwoman Caren Ray, and later followed me again as I returned to take care of Sage.

This stalking by Mr. Rice, who you know as your Mayor's sidekick, is legal. Nonetheless, I contacted the Sheriff and the SLOPD and I now have police protection. I will next have to seek a restraining order against Mr. Rice. [FACT CHECK: both the police and sheriff departments denied that they were providing protection.]

This is how ugly and dangerous this nonsense about a non-issue stirred up by your Mayor has gotten. It should appall you that I have to live with death threats and stalking as it appalls me and frightens my family.

Frankly, I don't care what you do about her anymore. If you want to keep her on the APCD Board she will continue to embarrass the city, and get the county sued. She has alienated me entirely, and I find her a disgrace to our community.

Sincerely, Adam

JULY 26, 2013
Grover Beach City Council Meeting

Hill was really working it. During public comment he said,

"Good evening, madam mayor, honorable council. Adam Hill. Since 2009 I've had the honor and pleasure to represent you and to serve you at the County and uh, I think all of you know that uh I have great regard for this city. I love the City; I love the people in it. I was a resident here for ten years um, and I would dare to say that you have never had a better friend uh at the County than I have been um. I have supported, I provided you with just a rundown just so to remind you of more than 37, almost $38,000 to city causes, directly to the city from parks to the fire department to the police department to our library. This community matters to me. It always has.

District 3 Community Project Funds Given To Grover Beach   (2009-Present)

Funds Given Directly to Grover Beach		*Funds Given Indirectly to Grover Beach*	
City of Grover Beach-Parks & Recreation Dept.	$ 6,400	South County Historical Society	$ 2,400
City of Grover Beach-Police Department	$ 2,000	Arroyo Grande High School Robotics Team	$ 1,250
Five Cities Fire Authority	$ 6,000	South County Youth Coalition	$ 2,200
City of Grover Beach Summer Concert Series	$ 2,000	South County Peoples Kitchen	$ 1,000
Grover Beach Community Library	$ 2,750	South County Performing Ars Center - Clark Center	$ 250
Arroyo Grande/Grover Chamber of Commerce	$ 4,250	Arroyo Grande High School Eagles Athletics	$ 100
		Five Cities Dog Park-SLOPOST	$ 1,000
		SARP Center	$ 600
		Arroyo Grande Hospital Foundation	$ 300
		5 Cities Homeless Coalition	$ 4,000
		Five Cities Diversity Coalition	$ 1,200

			Total Funds Given
$ 23,400		$ 14,300	$ 37,700

'District 3 Community Project Funds Given to Grover Beach'

Hill waved the above list at the council during his public comment and left copies on a side table for the public and councilmembers to collect on their way out. It was his list of donations to Grover Beach charities and what he could continue to donate if the council would remove me from the APCD. Of course, it wasn't his own money; it was an allowance provided to each supervisor to distribute in his or her district.

The legal term for someone threatening to take away support to your charitable institutions if you don't do as he wishes is 'extortion' (see Appendix 2).

Grover Beach City Council Meeting 8/5/13

Councilmember Nicolls proposed that the council remove me from the APCD board. He was hell-bent on discrediting me in any way he could to distract from his own misdeeds at the sewer district. Councilmembers agreed to agendize the matter at the August 5, 2013, council meeting.

AUGUST 5, 2013
Remove Debbie from the APCD

Around 100 people, including fellow APCD board members, attended the meeting, at least fifty of them waving florescent orange placards saying, "We Love Debbie" or "Keep the mayor on the APCD." I knew it would be a long and tough meeting. As I entered the council chambers, I saw florescent "We Love Debbie" signs everywhere. It was my birthday, but no one knew. It felt like the nicest thing anyone had ever done for me. Seven former mayors were there, five of whom supported keeping me on the APCD. The other two were Hill supporters; one his campaign manager, and the other Shoals. I made my case and then heard them out. Hill owned the other four councilmembers, two of them being County employees, another one a school board employee, all risking their jobs if they didn't kowtow to Hill. The ones who mattered, the people of Grover Beach, were with me. I made notes of what I wanted to say.

> *My job is to serve my community, and I love doing that. As your representative, I have a compelling constitutional right and responsibility to speak out when I know that the public is not being served.*
>
> *I agree that public health is number one.*
>
> *I had to summon up all my courage and conviction to talk with you tonight because on this issue I have been so badly treated by the local press and some of my colleagues who have not sought to understand my concerns.*

If there is anything that raises questions with you on any of this, please ask. Please challenge it. I am not afraid of hard questions. I am deeply moved by the spirit and intent behind our rights to free speech and the better outcome of this very cumbersome and difficult democratic process.

I outlined my concerns with the APCD:

1. Tunnel Vision: ten years focusing on one matter while ignoring the other factors degrading air quality
2. Not enforcing mitigation that could immediately improve air quality
3. Human and financial resources all funneled to one issue: vehicles in the dunes when there are elephants on the Mesa
4. 'Sensitive Receptors' addressed in air quality reports means 'People'—the monarch butterflies are better protected than the residents of the development
5. Bad legislation with impacts far surpassing the legislative intent and reach of APCDs
6. They are spending your money to monitor the monitors monitoring the monitors
7. Mitigate Don't Litigate
8. The Air Was Bad, Is Bad, and will Always be Bad
9. Deflecting
10. The council is under tremendous pressure from two supervisors who are trying to engineer a majority and want me off the board to achieve that majority
11. There is huge pressure to be 'collegial'—to go along to get along; not to rock the boat
12. Cynical manipulation of people they want to be popular with rather than doing anything to fix air quality
13. To support the above I would have to compromise my integrity and I will not do that. I care if people do not like me, but I do not mind.

I know you came here to get information. I can provide you with far more than we can cover today, so what is it that is important for you to walk away with?

I have always determined that no one else will dictate my behavior. How I behave is my choice and mine alone, so no matter how difficult the meeting, I keep my cool and maintain professional composure and courtesy. I am better able to understand when I listen rather than react. I gained a lot of respect and made a lot of friends that night.

One lesson learned came too late. State Code states that it is the mayor's choice who sits on the APCD! The council had no authority to remove me. Hill was circulating misinformation. The lesson? Always go back to the legislation to understand how things are supposed to operate.

SEPTEMBER 1, 2013

When I received reports of someone cutting down trees on the Mesa, I visited the site in question. I was so distressed by the magnitude of the air quality infractions I saw that I couldn't sleep for two nights. The APCD was compromising the health of the sensitive population in these developments by ignoring and not enforcing the significant factors contributing to bad air and attributing bad air to State Parks. While people were blaming vehicles for causing dust in their community, right in their own backyards were multiple known air quality detriments that I recognized because of my time as a planning commissioner.

The first sentence under 'About APCD' on their website, SLOCleanAir. org is, "*The San Luis Obispo County Air Pollution Control District (APCD or District) is the local agency working to protect the health of over 269,000 county residents by preserving good air quality*" and they weren't doing it.

SEPTEMBER 5, 2013
APCD Board Meeting Agenda Item, Rule 302

My comments at the May 29, 2013, meeting were not included in the record as requested. I read and provided a transcript of my comments for inclusion in the minutes.

California code dictates that legislators must make findings of legitimacy in order to implement legislation. If legislators cannot make such findings, the legislation is not legally defensible, leaving the agency at risk of legal challenge and the attendant costs.

I could not make the finding of Necessity or Consistency because it was not necessary to make a rule to achieve what nearby agencies were achieving with a Memorandum of Understanding. I was unable to make the finding of Clarity because it was unclear as to what the permit was permitting. I was repeating the findings required by state code straight out of the staff report. I wanted to be sure the record would reflect that the agency could not make findings to support the Dust Rule.

DECEMBER 16, 2013
City Council Committee Assignments

Meeting at which committee assignments would be made. Supervisor Adam Hill was there for his third visit of 2013. As the councilmembers took their seats, they saw a 'bronze' medallion key ring at their place on the dais. The medallion had Hill's name on one side and the County seal on the other.

20:14 Public Comment Adam Hill Finally if any of you have needs or things feel free community funds, I know Kathy just got one in … trying to help with the Christmas parade and my office is always happy to provide community funds for the city or for any nonprofits that the City or you are involved with Councilmember Lee has done so, so I encourage to do that."

Four former mayors attended the meeting and, along with most of the other city residents there, spoke in favor of retaining me on the APCD. The powerful alliance of off-roaders, Friends of the Oceano Dunes, took umbrage at threats to remove me from the APCD board and threatened to oppose the hotel because it blocked their ability to stop and prepare their vehicles for going onto the beach. Before the meeting, I called former mayor Shoals to see if he would join me to sit down with them to reach an understanding in order to prevent an appeal to the hotel. He was unresponsive, but it must have really wound him up because he and his best friend Lieberman came to the meeting and goaded the off roaders into suing State Parks, saying, "OK, sue us!"

The council voted as Hill wished, to replace me on the board with Karen Bright. The irony was that I had not once veered from the council position while on the APCD board, as very clearly set forth in 2011, while Councilmember Bright had blatantly refused to follow the council direction, instead acting as Hill wished. A second irony was that they removed me because they said I was too opinionated about what was going on at the dunes, a charge that could have been leveled at every single one of my accusers.

The Colonel

The battle with the APCD had been punishing, but for the fair and reasoned leadership of the General and Colonel. Waiting for coffee in Starbucks one day, I saw I had a call coming in from a Sacramento area code. The Colonel was calling before he retired to thank me for standing up for what I believed and standing up for my community; for being a political figure who truly represented my community with integrity. "You are my hero," he said.

I teared up, hearing that from the man who led the reconstruction of a nation's government following The Surge in Iraq. That's as much validation of my political worth as I will ever need. That's as great an example of good leadership as I will ever need. The colonel always took the time to affirm good people.

MARCH 12, 2014
Moxie

Adam Hill pursued the *LA Times* in an attempt to discredit me through national media. Hill did not account for my background in PR and experience working with the media. Hill had the ear and pen of the central coast editorial team, but the *Times* was the big league and Hill did not count on a good reporter or an experienced professionally trained mayor. When the *LA Times* asked me for an interview, I outlined the issues for them. *The City of Grover Beach made the front page of the LA Times* on March 14, 2014, for the first time ever, with accolades for the dunes and for the mayor, "a real estate agent, a single mom, and a free spirit," with "moxie and business experience" who "voters chose by a wide margin in 2012." Hill's plan backfired.

2015
The Coastal Commission Comes to Town Again

Despite promises of my council colleague Bright and County Supervisor Hill who "never wanted to close down the dunes to vehicles," less than two years had passed before the APCD petitioned the Coastal Commission to close the dunes to OHVs.

JUNE 17, 2015
APCD Meeting

State Geological Survey Senior Engineering Geologist and Hydrologist Will Harris had the audacity to stand up during public comment to speak to the matter. His comments were respectful and professional. He called for the agencies to work together. Hill and Gibson badgered Harris from the dais and Hill closed the meeting saying, "Perhaps somebody will talk to your bosses in Sacramento about your appearance here today."

And so, Gibson did, using SLO County letterhead, without the authorization of the other ten members of the APCD board, the majority of whom were supportive of much of what Harris said.

It seems that Hill forgot his 2013 promises that he didn't want to close the dunes and that if the board elected him chair, he would not send anymore correspondence without board consent.

Hill and Gibson were outnumbered by the rest of the board and most of the audience and were seeking to regain the majority, just as they did in 2013 when they staged the board meeting "no show" and emailed and called the Grover Beach councilmembers seeking my removal from the APCD board for the same reason—to silence views that differed from theirs.

I emailed my supporters asking them to let Harris's boss know that Harris always behaved professionally, that he was dedicated to the public good and that's just the kind of true public servant we need, one with the courage of his convictions and the qualifications to stand by the scientific facts, reminding them, "If you happen to be a Democrat, tell him so, because Hill and Gibson will dismiss any correspondence by saying it is all [right wing] party politics."

Even the character, courage, and sincerity of Harris and his supporters were not enough to keep him in his role as the geologist working with State Parks. The correspondence that follows demonstrates Harris's and his supporters' passion for the truth and for open and transparent public discourse, as well as a historical record of the science and events surrounding the Dust Rule and the charlatans who put it in place.

Hello, I'm Will Harris with the California Geological Survey. In the continued hearing on Rule 1001 document Larry Allen submitted to the Board for this meeting, Mr. Allen states "the intent and design" of the rule is to reduce dust to "natural background levels." The trouble is those levels are unknown and so a rule that seeks to achieve an unknown is pointless. But what is of greater concern is that the APCD has never attempted to find out what the "natural background levels" are of dust generated from saltation. If they did, they would actually discover that dust levels from dune saltation were much greater in the past than they are now. That's because Parks began planting native vegetation in the dunes in 1982; the year it took over management of Oceano Dunes Park. And as a result, much more vegetation covers the dunes now than ever before. A comparison of 1930's aerial imagery confirms this. More vegetation means less open sand exposed to the winds, and consequently less saltation of sand. Less now than there ever was in the past. The past and present dune vegetation differences were pointed out to the APCD and to this Board beginning in November 2011. But the net dust reducing benefit from the increased dune vegetation coverage has never been acknowledged by the APCD or the Board. And Mr. Allen continues to advocate for the confounding mandate to reduce dust levels to "natural background levels" that were actually higher in the past than they are now. Small wonder this Catch-22 construct of a rule has generated so much litigation. Considering this if I was a Board member, moving forward, I would want 1. To end litigation related to the Rule. The Rule and consent decree are invalid in the eyes of the court. If status quo reigns and the Rule consent decree remains in place, the action taken under the Rule such as a fine or a mandate to cover over sand with wind fencing or a surface treatment known as soil cement, we see APCD has advocated for, those mandates could easily be challenged and successfully challenged in court. This makes it clear that the status quo only ensures continued litigation. Additionally, a significant amount of money and staff resources and time have gone towards monitoring of ride and non-ride portions of the dunes. This monitoring is set up as a mechanism to fine State Parks for any perceived "violation per the Rule," whether then devoting so much money and resources to punitive aspects of the Rule which again can easily be challenged in court, I would rather see those resources devoted to best management practices identified in a new Memorandum of Understanding (MOU) and 2. I would want to see collaboration rather than confrontation. State Parks has entered into successful insightful MOU's with air districts from Monterey Bay and Imperial County. I would hope this County could achieve a much more positive relationship with State Parks."

Adam Hill, Chair "Mr. Harris can I ask on whose behalf are you speaking?"

Harris "I'm speaking on behalf of myself."

Hill ""and who employs you?"

Harris "California State Geological Survey."

Hill "Who asked you to come here today?"

Harris " Why would you ask?"

Hill "Seems like a reasonable question if you are before this Board on behalf of the Geological Survey."

Harris "Because I have advocated for a position based on my professional evaluation of the Rule, based on my professional experience in the Dunes since 2008 working with State Parks, I felt my point is valid to give to the Board and I think you should hear it unvarnished."

Hill "So you were not asked to make this statement today by anyone?"

Harris "That's correct."

Hill "and did not clear this with anyone at the Geological Survey? You're here on your own time?"

Harris "I'm not here on my own time. I'm here on State time."

Hill "you are here on state time?

Bruce Gibson, Board Member "advocating on your own behalf? Continuing to attempt to undermine the science Mr. Harris, this is appalling, frankly."

Hill "that's it, thank you."

Harris "thank you very much for your consideration of my comments."

3:09:00 Mr. Harris leaves the lectern.

3:20:53 While Board members and Counsel are discussing Board Members' Items, Mr. Harris starts walking back up to the lectern.

Hill "I'm not going to give you a microphone Mr. Harris if you're coming."

Harris "I just wanted to let the Board know that the words I spoke were my own I am not an advocate of anybody other than (unintelligible).

Hill "Mister you are out of order. Mr. Harris you are not given permission to speak. You are out of order, perhaps somebody will talk to your bosses in Sacramento about your appearance here today."

BOARD OF SUPERVISORS
1055 MONTEREY, ROOM D430 SAN LUIS OBISPO, CA 93408

BRUCE GIBSON
SUPERVISOR DISTRICT TWO

June 20, 2015

John Parrish, State Geologist
California Geological Survey
801 K Street, MS 12-30
Sacramento, CA 95814

RE: Public Comments by Will Harris, California Geological Survey (CGS), on June 17, 2015

Dear Dr. Parish:

I write to register my objections to public comments made by Will Harris of CGS at the June 17, 2015 Board meeting of the San Luis Obispo County Air Pollution Control District (APCD).

In comments regarding APCD's efforts to control dust pollution coming from the Oceano Dunes State Vehicular Recreation Area (ODSVRA), Mr. Harris disparaged the integrity of the District's technical efforts and the competence of its Air Pollution Control Officer, Larry Allen. In addition, he improperly advised the APCD Board of his personally-preferred regulatory approach, and in the process, contradicted an agreement between the APCD and the State Department of Parks and Recreation (DPR). A transcript of his comments is attached for your reference.

As I'm sure you're aware, it is the APCD's mission to protect the public's health through the regulation and reduction of air pollution. For many years, areas downwind of the riding area of the ODSVRA have seen measured levels of airborne particulate matter (PM10 and PM2.5) pollution that regularly exceed state and federal standards—exceedances of the state standards typically occur 60-70 times per year. Measurements downwind of non-riding areas show far fewer exceedances.

Technical studies in 2007 (Phase 1), 2010 (Phase 2) and subsequently have confirmed that open sand sheets are the major source of particulate matter pollution in the area and that the riding areas of the ODSVRA emit far greater amounts of particulates than non-riding areas. Importantly, the Phase 2 study was peer-reviewed by noted experts in airborne particulate pollution, who confirmed the findings. Copies of relevant studies are available on the APCD web site, www.slocleanair.org.

In response, in November 2011, APCD adopted Rule 1001, that requires DPR to put measures in place to reduce dust pollution levels to natural background levels. Rule 1001 clearly states that the background dust pollution levels are to be measured at a control monitoring station downwind of non-riding areas. The performance measures of Rule 1001 require dust levels at a monitoring site downwind of the riding area to be less than 120% of the control site levels.

Given this background, I take considerable exception to Mr. Harris's comment that background levels are "unknown" and that therefore Rule 1001 is "pointless." His further comments regarding historical vegetation patterns and sand movements are diversionary and irrelevant.

Since its 2011 adoption, progress toward gaining DPR's compliance with Rule 1001 has been slow, due to technical disagreement, general public controversy, and litigation. Recently, however, DPR and APCD have been making progress under the auspices of a Consent Decree Agreement. This legal instrument, facilitated by the California Air Resources Board, provides a means of reaching compliance with Rule 1001 and includes a structured dispute resolution process.

Mr. Harris's comments regarding this agreement (the "status quo" to him) and a speculation regarding potential future litigation are highly inappropriate. DPR has embraced the Consent Agreement as "collaborative," "cooperative," and "workable". That he should contradict DPR's position by advocating some other arrangement (specifically, an MOU, which lacks necessary enforcement authority) seems unacceptable for his role as technical advisor.

Finally, while not explicit in his June 17 comments, I believe Mr. Harris's personal biases have affected his technical advice to DPR, and thus delayed the protection of the public's health. Mr. Harris has consistently sought to discredit the Phase 2 study in particular, posing specious arguments and hypotheses in an effort to undermine the conclusion that off-road vehicles have a role in this serious pollution problem. His arguments have been consistently rebutted by experts.

A full analysis of our technical disagreements on the Phase 2 Study would require more space than this letter allows. I would be happy to discuss this further if you'd like, but let me observe that 1) the fundamentally-important Phase 2 study conclusions were peer-reviewed by air pollution experts; 2) while Mr. Harris is a geologist, he is not to my knowledge an expert in particulate matter pollution, and 3) while I am not an air pollution expert either, I do hold an undergraduate degree in physics and doctorate in geophysics, which I have used in a careful reading of the technical issues.

The conflict of Mr. Harris's personal and professional roles is evident in the latter part of the transcript. Mr. Harris identifies himself as a CGS employee, and proceeds to make aggressive personal comments, on state time, without the authorization of CGS or DPR.

In conclusion I believe Mr. Harris owes the APCD and its APCO Larry Allen an apology for his grossly inappropriate commentary. I would also urge you to review Mr. Harris's role I advise DPR to ensure that the public's interest and health are protected.

As you know, I have worked with other staff members of CGS on technical matters of great importance to public policy and have the highest regard for their technical expertise and demeanor. I regret having to bring this matter to your attention and hope for productive future relations.

If you have any questions or need further information, please don't hesitate to contact me.

Sincerely yours,

BRUCE GIBSON
Supervisor, District 2
San Luis Obispo

Cd: Adam Hill, Chair, APCED
Larry Allen, APCO

From: Harris, Will@DOC
Sent: Tuesday, June 30, 2015, 3:53 PM
To: Conlin, Christopher@Parks; Marshall, Brent@Parks
Subject: Oceano Dunes—SLOAPCD Consent Decree/Rule 1001 concerns

Dear Chris and Brent,

Please see the attached memo regarding technical and practical concerns with the implementation of the Consent Decree/Rule 1001 at Oceano Dunes. I alluded to these concerns in my comment given to the SLOAPCD Board on June 17, but I think it's fair to say the dialogue following my comment distracted from the message. To bring it back to the message, and in keeping with my professional responsibility, I've detailed the concerns in the memo.

As always, I'm happy to discuss the memo and broader Oceano issues at your convenience.

Best, Will

Will J. Harris
Senior Engineering Geologist
California Geological Survey
801 "K" Street, 13th floor
Sacramento, CA 95814

DEPARTMENT OF CONSERVATION
CALIFORNIA GEOLOGICAL SURVEY

June 30, 2015

To: Chris Conlin, Deputy Director
California State Parks
Off-Highway Motor Vehicle Recreation Division
1725 23rd Street, Suite 200
Sacramento, CA 95816

From: Will J. Harris
California Geological Survey
801 K Street, Suite 1324
Sacramento, C 95814

Subject: Practical Concerns Regarding the Implementation of Rule 101

Below are two aerial images depicting the same area of coastal sand dunes in south San Luis Obispo County, California. One image depicts the dunes in the 1930s, and one shows the dunes in 2014, more or less the present day. Also shown on both images is the line trace marking the southern portion of California State Parks (State Parks) property, which is the dune and Oso Flaco Lake Preserve area found in the southern portion of the Oceano Dunes State Vehicular Recreation Area (Oceano Dunes).

A glance at the two images reveals a difference. The image from the 1930's shows there was once much more open sand than there is now. The present day image reveals that much of what had been open sand dunes is now covered over with vegetation. I bring this up because the Air Pollution Control Officer (APCO) for the San Luis Obispo Air Pollution Control District (SLOAPCD) submitted a document to the SLOAPCD Board for its June 17, 2015 meeting which states, "the intent and design of the Rule [1001] is to reduce dust emissions caused by vehicle activity at the ODSVRA [Oceano Dunes] to natural background levels..." (SLOAPCD, 2015).

As you know, Rule 1001 is a regulation SLOAPCD has imposed on State Parks that seeks to limit the amount of saltation-derived dust emanating from the OHV riding area of Oceano Dunes Saltation is the geologic, dune-building process in which strong prevailing winds push sand shoreward and cause sand grains to creep and bounce along dune surfaces. Larger grains bounced by the saltation process can release finer grains, including dust particles, which are then blown inland. Dune vegetation not overwhelmed by blowing sand will hamper the saltation process. Where there is more dune-covering vegetation there is that much less dust produced from saltation.

Oceano Dunes Vegetation 1939   2014

1939 and 2014

The "natural background" distinction is of concern because the southern portion of Oceano Dunes depicted in the above images is considered a "control" location per Rule 1001. An air monitoring station (approximate location shown on the 2014 aerial image has been placed downwind of this area. Per the APCO's document, and subsequently reiterated by SLOAPCD staff in the press (Lompoc Record, 2015), dust readings from this monitor will be considered "natural background levels" to be compared to readings downwind of the riding area of Oceano Dunes. Higher readings from the riding area of the dunes will be considered "violations", and State Parks will be subjected to fines per the Rule.

There are two things wrong with this. I have alluded to one of them—dune vegetation. When State Parks took over management of Oceano Dunes in 1982, it began planting native vegetation in the dunes. Today, within the boundaries of the park, there are 650 more acres of dunes now covered with vegetation than in the 1930's (CGS, 2011), a time that predates OHV recreation in the dunes. Putting this conversely, in the 1930's there were 650 more acres of open and subjected to dust-producing dune saltation. By this measure, State Parks has already reduced saltation-derived dust below "natural background levels." More to the point, the air monitoring station downwind of the "control" area cannot measure "natural background levels " of saltation-derived dust because the lesser amount of open sand in the area is not representative of natural conditions.

Secondly, Rule 1001 makes no mention of determining "natural background levels" of dust—the terminology is not present within the rest of the Rule. The is only the latest migration from the actual language of Rule 1001. In previous emails to you, and in several meetings we have had in recent months, I have pointed out that the Rule allows Parks to choose locations to place air monitors downwind of the OHV riding area and downwind of a "control" location where no riding occurs. Despite this appearance of choice, the de-facto riding area monitor has become the SLOAPCD's air monitoring station at 2391 Willow Road, which is a California Department of Forestry (CDF) fire station in Arroyo Grande. The CDF station is well away from the Oceano Dunes, does not accurately record the strength or direction of regional prevailing winds due to near-station influences, and it's influenced by other dust sources that lie between it and the park (CGS 2010). The SLOAPCD air monitor at the CDF station was never formally chosen by State Parks or its technical team as a riding area monitor per Rule 1001, nor was the location formally approved by the APCO, as is required by the Rule. Similarly, no formal choice was made for the control monitor location. Its location was determined by SLOAPCD staff who squeezed it into the easternmost point of State Parks property. (Additionally, the control monitor location does not align with upwind open sand along the prevailing wind direction line, a misstep that will likely cause lower dust readings at the control monitor. This in turn will skew greater differences with the riding area monitor, triggering more "violations" per the Rule.)

Due to litigation related to Rule 1001 that has continued to the California Court of Appeal, State Parks and SLOAPCD entered into a Consent Decree brokered by the California Air Resources Board (CARB) so that compliance with Rule 1001 could continue without opposition from California State Parks. But the Consent Decree was not approved by the court, presumably because the plaintiff, Friends of Oceano Dunes (Friends) was "specifically excluded" from consent/settlement discussions (New Times SLO, 2014). More recently, of course, the Court of Appeal ruled in favor of Friends (California 2nd Appellate District Decision, 2015), effectively invalidating Rule 1001 and the Consent Decree, and the SLOAPCD Board seems intent on not appealing this ruling to the State Supreme Court. From a lay perspective, it would seem State Parks is no longer required to comply with Rule 1001. From my technical professional perspective, given the concerns I detailed above actual compliance with Rule 1001 is simply not possible.

Should you have any questions, please feel free to call.

Respectfully submitted,

Will J Harris, PG 5679, CEG2222 CHg750
California Geological Survey

From: R Holt
To: "john_parrish@conservation.ca.gov
Sent: Sunday, July 12, 2015 9:18 PM
Subject: Will Harris status

Mr. Parrish,

I have been on vacation and am not familiar with the incident which has apparently resulted in the removal of Mr. Will Harris from involvement with the issues dealing with air pollution from blowing sand at the Pismo Dunes SRVA. However, I am quite familiar with the political tactics in which Mr. Gibson and Mr. Hill of the SLO County Board of Supervisors engage. They are, to put it bluntly, arrogant bullies who have no sense of fairness or justice in dealing with people who disagree with them. Anything they state about the incident should be examined thoroughly and carefully for half-truths, distortions, and other forms of bias before acceptance. They are a disgrace to those who value civil political discourse. I say this as someone who agrees with their general political positions about half the time.

Additionally, they do not represent the APCD as a whole in their opinions and their views on this subject are not the views of the entire Board of Supervisors either. As for Mr. Allen, I have great distrust for the objectivity of someone whose salary and position is largely dependent upon fines generated by his department. It may not be his fault that the APCD is setup to operate this way but I remain unconvinced that he is not abusing his authority for reasons other than environmental protection. His views on the issues should also be taken with a block of salt.

Please reconsider your actions regarding Mr. Harris. If he was indeed out-of-line with the presentation of his comments, I would think that a minor reprimand would be in order. Someone who is both knowledgeable and willing to present that knowledge clearly is valuable in arriving at an honest and reasonable conclusion—particularly when others present weak or erroneous information aggressively to support their political goals.

Ron Holt
Arroyo Grande, CA

From: Harris, Will@DOC
Sent: Monday, August 31, 2015, 9:49 PM
Subject: Working with you

Hello Oceano Dunes colleagues,

As some of you may have heard by now, I am no longer working on OHV projects. It is a bitter pill to swallow as it has been wonderful, challenging work, with Oceano Dunes being the most wonderful and most challenging. The decision to remove me from all OHV work is internal to CGS and based on the three-minute comment I gave at the June 17 air district board meeting. I gave the comment without asking permission and subsequently Supervisor Gibson complained to my bosses and, I was told, to John Laird of the Natural Resources Agency. The basis for my comment is detailed in the attached memo. I did not have time ahead of the meeting to prepare the memo, but I knew it would be important to detail my concerns in some fashion given how distracting the discourse that followed my comment was.

You may be wondering about the work I have been doing with Scripps, if there are any preliminary results. All of you had a hand in helping that collaboration come together, so I wanted to give you some early news.

It turns out there is DNA from a particular diatom that has been detected in the seawater, in the frothy, shaving cream-like foam that blows up from the lapping waves along the shoreline, and in the air filter strip taken from the BAM air monitor located in the deep interior of the dunes. And most importantly, that DNA is not in the sand itself, meaning that once the wind blows the diatoms become entrained in the air, blowing downwind and never becoming part of the dune system.

Now, granted, these are preliminary data, and Scripps will need to replicate the results next spring, but it is nonetheless huge news. Diatoms are tiny plankton—they can be smaller than 2.5 microns and they are composed of silica. Plankton bloom excessively offshore due to upwelling associated with the strong spring winds. The air district has detected an unusually high fraction of silica PM2.5 in their PM10 measurements, but they can provide no rationale for why that is. The DNA data, along with the upwelling backstory, potentially provide that rationale, one that has nothing to do with OHV recreation and everything to do with the natural environment.

That's the latest on the planktonic DNA investigation. I only hope it will be allowed to continue.

With that I will sign off. You all have been a great joy to work with, even if briefly (and for some not so briefly—Ronnie and I have worked together since 2007!) All of you have demonstrated a dedication to your job that is admirable, and I have learned much from you. I do hope our paths cross again.

Best to you all,

Will J. Harris
Senior Engineering Geologist
California Geological Survey
801 K Street, MS 1324
Sacramento, CA 95814

At the next APCD meeting Kevin Rice made the statement below during public comment, following it up with correspondence.

7.9.15 USING POLITICAL AFFILIATIONS TO TERMINATE PEOPLE YOU DISAGREE WITH IS NOT "CIVIL" DISCOURSE.

This is the SECOND TIME Mr. Gibson has used back-room politicking to cause a person to lose their job.

On December 5, 2011, Supervisor Gibson traveled with Air Pollution Control Officer (APCO) Larry Allen to meet with Secretary of Natural Resources John Laird. Secretary Laird's agency oversees State Parks, the Coastal Commission, and the California Geological Survey (CGS), and others.

FOUR DAYS after Gibson's meeting with Laird, Daphne Greene—a high-energy and accomplished Democrat appointed by Gray Davis—was terminated from her job as Deputy Director of State Parks Off-Highway Division. It was extremely obvious at that time that APCD, Gibson and Larry Allen disliked Daphne's positions on the APCD "Dust Rule" (Rule 1001).

Article: http://thegeneralsrecreationden.blogspot.com/2011/12/ca-governor-makes-political-decision-to.html

Rice went on to detail the story of the Gibson/Hill attempts to have Harris terminated and Hill's libel of Harris on Facebook.

Harris is a state licensed professional Engineering Geologist (Lic. #2222), Geologist (LIc. #5679) and Hydrogeologist (Lic. #750), yet, on June 24, Supervisor Hill posted on Facebook, "Mr. Harris is not an expert" (https://www.facebook.com/calcoastfraud/posts/1624556647787399?comment_id=1624635064446224). Hill's libel is both outrageous and FALSE.

EXTREME DANGER TO PUBLIC TRANSPARENCY, CIVILITY AND HONESTY:

(1) Using political clout to terminate a person's livelihood places an extreme "chill" and fear upon any public employee involved in a public debate. Do we wish scientists to be afraid to express their professional views? Do we wish agency employees to bend to fear and political pressures anytime they fear a single board member wields higher clout?

(2) It is OUTRAGEOUS, in my view, that Supervisors Gibson and Hill have taken on this unilateral and extra-curricular pursuit without APCD Board deliberation, public input and majority, democratic direction of the Board.

(3) PUBLIC LOCKED OUT. If legislators may freely and individually "interfere", what quells all twelve directors of the APCD Board from individually lobbying and interfering with every matter that comes to the table? And, if that occurs, the discourse and debate move from the public boardroom into the realm of behind-the-scenes individual power plays and lobbying. The public never sees the debate and is not opportuned to participate in the debate of these highly contentious public issues.

For years, I've worked to get the APCD Board to honestly air and debate the issues Will Harris brought. Supervisors Gibson and Hill, once again, cut off honest debate and made a very personal attack on this science professional.

How am I (and others) expected to remain "civil" in this atmosphere of personal persecution?

Please let me know how I can bring this issue to the attention of the League.

It was out of sheer frustration that Rice addressed the League of Women Voters because of their well-publicized campaign to restore civility to public debate.

2020
APCD PROPOSES TO SHUT DOWN THE DUNES

As locals have known for decades, and as expressed by the business group that circulated the petition in 2013, the truth was that the APCD wanted to shut down riding in the dunes. Despite the denials by Hill and Councilmember Bright that they did not wish to, their actions with the APCD and the Coastal Commission are shutting down riding in the dunes. Residents of the Monarch Dunes development elicited sympathy with their stories of not being able to go outside and of dust-covered furniture on high wind days; however, this phenomenon exists near all the beaches and dunes nearby. In fact, the wind blows so much sand up Grand Avenue that it begins to pile up in the streets and sidewalk planters. Locals in every neighborhood experience constant build-up of dust on inside and outside surfaces, especially on vehicles parked outside. Added to the dust from high winds in sandy areas is the ash from forest fires that has plagued us for the past ten years. Travelers through the area in the 1860s documented the miserable conditions as noted in the excerpts below from *Up and Down California in 1860 to 1864*, the journal of William H. Brewer, Professor of Agriculture in the Sheffield Scientific School from 1864 to 1903.

Nipomo Ranch
Wednesday, April 10, 1861

Tuesday, April 9, we came to Nipomo Ranch. Our road struck into the valley of Santa Maria River. This river is now entirely dry, not a drop of water, its valley a perfectly level plain, with the exception of an occasional terrace or old riverbank, about six or eight miles wide. We struck down and across this valley about ten or twelve miles, a most tedious ride. We were dry, but no water was met with for the twenty-two miles traveled except a sinkhole with stagnant, alkaline, dirty, stinking water. The ride was very tedious as we wound our slow way over the plains, here drifting sand, there a partial pasture. Nothing relieved the eye; the senses tired with the level scene...**wind filled the air with gray dust, sometimes shutting out the sight of the hills like**

drifting snow. Lovely green hills lay on each side at the distance of a few miles. Many cattle and horses were feeding on the hills or on the plain. Water every four to six miles in the side canyons was sufficient for them. They seemed mere specks on the plain—a herd of a thousand like a few flies on the floor. This valley runs to the sea, and in that direction a mirage kept ahead of us in the hot air...

The Coastal Commission voted in March 2021 to shut down the dunes within five years, a decision based on the lie contained in a March 27, 2017, letter from APCO Allen to California Coastal Commission Deputy Director Dan Carl.

"Public exposure to unacceptably high levels of particulate matter, much of which occurs in the form of highly toxic crystalline silica, have continued to impact downwind residents."

The State Attorney General (at the time, now Vice President Kamala Harris), represents state agencies, i.e., State Parks and the APCD. The Attorney General's office has taken the State Parks' position against the APCD in every case brought against the APCD regarding the Dust Rule. Scripps Institute supported what the locals and State Parks knew all along: particulate in our dunes is a natural process upon which vehicles have no impact. It's Mother Nature's fault. The state park has already spent $15 million on the matter. The SLOAPCD has spent over two million dollars in court.

APCD Science Debunked

Finally, in 2020 the word came out. Lynn Russell, Ph.D. chemical engineering, California Institute of Technology, 1995, postdoctoral investigator at the National Center for Atmospheric Research, faculty member at Princeton University; now at Scripps Institute of Oceanography, Fellow of the American Geophysical Union for "pioneering contributions to the fundamental science of organic aerosols through innovative theory, instrumentation, measurements, and modeling" used DNA technology to determine the content and source of the notorious particulate. Scripps confirmed the information that Will Harris had so desperately wanted to convey in 2015.

OCTOBER 1, 2020
Scripps study on dust at Oceano Dunes "Dust emitted from the Oceano Dunes is less harmful than previously thought"

The ongoing Scripps Institution of Oceanography released preliminary findings in its second of the three-year research study into the sources and composition of the airborne particulate that has been the subject of so much angst in the community, telling reporter Kasey Bubnash of the *SLO New Times*, "We're just interested in getting the right science out there, so that people can make informed decisions."

Federal clean air standards regulate the amount of particulate matter (PM) with a diameter of 2.5 and 10 microns. At high concentrations, depending on the composition of the particulate, it compromises health and can be deadly. Particles with a diameter of 10 microns or less are inhalable. Combustion particles, metals, and organic compounds are considered to be most dangerous. Dust, pollen, and mold can also be harmful. The Scripps report reassured us, "It is worth noting that **there is no evidence that toxic compounds are associated with the two major PM2.5 sources (dune dust and sea spray) during windy conditions at Oceano Dunes, so association of PM2.5 with detrimental health effects may be without foundation."**

Coming under public pressure, after ten years of warning Nipomo residents of the dangers of silica dust, despite having no scientific evidence of such, the APCD ran tests for silica in the air. Their tests found none. So the APCD changed its messaging to say that nevertheless, the vehicles were creating gas fuel emission particulate that was blowing downwind. While it can't be argued that vehicles do not cause emissions, even this next unsubstantiated argument that the particulate downwind was caused by fuel emissions was also debunked.

Scripps found that the sources of PM 2.5 at the Oceano Dunes, previously attributed to harmful mineral dust and vehicle emissions, only accounted for a fraction of PM 2.5 detected at the dunes. **The majority was attributed to sea salt, ammonium, and nitrate blown in from the ocean.** None of us expected that! We had all assumed the particulate came from the dunes.

The interim report concluded that even when recreational vehicles were not allowed in the dunes for several months during a COVID shutdown, there were high PM10 and PM2.5 measurements and therefore, "dune-derived mineral dust is more likely to be caused by natural forces rather than human activities." While the short duration of the interim study provided only limited statistics in support of this result, the report concluded, "the longer records provided by APCD provide additional confirmation. For this reason, the high dust concentrations measured on high wind days in and downwind of Oceano Dunes are likely dominated by natural saltation processes associated with the indigenous geomorphological dune structure."

We were right. The furor and panic that was scaring senior golf resort residents was nothing more than political fear tactics and attempts to fund an agency with a fine retirement for an overpaid chief executive. In the meantime, Harris's superior sidelined him for over a year because he dared to speak the truth publicly. The Colonel, upon his retirement, asked for Harris's reinstatement. We are all vindicated, and Adam Hill and his cronies who I have called the "bad dems" left a trail of destruction, anxiety, and financial detriment to the very individuals and taxpayers they claimed to serve.

NOVEMBER 15, 2021
Court ruling voids Dust Rule implementation agreement /Opens door for public to claim reimbursement of $10m from SLOAPCD

Friends of the Oceano Dunes, the not-for-profit grass roots organization that seeks to preserve camping and off-highway vehicle recreation at the ODSVRA for 28,000 members and users of the park, has yet again been victorious in court against the SLOAPCD.

The San Luis Obispo County Superior Court ordered the APCD to pay the group's attorney fees and costs of $121,241 after determining that the

APCD's method of implementing its dust rule is void and against public policy because the APCD changed the rule without public notice as required by the state's air quality statutes. Instead, the APCD adopted the agreement in closed session, out of view of the public and without public input.

The Court also ruled that APCD staff didn't have authority to change the mechanism for determining compliance deadlines for the Dust Rule's requirements, because that must be presented to the full APCD Board.

The ruling also throws into question certain aspects of dust control and allows the public to ask the Air District to reimburse the State of California for monies expended under the void agreement, which could amount to more than ten million dollars.

When does the nonsense stop? Every outside agency and even inside studies now concur that vehicles in the dunes are not causing dangerous air conditions. The State Park's good-faith effort to comply with the Dust Rule now leaves two hundred acres of previously pristine dunes littered with orange plastic fencing and hay, wasting upwards of millions of dollars of taxpayers' money and an incalculable number of employee, agency, and public hours which could have been so much more constructively used.

The sensible Sierra Club founder and State Parks solution and legislation of the 1980s that remains in effect has stood the test of eminent scientists and the courts. It has stood the test of time. Adam Hill has not. The APCD has not.

NOVEMBER 21, 2021

Karen Velie, of *CalCoastTimes* reported that the APCD website continued to tout the misinformation it had perpetrated for the past ten years:

> "The APCD has been investigating the source of the high particulate matter concentrations on the Nipomo Mesa for the past decade. Several studies performed by the APCD in the Nipomo Mesa area have shown the source of the elevated particulate matter pollution to be windblown dust from the open sand areas of the Oceano Dunes State Vehicular Recreation Area."

The APCD has now admitted it never analyzed the particulates for mineral dust content. In 2017, after 10 years of warning Nipomo residents of the dangers of silica dust: that it causes cancers and lung and kidney disease, and asserting that discontinuing vehicle use in the dunes would save citizens from these evils, the APCD decided to run tests for silica in the air. The testing refuted the APCD's earlier claims, concluding the dust blowing from the dunes did not contain dangerous levels of crystalline silica.

In response to the APCD's claim, the state of California has spent more than $22 million to reduce dust from the Oceano Dunes in an attempt to protect people from a public health hazard that didn't exist.

The prestigious Scripps Institution of Oceanography analyzed the particulate and determined only 14% of the particles blowing on the mesa consist of mineral dust. In other words, neither State Parks nor the vehicles are to blame for bad air quality on the mesa.

The study determined that particulate concentrations are highest during high wind conditions, even when off-road vehicles were banned from the dunes during the pandemic. Researchers also determined the mineral dust blowing on the mesa is more likely caused by natural forces such as wind than off-road recreation. Based on the content of the particulate, the study determined that the main component of the particulate—saltwater—indicates that it comes not from the sand, but from waves.

The APCD says that during the pandemic when there were no vehicles in the dunes, although a particularly windy time period, there were fewer days of bad air quality. All along, studies have focused on only one factor and one assumption, attempting to prove or disprove it, without looking at other influences. As a result, assuming particulate was derived from onshore sand, no one tested the particulate content. It is at best tunnel vision, at worst, machinations intended to shore up agency income; it is certainly bad science.

It is possible that the attempts to remediate particulate entrainment in the dunes has made a difference. There is no argument about the location and intensity of the plume, and it's clear that anything that thwarts the northwest winds and thwarts entrainment of sand will reduce the amount of particulate reaching homes downwind.

The other clear science that has been ignored and unenforced is the effects of the dirt roads, highway one, train tracks, open plowed fields, and construction upwind of the strongest part of the plume and nearer, or inside, the developments most affected. Since 2015, decreased construction and decrease in open dirt fields, with conversion of open fields to cannabis production in hoop houses, has significantly reduced the amount of localized pollution from known particulate sources. This may be the answer to the APCD's question of why it appears that closing the dunes to vehicles improved levels of particulate.

CHAPTER 6

THE INGRATE WASTE MANAGEMENT AUTHORITY
Embezzled

Why didn't the mayor want our recycling agency investigated?

The Integrated Waste Management Authority (IWMA) is responsible for recycling in SLO County. Grover Beach Mayor Jeff Lee served as the board president for four years. During Lee's tenure there were many public calls for an investigation, including one from Wayne Hall, the assistant county administrator who helped author the agreement that created the IWMA twenty years earlier. Writing to the board in April 2018, Hall accused chief executive William Worrell of "blatant disregard for statutory requirements for spending, contracting, and accounting," asking if the board was providing proper oversight of Worrell and the agency.

The board's refusal to act prompted a citizens group to hire government fraud expert Carl Knudson. Knudson reported that even after a cursory glance, the IWMA's financial offenses appeared much, much worse than those he found at the SSLOCSD three years earlier.

President Lee told the press, "When the information came forward, we took action." However, the IWMA auditor had alerted the board to problems during Lee's four-year presidency. The 2018 audit contained a warning that despite its responsibility to express opinions of financial statements, the firm could "express no such opinion on the effectiveness of internal controls" and *could not provide any assurance because limited procedures do not provide us with sufficient evidence to express an opinion or provide any assurance."* This alone would have triggered a forensic audit by most boards.

Even with difficulty obtaining information from the IWMA due to delays to public records requests, confounding responses, and destroyed agency records, Knudson found "huge accounting discrepancies and irregularities involving its entire budget." He reported a "lack of documentation for $445,077 in expenses on the IWMA credit card..." and several transactions that "appeared to be personal in nature." Knudson also noted "large contracts granted without competitive bidding." Knudson's report pointed out that chief executive Worrell, legal counsel Raymond Biering, and the agency's auditors ran the agency from its inception until its downfall, never changing in the 20 years of its existence.

As the agency and President Lee continued to obstruct disclosure, the FBI and District Attorney's office requested Knudson's report. By July 6, Worrell was corresponding with Deputy DA Michael Frye regarding a request for documents. Soon thereafter, the board suspended Worrell and clerk Carolyn Goodrich resigned and moved to Tennessee. Within weeks Worrell and Beiring "retired."

Knudson reported that Worrell had run the agency for decades with virtually no supervision from its governing board or the SLO County Auditor Controller's Office, which was responsible for financial oversight.

On July 25, Board member Tim Brown emailed the board calling for a meeting "to discuss allegations that have prompted the District Attorney's office to open an investigation" saying, "Board members have a legal obligation to inquire and can be held personally liable for not doing so."

On August 8, Assistant DA Eric Dobroth confirmed that his office was actively looking into the allegations. Having failed to stifle an audit, President Jeff Lee announced that the "executive committee would perform a forensic audit." None of the committee members had accounting or audit qualifications.

Finally, on August 29, when it became impossible to ignore the scope of the concerns, Lee told the local TV station *KSBY*, "The board agreed to hire an independent firm to conduct the audit, but will put out bids for the process," adding, "It will take several months before an audit can begin."

Supervisors Gibson and Hill argued against an audit. "There is no need for an audit," Gibson said. "There have been no improprieties."

As of 2020, more than two years later, the board had not publicized the results of the audit and the DA's office had not completed its investigation, prompting widespread public skepticism as to the efficacy of the DA's office, which has not entirely died down.

AUGUST 5, 2021
Former SLO County IWMA employee charged with embezzling public funds

Three years after *CalCoastNews* broke the story exposing the IWMA executives' questionable use of an unauthorized agency card to charge over half a million dollars, San Luis Obispo County prosecutors charged the former board secretary with ten felonies—nine for embezzlement and one for destruction of public records.

In 2018, *CalCoastNews* reported that public records requests turned up documentation for only twenty percent of the charges. Knudson discovered that credit card receipts for 2012 through 2016 were at the home of IWMA president (now Grover Beach Mayor) Jeff Lee. Lee returned the records to the agency, according to staff.

In August 2021, the SLO County Board of Supervisors decided to withdraw from the IWMA. The public commentary on that date underscores the importance of public participation.

AUGUST 11, 2021
County Board of Supervisors—Cost Benefit Analysis of IWMA Split
Agenda Item 47

4:32 p.m. Wayne Hall, County Analyst (retired)
I'm here to give a little history on how we got to the IWMA as a regional entity. This goes back to the late eighties. I was in the administrative office as a staff person and one of my as-

signments was to work with regional agencies. Back then the County provided staffing, facilities, all the overhead expenses, and services for regional entities, including the California Air Resources Board (now the Air Pollution Control District), the Local Agency Formation Council (LAFCO) and San Luis Obispo Regional Transit Authority (SLORTA). That preceded the IWMA coming into being. This is what happened in the late eighties, from an analyst's perspective.

Staff working for these agencies wanted bigger jobs and better pay. They asked for reclassification studies. We studied their positions and determined their positions and salaries were correct and that didn't satisfy them, so they went to the cities and city staff and started complaining about the county and started creating a poison between the cities and the County and strained relations so poorly that the County gave into the idea of going along with independent agencies where the County wouldn't provide services anymore.

From that point on all of these entities became locally-based agencies with their own facilities and personnel systems and accounting systems and so forth. Costs exploded. Staffing exploded. Empires started getting built outside of the county. Then the IWMA came along, and the staff involved in that wanted another regional entity. I recommended against it because we were having economies of scale in providing overhead, facilities, so forth. I also was worried about an unwieldy board with members not doing what they really want to do; they have a primary job somewhere else and now they're doing it with the IWMA, and I was worried that you could have things go wrong with the IWMA, maybe even malfeasance. That's what we saw. That actually came to fruition. We had an IWMA with misappropriated funds and corruption. Now is the time to get out of the IWMA. You're not going to get out of the others, but this is your chance to get out and get away from corruption. Put some distance between yourselves and this regional agency that should never have been formed to begin with.

4:38 Carl Knudson, Forensic Accountant/Auditor/Investigator
I'm a private investigator, certified fraud examiner, and forensic accountant. I was the one who did the investigation of the IWMA. My findings were published June of 2018 which included amongst many other things, the embezzlement of funds. There was a history of the IWMA awarding contracts without any bidding process whatsoever, no competition.

Most of the big awards were awarded to personal friends of the manager of the IWMA. There were conflicts of interest, there was destruction of records without any record keeping of who authorized the destruction of records. This was an agency running without any oversight or supervision. There were no auditors of the books. There were no audits of the billing process of large vendors who were putting in $80-$90,000 requests for reimbursement on a monthly basis—no audits, no challenges. During my examination of those billings, I could see lots of billings by the vendors with no description of what was being done. No dates, no duration, nothing as it related to the contract with the IWMA.

Today we still have outstanding requests to the IWMA for a computer forensic audit of the IWMA computers right after Mr. Worrell left. Those results were given to the IWMA, and subsequently to the DA's office. We were unable to get access to any of that. We understood at the time that the IWMA was changing leadership, that the DA went in and asked them not to destroy records and they did it anyway.

Our preliminary examination of the computers at the IWMA showed that some of them had been wiped clean. We looked at emails and attachments to emails were gone; emails were erased. We suggested to the interim manager at that time that he do a computer forensic analysis of all the IWMA computers. He did that and published a report, but I don't know if you got to see that report of what was missing and what was changed.

4.52.40 Stew Jenkins, Attorney

I had the privilege of managing some industrial property we own in Santa Barbara County. A lot of it had to be repaired and rebuilt so we had a lot of waste to get rid of. What I discovered is that going to the dump in Santa Barbara County was 40-50% less costly than in San Luis Obispo County. We had florescent tubes to recycle via SB Co. but by getting a private company to do it, it was only 20% of the cost of what Santa Barbara County would charge us and they were cheaper than San Luis Obispo County. Those are some practical things.

Some of you know that I do election law, but aside from election law we also do estate planning. We all get a lot of practical experience in estate planning. All five of you inherited the IWMA. It existed before you got on. If you inherit a barn where a barn has been neglected so long that the wood has been infested with termites and wood rot so that it is collapsing, what do you do? You do the practical thing. You tear down the barn and rebuild it from the foundation up. That's what you need to do with what you've inherited here. You don't waste money or effort or time trying to shore up the rotten structure. The IWMA is in a state of collapse like that old rotten barn because of previous documented corruption. It should be dismantled and replaced with one or more new structures that will provide residents with efficient trash disposal and recycling. Everybody wants to recycle these natural resources and plastic and polystyrene. It can be done. But it can be done without the higher cost and certainly without the cost of the inherent corruption.

I would urge the board to formally ask the SLO DA to bring action against those former staff members of the IWMA and contractors who benefited, to recover funds that have been misappropriated. Government Code Section 12651 provides the SLO County DA to civilly recover the funds for the public agencies that have been defrauded, along with along with treble damages unless there is an unjustifiable delay.

AUGUST 11, 2021
IWMA board meeting

The following day the IWMA board met. It was a long and convoluted meeting as the board struggled with how to move forward, having lost its biggest customer, the County of SLO, the day before. Board members spoke their minds.

Supervisor Gibson said, "The board majority trashed the reputation of the agency and by extension former members of the board, and that is the most egregious error of governance that I have ever seen."

Gibson was the board member who had snorted previously that there was no need for an audit; there were no improprieties.

The President of the IWMA Board called the board of supervisors meeting "a toxic environment."

A member of the executive committee, Jan Marx said that they were "spewing hatred."

Adam is gone, but it's clear that he wasn't alone in his mischaracterizations of anyone who disagreed with his agenda. The culture of the SLO Democratic Party is that it is against the rules not to agree with them, which corrupts the rooting out of corruption.

AUGUST 31, 2021
Former SLO County waste management employee posts bail

Calcoast News reported that the former board secretary of the IWMA posted $20,000 bail after being charged with ten felonies.

SEPTEMBER 2021
SLO County's waste agency settles records lawsuit for $44,670

Calcoast News reported that the IWMA agreed to release records and pay the $44,670 legal costs of investigator Carl Knudson in order to resolve the public records request lawsuit he brought against the agency in 2019. The court will retain jurisdiction over the case so that if the IWMA fails to release the public documents, Knudson's attorney can bring the issue back to court. As of November 2021, Knudson told me that the agency was still obstructing the release of information.

The District Attorney completed his review of Knudson's reports on the IWMA

In what could be considered a somewhat defensive report, the DA upheld charges against the agency secretary. As for findings regarding perjury, lack of oversight, mismanagement, and failure to retain records, the DA's office found that the errors had been corrected by the board, or the party involved, or didn't rise to the level of charges, or that documentation had been destroyed and therefore the evidence did not exist. Responsibility for agency oversight bounced back to the board and to the county auditor. The auditor's office said it was not responsible for retaining records, that it was up to the agency to do so. The agency said the auditor was responsible for retaining records. The bucks around that place sure do get passed around.

I am not privy to whether or not there will be any further lawsuits regarding this matter, but I suspect that this is not the end of it. Professional videographers are publishing teasers in advance of the launch of a documentary into the agency at LyingInTrash.com.

CHAPTER 7 WHO OWNS THE WATER?
Snakes, Ladders, & Laundering

Relationships in SLO County are tangled and hidden, much as I suspect the water pipes are underlying county soils. Knudson had forewarned me that county corruption would be a network deeper and wider than I could imagine; a kind of snakes and ladders.

I have struggled to find a model that illustrates how the corruption permeates agencies, contractors, politicians, and staff members—so far without success. Any model would have to be 3-D. A kaleidoscope works because every time you turn it, the picture changes, but it isn't three dimensional. Nor is a spider web, but it does have the spider! The convoluted models of brain synapses and neurons are close, but are not yet understood and are unpredictable and too confusing to demonstrate something which is predictable and which we CAN understand if we choose to.

The best model is the unseen network of conduits and pipes that run below us, installed by unknown agencies and contractors decades, and sometimes even centuries ago. As board members and staff members cycle through the system, the poorly documented infrastructure is soon forgotten, lost from institutional memory, gone to the graves of city engineers, and sent to damp storage units, archives, and shredders.

Forgotten pipelines deliver a compelling directive to government agencies to perform postmortems on projects. Failure to do so can lead to postmortems on people and the environment, as it did in San Rafael when a whole neighborhood exploded because no one at PG&E was keeping tabs on old gas lines. Project postmortems would go a long way to preserving institutional memory and would better provide for the safety of residents, especially now as politicians pass through institutions more quickly due to term limitations, as do, in turn, the chief executives who serve at their pleasure.

Underground pipes and conduits are placed by a variety of agencies, and even if they are well documented within the agency, rights of way can change…passing from private ownership to the federal government, to the railway, to the county, to the state, or to cities, or simply abandoned and never decommissioned. There is little motivation for staff to track down information buried in the annals of time, and there is inconsistent oversight to ensure that the records that document the lines that have been placed in rights of way pass cleanly from one agency to the next. Union Pacific acquired millions of monopoly miles of right of way from the federal government when they laid their tracks, and now makes a huge profit selling space along their tracks to utility companies, contributing to more than a 25% after-tax annual profit for the company. Even government agencies find it nearly impossible to get information and access to what's in that right of way.

The underground tangle is illustrated by the additional $400,000 my city spent on an $800,000 project to run a six-foot diameter storm drainpipe under the Union Pacific Railway. There was a misunderstanding as to lines that ran below the tracks, and the city had to pay for a larger conduit resulting in the fifty percent increase in project costs. The council and the public never heard about it. After finding the discrepancy, I insisted that the city obtain a title report prior to undertaking new projects. Sometimes a simple $300-400 report can save a thousand times its cost.

No one sees what's underground. No one wants to unearth a labyrinth of things that are underground and already dirty, or infiltrated by vermin, fungus, and mold. The darker the deed, the deeper it is buried, and the harder it is to see. Private companies performing government work are immune to public records requests, even as they install miles of infrastructure underground. This opens the door for all kinds of things to go on without anyone knowing. For example, if you owned the company that designed and installed nearly every public and private water line in the county, and set up several water companies and sewer systems, some of which you own, you could divert water for your own use, or sell it to cannabis producers, or bottle and sell it to the highest bidders. You could farm the water in aquifers that no one has mapped. You would resist any public effort to map water flow or aquifers. You would make sure that you were always a lead consultant or participant in water studies and infrastructure planning, development, and management. You could exercise control over the water supply and infrastructure and operate, in essence, as a private utility without the added layers of accountability of public utilities. You would make sure you or your sidekicks were appointed to the boards of agencies that control the water.

The following examples of people, their relationships, their companies, and employees illustrates the complexity of the web that I have stumbled across and that Knudson warned of based on his decades of tracking down government corruption. Not every connection, employee, or contractor associated with the project in any of these situations is corrupt, but the circumstances do nothing to discourage corruption.

In order to rout corruption, it's necessary to know, not just how the books are cooked, but also how it's carried out in the field. Agency employees relayed the following to me about how it was done in an agency they worked for.

HOW CORRUPT PUBLIC OFFICIALS CAN GAME THE SYSTEM TO STEAL TAXPAYER DOLLARS:

- ✦ Chief Executive (CE) of a government agency gives government agency contracts to 4 companies CE owns
- ✦ CE also gives contracts to another two companies owned with a retired government employee
- ✦ A current government employee has 3 private businesses:
  - ▫ 2 of employee's businesses supply government agency
  - ▫ 1 of employee's businesses uses government agency workshop alongside other government workers

- ✦ Chief Executive loans out government agency equipment to private individuals

- ✦ Chief Executive employs public agency chairman's and attorney's wives at one of his companies

- ✦ Chief Executive allows an employee to camp out in the premises

After a concerned citizen and I uncovered the following facts, Carl Knudson explained how it works.

LLC TRAIL

John Doe ('04) *is a* Board Member of Government Agency, *funded by* Taxpayers and *managed by* Govt Exec

Board approves $2m project *to be carried out* by **Private Company**

Govt. Exec *owns* **Private Company** that *works for* Government Agency

Private Company *subs out the project to* **Consulting Co. A**

Consulting Co. A *does $1m worth of work* and *charges* **Private Company** $2m. **Private Company** *charges* Government Agency (aka Taxpayers) $2m

Doe incorporates **B St Partners LLC** *('05) to buy* $1m B St property *from* mom of **Consulting Co. A Principals**

B St Partners LLC *borrows* $1m from bank and *pays* mom for B Street property

Doe *incorporates* **b street associates inc.** ('10) *owned by* **B St Partners LLC**

  B St Partners LLC *"loans"* $1m *to* **Seaside Land LLC**

   Seaside Land LLC *is owned* by **Property Manager LLC**

    Property Manager LLC *is owned* by **Consulting Co. A Principals**, *suppliers to* Government Agency as *subcontractors* of Government Executive's Private Company that *does work for* Government Agency where Doe *sits* on the Board

Consulting Co. A Principals *send $1m from* **Consulting Co. A** *to* **Property Manager LLC**

  Property Manager LLC *sends* $1m to **Seaside Land LLC**

   Seaside Land LLC *sends* $1m to **b street associates inc.**

b street associates inc. *sends* $1m to **B St Partners LLC**

  B St Partners *sends* $1m to bank, *thus repaying bank loan for the purchase of B Street.*

Knudson explained how it works. A public "servant" lobbies to award a government contract to a supplier. Then the public "servant" sets up a private Limited Liability Company (LLC) that borrows money to buy commercial property. The public servant's LLC then makes a "loan" (on paper, but never transfers any money) to an LLC owned by a chain of LLCs owned by the supplier. The supplier repays the "loan" through the same chain. Thus, the public servant's LLC has the money to repay the loan it got to buy commercial property.

This way, the public servant owns property and takes the profit investing nothing out of pocket to repay the commercial loan for the property. The public bought the commercial property for the public "servant" by overpaying for services. The public servant owns real estate without ever paying for it and additionally gets lease income from the property, as well as the full value plus the appreciation when it's sold.

A public servant can collect even more by delaying projects that then generate price hikes, or by approving "additional work" on the projects, or by allowing a supplier margin of 10% for unforeseen costs. That way funds just keep coming to him, unseen, through making sure there is enough in the additional charges to provide more kickbacks.

And of course, he can award more work to the supplier through other agencies he also "serves" and continue the cycle of kickbacks, price increases, and additional charges, with the added bonus that the higher costs of previous projects ratchet up the standard pricing on the next round of bids, and the next, and the next, meaning the "servant's" take also ratchets up.

Until honest public servants choose honest suppliers, public works costs will increasingly exceed inflation, creating a cycle in which ever more money is available for the public servant serving himself as the middleman between the government and those seeking government contracts.

Project costs increase exponentially higher than tax income, so the public coffers continue to decline until or unless taxes are increased. There is less and less money available for roads, bridges, and other public services, and we are the ones whose quality of life, health, and safety suffer, getting less and less bang for our buck.

Because private companies do not have to respond to public records requests, money laundered through LLC chains is not easy to document. In the examples above, public records from the California Secretary of State and the Santa Barbara County Clerk document LLCs, property owners, and the loan recipient and provider. Former employees disclosed the final supply chain contractor as having done work at the agency and a company owned by the chief executive of the agency. The leads grow cold when we try to find the property financed by the commercial loan because several states, including Delaware and Nevada, require so little documentation that it is impossible to determine the parties involved, and because lenders rarely record commercial loans.

These examples cover just one agency, one board, one chief executive, and one attorney. Consider the effect when these same contractors, suppliers, and public officials serve on multiple boards and supply multiple agencies. Their take from the public purse grows exponentially. Even if you think I am havering (an old Scots word for talking nonsense), if even one of each of the above situations is accurate (and we know several are because of prosecutions already completed), there would be be tens of millions of dollars involved that will never be returned to the service of the public.

Listen carefully because people tell you what they are doing. In 2015, a redevelopment agency interviewed a successful CEO. He formed his business as a one-person, home-based business after leaving a government job because he saw that he could work for many of the people the agency served. Even his former government employer offered him a consulting job.

He took advantage of an opportunity; admirable in private practice in the private sector, open to abuse in the public arena. The county's isolation gave him a competitive advantage, because it was too far from any big cities for competitors to travel for the work. His company took on the administration of several small cities and districts and now has the biggest share of the market, in part, because his firm understands the government system and the market.

Situations like this can go awry. A contractor that is too cozy with government officials can find itself in this situation. Suppose the contractor prepares a report assessing the water supply for a large housing development. The assessment doesn't agree with a previous report so the government agency asks the contractor to do another report, which shows water availability, even as neighboring wells are, in the words of locals, "sucking air." It was in the contractor's best interest to overstate water availability to ensure approval of the extensive new development because the contractor would design and install the water and sewer infrastructure, and once complete, would manage the sewer and water systems.

2021

Water, power, and cannabis go hand in hand; an invincible and inseparable threesome. A recipe for wealth. Morgan (whose name is changed to protect the individual from retribution) relayed to me that landlords in the Grover Beach Cannabis Zone refer to a water supply company owned by a former mayor and his crony as their "gold."

The cannabis industry needs more than just copious amounts of water. When I was in office, the PG&E government affairs representative told me that PG&E had doubts about there being sufficient infrastructure to supply the industry in our cannabis zone. According to Mark Arax, author of *West of the West* and longtime observer of the people and history of agriculture in California, "It takes seventy-five gallons of fuel to produce one pound of indoor pot. That is the same as the average car making one trip from California to Texas."

None of the online California reports on agriculture, land use, or water include cannabis as a commodity, nor do they track cannabis acreage, so the only available information comes from taxable sales reporting. In 2021, sales of legal cannabis in California will be over $5 billion based on tax revenues. *Marijuana News* quotes cannabis insiders who estimate that the real numbers of legal and illegal grows are nearer 9.2 million pounds grown each year. Legal grows represent only about 25% of total cannabis grown statewide, making the total 2021 California market for cannabis over $20 billion; four times the 2019 total grape production of $5.41 billion tracked by The California Department of Food and Agriculture.

Cannabis producers assured the Grover Beach City Council that they were using far less water, but given their history and the size and breadth of the industry, I am certain there are still huge issues surrounding water. It gives me pause when I consider our current drought. During a drought, when there is no state reporting on the actual water or land use for the water-intensive cannabis grows and production, we have a problem of gargantuan proportions.

When I was a new member of our local reservoir board, I asked why the reservoir wasn't filling as it had in the past. The response? It was being used upstream of the lake, so there was less flow into the lake. That tallies with reports of real estate professionals living upstream. They report that the amount of cannabis now being produced is "beyond belief."

It didn't dawn on me until I ran for a county supervisor position against Adam Hill and began going to supervisor board meetings and poring over agendas that one man "owns" the water in our county. I don't mean he necessarily has title to the water, although in some cases he does; I mean he has the beneficial use or control of it. His name came up repeatedly. He was managing projects for public water companies,, working for developers, building dams, building roads, serving on boards, running agencies, and running water and sewer districts.

How do you control the water, or, for that matter, anything? Get some solid experience as a government employee. Go out on your own. Get contracts to design, develop, manage, or administrate almost every government, private, and commercial water system. Befriend the corrupt and corruptible politicians and attorneys. Grow pot. Allow cannabis grows on your property. Ratchet up costs for public works, hold off on projects so the cost grows exponentially, far exceeding the inflation rate, creating ever more booty for compromised public officials. Frighten staff who just want to keep their jobs. Buy employees with fear of guilt by association, or if they sound the alarm buy them off with golden handshake exit payments, silence clauses, threats of exposure of 'failings,' career blacklisting, or public derision. Or take them under your wing, bringing them into the fold. Groom agency attorneys over decades of employment.

Years ago, when traveling in Sicily, the exquisite and abundant resources of the island mesmerized me. The island had the loveliest, largest, tastiest produce I had ever encountered, even in the San Joaquin Valley where I grew up, plus world-class cuisine, views and scenery, abundant seas and ports, and a rich history and civilization. And yet, poverty was rampant and the cities were dirty. As our car wound through verdant citrus groves, I wondered if poverty was the result of a mafia that had a monopoly on the resources, thus depriving the residents of the island.

We were headed to my then-husband's ancestral hometown. As we stood in the hot summer sun on the sandstone steps of the medieval townhall, the assistant chief of police, Lino, approached us and confirmed my hunch. He told us to wait in the square, that we must meet with the Comandante (chief of police), who we learned had the same surname as my husband. The Comandante was delayed because he was sorting out a water leak. In Sicily it is not plumbers who take care of water issues, it is the police.

In SLO County, if one organization alone knows where all the pipes are buried, we face the same risk of ceding over our riches to a corrupt monopoly. Just as in Sicily, if you own the water, you control the agriculture and the health and safety of the population, and most people won't risk speaking out against someone who controls their water, agriculture, and sewage systems.

A digital list of water companies, projects, and agencies owned by, managed, engineered, constructed, or consulted for by just one company in a quick search of the county website in 2020 raises questions of conflicts of interest.

- The company prepares ground water studies and ground water availability evaluations for the subdivisions for which the company either/or:

- □ designs, engineers, installs, manages water and sewer infrastructure,
- □ owns or manages the private water company, or
- □ sits on the board that manages the public water supply.

+ The company works for or has worked in one or more capacities outlined in the previous bullet points in ten special districts in SLO County, including a flood control district, and one in Santa Barbara County.

+ The list includes two private subdivision wastewater and water systems, a community charitable foundation, and contracts in the county, all cities in the county, and two cities in neighboring counties. In three cities, the company was the director of public works, and there are citizen claims that the planning and building divisions directed work to the firm owned by the director of public works.

+ The projects include:
  1. Stormwater in a neighboring county
  2. Master Water Plan for SLO County
  3. Administering and managing a plumbing retrofit program
  4. Projects on personal property
  5. Planning projects (2017)
  6. Management of a water basin
  7. A cannabis water management plan
  8. Plans for a cannabis plant
  9. Projects associated with a developer now under investigation by the FBI
  10. Plans for a commercial center in a residential resort development
  11. Appointment to a committee that manages the water supply to multiple special districts
  12. Wholesale Water Agency Flood Control and Conservation Plans and Reports and Water Management Plan for three cities
  13. Underground utility district establishment in a SLO Community Services District

These overlapping roles demonstrate the challenges of operating without conflicts of interest in small communities, made greater because it is simpler to keep the same supplier than it is to put projects out to bid, and it feels safer to work with known entities rather than new entities.

However, it is in the public interest to choose alternative suppliers, even if not the lowest bid, in order to avoid all contracts going to one contractor, or perhaps set a 'not to exceed' percentage of how much of an agency's work any one supplier is allowed to perform. Not all entities have bidding ordinances or rules for contracts, and many don't regularly perform reviews of administrators and attorneys. Most agencies do not require bidding for expenditure under certain limits or for some administrative or consulting contracts.

This practice of obtaining multiple overlapping services and contracts as the sole or primary supplier in any one market is admirable in private commerce so long as it is not a monopoly. It is another area where what works and is respected in private companies is not or should not be legal in the people's service because it thwarts transparency and oversight and is fraught with opportunities to abuse the system.

While business owners make excellent local representatives because of their business knowledge, acumen, and grasp of financials, they often approach government service in the same way they run their own company, without grasping the differences in private and public ownership.

Good government and best business practice demand attentiveness to the amount of power granted to any one contractor, whether it is geographical—across a locale or venue—across an agency, or across a sector. It is the easily grasped "don't put all your eggs in one basket," or the business principle of not having all your business with just one customer. Sound management of our government agencies and the business of the people demands active oversight by our elected representatives, and each of us who elect them to protect against over-concentration of power in one area or by one individual or contractor.

It is dereliction of duty for elected representatives to take the view, as did the current mayor of Arroyo Grande in a radio interview, that,

"We are just volunteers. We're not activists." Or the mayor pro-tem of Grover Beach, who said in a council meeting, "I just listen to what staff tell me." Or the Grover Beach council woman, who said as a district board member, "I don't understand this and can't read it all, so I just go with the staff recommendation." If our elected representatives won't exercise oversight on our behalf, who will? The district attorney notes that dereliction of duty is a crime.

It is easier to take the "we should put all this behind us" approach when something goes wrong. The problem is that graft doesn't stop with one little bribe or theft that the public can put behind themselves and forget. When board members don't question, when staff don't blow the whistle, when agencies and their attorneys and insurers cover up misdeeds of public servants and officials behind the cloak of human relations or attorney privilege or closed session meetings, when the courts and police don't prosecute, when the public fails to pay attention or doesn't want to believe it could happen, crooked public servants become bolder and bolder and find more and more ways and create better and stronger schemes to steal from the public.

And they make sure to protect their booty. They make sure to get their own people in office or on staff, and to keep honest suppliers and honest public servants out through whatever means necessary. They threaten and attempt to destroy families, businesses, and reputations through whispering campaigns, manipulating the media, public derision and putdowns, and worse. Eventually, such bad practices leave the public too financially stretched to fully staff police and fire service, or to provide rehab beds and mental health beds to curb the problems of public health and homelessness. We are left unrepresented and unserved while the opportunists self-serve, representing their own interests first.

Look everywhere lest you be the customer of not just a monopoly, but a hidden monopoly. The next two chapters tell the story of opportunists and their decades-long control of two quite different communities and how the citizens took their cities back. Often they closely parallel the situations I have encountered in my own backyard.

Postscript

In 2016 I opined, "My concern is this is not an isolated incident. In the interests of transparency and accountability to the citizens of this county, and further afield, it is critical that all agencies 'served' by these parties be investigated in light of this information to be sure the agencies are fiscally healthy and transparent. The public and their representatives must become aware of the practices to guard against and ensure ratepayers recover misused funds so they can carry out the health and safety mission of their sanitation district." Soon after, the sewer district administrator in my town and nearby Avila Beach was charged with multiple felony and misdemeanor conflicts of interest.

CalCoastTimes reporter Karen Velie wrote in November 2020 that the agency referenced by Nicolls as having no conflict of interest—San Simeon Community Services District (SSCSD), lost a grant after the administrator, directed his engineering firm to make unpermitted repairs at the agency and to the agency chair's home next door. And that's not all—it usually isn't. The deeper you dig, the more you find. Attentive citizen Henry Krzciuk reported in a November 13, 2021 *CalCoastNews* opinion piece that since 2016, SSCSD had been in trouble with the county for building a treatment facility that encroached on land owned by the Hearst Corporation and on a public road right of way without permission.

In April 2020, the board failed to provide an accurate link for public access to a virtual meeting and received a letter from the DA asking them to correct the matter on their next agenda. The agency failed to do so. By 2021, the FPPC had six open cases regarding the SSCSD; the county had turned down a second grant due to these concerns; and the SLO County district attorney had filed a suit against the district charging conflicts of interest.

The district serves the San Simeon area, a small unincorporated community of five hundred people on California's central coast—the home to Hearst Castle. It owns a wastewater collection and treatment system with five miles of sewer lines, water supply, storage wells and tanks, up to 250 connections, an office building, less than five miles of distribution lines, less than five miles of local roads, and a street lighting system with approximately 50 active streetlights. Since 2004, the district has contracted out all services. In the past five years, the district has lost numerous grants and several board members have resigned, disadvantaging the tiny community and costing residents thousands of dollars to prosecute people they should never have elected or appointed in the first place.

SEPTEMBER 28, 2021
DA's Special Prosecution Division Public Integrity Suite Files a Civil Suit Against San Simeon's CEO/Management Company

The District Attorney filed a civil lawsuit against Grace Environmental Services, LLC, (GES) and its owner Charles Grace after concluding a one-year joint investigation with the Fair Political Practices Commission.

The civil complaint alleges that GES and its owner had violated state laws since 2014 while providing day-to-day management, operation, and services for the SSCSD.

The lawsuit was filed after the DA investigating the case, responding to months of public confusion and questioning whether or not Grace was the general manager of the district, was unable to elicit a clear response to his correspondence or to his conversations with Grace's attorney.

The civil lawsuit seeks a court order to stop the violations, and civil penalties of alleged violations of California's Unfair Competition Law and False Advertising Law. "Unfair competition" includes any unlawful, unfair, or fraudulent business act or practice. The lawsuit lists nine issues of unfair competition, including allegations that Grace and his company, GES, sent threatening letters to a resident, sought to mislead the board of directors concerning the district's investigation of potential conflict-of-interest violations, and engaged in accounting practices that unfairly interpreted contractual provisions and financially benefitted GES.

The release states that the filing of this civil lawsuit is consistent with the stated purpose of the Political Reform Act of 1974:

Public officials, whether elected or appointed, should perform their duties in an impartial manner, free from bias caused by their own financial interests or the financial interests of persons who have supported them.

I appreciate the efforts of the District Attorney's Office Public Integrity Unit, part of whose stated mission is to increase the public's level of trust and confidence in its elected and appointed officials, and to "use all resources at its disposal to detect, investigate, and prosecute criminal misconduct at all levels of public service with the commitment that all matters referred to the Unit for consideration will be thoroughly and fairly reviewed, filing criminal charges or civil cases in all appropriate cases."

SEPTEMBER 29, 2021

Grace's attorney, Greg Sanders of Leucoma Nossaman Guthner Knox & Elliott in Orange County, is well versed in SLO Coastal CSD practices, having served on the Cambria Community Services Board of Directors from 1993 through 2010, and as an appointee in 2015 after a board member resigned. Claiming the charges were politically motivated, Sanders told the *Tribune*'s Kathe Tanner that he was very disappointed in Dan Dow as district attorney, claiming that he and Grace had worked in good faith with the DA's office and that Grace had done nothing wrong, and had performed diligently and professionally for the sewer district.

The DA's office reminds us that a civil complaint contains allegations that must be proven in a court of law by sufficient evidence.

FAIR POLITICAL PRACTICES COMMISSION (FPPC) MAKES HISTORY, CHARGING CONFLICTS OF INTEREST

Meanwhile, the FPPC was making its own history. The DA had referred Grace to the FPPC in 2020 for violating Assembly Bill 1090, passed in 2013, which prohibits a government official from having an interest in negotiating a contract with a government agency. The DA's referral included several sworn complaints filed against Grace, received by the Enforcement Division in mid-2020.

This is the first time in FPPC history that it has prosecuted a violation under Section 1090, and while the Commission's decision is not admissible in court, it can render a contract made in violation of section 1090 void, which would entitle the SSCSD to recover $393,734 compensation paid to Grace. Furthermore, the courts will not entertain any rights growing out of the contract. Although Grace has been associated with the district since 2005, statutes limit the FPPC from prosecuting anything more than five years after the act, thus limiting any action against him to actions taken since 2015.

Grace and FPPC staff reached a stipulation that the commission considered at its October 2021 meeting. The Commission refused approval, stating that they would start as they intended to go on with this first fine, and demanding that staff return with clearer statements as to how Grace's actions harmed the public. As to the extent and gravity of the public harm caused by the specific violation, Government Code Section 1090 codifies a prohibition against "self-dealing."

Grace contends that there is no evidence to suggest that the district was defrauded by this contractual agreement, suffered any actual unfairness or loss, or that he was dishonest in his dealings. However, such a finding is not necessary to prove a violation, nor would such a finding be sufficient to show that there was no public harm. The enforcement arm of the Commission determined that there is public harm inherent when a public official is acting on both sides of a transaction, as Grace did. Such actions erode the trust the public has in their governmental officials and contractors. In his role as general manager for a public agency, Grace has filed financial disclosure Form 700s, or Statements of Economic Interest, since at least 2011. Grace is or should be familiar with the conflict of interest provisions.

FPPC Case No. 2020-00416 STIPULATION, DECISION AND ORDER describes the Commission's consideration and findings. The

Commission considers factors that apply to the making of contracts. First is that public officials are to be guided solely by the public interest, rather than by personal interest. Public policy goals include eliminating temptation for public officials and independent contractors, avoiding the perception of impropriety, and obtaining their undivided loyalty.

Public officials may not be given the opportunity to influence the execution of their own contracts directly or indirectly, including involvement in planning, discussions, reasoning, preparation of plans/specifications, solicitation of bids, negotiations, compromises, and give and take. If such involvement causes government business and money to go to an entity or person in which the official has an interest it violates Section 1090.

The statute is more concerned with what might have happened than with what actually happened. It protects the actual and perceived integrity of the public treasury. As a result, criminal liability can accrue without actual fraud, dishonesty, unfairness, or loss to the governmental entity. Forbidden interests include indirect interests and future expectations of profit (or loss) by express or implied agreement, which may be inferred from the circumstances.

Grace had worked with the district since 2005, stepping in to cover operational field services for the district in 2014, when his employer ceased work with the district. The board approved an emergency professional services contract for the same services provided by Grace's former employer and extended it until 2016, understanding that Grace was a sole proprietor. The minutes for the December 9, 2015, board meeting note that District Counsel Whitman reported to the board that she had begun negotiations with GES for a new contract. However, the board voted to approve the contract with no agendized discussion item or vote directing the attorney to conduct negotiations, no discussion of alternatives to the contract, and no public consideration of putting the contract out to bid.

At the board meeting, Grace presented the contract, including several changes, sitting in front of a placard that read "General Manager" at a table adjacent to board members. When the board discussed his contract, Grace remained in his seated position and did not distinguish that he was acting in his personal, and not his official, capacity.

When advising the board and the community of the terms, Grace failed to take any steps to distinguish his role from that of the general manager, such as by hiring his own attorney to negotiate, or by stepping down from his ordinary seat at the table, or by deferring to the district's counsel to discuss the terms and provisions of the contract. The contract remains in effect. As of the date of going to print the Commission has not reported whether or not Grace's contract will be considered legally void.

The maximum penalty is $5,000 per count based on the FPPC's consideration of the facts and circumstances. These include the extent and gravity of public harm; the violator's level of experience of the requirements of the Political Reform Act; penalties previously imposed in comparable cases; the presence or absence of intent to conceal, deceive, or mislead; whether the violation was deliberate, negligent, or inadvertent; whether the violator demonstrated good faith by consulting FPPC staff or any other governmental agency; whether the violation was isolated or part of a pattern, whether the violator has a prior record of violations; and whether the violator, upon learning of a reporting violation, voluntarily filed amendments to provide full disclosure.

FPPC Staff found no evidence that Grace had any intent to conceal, deceive, or mislead with respect to the formation or presentation of the contract at issue. The contracts discussed were matters of public record. The FPPC determined that actions taken by Grace appear to be the result of inadvertence as opposed to deliberateness or negligence. The Enforcement Division's investigation did not find that Grace's actions were intended or deliberately violative of conflict of interest statutes.

However, the district failed to solicit competitive bids or demonstrate good faith by consulting FPPC staff or any other governmental agency. Grace has no prior history with the Commission and although Grace contacted the Commission's Legal Division after the fact, FPPC legal staff cannot advise on past conduct. As part the settlement, Grace completed the Local Officials Ethics Training Course required by AB 1234. Staff recommended a penalty of $4,500, payable to the General Fund of the State of California.

NOVEMBER 29, 2021

Grace faces legal fines and fees on top of the $400,000 he may have to refund the ratepayers. The Agency went into closed session to discuss indemnifying Grace.

Next, the DA caught the SSJWD violating the law

The examples in this chapter are but a few of the many, many violations countywide. They go unreported because often the public and even their elected representatives do not know there has been a violation, and because of intentional choices by officials to operate behind closed doors. More often, numerous citizens over decades have reported violations that their elected representatives, staff, or law enforcement never addressed.

NOVEMBER 4, 2021

In a cease and desist letter to the board members and secretary/treasurer of the Shandon-San Juan Water District (SSJWD), Deputy District Attorney Public Integrity Unit Michael S. Frye directed the board to follow the open meeting requirements of the Ralph M. Brown Act. The agency's attorney was not included as a recipient, although it is the attorney that the board and staff rely upon to ensure they act within the confines of the law.

According to the letter, the board violated the Brown Act by going into a closed meeting to discuss matters that should have occurred in open session. In such circumstances, the DA is authorized to file an action to determine whether past board actions have violated the Brown Act, but must first send a cease and desist letter describing the past action and nature of the violation.

In order to avoid a civil enforcement action, the agency must respond in writing with an unconditional commitment to "cease, desist from, and not repeat the prior action." This means that the agency will refrain from entering closed session to discuss matters that should occur in open session.

The Brown Act requires all meetings of a legislative body of a public agency to be open and public. The entire deliberative process by legislative bodies, including discussion, debate, and the acquisition of information, must be open and available for public scrutiny. Gov. Code § 54950 emphasizes the right of the public to acquire information and participate in the decision-making process. For purposes of the Brown Act, a "meeting" occurs whenever a majority of a board gathers to "hear, discuss, deliberate, or take action on any item over which the legislative body has authority."

The Brown Act limits closed session meetings to a very narrow set of circumstances. One is "pending litigation" in order to protect the attorney-client privilege between a board and its counsel when a discussion of those matters in open session would "prejudice the position of the agency" in litigation. "Pending litigation" is defined as: based on existing facts and circumstances, the legislative body or the local agency has decided to initiate or is deciding to initiate litigation.

The DA alleges that based on a review of the agenda and the minutes from the March 16, 2021, meeting, the board of directors went into closed session and discussed matters that did not involve "pending litigation." Rather, in a closed session lasting more than an hour, the board discussed its application to the State Water Resources Control Board (SWRCB) to appropriate water rights and authorized the board president and legal counsel to enter into an agreement with NRWMAC.

The DA wrote that these were matters that fell within the "subject matter jurisdiction" of the board—the board for a water district—and included taking steps toward establishing water rights. As such, any discussion about these matters by a majority of the board—even if a decision was not made—should have occurred in open session.

The board's decision to go into closed session appears to have been for the sole purpose of preventing others from learning that it was attempting to appropriate water rights. This was made clear when Board member Steve Sinton gave a presentation to the Water Resources Advisory Committee (WRAC) about its applications to the State Water Resources Control Board. During his recorded presentation, he said, "Our district decided to apply for the water. And since this would be an appropriative water right, and under appropriative water rights first in time has the highest priority, we couldn't discuss our plans and thoughts with anyone until we had the application in place. If we had discussed it prematurely there wouldn't have been any water to apply for."

By all appearances, the board also improperly entered into closed session at five previous meetings prior to the March meeting. These were the five meetings when the board was submitting its applications to secure the water diversion. These discussions should have occurred in open session. While the board may have had its own reasons for going into closed session(s), they did so in violation of the Brown Act. The Brown Act is clear: "There has been a long and vigorous battle fought against secrecy in government...Local governing bodies, elected by the people, exist to aid in the conduct of the people's business, and thus their deliberations should be conducted openly and with due notice...."

NOVEMBER 10, 2021

CalCoastTimes reported, "The water district's subversion appears to have backfired. The California State Water Control Board rejected the water district's applications to appropriate water rights because of multiple deficiencies, which included not informing other shareholders of their plan. The shareholders include those with rights to Lake Nacimiento and Salinas River water and those who paid for the Nacimiento pipeline."

APRIL 14, 2022

And now this, just days before going to print. In 2017 the Department of Toxic Substances Control (DTSC) found 86 illegally buried drums of toxic waste in the yard of the Panoche Water District (PWD). PWD's primary purpose is to distribute water for irrigation, municipal and industrial uses, and to own, operate, and maintain a water delivery system for Central Valley families.

According to California Attorney General Xavier Becerra, Jack Hurley and Dubby West buried the drums of hazardous waste without permits or authorization, acting under the direction of the PWD general manager Dennis Falaschi. By 2018 Becerra had estimated a loss of more than $100,000 in public money. The DTSC kept digging and called in reinforcements from several state and federal agencies. including the U.S. Department of the Interior's Office of Inspector General, the IRS-Criminal Investigation, and the Federal Bureau of Investigation.

Together they uncovered a wide range of scams totaling $25 million over 23 years. The feds stepped in with a grand jury. In a Department of Justice press release dated April 14, 2022 U.S. Attorney Phillip A. Talbert announced a five-count indictment against Dennis Falaschi, charging him with conspiracy, theft of government property, and filing false tax returns, totaling $25 million.

Five PWD employees were booked and charged in a felony complaint with a total of ten counts, eight counts relating to the theft of public funds and two counts involving hazardous waste disposal. The employees allegedly spent public money for personal expenses, such as illegal slot machines, kitchen remodeling, and residential landscaping.

"In California, those in public posts who abuse the public's trust for personal gain will be held accountable," said Becerra. "The California Department of Justice will investigate and prosecute those who embezzle and misuse public funds. We will work with our law enforcement partners to get the job done."

The criminal complaint alleges that Dennis Falaschi, the ex-General Manager of PWD, ran the District as his own personal operation and bank account, spending excessive amounts of District money using credit cards issued by PWD. Under the direction of Dennis Falaschi, Julie Cascia used PWD credit cards and money orders for personal expenses, while mischaracterizing the charges as business expenses. Dennis' son,

Atomic Falaschi, took items from PWD, including trees, equipment, and other goods, and used them on his own personal property.

According to court documents, in 1992, Falaschi was informed that cracks in cement in a gate that had been cemented closed years earlier were leaking water from the Delta-Mendota Canal through a drain that flowed into a parallel canal that the PWD controlled.

Falaschi instructed an employee to install a new gate inside the standpipe that could be opened and closed on demand. He later instructed the employee to install a lid with a lock on top of the standpipe and an approximate two-foot elbow pipe off the valve of the standpipe that angled down 90 degrees into the PWD canal. The lid prevented people from seeing that the gate inside the standpipe was functional. The submerged elbow pipe further concealed and expedited the theft because it enclosed the water flow from the Delta-Mendota Canal into the water district's canal.

Falaschi instructed employees to use the site to steal federal water from the Delta-Mendota Canal on multiple occasions until the site was discovered in April 2015. He used the proceeds of the theft to pay himself and others exorbitant salaries, fringe benefits, and to reimburse personal expenses.

Additionally, Falaschi is charged with filing false tax returns when he failed to report over $900,000 in income that he received from private water sales.

If convicted of theft of government property, Falaschi faces a maximum penalty of ten years in prison and a fine up to $250,000. If convicted of conspiracy, he faces a maximum penalty of five years in prison and a fine up to $250,000. If convicted of the tax charges, he faces a maximum penalty of three years in prison and a fine up to $250,000. Any sentence would be determined at the discretion of the court after consideration of applicable statutory factors and the Federal Sentencing Guidelines.

But that's not all. Guess who pays for the $25 million diversion of public funds. The public (self) servants who lived high off the hog with salaries and benefits of up to $925,000 a year? Nope. The board that somehow failed to notice despite years of auditors qualifying the accounts.

Nope. It's the ratepayers of the PWD who elected the board that hired and overlooked the alleged criminal activity. Just as happened in my own sanitation district, and our IWMA, although employees were charged, the boards were able to wash their hands of it. Despite whistleblowing employees, and auditor warnings the boards whose responsibility is oversight, walked free. The perpetrators paid fines and penalties to other government agencies, but did not have to reimburse the agency they served so poorly. Per the audited accounts, the board president remains in office and continues to enjoy interest-free loans from the public agency to two of his companies.

Meanwhile, the PWD ratepayers are encumbered with a bond of $8,545,000 to cover the cost of issuing the bond and the $8,261,461 legal settlement to the federal government.

PART 3

PANTOMIMES, KINGS, AND MACHINES

"If you want to have hope and faith
in the future, you first must stand
on the shoulders of the past."

–Famous Māori Saying

CHAPTER 8

THE FRESNO PANTOMIME
Ghosts of Christmases Future

> "Like zombies in 'Night of the Living Dead' they just keep coming."
>
> —Kevin Rice, Activist

I grew up in Fresno, California. It is the county seat and California's sixth largest city, with an estimated area population of 600,000 at the time of the events that follow. The web of corruption extended beyond the city of Fresno to Clovis, on its eastern border, and even to a county supervisor.

Once the FBI indictments of Fresno County politicians and big-name developers began, they just kept coming. Substitute "SLO County" for "Fresno" in the following 1994 article and you could easily be describing Oprah's Happiest City in America. Mark Arax, a Fresno native, and *LA Times* Central Valley desk editor at the time of writing, described the situation in Fresno:

> "Whether a function of its detached geography—180 miles south of San Francisco, 210 miles north of Los Angeles—or its complacent citizenry, Fresno has long been considered by the feds to be one of the most lawless cities in the country. Its Chinatown opium dens and gambling halls were among the nation's busiest in the early

1900s. During Prohibition, a quarter of its police force—the chief and several of his top men—resigned after federal authorities caught them taking $120,000 in protection money from three bootleggers. Latter-day Fresno has limped from scandal to scandal with nary a housecleaning. In 1950, vice lords devised a fantastic scheme to use a chinchilla farm to launder prostitution, gambling, and drug proceeds for friendly politicians. In separate court cases in the 1970s, one developer was convicted of giving a $4,000 bribe and the councilman in question was acquitted of taking it."

If, as I am, you are a baby boomer, you will remember the primetime soap opera cliff hanger *Dallas*, a program about a dysfunctional Texas oil family. You may even remember *Fresno*, the *Dallas* miniseries spoof starring Carol Burnett. The characters owned a ranch and treated their farm workers, one another, and neighbors dreadfully, and spoke with Oklahoma accents. My friends and I roared with laughter when we watched it. It was *Dallas* and *Fargo* and Archie Bunker all rolled in one.

My favorite line was from the disgruntled son and heir at the kitchen table. The family was discussing kinfolk over breakfast. The son blows up and says to his cousins, "Your mama's dead, *your* mama's in jail, *my* mama's crazy. Now that we know where everybody's mama is, can we finally get back to saving this ranch?"

My other favorite scene is repeated in nearly every episode: Carol Burnett, dressed as an 1800s Southern belle, sun umbrella and all, encounters subservient ranch hand Juan, who regularly asks for a raise, is always denied, and finally asks why he cannot have a raise. Carol explains in an overacted southern drawl, "Because there are the 'haves' and the 'have nots.' I am a 'have' and you are a 'have not.'"

Black humor, social satire—both tragic and funny at the same time. I didn't know it was TRUE! It was funny—a good fun-poking little Fresno story modeled on *Dallas*. Did the script writers have any idea how close to the truth their story would turn out to be?

The true story of Fresno shenanigans plays out like the *Fresno* parody—or like a script from our coastal Oceano Melodrama, an old-time

Victorian 'who dunnit' comedy theater as popular with locals as it is with tourists. In Scotland, the same type of entertainment comes around every Christmas season and it is called "Pantomime." The Fresno story that follows is a true spectacle with a tangle of never-thwarted villains who outplay the best melodrama or pantomime characters. Journalists were the local heroes, writing eloquently, as did FBI Agent Wedick in his case notes. I have reconstructed much of the story that follows from their accounts.

The Shrimp Scam Sham

FBI agents James Wedick and Howard Moline made their names as FBI greats when they netted California legislators in a sting they called the Shrimp Scam.

Wedick and Moline formed two fictitious seafood companies that gave $90,000 in campaign contributions and honoraria to several legislators. The legislature approved bills (later vetoed by the governor) giving the sham companies business advantages, thus exposing the corruption and taking down fourteen public officials.

The Shrimp Scam motivated California voters to pass Proposition 112 in 1990, a constitutional amendment banning honoraria, setting gift limits, restricting travel payments, and strengthening laws prohibiting personal use of campaign funds.

Christmas 1993

Although the well-publicized Shrimp Scam tale reached Fresno, Proposition 112 seemed to have no effect there. *The Fresno Bee*, with a premonition of ghosts of Christmas yet to come, published a cartoon depicting three developers, John Bonadelle, Patrick Fortune, and Kenneth Crabtree as wise men bearing gifts just before the investigation that triggered the demise of a whole generation of Fresno developers. In less than a month it all started coming out—an overflowing Santa's bag of money, big boy's toys, donations, and self-dealing.

January 1994

Bill Tatham received an early morning phone call from consultant, Jeffrey T. Roberts, who was helping him to rezone forty acres of farmland. Tatham had more than $110,000 tied up in the project. Roberts was calling to tell him that the council had voted against him. Roberts couldn't explain why Leif C. Sorensen, the leader of the council trio that always voted in favor of developers, voted to deny the project.

Only Mayor David Lawson, and Councilman Glynn Bryant voted in Tatham's favor.

Roberts, a planning consultant, land developer, and lobbyist had sway over nearly every major zoning change and general plan amendment in Fresno and Clovis in the 1980s and 90s. The grandson of John E. Roberts, who helped shape post-World War II Los Angeles as the head of city planning, the younger Roberts grew up in Southern California and studied urban planning at Cal State Fresno.

In 1980, when Roberts was laid off by Fresno County, James W. Logan & Associates hired him to lobby elected officials on behalf of builders and developers. Logan was a former Fresno planning commissioner and councilmember (1969-72) who started his planning consulting business after leaving the council. Roberts outdid all others in winning zoning changes and general plan amendments for his wealthy clients. He dressed in flashy clothes and drove around town in a classic Corvette with a license plate that read 'REZONED.'

A few hours later Roberts called back with a solution. If Tatham donated $10,000 to three Clovis City Council candidates in the upcoming city elections, Sorensen would ensure that Tatham's re-zoning "would be approved so fast, it would make his head swim." That sounded like a bribe to Tatham and he wrote to the FBI to report it.

William Tatham, Jr., sometimes known as "Wild Bill," had returned home and trained as a lawyer following a successful football career and ventures into ownership of The Tampa Bay Bandits and Arizona Outlaws.

FBI case notes explain, "In the 1980s, greater Fresno County was one of the fastest-growing regions in the country. Farmland was worth $3,500—$8,500 an acre. Rezoned with improvements it could resell "for up to $100,000 an acre." With 'shopping center' potential, it could soar to more than $250,000 an acre."

Sacramento—Agent Wedick responded to Tatham's letter by launching what Arax described as "a wide-ranging FBI and IRS investigation to root out an entrenched—and barely concealed—system of buying and selling land use votes, and long-rumored corrupt ties between some politicians and builders."

St Patrick's Day 1994, Clovis

Wedick and IRS Special Agent Moline equipped Tatham with a hidden microphone. Tatham then turned over the secret recordings of meetings between himself, his consultant, Jeffrey ("REZONE") Roberts, and Clovis City Councilman Sorensen, who had promised to "make Tatham's head swim" with the speed of his approval of Tatham's project once he received a $10,000 donation. Roberts asked Sorensen in what form he wanted the payment, and the councilman allegedly responded, "I think in the spirit of St. Patrick's Day, you just do it in green."

What followed, according to Arax, may be "the most improbable chapter of all in the Tatham family's saga. 'I've taken a huge risk and I know I'm going to pay a big price,' said Tatham, 'I may never do business in this town again. But the bottom line is I had no choice but to go to the FBI. It's one of the few things I've done in my life that feels good.'"

The reputations of the two investigators heading the case made Fresno developers and politicians skittish. The authorities were predicting they could indict as many as twenty-five elected officials, lobbyists, and developers in Fresno and neighboring Clovis before the investigation was over.

According to Arax, the land of raisins was heading for its first bloodletting since the great liquor scandal of 1925, thanks to the local football hero come home. Arax's sources said federal agents marveled at the riches up for grabs and the stranglehold big builders appeared to have had on the political process.

Agent Weddick's file notes logged a call for reinforcements, stating, "Sacramento has agreed with United States Attorney Charles J. Stevens and Assistant US Attorney John K. Vincent, Eastern District of California, that the sheer number of individuals… mandate that the case be presented to the Federal Grand Jury for indictment in several stages so that… the matter could be manageable…."

Local Assistant US Attorney Vincent was remarked upon for his inspiring leadership, commitment, and character. His colleagues held him as the heart and soul of his office, exemplifying integrity; someone who personified the principle to always do the right thing for the right reason.

Vincent's boss, U.S. Attorney Charles Stevens, was the Department of Justice official overseeing the case. He said, "The problem is way too deep and way too broad to have developed overnight. It's the kind of corruption that has developed over decades, if not generations."

Stevens said the government was prepared to "shut down the development industry in Fresno" to root out the corruption. He was good for his word. "What flabbergasts me is not only the scope of the problem and the number of people involved, but the brazenness of it. It's a type of old-fashioned corruption that you would think just doesn't exist anymore, at least not in California." Apparently he had not been to SLO County.

Hundreds of charges from the Federal Grand Jury, the assistant federal bankruptcy trustee, California Inspector General, and the Office of Agriculture included violations of the RICO Act, money laundering, obstruction of justice, extortion, false tax returns, perjury, witness tampering, fraud, bribery of a federal agent, submitting fraudulent documents to obtain farm subsidies, concealing assets, and false testimony to a bankruptcy court.

Media reports noted, "Investigators say they have uncovered a decades-long practice of developers subverting local zoning and environmental laws by buying off politicians in this fast-growing farming region.

In some cases, the alleged cash payoffs were delivered the old-fashioned way in bags."

As a kid growing up in Fresno in the late sixties, I dismissed neighboring Clovis, with its population of fewer than 30,000, as a cow-town. As I grew into my teens, the town gained my grudging respect because of the excellent new Clovis High School. Now, the village center is a destination—a charming bustling small town surrounded by big box stores, medical developments, and housing subdivisions. In the 1980s, neighborhood groups opposed to suburban sprawl complained of councilmembers and supervisors being "bought off" by developers, with Roberts as their conduit, telling stories of country club back-room meetings of politicians and developers and cash payments hidden in the folds of building plans. The city attorney for my town recounted to me his recollection of black limos with tinted windows pulling up to city hall at lunchtime to pick up councilmembers. Their stories were corroborated when Tatham blew the whistle.

Clovis City Councilmembers and Jeffrey "REZONE" Roberts were the first to be indicted. The investigation then spread to the county seat of Fresno. Roberts was quick to turn on the clients and politicians who had bankrolled his flashy lifestyle. He made one last deal—on his own behalf. He would give the FBI a written confession and cooperate while serving his sentence in exchange for reducing a potential 24-year sentence to 24 months. Roberts pleaded guilty to one count of aiding and abetting extortion and one count of tax evasion.

Roberts divulged that Williamsburg Manor Homebuilders' Pat Fortune and Ken Crabtree, and Clovis City Councilmember Sorensen had hatched a plan to cover up the $10,000 Tatham extortion. Fortune, Crabtree, and Sorensen maintained their innocence, although eventually Crabtree pleaded guilty to interfering with a witness in another aspect of the case. Roberts owned up to:

- Giving Fresno City Councilman Robert Cooper Smith (1991-94) $250 and a half case of scotch at a Denny's

Restaurant after Smith called asking for money. He also gave Smith money from a restaurant that was asking for approval for a drive-through lane. Roberts told the FBI that he did not mind helping Smith because Smith voted for Roberts "approximately 90 percent of the time." Smith then pleaded guilty to extorting $10,509 from developer Jon Thomason and subsequently attempted to withdraw his admission of guilt. Smith's lawyer, referring to his client's extorting money from a developer, explained, "That's the political process ... money changing hands."

+ Roberts' colleague Logan paid for a hotel room for a fundraiser to re-elect Fresno Councilmember Lung. While there, Roberts and developer Thomason, who had projects pending before the city councils, sold a Harley-Davidson motorcycle "under very reasonable terms" to Clovis City Councilmember Sorenson. After Thomason bought the bike with a loan under lien, Roberts created an entity, CTL Leasing, for the motorcycle's registration to conceal its real owner, Thomason. Roberts said the motorcycle, just before Sorenson's fated reelection bid in 1994, "was a big happy pill that Sorenson could just not resist."

+ Giving cash to Mayor Doig, who served on the Fresno City Council between 1973 and 1989.

Williamsburg Manor Homebuilders developer Gerald Hamel spilled the beans on the other developers, consultants, and councilmembers in Clovis and Fresno. Hamel was charged with perjury, bankruptcy fraud, preparing a false tax return, and filing false political statements of economic interests. He told in a written confession how the crimes went down. "From 1991 to 1995, I, and others, including Patrick Fortune, made up a plan and acted with intent to deprive the City of Clovis and its citizens of their right to honest services."

+ Shortly before a Clovis City Council vote on a property he and Fortune owned, they arranged for their company,

Williamsburg Manor, to get a $27,000 loan from California Valley Bank for then-Clovis City Councilmember Lawson, knowing that Lawson could not have gotten the loan otherwise. They laundered the transaction by securing the loan with a CD through Hamel's personal bank account and then cashing in the CD and having Williamsburg Manor make the loan to Lawson. Hamel and Fortune then arranged for repayment of the loan through an entity known as the ASC Corporation, his brother-in-law's company, to hide their involvement. Despite his conflict of interest, Lawson and councilmembers Bryant and Sorensen voted in favor of the Williamsburg Manor project.

+ He and Fortune handed Clovis City Councilmembers Bryant and Sorenson $5,000 just before a vote on a Williamsburg Manor project, knowing they would not disclose the payment.

+ On two occasions Hamel, to disguise the source of the payments, used his Williamsburg Manor checking account to send campaign contributions through ten intermediaries to then-Clovis City Councilmembers Bryant and Sorensen. To avoid paying taxes, he also claimed $23,560 for two campaign contributions as write-offs through his company Williamsburg Manor.

+ On three occasions he and Fortune cashed and split $58,840 of PG&E refund checks for their companies, Williamsburg Manor and Hamel Development, not claiming them as income on their personal or business tax returns.

+ Fortune hand-delivered $15,000 cash to Sorensen, obtained by cashing a Williamsburg Manor check for $15,215.17. On the check he wrote "Scaffolding & Planks, etc." so he would not be connected to the money, and it was deducted as a business expense. For this he was convicted of witness tampering, honest services mail fraud, and filing a false tax return.

> ✦ When Hamel filed for bankruptcy in October 1992, while receiving $120,000 a year from his company, he had claimed he had no income. He also said he had not transferred any property after transferring seven properties to an entity known as KMA. He said he only had a single checking account containing $2,300, whereas he had a checking account with over $60,000 in it. When the Federal Bankruptcy Trustees recommended that there was a right to recover $3 million, Hamel agreed to return $1.9 million.

Meanwhile, aside from preparing for the HAMEL/BRYANT trial, Wedick and Federal US Assistant Attorney Vincent were examining a voluminous number of records and documents.

Longtime Clovis City Manager Kathy Millison, when leaving Clovis for a new job in Santa Rosa, described the unscrupulous times in Clovis in a 2010 *Fresno Bee* article, saying that city staff became suspicious when the council majority prohibited the standard practice of city staff report recommendations to vote for or against development projects. According to Councilmember Wynne, the trio planned to fire the city manager, assistant city manager, and the planning director. They had already replaced the city's attorney and the public works director had resigned.

APRIL 1994
Clovis City Council Election

When Operation Rezone came to light just weeks before the election, Clovis voters expressed their anger by electing two slow-growth advocates, one of whom was Kent Hamlin, a Fresno County Prosecutor, now a Fresno Superior Court Judge. The city was then able to regain the community's confidence by overturning land-use decisions passed in the earlier 3-2 votes.

As prosecutors followed up on indictment after indictment, locals weighed in.

Fresno City Councilmembers:

Former Councilman Tom Bohigian—"I suspect there are quite a few politicians and developers around here who aren't sleeping so well at night."

Councilman Michael Woody—"Getting a majority vote on a council easily nets any developer $500,000."

Former Councilman Rod Anaibrian called developers and councilmembers "a tag team for so long that councilmembers counted on developers as their piggy bank."

The Building Industry Association Head:

Jeffrey Harris was "…surprised by the allegations. I guess maybe I was naive, I just didn't think that kind of thing was going on." But he cautioned that, "an indictment is certainly not a conviction. From my perspective, to think it is as pervasive as the FBI is indicating, I find that hard to believe."

The Politicians:

Some politicians denied that the problem was as widespread as the federal agents alleged, but others did not wait to act. The Fresno City Council passed an ordinance requiring lobbyists to register. Fresno Mayor Jim Patterson, after developers bankrolled his 1992 election, announced that he would not accept money from the building industry for his reelection campaign.

Planning commissioner:

Jim Klein, let go by Patterson for voting against the building industry said, "You will not find a place with more tangled relationships."

One Mayor:

Got a good rap. Roberts told the FBI that Fresno Mayor Jim Put had never asked for money in exchange for voting on council issues. He described Put as a "straight, nice guy."

The Indicted:

Sorensen proclaimed his innocence and went on to project his outcome, quoting Proverbs to shore up his claim, "A false witness shall not be unpunished, and he that speaketh lies shall not escape."

JUNE 1996

On the eve of their federal trial, Sorensen, Crabtree, and Lawson, following two weeks of government testimony, short-circuited a trial by changing their pleas of 'innocent' to 'guilty.' Convicted of extortion of William Tatham, Jr. under color of official right and obstruction of justice, Sorensen bore false witness and did not go unpunished; he spoketh lies and did not escape.

Restauranteur Militinovich (obstruction of justice), real estate agent Williams (obstruction of justice, filing a false tax return), and his son David (perjury), having been ratted out by Rezone Roberts and Hamel, pleaded guilty mid-trial.

But that wasn't all. The San Francisco Inspector General Special Agent and the US Department of Agriculture (USDA) suspected Hamel of scamming USDA subsidies in excess of hundreds of thousands of dollars by submitting fraudulent farm subsidy documents, and the Federal Grand Jury was examining allegations of bribing a federal agent.

The feds then moved on to the Fresno City Council:

FEBRUARY 20, 1998

FEDERAL GRAND JURY INDICTS FRESNO AREA DEVELOPERS JOHN BONADELLE, FRESNO COUNCILMEMBER LUNG, AND FORMER COUNCILMEMBER LOGAN CHARGING CORRUPTION AND WITNESS TAMPERING (Press Release)

> In announcing the indictment, US District Attorney Paul Seave said, "The Department of Justice is committed to the eradication of public corruption at all levels of government. This latest indictment focuses on two who allegedly supplied the money and one who took it."

The grand finale of the investigation was the conviction of the developer that we baby boomers from northwest Fresno thought of as the granddaddy of the city, John Bonadelle. Reporter Mark Arax grew up in the shadow of Bonadelle subdivisions and described Bonadelle's influence:

> "…Bonadelle, 81, openly and often, boasted about his corrupt influence with local officials, suggesting to many he was "untouchable" with respect to law enforcement. Bonadelle confided to several individuals that the reason he was "untouchable" was because over the years he has had every politician, elected official, judge, and/or prosecutor in his back yard, 'shaking hands and/or jawboning about something.'"

Bonadelle's alleged bribes of government officials included:

+ Offering to testify on Fresno County Supervisor Stan Oken's behalf in a civil action in exchange for Oken's favorable influence on land in the outlying areas of Clovis coming up for consideration by the Fresno County Board of Supervisors.

+ Giving Lung $9,800 to get his approval regarding land in the outlying areas of Clovis, which the Fresno City Council was considering. Bonadelle overpaid Lung for a truck, tractor, and other equipment through an intermediary, thus laundering the gift. Lung never reported it as a conflict of economic interest on his annual financial disclosures.

+ Making $10 million dollar deposits with Logan at former Clovis Councilmember Bryant's branch bank so Bryant would vote in favor of rezoning two Bonadelle parcels planned as subdivisions, and then trying to convince Bryant not to communicate information to law enforcement authorities. The charge included a forfeiture provision, as the county had rezoned the property and Bonadelle had sold the subdivisions.

Bonadelle's other alleged witness tampering included trying to persuade Tatham, Sorensen, and Roberts not to communicate information to federal law enforcement authorities.

Bonadelle was the ringleader of the failed scheme during the 1994 election to pack the Clovis City Council with pro-development members by having each developer contribute $10,000 to three candidates. Clovis City Councilman Sorensen spearheaded the fundraising and backed the elections of Mayor Lawson along with first-time candidates Shirley Ingalls and Glenda Lowe. Developers Bonadelle, Fortune, and Crabtree hand-picked Ingalls and Lowe, who they expected to vote their way.

According to Wedick, the developers designed the re-election scheme to orchestrate the "yes" and "no" council votes in order to redirect the suspicions of the general public piqued by the constant "yes" pro-development votes from the same three Clovis councilmembers. "Squeaky" 3-2 votes weren't enough. They wanted to stack the council with their own candidates so they would have four or five of the votes on the council, secured with bribes or hefty campaign contributions.

Agent Wedick hadn't been the only intruder on Bonadelle and his cronies' turf. California's largest developers, Kaufman & Broad, ventured into town in 1992. Tatham planned to use Kaufman & Broad to build his subdivision. City councilmembers reported that Bonadelle and his sons-in-law Robert McCaffrey and Jerry DeYoung pressured them to obstruct Kaufman & Broad projects. Tatham reported that the Clovis council told him to "get rid of Kaufman & Broad" if he wanted his project approved. Tatham was therefore all the more dependent on the expensive consultant Roberts to get his project through.

Equal opportunists, local politicians were shaking down Kaufman, too. News agencies reported that Kaufman & Broad fired their Fresno director in April 1994, after federal authorities began asking questions. A company spokesperson said the firing was related to "inappropriately" generating a $10,000 check for a proposed housing subdivision. The spokesperson would not identify the real estate agent or the elected official for whom the payment was intended. However, real estate agent Williams later pleaded guilty to obstruction of justice and subscribing to a false tax return, and his son David Michael Williams to perjury and obstruction of justice.

Arax reported in a 1994 *LA Times* article that Fresno City Hall observers recalled only one time—during a period of 14 months and hundreds of votes—when the city council or planning commission had denied a developer's request for a plan amendment or rezoning, and that was a Kaufman & Broad project. Federal agents also investigated that vote. Councilmembers initially opposed the request, with Councilman Lung leading the charge. Campaign records showed that nine days later, Lung received a $500 campaign contribution from Kaufman & Broad. The council passed the project at its next council meeting without a word of discussion. "I happened to have a fundraiser and they donated to my campaign," Lung said. "There was no quid pro quo."

Every one of the sixteen convicted politicians and developers was a party to false financial statements or false campaign reports.

A week before the trial, Bonadelle pleaded guilty to a single felony in exchange for which the government would drop ten remaining counts of corruption and witness tampering, bribery of a federal agent, mail fraud, money laundering, and a RICO (Racketeering Influenced Corrupt Organizations) charge. Bonadelle's lawyer, Christopher Wing, characterized the guilty plea as "a business decision."

Logan, seventy-four, made a deal, too—but his was just keep one, drop one. Bonadelle got nine months in a halfway house with a $300,000 fine and Logan three months in a halfway house, three months of home detention, and a $5,000 fine. It didn't really go that badly for the house of Bonadelle. His sons-in-law continued the family business.

1998

Weddick's case notes say that after Bonadelle was indicted, he intended to pursue charges against Randy Joe Hill and Kenneth Gary Crabtree, but the story is getting too repetitive, so I will finish with one Fresno councilmember who rose to a high position and ran into trouble with the law around the same time.

In November 1998, former Assembly Speaker Brian Setencich was charged with taking a bribe when he was a Fresno Councilman, taking money from a businessman in exchange for waiving rental fees at the Fresno Convention Center, and using a check-cashing scheme to take $30,000 from a campaign account, and funneling the money back to himself through an intermediary. The star witness pleaded guilty to bribery, fraud, and witness tampering. The jury did not convict Setenich, who was reported by *SF Gate* in 1999 as saying, "This is a creation of a conspiracy that was never there. My job is to dispel something that never happened." Then in June 2000, Associated Press reported that a U.S. District Court jury convicted Setencich of filing a false tax return understating his 1996 income by $19,300.

Finally, crime did not pay out for the Fresno County developers and politicians. It didn't win elections when exposed. Their 'investment' in votes failed. In Clovis, the decisions they had bankrolled with big boys' toys, whiskey, loans, bank deposits, and cash were reversed by the next, more transparent city council.

By the time it was all over, more than 450 Federal Grand Jury sub-poenas were issued, 150,000 documents examined, twenty-two people charged, and sixteen acting and former elected officials, intermediaries, and developers went to jail. Fellow brokers tell me that nowadays, when developers from Fresno buy real estate in SLO County they adamantly refuse to follow the standard money-under-the-table practice to get developments approved. The Fresno lesson has held for thirty years now. Grover Beach and Arroyo Grande developers who passed no money to their respective mayors reportedly faced strong opposition from the mayors.

Bill Tatham went on to develop more companies, all apparently still trading.

Who brought them down? The Sacramento Division of the White-Collar Crime Program (WCCP). Its website states it is the number one such program in the United States. The Sacramento Division lists public corruption as the number one crime problem within the WCCP ... a pervasive problem that permeates ... the Legislative and Executive branches of government. The program investigates public corruption by legislators, regulators, contractors, courts, and law enforcement.

This is a case of the enemy within, against whom we must also guard.

SEPTEMBER 2011

The 20 years following 9/11 was perfect timing for opportunistic government fraudsters. Mark Arax wrote, "The war on white-collar crime was suddenly an indulgence ... In FBI offices across the country, the shift to counterterrorism was swift and unmistakable. In Sacramento alone, dozens of agents from public corruption and other squads were now working foreign intelligence, domestic terrorism, and international terrorism. Federal prosecutions of white-collar crimes would drop by one-third over the next five years. "With everyone looking for bin Laden," Wedick told friends outside the Bureau, "there's no better time for the good old-fashioned American crooks to steal from the people."

Government officials swear to protect from enemies within and without. The enemies within are running rampant and our elected public servants are serving them at best and being them at worst. It is these enemies within who forever change our country from the one we remember as kids. It was the other countries—the third world countries—where you had to bribe your way to anything you wanted from the government. The 'it can't happen here' belief left the door wide open for it to happen here.

CHAPTER 9 THE KING OF KANSAS CITY Meets the Mayor for the Ages

"You have turned your city over to a gang and given it into the hands of crooks and racketeers because you are asleep."

–Rabbi Samuel Mayerberg, May 24, 1932

The words above are the challenge issued by the rabbi to the Kansas City Republican Women's Study Group. Mayerberg writes in his autobiography, "The reception given at that address amazed me. Those gentlewomen, leaders in the club life of the city, arose and shouted their approval."

These women were to become, in the words of a former mayor, Kay Barnes, the city's "civic housekeepers."

The Kansas City story finished longer ago and farther away than the Fresno or current San Luis Obispo stories, but is remarkably current even a century later; particularly for me because I lived there for all the years I can remember until I was ten years old. Kansas City referred to itself as "The Heart of America." San Luis Obispo calls itself "The Happiest Place in America." The Kansas City history teaches reform from failure to finish. It illustrates the power of family traits in determining leadership for good or for ill, showing how vice, left unchallenged, can

255

grip a city for decades, and that bold effort and persistence over time can turn entrenched criminal systems into generations of good governance.

The Apple Didn't Fall Far

Three weeks before my mother died in 2014, she told me that back in the 1930s, her parents collaborated with independent Democrats in Kansas City to form a new political party to end the corrupt drug cartels of the Democrats there. For two years I had regaled her with my frustrations with my own Democratic party in San Luis Obispo County. I referred to some local Democrats as the "Bad Dems" and the independent Democrats I knew and respected as the "Good Dems." I asked why she had not told me sooner. She said she only just remembered it: she had been just a little girl in the '30s and didn't know much about it. Her sister, six years younger, has no recollection of ever hearing about it. My grandparents on my mother's side were (almost) lifelong staunch Republicans and members and leaders of their party in Kansas City, Missouri.

My mother's recollection sheds light on my experiences eighty years later; not just on the values that I inherited, but also as strong encouragement that we can defeat even the worst corruption in our system of government if we live up to the ideals that create it. I did not come by my political service consciously, but with a historical perspective, I understand that I came by the values that motivate it by generations of nature and nurture. There were hints that all had not been well in the Kansas City of my grandparents. My brother and I wondered why my grandfather was so anxious that we might come under the influence of drugs at school. My mother and aunt have both said that my grandfather questioned them too about being pressured to use drugs, and they never understood why. None of us ever felt that pressure. We lived the sheltered upper middle-class lives that our grandparents and parents worked so hard to provide for us.

I was eager to find out about my grandparents' youthful mission. Heartened that the Republican grandparents who I had thought were joined at the hip with their party had been willing to lay aside party loyalties in the best interest of their community, I started Googling. In 2014, I came away disappointed. I could find nothing. I looked again in 2019, and there was a plethora of information, including source materials (see the end notes) that I could buy online at used book prices, some long out of print.

I know why my mother didn't tell me about her parents' experience of cleaning up Kansas City, but why didn't my grandparents talk about it more with their daughters, or with their grandchildren? Were they afraid for our safety, or was it just that it was long ago and far away, and they believed they had put it to rest? Did they not speak of it because they no longer wanted to remember the hard times of two wars, in which my grandfather lost his youngest brother to suicide brought on by "shell shock" in World War II, and also lost his oldest brother, a World War I medic? Why did they never speak of the Spanish flu in which both sides of my family lost young mothers?

I remember hearing my grandfather express his gratitude that he could retire at 65 thanks to social security—a construct new to his generation. He never lost his passion for honor in politics. After he retired, he went on to chair the Jackson County (Missouri) Republican Party and was a delegate to the convention that nominated Ronald Reagan for the presidency. He proudly relayed to me that he and a consortium of Kansas political leaders travelled to Washington, D.C. with other Republican luminaries to confront Nixon during the days of Watergate; to tell the President that he had let them down. Nixon's diary records the meeting, if not the content: "March 22, 1974, 12:10—12:16 Marion "Zeke" Ramsey, retired executive of the General Motors Insurance Corporation."

I was proud of my grandfather then, and I am now proud to share with my son this historical record of his great grandfather. I also felt sorry for my grandfather, that he had worked so hard for his party and was so disappointed, but he took it all in stride. In my mother's mementos were letters and speeches from my grandfather's time as his party leader. He and I landed in different parties, but as I read my grandfather's speeches,

THE WHITE HOUSE				PRESIDENT RICHARD NIXON'S DAILY DIARY
				(See Travel Record for Travel Activity)

PLACE DAY BEGAN

THE WHITE HOUSE
WASHINGTON, D.C.

DATE (Mo., Day, Yr.)

MARCH 22, 1974

TIME   DAY

8:51 a.m. FRIDAY

TIME		PHONE P=Placed R=Received		ACTIVITY
In	Out	Lo	LD	
8:51				The President went to the Oval Office.
10:23	10:30			The President met with Secretary of State Henry A. Kissinger to discuss the Secretary's forthcoming trip to the U.S.S.R. Members of the press, in/out White House photographer, in/out
10:33				The President and Secretary Kissinger went to the Rose Garden.
10:35				The President and Secretary Kissinger returned to the Oval Office.
10:35	10:51			The President met with Secretary Kissinger.
10:57	11:37			The President met with his Counsellor, Dean Burch. White House photographer, in/out
12:10	12:16			The President met with a delegation of "Friends of the President" from Missouri: W. Marshall Giesecke, retired Chairman of the Board of the Bruce B. Brewer Advertising Agency Albert Rendlen, attorney and Chairman of the Missouri Bar Association Joseph Stevens, attorney Marion E. "Zeke" Ramsey, retired executive of the General Motors Insurance Corporation S. Bruce Herschensohn, Deputy Special Assistant White House photographer, in/out
12:17	12:22			The President met to discuss the settlement of investment disputes with the Government of Peru with: James R. Greene, Special Envoy from the U.S. to the Peruvian negotiations and Senior Vice President of Manufacturers Hanover Trust Company Peter M. Flanigan, Executive Director of the Council on International Economic Policy (CIEP) Members of the press, in/out White House photographer, in/out
12:22	12:30			The President met to receive an invitation to dedicate the new National Housing Center in Washington, D.C. with: Lewis Cenker, President of the National Association of Home Builders (NAHB) Lloyd Clarke, former President of the National Association of Home Builders Col. Dana G. Mead, Associate Director of the Domestic Council Kenneth R. Cole, Jr., Executive Director of the Domestic Council White House photographer, in/out

President Richard Nixon's Daily Diary recorded my grandfather "Zeke's" visit at 12:10 pm
www.Nixon Library.gov

unknown to me until fifty years later in 2020, I was amazed to find that our words and style were almost identical. I have the same passion for honest government. I had no idea that I had channeled my grandfather and dozens of generations that preceded him, now made known to me by Ancestry.com.

Internet searches for my grandparents' political activities brought up sites indicating that they had cleaned up Kansas City, but when I told a friend from Chicago the same, his response gave me pause. The good citizens had not completely stamped out the "Bad Dems" of Kansas City, who continued their voter fraud, albeit with less violence. As an example, I have included the speech and news release that my grandfather, an election judge and the new Chairman of the Jackson County Republican Committee, made challenging the Board of Election Commissioners.

My brother remembers my grandfather in his dimly lit office in the basement of their Kansas City home, typing away on his manual typewriter wedged between the washer, the dryer, and the furnace. I remember his prize Florida swordfish catch mounted on the wall above the old couch and the musty smell of dried laundry soap and damp dryer lint. Many of his letters and articles were edited in my grandmother's handwriting—I suspect her journalism degree must have come in handy. My grandmother kept a low profile in politics, preferring her women's groups, but she clearly had some influence. A note from a friend when she passed said she remembered my grandmother's generosity as, with a sweet smile on her face, she wrote a check for a charity. I remember more of a Mona Lisa Smile—a little bit cheeky—as if she knew something no one else knew. Somehow, I think she did.

In 2009, retired British attorney John S. Matlin published his Ph.D. thesis, *20th Century American Local Government, the origins of the Progressive Movement, and the Role of Political Machines in Corruption* (University of Birmingham, England). A student of American government, Matlin is an informed outsider without local bias. Kansas City was the substance of his research. He brings to life early 20th century municipal history with women's suffrage, political action, investigative journalism, voting rights of African American men, the first progressives, and political corruption, all still forefront at the turn of the 21st century.

Hungry for knowledge of my grandparents' battle in the 1930s, I pored over several first-hand accounts. Each different perspective adds to the whole and reminds me of the parable about several people who, blindfolded, handled different parts of an elephant—one the tail, another the tusk, another the ear, none accurately describing an elephant. The diverse perspectives of the participants in the Kansas City cleanup have also helped me gain a clearer understanding of how the experiences of the few and the success of the many, working in concert over time, can slowly shift perception enough that change can happen. It confirms that not every effort will meet with immediate success, but repeated efforts eventually succeed. A little success here, a small tip there, and the huge immovable stone of impossibility budges. And with sufficient little pushes together, it starts to roll downhill and then rolls faster and faster.

The King of Kansas City Story begins in the 1890s and ends in the 1940s, the days in which the 20th Century was born and grew up. There are two Kansas Cities, divided by the Missouri and Kaw Rivers that create the east-west border between the states. The Kansas City of this story is Kansas City, Missouri. While the cities are in different states, there was much crossover between the two in both travel and attitude. My grandparents, raised in Kansas farm towns, had moved to Kansas City, Missouri, while my mother and aunt, raised in Kansas City, Missouri, lived on the Kansas side. What follows is the story they never told us; the mystery behind why my grandfather worried that we were at risk of narcotics pushers and why he, the small-town farm export to the big city, was such a worry wart where his daughters and grandchildren were concerned.

In order to understand the cleanup, it is necessary to understand the social and cultural situation that pre-dates it. I have pieced together the Kansas City story from several first-hand sources, including Matlin's thesis, books written soon after the cleanup, and local papers and libraries (see Notes), and formed a timeline to provide insight into the people and groups involved and the political and media mood at the time. The months or election dates in the accounts don't always match up, but the action and the stories all concur on the outcomes. Like the Fresno story, what follows is an impossibly corrupt challenge where sunlight eventually prevails.

1890 to 1940 The Pendergast Dynasty

An article published 8/6/15, "Byte Out of History, FBI Involvement in Early Election Fraud Case in Kansas City", sets the stage.

> Impartial and fair elections are the cornerstone of any democracy, and the FBI has a long history of investigating illegal activities that harm the elective process. One of our earliest investigations involved Kansas City political fixer and power broker Tom Pendergast. Pendergast aggressively promoted Kansas City ... as a "wide open" city where gangsters moved freely, and prostitution, gambling, bootlegging, and drug enterprises flourished, making Kansas City notorious throughout the nation. The ... James and Tom Pendergast era was marked by violence and corruption. During prohibition, Pendergast kept the bars open and the liquor flowing... Kansas City eventually made national headlines for its fraudulent elections, dishonest bookkeeping, and lack of accountability, to say nothing of the vice, racketeering, and lawlessness with which Kansas City's leaders were associated.

Background

The Civil War was pivotal in shaping the neighboring frontier states of Kansas and Missouri. Kansas was the home of John Brown—the one from the folk song whose body "lay a moldering in the grave"—the controversial abolitionist who started out with standards most of us would now embrace but who became so married to his cause that any means justified his end. Half of Missourians supported the North and the other half supported the South. Even so, Missouri had its share of the Lincoln party Republicans and mostly Republican social reformers who were the first to identify themselves as Progressives.

1867

Voter Registrations among African American men, even in Mississippi, were 67% of those qualified to vote.

1870

When the **15th Amendment to the U.S. Constitution came into effect**, prohibiting government from denying men the right to vote based on race, Abolitionist societies disbanded thinking they had completed their mission, and many Republicans believed the Amendment had made the Reconstruction successful. But the abolitionists gave up too soon and did not oversee the implementation of their reforms. The Republican Party gained an African American voting bloc in the North while white leaders in the South successfully ignored the new law. African American voters in the South encountered poll taxes, literacy tests, and threats of violence from the Ku Klux Klan.

JULY 22, 1872

Tom Pendergast, the mastermind behind Kansas City's darkest days, was born in a small town in Missouri, the youngest of nine siblings.

1876

The **Supreme Court ruled that poll taxes and literacy tests were legal.** African American voter registration in Mississippi dropped to four percent. This history of interference at the polls, whether by identification or intimidation, continues to fuel voter angst and activism.

FEBRUARY 24, 1887

Bailey "Jack" Gage, Pendergast's nemesis, was born on the 80-acre family dairy farm in Kansas City, the son of Ida Bailey Gage, a Harvard-educated lawyer, and Kansas City native dating back to frontier days. Bailey senior was renowned for impeccable ethics as city attorney during the acrimonious Civil War years. He later represented Kansas City in the Missouri General Assembly. Gage junior sold milk to local customers until, at 16, he began undergraduate studies at the University of Kansas, and then following in the footsteps of his father became a lawyer with a reputation for integrity. In 1909 he graduated from the Kansas City School of Law, running his own law firm and teaching evening law classes. He was widowed young when his wife died of the Spanish flu. Gage's career proceeded against brutal local politics controlled by the biggest political machine boss in US history; Democratic machine boss Tom Pendergast.

1889

By the time Gage was two years old, Pendergast was striding into a 50-year regime, going to Kansas City to work in his brother Jim's saloon, as had his siblings who worked in various aspects of the business, legitimate and otherwise, for decades to follow. The family had a strong work ethic, and along with it, Tom had innate organizational and business acumen. As the Chairman of the Jackson County Democratic Party, Tom developed a large network of local "workers" to elect politicians (through voter fraud in most cases) and hand out government contracts and jobs. He directed the appointment of city officials, from the city manager to the chief of police, right down to a force of over 1500 part-timers who did menial jobs or functioned as his operatives, all on the city payroll. One online source describes him as "A self-appointed, self-made, self-dealing man whose skill at organizing the poor for the trade-off of jobs and welfare, while shielding the rich from the seedy side of town, and municipal exploitation allowed him to establish an iron grip."

Pendergast was not a drinking man, preferring to keep his wits about him while he held court from 5 a.m. to 6 p.m. six days a week. Those same wits left him when it came to gambling. His brother Jim's gambling changed the family forever when Jim bought his first saloon with sizeable winnings. Tom's gambling losses would change it yet again. Tom's eye for the main chance, while myopic as a gambler, was prolific in other forms of money-grabbing, setting him up as the principal in charge of dozens of businesses and the recipient of protection money from nearly every other business and city employee in Kansas City, Missouri.

US Treasury Investigator Rudolph Hartmann wrote that the city council did not approve contracts for public improvements unless one or more of Pendergast's companies participated.

1892

The First Ward elected Jim Pendergast, Tom's eldest brother, to the post of city alderman, dubbing him "King of the First Ward." In this election, the unofficial count showed a clear Republican victory for the office of county prosecutor and marshal, but forged final returns put Democrats in office. When a Grand Jury returned twenty-one indictments for election fraud, twelve politicians fled town and one committed suicide. **William Rockhill Nelson**, the progressive personality and editor at the *Kansas City Star* daily newspaper, supported exposing the fraudsters, and in **1894** began a decade-long campaign for non-partisan elected representatives, declaring, "The non-partisan idea does not depend on the result of one canvas. It will succeed in the end because it is right."

1900-1904

My grandparents were born.

1911

Woodrow Wilson (1856—1924), statesman, lawyer, and academic, and the Governor of New Jersey broke with party political bosses and won the passage of several progressive reforms, and in **1912 became the first Southerner president since the Civil War.** Wilson's success in New Jersey gave him a national reputation as a progressive reformer, and he defeated Progressive party nominee Theodore Roosevelt and incumbent Republican President Taft to gain the presidential nomination at the Democratic National Convention. **He appointed Henry Morgenthau** as ambassador to the Ottoman Empire (now known as Turkey) in 1913.

Morgenthau's son of the same name, as Roosevelt's Secretary of the Treasury, would later appoint his best agent, Rudolph Hartman, to investigate and take down the Kansas City underworld. Arriving in Turkey, German-born Morgenthau, the son of German Jewish emigrees to the United States, discovered that a small group ran the empire, ruling the various ethnic regions of the country through fear and assassinations. He compared their rule to that of machine boss rule in American cities of the time.

Morgenthau's lifelong active advocacy for the Armenians brutalized by the Turks exemplifies political passion for the greater good on a world scale. Mogenthau's efforts matter to me because growing up in Fresno, California, in the 1970s, my family had warm friendships with descendants of Armenian families who emigrated to the area at the turn of the century. My father's best friend was an Armenian American WWII medic who had been injured in the line of duty. My dad shared with my brother and me that his friend was not only in constant pain from the injury, but fought a lifelong battle of recovery from the morphine used to manage it when he was first treated. I am thankful that both he and his friend raised that alarm with us as adolescents so we understood the danger of opiates, even when medically necessary.

One of my high school friends made sure I knew that Noah's Ark landed in Armenia, among other accolades, and my church helped a 95-year-old survivor of the genocide publish her memoire, *Olive Trees Grow* Again.

1914
Outbreak of World War I in Europe

American consuls all over the Ottoman Empire flooded Morgenthau's desk with hourly reports of an Armenian genocide, documenting massacres and deportation marches. After the outbreak of war, U.S. allies withdrew their diplomats and the American Embassy—and by extension Morgenthau—which had represented many of the Allies' interests in Constantinople (now called Istanbul). Morgenthau was haunted by the "Armenian Question." He held high-level meetings with the leaders of the Ottoman Empire to help the Armenians, but the Turks ignored his protestations. Morgenthau officially informed the U.S. government, asking Washington to intervene. The American government, not wanting to get dragged into disputes, voiced little official reaction.

A telegram he sent to the State Department in 1915 described the massacres of Armenians as a "campaign of race extermination". Morgenthau famously admonished the Ottoman Interior Minister Talaat Pasha, stating, "Our people will never forget these massacres."

Through his friendship with the publisher of the *New York Times*, he made sure that the massacres received prominent coverage. In 1915 alone, *The New York Times* published 145 articles.

1916

Morgenthau resigned his post, exasperated with the Ottoman government, and unable to continue to work with a corrupt regime. Looking back on that decision in his book, *The Murder of a Nation, Ambassador Morgenthau's Story—A Personal Account of the Aermenian Genocide* he wrote he had come to see Turkey as "a place of horror. I had reached the end of my resources. I found intolerable my further daily association with men, however gracious and accommodating…who were still reeking with the blood of nearly a million human beings."

Morgenthau's own people would suffer a genocide far exceeding these numbers just three decades later, during the time that his son would be Secretary of the U.S. Treasury investigating crime in Kansas City. I find myself wondering if our government, in 1914, had heeded this prophet, Morgenthau, and intervened in the Armenian genocide, would it have mitigated the Jewish genocide that followed later? Morgenthau went on to become the treasurer for President Wilson's successful campaign for a second presidential term and began work on a book on the genocide, re-released by Harper in 2017, the 100th year of publication.

1917
President Wilson led the United States into World War I

A Democrat, Wilson oversaw the passage of progressive legislative policies unparalleled until the New Deal in 1933, and established an activist foreign policy known as "Wilsonianism" and leadership in forming the League of Nations.

1918
World War I ended

Morgenthau published his conversations with Ottoman leaders and his account of the Armenian genocide, *Ambassador Morgenthau's Story—A Personal Account of the Aermenian Genocide*, and initiated a speaking and fundraising effort, warning that the Ottoman leaders were carrying out the "same wholesale massacre" against Greeks and Assyrians, and that two million Armenians, Greeks, and Assyrians had already perished. As the massacres continued, Morgenthau, assisted by his wife, son, and several other Americans formed a public fundraising committee to assist the Armenians—the Committee on Armenian Atrocities (later renamed the Near East Relief)—raising over $100 million in aid, the equivalent of $1 billion today.

MARCH 1918
The Faith community joined the battle for good government early

In March 1918, The Citizens Committee of Five Thousand met in the Tabernacle of the Men's Bible Class of the First Baptist Church and formed a permanent organization to take an active part in city elections as watchers.

Activism Among Women's Clubs

1896
The Athenaeum was founded

A well-established 2,200-member organization, the club advocated the creation of public playgrounds, kindergartens, juvenile courts, parent-teacher associations, and city jail matrons to oversee female inmates previously overseen by males, pure milk regulations, prohibition, and women's suffrage. Although unable to vote, women were ardent reformers, advocating for women's and children's health and safety. While men of all hues had the right to vote, they still legally classified women as "chattel" (personal property). Women of the day pursued "progressive" social policies. Even the Pleasure Seekers Art & Study Club engaged in politics by hosting a lecture by firebrand reformer Ida B. Wells in 1925.

In Kansas City, middle- and upper-class women founded the Women's City Club to improve social conditions in the community. The club embraced juvenile justice reform and favored aid to widows who were "morally and legally entitled" to aid.

The club also sponsored a speech by suffrage leader Carrie Chapman Catt, who held that U.S. policy undercut peace efforts. Women's clubs provided an organizational structure for women's activism, reflecting women's aspiration to participate in the governance of their city. Although overwhelmingly white and Protestant, the Athenaeum and Woman's City Club counted among their members Republicans and independent Democrats. They collaborated with Jewish members and the National Council of Jewish Women on the use of silver nitrate to prevent blindness in newborns.

My family history in Midwestern America brings me to tears as I look through old family portraits and note missing young family members; victims of two world wars, the Spanish flu, childbirth, typhoid, and diabetes. I no longer wonder why the women who survived childbirth show up in these portraits looking so drawn, so tired and severe, by late middle age. On the Norwegian side of my family who arrived in this country in the 1880s, my Peterson grandparents were both the youngest of eleven children raised by older sisters. The Spanish flu took one great aunt, a mother of two, at the age of twenty-six and her sister, a mother of three, at thirty-two, just five months later, and a great aunt on my mother's side. My grandfather's oldest brother died at the age of eighteen, his twin at three, and another sister at fourteen. Wells were too shallow, and many children died in typhoid epidemics as a result.

On my mother's side, my great grandmother, following the death of my great grandfather of diabetes at the age of thirty-one, married a widower whose wife had died a week after my great step-aunt Ruth was born. The doctor amputated a gangrenous leg and then went to deliver Ruth. My great half aunt Lavina, Ruth's older half-sister, said they did not know then that lack of hand washing spread germs. Pregnancy and childbirth were the most dangerous health issues facing women until birth control came into its own in the 1960s.

These tragedies are 'aha' moments for me. When you, your sisters, your friends, and your already deceased mother carry a child for nine months in their bodies and then breast feed and nurture that child for years after and experience as many as thirteen live births, and your children are dying, you would be passionate about crusading for social services.

In the Kansas City of the early 20th century, it was the Democratic machine that was conservative and the Republicans who pioneered a progressive legacy, although those who identified as "progressives" came from both parties and from non-partisan groups. During these times "muckraking," a new type of journalism, investigated and exposed the ills of society.

1919

The Athenaeum president addressed a meeting of the African American federated women's clubs because of their common membership in the General Federated Women's Clubs (GFWC.)

Finally, in 1920 women got the vote, 50 years after black men got the vote in 1870.

The Progressive party waned following the First World War, but during the Civil War and both world wars women took charge in new ways. The 1920s rolled in a lively sense of liberty and freedom from the ravages of World War I and the Spanish flu. African American branches of women's groups, including the Kansas City Association of Colored Women, the National Junior League, social sororities, and Masonic auxiliaries had deep roots in Kansas City and joined with the larger groups and with African American men's groups, seeking political leadership and attempting progressive reform.

The women fought for honest services, in contrast to the Pendergast machine that capitalized upon social problems to gain votes and control the vulnerable. Spouses of public employees affiliated with the political machines took part in and sometimes directed electoral fraud because they feared for the jobs of their husbands if they did not participate.

1922

Republican Mrs. Carolyn Fuller, a past president of the Athenaeum, was the first woman elected to the school board, and Emma Longan, an independent Democrat, and Democrat Margaret Doherty Shepard were the first women elected to city offices. The reformers, including African American women, found sustained success in school board elections, and advocated powerfully for municipal reform.

1924

Maisie Ragan had a long history of activism and was a grandmother and divorcee when she graduated from law school. Ragan represented the political and professional ambitions of progressive women. She was one of the winners of the 1924 city council Republican sweep. Republican women drove women to the polls and ran a telephone campaign to ensure that every Republican woman voted. Republicans won all the races except the city treasurer's position.

1925

Ragan served on the committee that wrote the 1925 city charter replacing the complicated 32-member city alderman structure with the now more common single council of nine people and a council-city manager structure. The new city charter required a vote the next year. In addition to nine councilmembers, the ballot included two municipal judges and city improvement bonds. The Republicans nominated Rose Ludlow and an African American clergyman, Reverend J.W. Hurse.

The Athenaeum and other progressive women selected Ragan as their representative on the city council. She secured the Republican nomination for an at-large council position with support from the Athenaeum. On the morning of the election, Pendergast's people distributed a handbill asking, "Who wants to vote for a colored woman on the council?"

Ragan was not African American. The bonds passed, but Ragan lost, leaving the progressive Mayor Beach alone in a council of Democratic machine politicians. Ragan's loss demoralized women candidates for city offices, and the machine no longer needed females to compete with Republicans and independent Democrats. **No woman served again on the city council until 1963.**

The 1925 progressives' loss was the machine's gain. Pendergast secured control of city government, including the police department, and held it until he was jailed in 1939.

The machine appointed Henry McElroy as the Kansas City town manager. Claiming "efficiency," McElroy made city purchases without competing bids, awarding contracts to 'worthy members' of the Pendergast organization. He joked about budget balancing, with a wink and a nod, claiming a touch of magic in his calculations. He quickly put an end to the nonpartisan 'nonsense.' His would be a Democratic administration he announced.

The Chamber of Commerce formed The Nonpartisan Committee of 1,000, an audacious undertaking to pass a colossal bond for Kansas City infrastructure, taking in all elements of the population and enlisting committees of the best engineering, business, and political minds to work out the details, lauded by KC Star editor Reddig as "a rare and stirring example of democracy in action."

Details of the public works plan were determined at a series of public hearings before the various committees. When plans were finally assembled, the program was presented to the public in a campaign that was notable for its effort to inform.

The committees chose projects based on need and a showing of popular preference. People went to the polls with the slogan, 'Make KC the Greatest Inland City' and voted for the bonds four to one, casting the largest ever number of registered votes at a special election. The plan called for city and county expenditure over a ten-year period of $50 million, including $11 million from the federal government. Out of it came a thirty-two-story city hall, a skyscraper courthouse, a new police building, a municipal auditorium that covered a city block, paved roads that completed one of the most extensive county highway systems in the country, trafficways and boulevards, hospital extensions, a new water works system, parks, playgrounds, sewer extensions, flood protection, and a public market.

Conrad H. Mann, CEO of the Chamber of Commerce, and the Committee of 1,000 counted on the city manager and citizens' advisory committee to restrain the politicians in the spending of the bond funds. It was hoped that the city administration could be prevailed upon to follow the example of the county government under the direction of Harry Truman, presiding judge of the county court. Truman's work with the citizens' advisory group and the stellar history of his administration were influential factors in the success of the bond campaign. Under a seven-million-dollar bond program authorized in 1928, Truman introduced planning, expert direction, and bipartisan control in a manner new to Jackson County politics. He hired two consulting engineers, one from each party, gave them a free hand in laying out a new road system, and saw to it that their recommendations were followed in building the highways and a new county hospital. Judge Truman followed the same standards in the additional county building authorized by the ten-year program. They built 244 miles of paved roadways—twenty more than originally estimated, leaving a tidy balance in the fund; enough to erect a statue in front of the courthouse and a public celebration of the bond's completion at a Jewish venue.

In the midst of the Great Depression, Pendergast established the Ready Mixed Concrete Company. Kansas City's unprecedented campaign of public works required vast quantities of concrete, all supplied by Pendergast companies, approved by City Manager McElroy and none documented in any obtainable records. In Kansas City, the depression was late in manifesting and never struck with full force, thanks in large measure to the employment provided by the passage of the bond.

1929

Rabbi Samuel Mayerberg rolled into town, recruited to lead the B'Nai Jehudah congregation. Advocating academic freedom, the new rabbi made his mark quickly when the University of Missouri suspended professors after a graduate student circulated an anonymous questionnaire about sexuality to sociology students. Religious fundamentalists took umbrage, pillorying one of the school's most eminent scholars for failing to intervene. They were not disposed to let him off, for they knew him as a confirmed freethinker. The Rabbi teamed up with Kansas City liberal protestant churchmen, the local newspapers, and other bold souls to take a stand against the fundamentalists.

Students protested and the American Association of University Professors made such a ruckus that the curators finally admitted that the University was under an oppressive regime and called for the president to resign. Mayerberg's crusading mood continued when the University did not reinstate two of the professors.

In the late 1920s, the State sued one hundred and thirty-seven Missouri Fire Insurance companies for overcharging policyholders, impounding the $11 million of excess fees (multiply amounts quoted by 20 to approximate 2022 values.) The Missouri Supreme Court required the insurance companies to repay excess premiums to policy holders. The insurance companies retaliated with substantial premium hikes. The State, acting for Missouri policyholders, responded by suing the insurance companies again. Pendergast owned several insurance companies, so it behooved him to have his long-time friend, Emmet O'Malley appointed as the Missouri Insurance Superintendent. The insurance debacle dragged through the courts for ten years.

Meanwhile, an officer of the U.S. Treasury Department Bureau of Internal Revenue passed on a tip to a Washington, D.C. Kansas City Star reporter who gave it to Missouri's Governor Stark. Although the machine had appointed Stark, he remained independent. Stark immediately contacted President Roosevelt and insisted that he move against Pendergast.

This tip set off a federal investigation of the insurance swindle. U.S. Treasurer Henry Morgenthau, Jr. (whose father served the Wilson administration) commissioned Special Agent Rudolph Hartmann, the Treasury Head of the Intelligence Unit and his top treasury agent, to investigate underreported income by Pendergast, whose family machine was in its 40th year. Hartman's team reported their findings to the criminal Grand Jury appointed by Maurice M. Milligan, the federal attorney for the western district of Missouri.

Researchers found Hartmann's treatise on the 10-year investigation buried in Roosevelt's presidential papers in 1996.

1929-1934
Prohibition

Pendergast bragged that the city was "wide open" and his machine and a bribed police force allowed alcohol and gambling. Kansas City was known as one of the most corrupt cities in America, in which political, social, and moral corruption was rife. Pendergast spun the corruption differently. While promoting Kansas City, he boasted that while gambling and slot machine complaints might be frequent, Kansas City afforded its citizens greater protection from violence and crime than any other American city;

i.e., he was running a protection racket and if citizens didn't put up with him, the mob he enjoined in his efforts would be worse.

The Dirty Thirties

This was the era of my parents' birth. In my father's father's carefully kept family photo album, I am shocked by my stick-thin big-boned Norwegian grandparents and father and uncle as children. My father's father led a Conservation Corps camp, but did not eat with his men, who looked much better nourished. I realize they simply did not have enough calories in the cold, unforgiving physical and financial climate of 1930's North Dakota. I understand now why they admired chubby babies, declaring them healthy. And yet, the photos my father's father carefully mounted in his albums also tell a story of a teacher who loved his charges, loved nature, kept all occupied in a wide variety of sporting activities, and made regular trips to visit his and my grandmother's surviving sisters and brothers.

My mother had a different early childhood experience of the depression in Kansas City, and family photos tell her story also. Both of her parents were proud that, even from farm families, all of their family members had college degrees. My grandfather had a secure job managing the insurance division of General Motors. Whereas my father spent his first days in small wooden shacks, my mother lived on a tree-lined paved street with sidewalks in a lovely Cape Cod-style three-bedroom, two-bathroom home next door to her great aunt Mame, a WWII widow. But she wasn't entirely sheltered. She taught us never to share utensils or cups with other children because we might get germs, and told us about how when she was a girl, children got polio from sharing drinking glasses. She explained that many of the Jewish rules in the Bible were related to health and safety and how important that is. She also said that sometimes she had felt so sad for the sweet lonely English children whose parents sent them to Kansas City to avoid the bombings in London.

The thirties were the "Gangster" era characterized by the "most successful bank robber in U.S. history," the dapper and personable Frank Nash (Wikipedia), who started his 200-bank robbery career in 1913 when he robbed a store with his friend, Nollie "Humpy" Wortman. He sent his friend to bury the money and shot him in the back. Nash was arrested and sentenced to life in the Oklahoma State Penitentiary. Nash convinced the warden he wanted to fight in World War I and was released, serving just the last two months of the war, thereby reducing his sentence from life to ten years. Two years after his reduced sentence and two-month war service, Nash was convicted of safe-cracking and sent back to the penitentiary to do 25 years. As the prison deputy warden's chef and general handyman, Nash had privileges. The *Brimstone Gazette* reports that he was sent outside of the prison on an errand and never returned. In 1923, Nash joined a gang of bank robbers as the "mastermind" of several criminal groups. He had planned various escapes while incarcerated. After his gang robbed a postal train in Oklahoma, Nash fled to Mexico, but officers enticed him across the border and arrested him. He got another 25 years at the federal penitentiary at Fort Leavenworth, Kansas, for mail robbery and assault. He escaped to Chicago and continued his criminal activities in major U.S. cities, helping seven prisoners to escape from Fort Leavenworth Penitentiary in 1931.

1931

Gage started the Gage and Hill law firm that became Lathrop and Gage, the oldest law firm west of the Mississippi River.

1932

Early in the winter of '32-33, the public was startled to read a report from Walter Matscheck of the Civic Research Institute showing that the city was renting machinery at excessive rates from favored concerns, letting contracts without competitive bidding, and otherwise ignoring proper regulation for the bond program. A group of Republican lawyers filed an equity suit to recover bond funds of $400,000 that they alleged city officials misspent. An advisory committee ordered an audit. The city manager managed to reinterpret the audit findings, showing an even larger overspend, and the committee accepted his explanation, giving him a light reprimand to do better bookkeeping and supervise the letting of contracts more closely. Thereafter there was little interference, even from the federal government. No one audited the bond program again until after City Manager McElroy retired in 1939.

The Civic Research Institute was not the only watchdog in town. Rabbi Mayerberg and women's groups were paying attention. So was the National Youth Movement (NYM), started quietly in 1932, calling themselves 'national' to create the sense of a larger movement and add an air of mystery. Their 'underground' approach had the advantage of appealing to the community's taste for melodrama, but reinforced Pendergast followers' fear of the unknown. The Movement's recruiters targeted young executives, and within a year, with more than four hundred members, they announced they would enter a nonpartisan ticket in the 1934 election. Heartened, Republicans vowed to cooperate with any group irrespective of party label to fight the machine. The Republicans joined the National Youth Movement, doubling their ranks, and formed the Citizens Party, which also included Democrats unhappy with the machine, later became the non-partisan Citizens-Fusion ticket. The NYM sent one of their finest, a Harvard graduate, to examine the city's garbage contracts and budget. He was welcomed and given a lecture on the beauties of the garbage contract, the budget, and the audit, but given no records. This treatment is uncannily like the treatment I and others have received in some SLO County situations—a pleasant invitation to tour the facilities and none of the requested information provided.

Rabbi Mayerberg was the most eloquent and outspoken of the people of principle who challenged the machine, thus raising the consciousness of the city. Mayerberg had spent three years learning his way around city and state politics and found that the local disturbances were but one aspect of a broad disorder in the Heart of America. By 1932, Pendergast's monopolistic control of Kansas City was so strong and widespread that Mayerberg could readily demonstrate that the local police department and the city manager were in Pendergast's pocket.

Mayerberg's fighting spirit was strengthened by a chance encounter on a train, when the stranger in the seat next to him said, "If you want to see a first-class lynching, come back here a week from today."

Mayerberg phoned the governor and convinced him that a genuine emergency existed. The governor dispatched the National Guard, who stood idly by during the lynching.

Mayerberg continued his crusade with an initial volley aimed at City Manager McElroy for his lack of regard for the rule of the city charter. McElroy declared in a May 1932 church meeting that election results were a mandate to continue a partisan administration, troubling words that haunted unlikely attendee Rabbi Mayerberg along with other religious leaders.

The Republican Women in their government study group and the feisty young rabbi Mayerberg took him on. A mélange of class, race, and ethnicity, women campaigned for city offices and the school board in the interwar period. Club members abhorred the influence of the Democratic machine and embraced a progressive spirit and a vision of good government.

MAY 24TH, 1932

A *Kansas City Star* cub reporter happened to be passing by when Mayerberg was publicly addressing the study group luncheon at a local hotel. Mayerberg told the women, who had been seeking to impose financial accountability on the city manager, "You have turned your city over to a gang and given it into the hands of crooks and racketeers because you are asleep. The time has come for action. The time for study has passed."

Mayerberg accused City Manager McElroy, a former judge and crony of the Pendergast family, of violating the city charter provision that "no person shall solicit political contributions from any officer or employee in the classified service of the city." McElroy supported the established practice that city employees "tithe" up to half of their salaries to Pendergast candidates in election years. Mayerberg went on to say, "If we had a county prosecutor who was not a part of the political machine, he himself would bring the charge against this man."

He concluded his speech by demanding to appear before the council to present his case for McElroy's dismissal. Mayerberg's 'clean-up Kansas City' campaign garnered significant public and press interest.

Former *Kansas City Star* editor Reddig called the righteous assault on the machine "the beginning of the revolt that overwhelmed" the Pendergast dynasty. This first salvo succeeded in demolishing the popular notion that ministers had no talent for politics.

Skulking Hyena

A week later in a speech to the Kansas City Lions club, the brave Rabbi repeated his charges against the city manager and revealed links between city officials, the Pendergast machine, and organized crime, accusing County Prosecutor Page of signing a parole application for Johnny Lazio, a member of organized crime and senior Democratic politico who controlled the north side Democratic Club of Kansas City.

Page, who had orders "from Washington" to drop investigations into Lazio, denied the allegation that later proved to be true. According to Pendergast biographers Larsen and Hulston, Lazio headed a "home-grown crime syndicate in Kansas City" and had an agreement with the Kansas City Police Department to protect fugitives from justice. In his speech that day, Mayerberg called Lazio, "a powerful leader, sentenced to twelve years in the state penitentiary for highway robbery" and Pendergast, "the big shot who cracks the whip," and suggested that the appropriate emblem for the Pendergast organization was a skulking hyena. The following year Lazio would go on to plan the Union Station Massacre, the fallout from an attempted breakout of Nash, the criminal mastermind.

In week three of his assault, Mayerberg announced that he was seeking a mandamus order against the city manager "for violation or neglect of official duty." McElroy had fired registered Republicans employed by the city for no reason other than exercising their franchise. McElroy denied the charges. The paper concluded that his "contention that men were not hired and fired for political reasons was a subterfuge" when they received a letter from Conrad Mann, President of the Chamber of Commerce, proving that this charge was, in the words of *The Star*, "a true bill," and concluding that the charter provisions had been breached and "a dangerous situation arose when a political organization had absolute domination." Later departing from the crusading spirit of its original editor Nelson, *The Star* chided Mayerberg for his assault on McElroy's personal integrity and efficiency.

The city council decided it would be prudent to go through the face-saving exercise of granting the Rabbi a hearing, allowing him ten minutes and responding with a resolution affirming its complete faith in the city manager and declaring the Rabbi's charges not worthy of further attention. Leaving the council meeting, Lazio approached Mayerberg who had called him a gangster, a racketeer, and an ex-convict, more amused than angry, saying he wanted to meet the "second Moses" and saying, "You did not get very far, did you, Rabbi?"

Mayerberg met with the Ministerial Alliance and enlisted 104 Protestant church preachers into the fight, stating, "If the churches of this city have not developed a laity that will rise up and correct conditions, they have no right to exist. I am not discounting the wide ramifications of political racketeering and am fully aware of the difficulties that will be found right in the congregation of the various churches."

The next day, his own board president made it clear that Mayerberg was speaking on his own behalf, and not on the behalf of his congregation.

Local ministers resurrected the 1918 churches' Citizens Committee of 5,000, renaming it the Charter League, headed by Rabbi Mayerberg to direct a recall movement to "defeat partisan city government." They started to fundraise and the Rabbi went to city hall to examine records.

He asked to see the latest audit, city payrolls, and personnel records. He got the runaround and was openly defied by city officials until he sought a writ of mandamus. He offered his hand to the city manager, "I don't care to shake your hand," said McElroy.

Mayerberg retorted, "My hand is clean while you have violated every provision of the charter except that providing for the drawing of your salary."

He further asserted that the fight against political conditions in Kansas City was just beginning, saying his fight was against corruption and asked, "decent citizens" to help him "rescue the city government from gangsters and racketeers."

A former police chief and a police officer, both fired for trying to right the ship, set themselves up as the rabbi's bodyguards and equipped Mayerberg's car with bulletproof glass. He received threats of character assassination, physical mutilation, and death, living a twenty-four-hour melodrama. At three o'clock each morning, he was awakened by a call from a man who identified himself as a gangster who called himself 'Pal' and offered the Rabbi information and tips.

In week four of his salvo, Mayerberg asked Police Chief E. C. Reppert for access to police records. Reppert denied him the records, using an excuse I have often heard in my own county, city, and district agencies, that he had to make the request in writing. According to *The Star*'s interpretation of the city charter, police records were freely open to the public. Mayerberg's claims were too powerful and too accurate to ignore. The newspaper followed up over the next few days with an editorial noting that interest in Mayerberg's "crusade" had been fanned by City Manager McElroy's and Police Chief Reppert's refusals to open the city's books, going further to say that McElroy's integrity was now in question and suspicion was growing about the business operations of the Democratic machine to the point of collusion between McElroy, the so-called "independent" city manager, and the Pendergast machine. Mayerberg believed that as many as seventy-five ex-cons were on the police force.

In week five, Mayerberg left Kansas City to attend a Rotary convention in Seattle. While there he sought legal assistance in the mandamus action against McElroy from Francis Wilson and Russell Dearmount, both attorneys and Democratic candidates for governor. Mayerberg reported that the Democratic attorneys "tremblingly told me they could not help me; it would mean their economic ruin."

The summer agitation continued as the preachers created an uproar from their pulpits.

Upon his return, Mayerberg tried again to get police records. Chief Reppert again refused with another excuse we still hear today—police records were for the police only. Finally, a week later, Pendergast gave the order to produce the records. However, no changes in the police department resulted. Mayerberg then sought to revive the Charter League movement, but it had lost momentum. Influential citizens applauded his efforts, but no important leaders outside the church and women's clubs came forward publicly to battle for him. Fear of reprisals kept sympathizers from joining the cause.

Businessmen and the regular politicians didn't relish the idea of working with ministers—the parsons were too difficult to control, too full of spirit, and too unrealistic. It was the women, the clergy, and young businesspeople who became the social conscience of Kansas City and revolutionized it by bringing people of all faiths and races together in the fight. My grandfather had often warned me about being too zealous in the expression of my faith, consistent with historical references to a strong anti-crusade sentiment in the business community.

At the end of August, following the state primary earlier that month, Mayerberg made his final disclosures of election board fraud. Although the accusations reached Governor Caulfield, he decided to make no changes to the composition of the election board due to "lack of evidence of election frauds."

The machine was too strong and the details of its operations too well buried. In the light of hundreds of federal prosecutions of Kansas City Democrat machine workers for fraud that would soon ensue, there is a high probability that Mayerberg's allegations were accurate, especially considering that every other charge he made was later borne out. However, Governor Caulfield, a Republican, seems not to have had the political will to act, like the election board my grandfather chided forty years later.

After just over three months, Mayerberg's campaign came to a sudden end when Mayerberg decided to set himself to the task of serving his congregation. The machine was powerful enough to stave off Mayerberg's challenge, but not so strong that Pendergast didn't give veiled direction to his machine workers: "Who shall rid me of this meddlesome priest?"

Mayerberg reported that his phone was tapped, that bribes were offered, and that one night his car was forced off the road and a shot was fired. For months he claimed never to go to bed without a loaded pistol by his side. In his words, "The pall of fear which encompassed the community in general and big businessmen in particular was impressed upon me."

Meanwhile, the head of the Chamber of Commerce, who had served the community so well with his programs, was prosecuted for taking a hefty personal cut of the proceeds from a marathon charity event he organized. A rousing celebration of his return following a pardon on the jail house doorstep was routed by the Parent Teacher Council, insistent that, "All good citizens should observe and respect the law. It is impossible for parents to instill in their children right principles of citizenship when prominent citizens who have disregarded the law are received with public acclaim."

The words of the PTA echoed throughout the next months.

NOVEMBER 1932

The state election proceeded without incident. The Pendergast Machine Democratic Party slate won the U.S. House of Representatives and the governor's mansion. Pendergast's stooge, Governor Park, would be in control for four years.

The attorney general in Washington, D.C., reopened the Lazio case on tax evasion, which had been deferred by Page on "orders from Washington."

Grand jury witnesses were threatened with reprisals in business and with bodily injury, receiving missives and phone calls telling them they were jeopardizing their lives and the safety of family members. The jury met in secret to escape surveillance and intimidating whispers.

The intimidation silenced people, causing reputable citizens to perjure themselves, thereby concealing evidence. Fear, incomprehension, bewilderment, and the habit of being ruled by political machines paralyzed the Democratic will. Kansas City Star Editor Reddig reported, "The grand jury returned a final report that should have provoked a wave of mass meetings, the ringing of fire bells, and at least one riot in a liberty-loving community. Nothing quite like that happened."

There were still a few individuals who had not lost their powers of indignation and initiative. One such was Judge Jim Page, echoed Mayerberg's sentiments:

> We have at the head of our city government a man who openly permitted violation of the law and made a public statement to the newspapers he was going to continue to do it and what could the people do about it?
>
> The community generally gets the kind of law enforcement that it wants and earns. The people can't sit still and delegate this to the public agents. The people themselves are responsible. When they are going to wake up to the situation I do not know, but it is time they ought to begin to help us. If they don't begin pretty soon it is going to be too late.

Page wasn't done. He called for another grand jury to complete the work of the first investigation. Instructing them to "go after crime" in all of its phases, Page said that "He who violates the law is neither Democrat nor Republican. He is a criminal."

His greatest scorn was for the so-called businessmen who perjured themselves, "They are racketeers just the same as the organization."

Warning the jury that they could count on threats of violence with no help from the police, Page closed, "If something should happen to one of us, we would only be making the supreme sacrifice that thousands of American boys made in order that this might be a country fit for you to bring up your families, and fit for your homes, that you might sit around your fireside without fear of anyone."

The jury included men prominent in business and professional life, and was the beginning of the belated revolt against Pendergastism in the business community. The jury returned sixty-one indictments. Criminal machines are hard to crack, and as is so often the case, the information starts to flow when federal agents from the IRS and FBI join forces and tax evasion convictions follow. Lazio started to talk; that is until just before his sentencing when former associates shot him in front of his home. Miller, who had also been involved in the massacre, was murdered a few months later.

The **"Union Station Massacre"** confirmed Mayerberg's Mafia depiction of Lazio, who was fingered by federal agents in a bungled attempt by "Pretty Boy" Floyd, Adam Richetti, and Verne Miller to free Frank Nash from federal custody. Two Oklahoma FBI agents learned that Nash was in Hot Springs, Arkansas. The agents drove to Hot Springs accompanied by Otto Reed, the police chief of McAlester, Oklahoma. FBI agents were forbidden from carrying weapons and making arrests. They arrested Nash, and that night, Nash, accompanied by the agents and Reed, boarded a Missouri Pacific train bound for Kansas City, Missouri. Word of Nash's capture and the destination of the agents got out, and Lazio and his Kansas City crime organization went to work. After arriving at the Kansas City Union Train Station, Nash was put into a car parked outside. Armed men approached the car and opened fire, killing Nash, Otto Reed, the Oklahoma Police Chief, an FBI agent, and two Kansas City Police detectives.

1934

The U.S. Congress passed legislation allowing FBI agents to be armed and make arrests following the massacre

The NYM plunged the community into a state of continuous uproar for the next six years, during which the principal aims of the challengers were realized. As of 1947 when he published his memoir, Reddig reported that the turmoil had not entirely settled.

The Fusion Movement members—the coalition between Mayerberg's Charter League (renamed The Citizens Association), NYM, young business professionals, students, liberal Republicans, and Democrats not involved with the Pendergast machine who wished to clean up their party had a common goal—good governance based on fiscal accountability and dispensing with politics in city governance. Pendergast wrote off the young business professionals, as "silk stocking college students," labeling the leaders, "a bunch of nice boys and girls misled by GOP soreheads."

FEBRUARY 1934
Citizens Movement office riddled with bullets

The "Bloody Election" of 1934 saw Pendergast machine thugs committing acts of violence and intimidation against opponents. Brutal psychological and physical violence escalated. The city election was the most violent on record in the annals of Kansas City. *The Star* reported, "witnesses stated they saw a car with NYM stickers used by gunmen."

Police Chief Higgins (a machine operative) claimed that NYM workers had staged the incident to arouse sympathy. This was a classic Pendergast political dirty trick, framing his opponents by labeling a car with opposition stickers and then raiding the office in the car appearing to be their own.

MARCH 1934
Kansas City Primary Election

The NYM, armed with cameras as their research tools managed to remove 88,107 "ghosts" from the voter register. A ghost is a name fraudulently registered and voted. The Citizens sent pleas to the governor to send the National Guard to the November election and went to the chief of police asking for better police supervision, but he refused to see them. Claim and counterclaim of vote rigging continued until election day, when the violence at the polls stole more headlines than the rampant vote frauds. Many "poll" workers had counterfeit credentials. The governor saw no need to send the National Guard, even after gangsters riddled the car of a *Kansas City Star* reporter with gunshots, and *The Star* editor's chauffeur was beaten and shot at while driving Citizen voters to the polls and a non-Pendergast Democrat candidate and deputy sheriff were killed.

When an Italian gang shot and killed a precinct captain who was trying to protect a poll worker from a beating, the Citizens again telegrammed the governor asking him to send the National Guard. Again, the governor refused. As terrorists and gangsters roamed the city the police made fourteen arrests. Twelve were Citizens suspected of "contemplating intimidation." In the end, the city elected two Citizens, one gaining office due to the murder of the competing candidate. The Fusionists won four wards formerly held by the Republican Party. The Citizens filed hundreds of affidavits of acts of terrorism and "sluggings" at the polls. Total machine control of Kansas City politics and nominations for state and federal representatives culminated in four deaths with no indictments. The fraudulent reporting of election results overthrew the democratic process, with precincts reporting astronomical participation rates. Vote totals for machine candidates exceeded the total population in several precincts!

The NYM held a post-election rally vowing to pursue permanent registration law and the impeachment of Governor Park. One of the proponents, William E. Kemp, became Kansas City's mayor on the Citizen's ticket in 1946. Even after having removed the 88,000 ghost voters in the city with a total population of 400,000, only half of whom were legitimate registered voters, conservative estimates of ghost votes in the election itself ranged from 50-60,000. False votes were almost equal to the legitimate votes.

Shootouts and Murder of an African American precinct captain on election day 1934 in Kansas City

The violence of the 1934 elections was finally enough to convince *The Star* to reclaim the fighting spirit of its founder, Nelson, to stop the graft in city government and to back the Citizens in the next three elections. *The Star* followed with an editorial demanding that the police force reorganize and ran features on attempts by independent Democrats to chase down the Election Day slayers and hoodlums, and of neighborhoods mourning for the murder victims, thus highlighting the police dereliction.

On Good Friday, the pastor of Linwood Presbyterian Church preached a "Black Friday" sermon on the crimes of Kansas City. His sermon ran on the front page of *The Star*, calling the Protestant brotherhood back to action. The next day the police director resigned. *The Star*, the Republicans, and the Citizens then turned on McElroy, the city manager, reinforced by blasts from Easter Sunday pulpits. On Easter Monday, all 104 Protestant church leaders called for the resignation of the city manager.

The city manager feigned remorse, pledging to purify the police force and create a permanent registration law. He then routed the good governance advocates by using crafty machine tactics and hiring a *Star* writer as the police chief, thus dampening the paper's appetite for further critical reporting.

1935

The insurance company customer over-charge litigation begun in 1929 was deadlocked. The insurance companies delegated authority to two respected insurance executives, Charles Street, Vice President of the Great American Insurance Company and Chairman of the Subscribers Actuarial Committee, and A.L. McCormick, President of the Missouri Insurance Agents Association, to make decisions regarding the court case. In secret negotiations, Street and McCormick offered Pendergast $200,000 (nearly $4,000,000 in today's dollars) to convince his old friend and appointee, Emmet O'Malley, the Missouri Insurance Superintendent, to settle the litigation.

Pendergast bid the bribe up to $500,000 (more than $9,000,000 in today's money) to be delivered in cash by McCormick. When McCormick delivered the cash, Pendergast kicked back a portion to be split equally between McCormick and O'Malley. Pendergast was slow to perform, so Street did a little incentivizing, upping the ante to $750,000 (over $14,000,000). That did the trick. Before long, O'Malley, who had hitherto enjoyed a good reputation as a public servant, agreed to the insurer's settlement terms. O'Malley agreed to return to customers twenty percent of the overcharges, less the insurance companies' legal fees and Pendergast's huge take. The remaining unskimmed 80% of the $11 million ($206,628,175) of ill-gotten insurance premiums was split between the 122 offending insurance companies.

Governor Park conferred with State Attorney General McKittrick, who advised against the 80/20 compromise. Two hours later, after a telephone conversation with Pendergast, Park approved the compromise. It is extraordinary to find the local press ignoring a twenty percent discounted distribution for the policyholders, wherein the individual taxpayer would continue to bear a monetary loss and where the monolithic insurance corporations would reap the benefit.

Before the full payout could be whisked off to Pendergast, all four men were under investigation due to that earlier tipoff from a Treasury agent that Pendergast had not declared, nor had he paid taxes on the $440,000 he had already collected in cash from McCormick. The money had shored up his income to cover his gambling losses.

Nevertheless, the O'Malley settlement reached in November 1935 was approved by the courts and the Missouri House of Representatives by 1937.

1936

The NYM and Fusionists disappeared from political view and "ghosts" became apparent. *The Star* turned "Ghost Buster," assigning two of its best reporters to develop an efficient spy and tipster system, putting them at risk of beatings or worse by hoodlums and the police force. Unexpectedly, Pendergast intervened with heavy protection to counter *The Star*'s negative reporting. In the two weeks before the election, the paper published a photo of a "ghost" husband registered to vote, whose "wife" of that name said he was not her husband. The reporters exposed a circuit judge who had upheld two ghost registrations. There were between two to eight "ghosts" in the homes of many city and county employees, some of whom were not aware of the haunting. *The Star* concluded, "… in numerous precincts and probably one entire ward, ghosts outnumber the legitimate voters."

Although the paper succeeded only in getting the machine-controlled election board to eliminate a few thousand ghosts who then found other ways to vote, they opened the door to the federal investigation that would follow.

As had been the case for three decades, corruption accompanied the elections of 1936. As Mafia-related shootings and election violence raged in Jackson County, U.S. Treasury Secretary Henry Morgenthau went after Mafia boss Charles Carrollo and Pendergast. Ignoring the Pendergast machine's influence in electing Democratic candidates, Morgenthau directed his subordinates to "let the chips fall where they may."

In 1937, the newly elected Governor Stark turned against Pendergast again, triggering federal investigations and removal of federal funds from Pendergast's control.

Milligan opened a well-prepared case against the ghosts, and finally the federal courts intervened. Federal Court Judge Albert L. Reeves appointed a new grand jury to investigate vote frauds in all Kansas City precincts, saying, "When a man casts a dishonest ballot, he cocks and fires a gun at the heart of America," instructing the grand jury, "Gentlemen, reach for all, even if you find them in high authority. Move on them!"

Mysterious individuals began to appear and turned out to be FBI agents sent by Washington to make this the greatest hunt for election crooks in American history.

The machine positioned itself as "caring for its people" by supplying money for bail, legal staff, and other purposes, doing everything except turning in the higher ups. Judge Reeves called on the puppet masters to surrender themselves in order to "rid literally hundreds of poor people of being humiliated and punished for doing their bidding. There should be some gallantry and chivalry, but so long as the higher-ups remain in the background the only thing for the judge to do is impose sentence on those who have followed their orders."

1938

Disgraced Missouri Insurance Inspector O'Malley, having collaborated with Pendergast, found himself out of public office. However, the machine took care of its own and made O'Malley director of the Kansas City Water Department.

A Cry for Freedom

The ministers, women, and progressives of the city, regardless of sect, whether liberal or conservative, had set a precedent of unanimity against corruption for more than thirty years, joining together to call for the cessation of the machine. Their example of a united front gained traction among the various groups who had worked to bring good government to their city—students, Republicans, independent Democrats, the Rabbi, National Youth Movement, Fusionists, Women's groups, African American groups of men and women, and their news publication. Businesses began to cowboy up, responding to the appeal, not financial as it had been in the past, focused on tax-savings and costs, but rather, on the universal cry for freedom.

As I consider historical precedent—the French revolution, the Declaration of Arbroath, first nations worldwide, our own Revolution, even in the face of poverty, the cry is not for income, or economics, but for FREEDOM. The clergymen questioned "whether free, democratic government shall endure."

The machine's adversaries had coalesced in even greater numbers, but yet again in the 1938 elections Pendergast's people won, even with less vote fraud and violence and even with a state-appointed election board. The machine had not yet lost its hold on honest voters. A New York sports reporter had come to town and in his writing, provided an apt description of the notorious Kansas City machine: "Good rotten government. It protected businesses from strike violence, kept tax rates at a moderate level, reduced robbery and car theft rates and diverted the energies of the criminal element into the vice rackets, all made possible by ties with the underworld and revenue from gambling and vice."

Crime statistics appeared low because when the police joined forces with the crooks, crime, while uninhibited, went unreported, including the diversion of funds from citizen bonds to finance a 1500-strong Pendergast machine and his $6 million gambling habit.

The federal courts kept the vote fraud issue front and central, parading the machine-dependent defendants through the courts in 1937 and 1938. Kansas Citians were alarmed by their appearance. They looked like ordinary citizens. Indeed, citizens who had never been in trouble with the law outnumbered the underworld types. They were yoked to the machine by their own employment or that of family members, by party alliances, or through fear of retaliation.

The courts hauled in election judges (aka poll workers) in batches. As the thirty-ninth conspiracy case concluded, the DA tallied 278 defendants, convicting 259 of them. In thirteen trials the jury acquitted none of the sixty-three accused. Thirteen offenders appealed their cases to higher courts, with only one reversal. Fines exceeded $60,000 with 72 defendants, including women, incarcerated for up to four years. The courts found voters registered at vacant lots, and small houses "occupied" by a hundred or more voters.

The anti-machine coalition, working behind the scenes, once again changed its name: from the Citizens-Fusion to Citizens Coalition and nominated a bipartisan ticket of five Democrats and four Republicans. A coalition including young people and liberal Republicans and Progressives formed to act against the absolute power and oppression of the machine. Known as the "Good Government Association" the group wanted to improve Kansas City's inner political system and its outer image as the 1940s approached. Supporters from the 1932 and '34 rallies, including Mayerberg, stepped up again. While subdued, supporters were bolstered by the local business community and *The Star*. Even then, not all businesses took part, still fearing retribution.

Who were these 20th century progressives?

1. Progressives regarded the business of government as the obligation of those who governed to concern themselves with economic and efficient municipal administration in the best interests of the entire community.

2. They believed non-partisanship was essential if the hold of machine organizations was to be destroyed.

3. Progressives argued that the removal of party-political influence would yield a more rational pursuit of the common good and free local government to work effectively on problems which were visible to the voter.

JANUARY 1939

Tom Pendergast, interacting with organized crime, had held Kansas City in his power for 28 years and had been the undisputed political boss for fourteen years, running local and influencing state and national politics almost unchallenged. He built his machine's profits and his personal wealth through increasingly sweeping corrupt practices protected by covert bookkeeping and an army of worker bees and, by extension, their families.

The gambling racket had grown into a major industry, netting today's equivalent of $360 million a year according to the governor. The 104-strong ministers' alliance had consistently spoken against it. One minister's brave wife campaigned boldly against the machine until it threatened her husband and children's lives. She lost her nerve and the family left town for quite a while.

The minister's wife was followed by Judge Southern, who met with similar reprisals, but had the power of the State behind him. Governor Stark decided that 1939 would be cleanup year, and ordered his attorney general to begin on January 1st. Twenty-four state grand jurors were called in a secret meeting to protect them. Only twenty showed up and ten gave excuses, a showing of how frightened residents remained. The judge excluded the county prosecutor from the investigation and kept the attorney general at arm's length, pointing out that neither had exhibited any awareness of crime conditions in Kansas City that needed investigation. The governor empowered the Grand Jury with three investigators and a $50,000 crime fund that he jammed through the legislature.

The jury appointed a founder of the NYM-Fusion reform as their foreman. Immediately, Judge Southern, a Democrat, received requests from public officials not to call a Grand Jury at this time because it would hurt them. Judge Southern advised the press of the requests and that he had received covert threats and warnings that those who were under investigation would frame him in such a way as to attack his character and personal moral integrity. He gave notice that if such were to happen, the framed evidence would be "false, malicious, and libelous."

Their targets in the unlimited investigation included the county prosecutor and Big Charley Carollo, who took over the Italian mob after Lazio's murder. The governor had backed the county prosecutor, but now fired him, saying, "His continued failure to prosecute ghastly felonies justifies his immediate removal from office."

The Grand Jury indicted the prosecutor for failing to prosecute when Lazio's lieutenant attempted to kill the sheriff in 1933. Despite his appeals, the state Supreme Court ousted him and his sheriff due to a breakdown in law enforcement.

Federal Judge Reeves stepped up with a Grand Jury concurrent with the State Circuit Court jury. Reeves was after the bigger fish, saying "Kansas City today is a seething cauldron of crime, licensed and protected."

His agents had been reporting big daily payoffs, hints of murder and frequent mention of 'The Big Man' who ruled the underworld. One operative said he had never seen any one individual in all the years he had been connected with U.S. government who had so much power as the 'Big Man.' By 1938, Carollo was collecting over $100,000 a year for Pendergast, who kept 40% and distributed the rest to five or six others in the syndicate.

MARCH 1939

The Federal Grand Jury issued 167 indictments, saying it had done no more than "*lift* the edge of the curtain."

The indictments included two bombings and charges that Corollo, fellow gangster, Gargotta, and a former judge of the county court, the presiding county prosecutor, approved $10,000 to remodel the Jeffersonian Democratic Club.

Governor Stark, on hearing that that Police Chief Higgins was headed to Washington, D.C. to plead with the President for clemency for Pendergast, called President Roosevelt warning "against the importunities of a man named Otto Higgins, who is a grifter."

The President refused to see Higgins.

APRIL 4, 1939

The US Attorney General and FBI Dept of Justice head J Edgar Hoover traveled to Kansas City to confer with DA Milligan and the FBI operatives gathered there.

The machine was under attack by the press, the federal government, the state government, and a groundswell of the combined campaign energies of political and civic organizations led by Kansas City Attorney John B. Gage as head of a fact finding committee.

The U.S. Treasury Department's insurance overcharge investigation initiated in 1931 began to pay off. Internal Revenue Service's (IRS) suspicion was aroused when agents discovered that Street had drawn huge sums in cash. Street had not reported to the IRS the $100,500 from the insurers that was intended to defray the insurance litigation settlement costs that had passed through his accounts. The identical sum was paid to Pendergast. Street had not benefited personally, and he avoided the indignity of prosecution by dying before the matter reached the courts.

McCormick had already confessed his part to Treasury agents. IRS agents passed their evidence to Milligan's criminal grand jury, leading to the indictment and trial of O'Malley and Pendergast. When Milligan announced Pendergast's indictment on income tax evasion, *The Star* proclaimed the news in headlines as large as the paper's 1917 declaration of World War I.

GOOD FRIDAY, APRIL 7, 1939

Pendergast maintained his cool until the day he was getting fingerprinted and one of his lawyers attempted to help him remove his overcoat. Pendergast lashed out angrily, and just as Clovis Councilman Sorenson had done, he used a religious reference to proclaim his innocence, "I'll take it off. There's nothing the matter with me. They persecuted Christ on Good Friday and nailed him to the cross."

APRIL 8, 1939

The Federal Grand jury indicted Pendergast on a second count of income tax evasion. District Attorney Milligan oversaw five federal agencies on special Kansas City assignment. US agents uncovered a narcotics ring that was taking an estimated twelve million dollars a year (2022 equivalent of $216 million) from addicts, and the Reeves grand jury returned thirty-three indictments.

APRIL 13, 1939

The diminutive Mayor Smith, who had for eight years been the subject of derision by City Manager McElroy, served notice on McElroy to quit his post. McElroy resigned and the mayor seized his powers. On his way out, McElroy admitted to a deficit of $1.5 million in the general operating funds. The final accounting showed a deficit of over $19 million ($344 million). It included illegal diversion of improvement bond money to pay wages, just as the SLO County sewer board and administrator/ treasurer had illegally diverted our capital improvement fund to pay wages. McElroy's books showed 3,200 to 3,500 employees—the actual number was 6,500. Another fraud involving McElroy was the payment of a machine operative $5,000 ($90,000) a month, totaling $365,000 to look for water leaks—akin to the current arrangement our county has with an engineering firm to verify that homeowners have installed water efficient plumbing fixtures; something that plumbers or purchase receipts can easily confirm.

Under the new mayor, the city opened its books. The council ordered an audit; the Civic Research Institute started a second audit and pressured the court for a county audit. *The Star* started a series of disclosures based on the analyses and findings of reporters now that the books were open. The Federal Grand Jury revealed that Pendergast's family held two fifths of the shares in the city sanitary service company. Once in city hall, the extent of the corruption the reformers found was overwhelming. There was something new every day.

Finally, the people who had been fighting for justice for two decades were free to coalesce. The business community, along with Progressive Republican and independent Democrat women, envisioning a city without Pendergast, created the Forward Kansas City Committee to transform city government.

O'Malley took a leave from his post as City Water Department director and Police Director Higgins resigned. The governor petitioned the general assembly for a bill to return control of the police department to the governor. In just months the mayor, along with a new city manager, reduced expenses, cut the payroll, ordered an audit, shifted personnel, fired eight powerful machine department heads, and reorganized, getting efficiency on all sides. The urging of the businessmen's committee and court action hastened the reorganization, but it wasn't quick enough for the Forward KC Committee or the ministers of the Mayerberg Charter League movement, and it was far too quick for the machine! Political maneuvering, over the course of the next six months, succeeded in ousting the tiny mayor and his city manager, but not before he found a new city manager, Cookingham—a man from out of town, who was to become the pick of the mayor who succeeded him also.

MAY 1, 1939

Pendergast and O'Malley went before Federal Judge Otis to enter formal pleas of 'not guilty' and have their trials set. Next was Charley Carollo for his gambling frauds, then three ringleaders in the narcotics racket. All pleaded not guilty.

MAY 2, 1939

Edward Schneider, the secretary-treasurer and a nominee shareholder of many of Pendergast's companies, mysteriously disappeared three days after making a full statement to the Federal Grand Jury of his transactions for Pendergast and Pendergast's financial dealings. Pendergast had just pleaded guilty to income tax evasion for not paying taxes on the insurance bribe received that had paid off his gambling debt. While a "suicide note" substantiates the story that Schneider took his own life, some accounts say he was driven to it by the pressure put on him by prosecutors, rather than his own guilt, but could that pressure have been greater than a lifetime of catering to racketeer and Mafia-friend Boss Tom? The circumstances surrounding Schneider's demise infer that at least some of Pendergast's business dealings, in which Schneider was implicated, were criminal. Schneider's last known contact had been the police chief, who had come to his home. His body was recovered from the Missouri River five days later. Over the years reports came out of threats of being "taken for a drive" such that it leads one to wonder if rather than committing suicide, Schneider was taken for a drive.

MAY 24, 1939

"A gross betrayal" is how *The Star* characterized the Pendergast involvement in the insurance swindle. In line with similar cases, and due to severe ill health, the judge sentenced Pendergast to fifteen months in the Kansas Federal Penitentiary and allowed his release after twelve months for 'good behavior.' Pendergast was forbidden to enter into politics or to gamble. He appeared not to be involved in politics, retaining anonymity, but continued to gamble for huge stakes. Although charged with tax evasion, the details of his part in the insurance deal remained a secret. The House ordered its insurance committee, which had approved the settlement, to inquire into the insurance payouts. The committee did not have the benefit of knowing all the facts surrounding the settlement. Similar to the Charter League's difficulties in 1934 investigating Mayerberg's claims, they found themselves shy of full documentary proof needed to convict.

Savvy criminals know better than to leave a paper trail, which is why so often only the U.S. Treasury has been able to convict—for failure to pay taxes on ill-gotten gains. In this case it took ten years of FBI surveillance, the U.S. Treasury's best agent, and mandates from the governor and the president from within Pendergast's own party to take Pendergast down. Larsen and Hulston note that in 2009, "the archives at Western Historical Manuscripts hold many records of the so-called Ten-Year Project, but there is no reference to Pendergast or his machine and no mention with whom contracts were placed or at what price."

Kansas Citians had had enough. While the punishment may have fit the crime for tax evasion, it didn't come near the punishment the public thought the villain Pendergast deserved for over half a century of crime and corruption. Kansas Citians were emboldened, critical mass was building, and a new sheriff was on his way into town.

Meanwhile, McElroy died, thus avoiding prosecution, as had Street, and then McCormick of insurance laundering fame, as well as Pendergast's company secretary, and gangsters Lazio and Miller before him. Whether it was the machine, or personal expediency, or age, or high living taking its toll, there were an inordinate number of friends of the machine who escaped earthly judgment by dying. Involvement in government corruption has a profound effect on life expectancy.

AUGUST 1939
The Citizens Movement surged to 1,000 members

Rabbi Mayerberg had been the voice calling in the wilderness that spurred others to organize and act. Now that the state and federal governments had stepped in, the clergy, women, African Americans, the Jewish community, young professionals, and "old white men" could come together to root out corruption in Kansas City. Women served on the executive committee as well as in wider committee roles. Despite the mutual respect and civility, those in social and professional circles rarely crossed lines of class, color, race, and gender. White women had acted separately from white men, so too did African Americans—both men and women. White women's organizations such as the YWCA remained active on such issues as anti-lynching, housing, and jobs legislation. The women coalesced to adopt a 10-point platform within the larger movement calling for fairness in public employment, housing, education, training, juvenile and adult corrections, and representation on the school board.

Businessmen organized under the Forward Kansas City banner, a nonpartisan group growing to more than three hundred members in concert with the Chamber of Commerce included a women's division. They conjoined the Republicans, two independent Democratic groups, the Ministerial Alliance, and the Charter Party under the name of the United Campaign to champion the charter amendment election in February 1940 that, if successful, would reduce council terms from four to two years and require a follow up election of new city councilmembers in April 1940. The State Legislature assisted by amending Kansas City's charter to cut short the terms of all city officials, making possible the 1940 election.

1939-1945
World War II September 19, 1939, Germany invaded Poland

Fifty years of machine rule and over forty years of reforming idealist effort culminated during the six years of World War II.

The Wizard of Oz premiered in movie form in 1939, the year Pendergast went to Penitentiary

"'I am Oz, the Great and Terrible,' spoke the Beast, in a voice that was one great roar. 'Who are you, and why do you seek me?' And the next moment all of them were filled with wonder. For they saw... a little old man, with a bald head and a wrinkled face."

L. Frank Baum, *The Wonderful Wizard of Oz* (1900)

When I was a child, *The Wizard of Oz* aired every year around Hallowe'en time, and I remember watching, perched on the loveseat in my grandparents' family room at the back of the house, which was also their informal dining room. It was, of course, based in Kansas. Film and television scripts often weave in current events. In the same manner that the silly *Fresno* spoof mirrored reality, and English nursery rhymes satirized politics, *Oz* had parallels with Kansas City.

There is a physical resemblance between Pendergast and the wizard—the one who was hidden but controlled the levers that ran the evil un-transparent empire of Oz who got taken down by an unlikely crowd of commoners, including minorities and young people. There were narcotics (poppies=heroin), and the munchkin minions who, walking in Hitler-esque lockstep, did the bidding of the machine, and were finally freed. In the end, when the travelers found courage, heart, and a brain they were able to free the land from tyranny.

Courtesy of: Missouri Valley Special Collections, Kansas City Public Library, Kansas City, Missouri. John B. Gage, Mayor of Kansas City, MO 1940-1946

FEBRUARY 1940
Charter Election

Coming together with the men under the 'Forward' and 'United' banners, women's political activity in municipal reform began to reflect a more evolved partnership with men. The Women's Forward Kansas City Committee assigned 1,500 women to polls, five hundred women to work the telephones, five hundred women who provided transportation for voters, and others who prepared lunches for the election judges and clerks. The charter amendments won by a margin of six votes to one.

The non-partisan United Campaign was composed of a ticket of five Democrats and four Republicans for the council places, all members of its Citizens Association Party headed by John B Gage, the Democratic lawyer who had led the Forward charge. Among the candidates was also one of the 1934 leaders of the NYM. Gage's childhood as a young entrepreneur selling milk from his family's dairy throughout Kansas City and a generational history of integrity were factors in the vital role he played in city affairs. His pedigree established him as a principled, second-generation Kansas Citian. Gage called his candidacy "the silliest thing in the world."

His distaste for politics and devotion to ethical, transparent city government made Gage an ideal leader for Kansas Citians burdened by a generation of corrupt elected officials. His second wife and widow Marjorie spoke in recorded interviews archived at the Kansas City Library. She said apathy and fear exacerbated in 1934 continued through the 1940 election, and that her husband had planned to leave the city if defeated due to personal threats to the family at speaking engagements. She said there was a populace keen to have a non-partisan election and a merging of factions into a non-partisan group and of women's activities in the Citizen's Association.

The women organized vigorously. They were powerful allies and powerful enemies. Former Senator Reed, who had earlier incurred the wrath of the national Athaneum women's group for opposing the renewal of the Maternity Protection Act of 1892 that provided prenatal and postpartum care to mothers and infants, seemed to have come to an understanding of the importance of women in the political process. He suggested that the United campaign give women a significant role, and the campaign admitted three women to the inner circle of the Forward Committee. The women adopted the broom as their symbol and worked it with style. Their leaders were the darlings of the *Kansas City Star* and the affluent South Side of the city. The leading organizer, Mrs. Gorton, won praise for her "capacity for facing dark facts."

The campaign was designed to appeal to housewives with the slogan:

Wanted: 75,000 women with pioneer courage…let us keep faith with those who blazed the trail.

This campaign, billed as the "Battle of the Brooms," included a band of 7,500 women who demonstrated by marching around city hall each wielding a broom as a drum major wields a baton, signaling the directive to sweep clean city hall. Under Gorton's leadership the women staffed 4,500 phones; an impressive number considering that only 37% of homes in the US had phones at that time. They also drove 5,000 cars to carry citizens to the polls, also impressive because households with cars had only one and women were still not widely considered the entitled driver, if considered at all. The United Campaign succeeded in a comfortable win for Gage and public recognition for the women's efforts.

The men looked on with admiration mixed with some trepidation. The United candidates, who wore broom-shaped lapel pins to symbolize their promise to make a "clean sweep" of city hall, did just that, taking seven of eight city council seats. Nonpartisan reform smashed the partisan machine after a half-century of partisan machine rule.

The Democrats retained control in the Pendergast precinct, but Boss Tom was in prison and the cleanup movement had been intensifying for decades despite election-day intimidation. Mandates and prosecutions by state and federal courts, the dedication of the clergy, the press, women's groups, minority groups, and the business community who made up the United Campaign Committee put a new reform government in office. The Citizens Association that had its roots in the election watchers of the 1918 Men's Bible Class of the First Baptist Church became the dominant force for reform and good government for the next 65 years.

Upon taking office, Mayor Gage found that things were worse than even the Rabbi's fiercest accusations forewarned. The $19 million that McElroy had "misplaced" over his years of office, through what he called his own method of "country bookkeeping" equated to twice the city's annual budget in 1938.

New City Manager Cookingham of Saginaw, Michigan, provided an unbiased perspective. Together, without burdening their citizens with large tax increases, Gage and Cookingham cut the city budget by $700,000, restoring the finances of one of the nation's most indebted cities, and increased the city's footprint fourfold. They reduced the payroll and created a large surplus even with increased wages, debt pay down, and the tax rates they lowered by reducing real estate tax valuations by $30,000,000.

Here's how the Citizens Association Facebook page describes Gage:

> Dubbed the "Clean up Mayor" and "The Prince of Kansas City," his task was to clean up the remnants of "the dirty thirties." They instituted fair, honest government.

1941

The 10-year investigation completed by US Treasury Agent Rudolph Hartman under the direction of Henry Morgenthau resulted in the convictions of at least 267 Pendergast political operatives, Pendergast himself, and murdered gangster Johnny Lazio.

1942

Gage was re-elected. Hartmann published the account of ten years of research and successful prosecution of Pendergast, *The Kansas City Investigation.* The Charter Party and United Campaign Committee became the Citizens Party.

1943

Remember the insurance company scandals that started in 1929? The state case collapsed, a victim of statutes of limitation.

1944

A federal judge took the initiative to return the eighty percent of the $8 million overcharges that Pendergast and O'Malley granted the insurance companies and added another $2 million in fines, issuing checks to policy holders fifteen years after the companies first gouged their customers. Gage was re-elected.

JANUARY 26, 1945
Tom Pendergast is dead

His wife, who had lived in an apartment in stylish downtown Kansas City for years, did not attend his funeral.

SEPT 2, 1945
World War II ended

1945

Women continued to strengthen the good fight. Nonpartisan efforts were so successful

Tom Pendergast 1939 Kansas Federal Penitentiary
National Archives at College Park

and so touted that the machine was overlooked but the retreat was not so extensive or fast as was supposed; witness my grandfather's experience in 1970. According to Reddig, the nonpartisan experiment attracted national attention. It endured longer and accomplished more than any similar effort in the past.

One distinguishing feature of the nonpartisan administration is that it was a businessman's government, but it was also the reformers government—an alliance of honest businesspeople, local churches, and reformers, so different from the McElroy regime; a businessman's government ruled by just one boss and his business machine. This aspect of the change is most striking when compared to earlier reform efforts. In his investigations of the battles against the great city machines of the turn of the 19th century, muckraking journalist Lincoln Steffens found that the do-gooders invariably encountered major resistance from the dominant economic interests.

The 1946 fiscal year closed with Kansas City better off by $22,000,000 than in 1940

The Kansas City comeback brought as much national attention over the next decade as had the organized crime and gangsters of the preceding ten years. For municipalities across the nation, Gage's leadership heralded profound advances in fiscal management, planning, personnel, social welfare, recreation, and an evolving concept of balanced civic infrastructure development and functions in a modern city.

In a sense, the Nonpartisan Citizens Party became a party not of one strong individual, but a group—singly successful in not identifying itself with one individual or with one traditional party. Nonpartisanship may not yet translate on a state or national level, but locally the businesspeople, the press, religious leaders, minority groups, and the women with the brooms kept it going, much as the mixed and motley crowd in my own county, bolstered by the courage of their convictions, despite retribution and payback, have joined forces to champion good government. Mayerberg remained active in voter reform in Jackson County.

Gage, who had once described himself as "forty percent farmer" stepped down after completing his third term as mayor, returning to his private law practice and his 700-acre farm in Kansas, ignoring calls to run for governor of Missouri.

1959
The Citizens Association lost its council majority

Reform efforts had remained strong in city government.

JANUARY 15, 1970

> **KANSAS CITY, (AP)—John B. Gage, died today,** the mayor of Kansas City for three terms in the turbulent days after the smashing of the Tom Pendergast Democratic organization.
>
> When he died at age 82 on January 15, 1970, three decades of good government in Kansas City had disproved skeptics who believed Gage's reforms would not last, and he became known in history as one of the twentieth century's most important U.S. mayors.
>
> He died of injuries suffered Dec. 11 when he was struck by a truck near his downtown law office.

I cannot help but wonder if the machine had finally caught up with him.

One thing I know for sure is that the bad dems were not altogether gone. My grandfather went to battle with them that same year.

1970
My grandfather, Zeke Ramsey, was elected the Chairman of the Republican Party of Jackson County

MARCH 16, 1971
Kansas City

Chair Ramsey addressed the Jackson County Elections Commission regarding election fraud, releasing his speech to the press.

> I visited a great many voting places in the 1970 General Election and the primary just passed. I found violators influencing voters in a great many of the polling places visited. I found many factional precinct captains of party representatives in charge of the polling places—meeting voters on the outside, taking them inside over to the judges [in California they are called poll workers and hereon I am substituting for ease of understanding] and then walking with the voters to the voting booths. In other cases, poll workers would accompany the voters to the voting machines, stand there with the curtains partially parted or even go in with the voters and pull the levers.
>
> When questioned, the poll worker would make known to me she had always done it and was only helping the voter and not influencing him in any way.
>
> In the 4th Precinct of the 1st Ward, in the 1970 election, a violation was reported. A few hours later, I visited this same precinct and found the same violation, namely the poll worker going into the voting booth alone with the voter. I again called in the complaint.
>
> I visited this same precinct during the primary just passed. I found an individual other than a poll worker in charge of the voting place. He was outside at the door when I arrived. He came in also and asked to see my credentials. I showed him mine and asked for his. He pulled out a stack of credentials, but none were signed by his county chairman.
>
> A deputy commissioner was there but showed no interest and made no comment. A few seconds later, this man in charge came back to me and showed credentials which were signed by the Democrat county chairman, but they would not let me see what

they were for. The deputy went to his car and drove away with no comment. The precinct captain or representative again took charge. There was no protest by any of the poll workers.

In many instances, the Republican poll workers are so intimidated they will hardly admit they are Republicans and would certainly hesitate to report violations or demand that proper procedure be followed. I admit we should do a better job of finding strong poll workers.

A Republican committeeman informed me on Election Day in 1970 he had numerous precincts where individuals other than poll workers were completely running the voting places and as soon as a deputy left after a complaint, they resumed their unlawful activities. I visited a number of his precincts and found the situation to be exactly as he reported it.

I found poll workers in numerous places wearing large badges of a faction. This must have been observed by deputy commissioners since it was so widespread.

In one precinct, it was reported to me by a Republican poll worker that a poll worker in that polling place was handling a carpool by telephone at the same time she was serving as a poll worker.

I doubt if there is a person in this room who doesn't know these violations go on year after year for as far back as most of us can recall.

We are placing inside and outside challengers in many of the voting places in the areas involved. They are being schooled in the duties of a challenger. If violations are observed again, challenges will be entered, and our challenger will demand the voting stop at that polling place until the arrival of a deputy and the infractions eliminated. If necessary, we will resort to a lawsuit naming the offenders.

This situation has gone on for far too many years. Kansas City is entitled to an honest vote. The voters are entitled to visit voting places without annoyances, fear, or undue influence. I commend the Board of Election Commissioners for the efforts in preventing these violations and urge committee people to appoint judges who cannot be swayed and then train them so they will know the law.

I urge voters to report all violations.

I ask the news media and the Board of Election Commissioners to inform the public so voters will know when violations occur.

I believe most voters want an honest election but do not always realize they are being used by unscrupulous politicians.

1972

Ramsey, Marion E. (my grandfather) —also known as **Zeke Ramsey** —of Kansas City, Jackson County, Mo. Republican—Delegate to Republican National Convention from Missouri. One of the many who created a new political party in the 1930's to oust the corrupt machine in Kansas City, my grandfather, upon retiring took on the chairmanship of the Jackson County Republican Party, nominating Ronald Reagan for president in 1976.

2018

Henry Morgenthau Senior's book on the Armenian Genocide that he had witnessed when he was the American ambassador to Turkey, had been printed and reprinted for over 100 years—a plea for fairness and humanity that transcends the centuries.

DECEMBER 12, 2019

One of the last countries in the world to do so, The United States Congress officially recognized the Armenian Genocide, more than 100 years after Morgenthau's first pleas for recognition of the situation.

2021

My grandparents' legacy lived on in the Citizens Association of Kansas City; Kansas City's oldest non-partisan political association, the offshoot of the early associations of concerned citizens. The Citizens Association, remembering and honoring the work of those who came before them, describes how it now carries out its 100-year mission:

> The Citizens League of Kansas City…under the leadership of men and women representing diverse socioeconomic, political, religious, and racial backgrounds, … is committed to promoting open, honest government at City Hall and broad participation in the local political process.
>
> Today the Citizens Association carefully screens and endorses candidates for the mayoral and city council elections held every four years, recommending only those persons who have demonstrated a high level of integrity and commitment to open, honest, and fair government. In non-election years, the Citizens Association identifies, tracks, and takes positions on important issues facing Kansas City.

CHAPTER 10 THE MACHINE ISN'T DEAD HERE
Fear Fuels it and Greed Runs it

"…you can't trade on your office, embrace a corrupt pay-to-play culture, and get away with it."

–FBI Special Agent Joseph R. Bonavolonta

As the country moved westward, local government made its way off the frontier, dealing with the day-to-day issues affecting citizens, such as streets, planning, water supply, sanitation, and trash disposal. City management became more sophisticated, as did the standards surrounding it.

The problem in Fresno County until Operation ReZone rebooted it, and in SLO County still, is that we are still accepting the wild west norms of the 1850s to the 1930s.

Historically, cities have operated separate from state and federal government, using committees to regulate and oversee schools, police, water, and fire services. In California, these committees take the form of special districts. The boards of these special districts are made up of councilmembers and county supervisors. The public is often only vaguely aware of these "ghost" districts and unaware of how much these districts can impact their quality of life. The APCD and SSLOCSD covered in chapters four and five are good examples of the impact of special districts. The Air Pollution Control District has the power to shut down the economic engine of the county. Sewer district rates have increased tenfold as a result of the graft of the board and administration.

Opportunists are able to turn these unseen and minimally overseen enterprises to powerful advantage, realizing easy money at the expense of residents. A tax base is an ongoing source of money that can be accessed repeatedly because it is replenished every year. With districts out of sight and out of the minds of the state, counties, cities, and residents, graft can flourish. A similar delegation of responsibility down the line is playing out with the recent California cannabis legalization. The high level of independence that comes of hundreds of cities and counties implementing their own regulations can lead to a low level of oversight, providing opportunity for crime to start and proliferate.

The Progressives vs. The Machine

Early good-government reform progressives wanted efficiency and honesty rather than machine rule. Progressive reformers, many of whom were women, got in the way of the machine, competing with the services the machine offered, by which they controlled their constituents. Until the country implemented social reforms, the machine was able to retain power. The hard fought, long lasting, and extensive Progressive reforms to local government of the late nineteenth and early twentieth centuries were an ongoing battle between liberal (mostly Republican) reformers and conservative (mostly Democrat) machines.

There is a popularly held misconception that political party machines started to fade out with the advent of the New Deal in the 1930s. This is wrong. It was not until the Great Society years of Lyndon Johnson (1963-1969), when federal welfare programs took over much of the machines' work, as immigration numbers fell, and as Americans sought a different type of local government more responsive to democratic values in those affluent economic times, that second phase machines began to leave the political scene.

For those who criticized machines as a public ill, the machines could point to the help provided to large sections of the public in the form of welfare. The machine has not died because human nature has not changed. It just shows up differently—still politically, but now as lobbyists, and still with corporate monopolies that put lives at risk, as with the large utilities, PG&E with outdated infrastructure and a system that encourages over-budgeting, requesting allocations year after year whether or not they need them, overbilling, and under-working according to ethical contractors who have shared their frustrations with me. The machine that operates for the advantage of the few uber-rich—the one percent—is the primary campaign funding source of our state and federal governments.

It's easier to grasp the cause and effect of machine activity at the local level. Take a drive or a walk in the national forest or the less populated areas of the county, or even along our highways, and you will see that vast amounts of cannabis are being grown—with the illegal trade still equal to or greater than the legal trade. In SLO County, tens of thousands of cannabis dollars have been donated to candidates for our board of supervisors and several thousands to city council candidates, making up 25–75 percent of the money many of the candidates raise. These same local donors donated tens of thousands to our lieutenant governor's campaign, as well. The local candidates when elected demand that cannabis industry applicants do charitable works as one of the qualifiers for a dispensary license. Then if there is criticism, the elected and their cannabis picks can point to the good works that they do for the homeless as a diversion from the bad works that steal from us and would provide for services needed by the homeless if graft wasn't diminishing the public treasury.

The references to Progressives are to the original progressives. In my county, the new progressives were co-opted by the machine, rising in power largely due to its social media whiz kid. As the news stories break of the illegal activities of some of their proponents, local progressives appear to be more cautious in their associations.

Characteristics—Political Party or Political Machine?

Michael Johnston, in *Patrons and Clients, Jobs and Machines: a case study of the uses of patronage* defines corrupt political party machines as "tightly organized parties whose members and followers are motivated by money, gifts, or favors, where votes, money, and control over public authority are the currency."

A political party machine relies both on favoritism, perks, or threats that they selectively mete out, and material temptations such as money, jobs, or real estate. Edward Banfield suggests a machine's political head must employ incentives to secure cooperation. Debts of influence owed to a boss cannot be collected through the courts, and the boss will reach beyond the law to secure enforcement. Such enforcement includes intimidation and threats of violence and reprisal. Banfield distinguishes the political party machine from other political organizations by the "emphasis placed on inducements, or the appeal to human frailty and greed through the possibility of power or advancement."

Lack of interest in the qualities of strong moral principles, honesty, decency, and efficiency are hallmarks of a machine.

Monopoly Gone Maverick

Machines are monopolies. They are anti-competitive and anti-market diversity, having a single seller within an industry. Historically, machines dictated the way in which the town conducted its business. A monopoly blocks and undermines competition and imposes costs on a third party. When a monopoly such as PG&E (Pacific Gas & Electric) fails to maintain its infrastructure, sparking wildfires that kill hundreds of its customers and destroy billions of dollars of their property, the third-party cost of such neglect is not borne by its shareholders, but by its customers, some of whom already lost everything and then, along with the rest of the populace, continue to pay the higher premiums, deductibles, and energy costs to cover the negligence caused by the monopoly in the first place. A monopoly machine business seeks to gain and retain power with a view to provide benefits for its players, just as the corporate or quasi-governmental monopoly provides earnings for its shareholders, placing shareholders above stakeholders: customers, quality of life, and the environment.

Organizational Deniability

An organizational chart of a machine has similarities to that of the American mafia. Both the machine and the mafia operate a pyramid organizational style with clear lines of reporting and levels of 'deniability', where the boss is isolated from any association with wrongdoing because those at the bottom of the pyramid do all the dirty work. As this relates to SLO County, be assured that when you see the dirty work, someone up the line has put out the word. When considering Adam Hill's antics and social media trolls, look to who lurks quietly behind inciting and manipulating that behavior. Ask in whose interest it was to stir up his acting out. In the case of a 'hit', find out who asked the thinly veiled question, "What are we going to do about this problem?" that signaled the order to act.

Although a machine was not averse to using mafia-style tactics such as intimidation and threat of physical violence to get its way, bosses like Pendergast realized that an abundance of carrot and a minimum of stick produced better results. The key was preying on the 'self-interest' of sufficient numbers of people so that no one got in the way of the power-broking of the machine.

Operating Methods of Bosses:

CONFRONTATION OR A COMPROMISE

Per Matlin: machines "treated the conduct of business as either a confrontation or a compromise and were unlikely to engage in authentic discourse. While an air of amicability may cover interactions, rarely is there a position of equality in dealings with the machine. The machine monopoly exercises and retains control, while placing people it deals with at a disadvantage. This is the art of the deal, weighted in favor of the boss." It is a win-lose proposition.

Matlin observed, "At a local government level, if one estate abuses power and the other two estates are unwilling or unable to stop such abuse, the citizen is left unprotected."

In Kansas City, Pendergast controlled all three estates—he appointed the city manager (Administrative), he controlled the polls, thus controlling the city council (Legislative,) and he controlled the police and the election of judges (Judiciary.)

Businessmen faced a double jeopardy—they paid 'protection' to the criminal fraternity that then saw to it that the businesses had no lawful protection from the authorities. Without local police protection, if the federal government's criminal investigation arm would not use its resources to stamp out organized crime, and if state and municipal criminal law enforcement was weak, or worse, if state and federal authorities were elected by the machine, it could expand unfettered. Machine control of the three estates of government at a local level made the machine immune from prosecution or lawsuits. Business owners knew their businesses would suffer, if not cease to exist, if they stood up to the machine.

In my city, as in many, the estates are not set up to hold one another accountable because they aren't separate. The city council (legislative) hires and controls the administrative estate (city manager). The city manager then hires the police chief. Only the voters in a recall election can remove councilmembers (legislative).

Mediators Between Poverty and Power

The boss sets himself up as the mediator between poverty and power whose chief function is as a broker between those wanting public favors and those able to give something in return. As do SLO County boss figures, Pendergast acted both as a political and a business broker. In this role, the boss recoups his funds by acting as a silent partner with contractors, for example by serving as local agent for developers and cannabis concerns and as a negotiator for the sale of planning permission and permits. In addition, the boss also helps friends who are down on their luck, is generous to the poor, and is a liberal subscriber to neighborhood charities.

In SLO County, the bosses positioned themselves as "consultants" for developers, shepherding projects through the system and brokering

ownership in one form or another in the newly regulated cannabis industry. When it became apparent that the state would legalize cannabis, the
brokers got to work. They contacted growers and dealers countywide and
further afield with promises of permits. Black, a political consultant, set
himself up as the campaign manager for a measure for the City of Grover
Beach (Yes on Measure L) that would tax cannabis businesses, thus paving
the way for ordinances that would permit and license cannabis businesses.
They found a city manager for Grover Beach in Northern California with
experience of legalized cannabis businesses. They met with administrators
in municipalities throughout California and Colorado who were already
engaged in the industry. They recruited cannabis businesses to Grover
Beach, demanding from them large campaign contributions for their
chosen candidates and the cannabis measure campaign that Black solely
managed. Cash-based bribes and extortion are facilitated by the fact that
cannabis businesses cannot work with banks.

Once Measure L passed, Black visited property owners in the desig-
nated "Cannabis Zone," offering them triple the market value for their
property, with the message that he was the campaign manager for Mayor
Shoals and had the mayor in his pocket. He formed and retained sole
control of multiple LLCs with cannabis-identifiable names. He had his
hand out at every stage of the process of bringing a cannabis industry not
just to Grover Beach, but to the whole county. Black parlayed his political
consultancy into a brokership of cannabis permits, property, relationships,
power (in this case electricity), water, and business ownership. His
cohorts, the mayor and mayor pro tem, set themselves up (unlawfully)
as the council committee that would oversee the process with the city.

They hobnobbed with the investors and businesses at lavish parties
and dinners. Black consulted for investors and businesses, drafted the
ordinances, influenced who would get the prized dispensary licenses,
set up LLCs, set up his own distribution company, and recruited the
company the city hired to oversee selection of cannabis licensees and
subsequently manage the tax collection. Along with Supervisor Adam
Hill at the county level, they were political brokers angling for donations

and political sponsorship for their allies, moving them into positions of political power, and granting their hearts' desires whether they be pharmaceuticals, sex, political power, a position, a judgeship, or a cannabis supply, and sidelining and maligning those who wouldn't play along. If a businessperson decided to avoid paying to play, then no license or permit would be forthcoming. As a result, the local cannabis companies with clean records either moved their businesses out of town or shut them down altogether. They orchestrated the cannabis cabal from start to finish, assisted by the scared people who go along to get along—contractors and developers who could rationalize playing along by believing that "this is how it has always been and always will be" or as retention of their livelihood.

The corrupt and the scared in effect work in a symbiotic relationship—the corrupt need the scared, and the scared need the corrupt not to hurt them, in the same way that addict and dealer do a symbiotic dependency dance. It is difficult to fault contractors who believe they must follow a certain financial course of action—the price of doing business—to get work or have projects approved. They consider it a budget item; an extension of a marketing plan. The dealer needs the addict, and the addict needs the dealer, until one of them is left, as Adam Hill was, in a game of musical chairs when the music goes off and the chair is pulled out from under him and he is left exposed with nowhere left to go but out.

Jobs for the Boys (and Girls)

In Kansas City, the machine appointed lowlifes to city jobs, not for their ability but in return for political services past, present, and anticipated. In SLO County, Adam Hill's campaign manager said he wanted one thing more than any other. He had been a volunteer fire fighter and wanted to be a fire chief, but had no formal training for the position. Hill created an emergency services manager position at the County made and made sure he was appointed to it. Then, when the fire chief retired just before an election, Hill's cronies quickly shoehorned his campaign manager into the position via councilmembers who would be termed out within the month, overlooking a qualified career firefighter who had reached the career pinnacle through hard work and competence. Appointees would be loyal to the machine, without which they would not be employed. Beneficiaries of patronage know that if they are disloyal, their jobs are in danger.

The former Oceano Community Services President, Matt Guererro, wanted one thing more than any other. He said so often. He wanted to be a judge. That happened when he teamed up with the cabal to tarnish the reputation of his former colleague, Mayor Jim Hill. His cohorts, Mary Lucey and Patty Welsh, were open about their cannabis habits. They were easy cabal converts.

Just as we have heard it was in Arroyo Grande, Wolfinger said in traditional machines it was commonplace for city or party officials under the rule of political bosses to advise contractors as to the acceptable sub-contractors and suppliers to patronize. In Kansas City, main contractors would sub-contract to one or more of the many companies owned or controlled by Pendergast. When a main contractor was entering into terms to construct a municipal building in Kansas City, senior city employees or machine operatives would have encouraged him to enter into sub-contracts with machine-connected companies and to purchase the requisite performance bonds through an insurance agency recommended by the Democratic Party Committee.

It is one of those near perfect crimes—the advice as to which contractor to use is given verbally by a public works or planning staffer, and the contract is laundered by sub-contracting it out from the main private contractor to a subsidiary of the contractor or to a contractor friendly with the cabal, neither of which is required to comply with a public records request, although honest companies handling government contracts often will comply as a matter of integrity and usually keep good records. When contracts are being laundered, private companies can control the recording of transactions, if any, making any kind of audit trail difficult to follow, although in some ways, the use of digital media has helped because it is not possible for most people to completely "disappear" information from a good electronic forensic investigator.

When something is amiss there are financial indicators. An experienced auditor or businessperson can "ballpark" the cost of jobs and know if charges are within a usual and customary range. Then, by looking at government records of a business's charges and the number and depth and breadth of their transactions, infractions can be identified. For instance, as Carl Knudson reported in the SSLOCSD audit, if a contractor has 100 employees and 20 known government contracts and is charging out the equivalent of 28 of those employees to manage one small agency which has previously been managed by nine staff members, all of whom are still employed by that agency, one has to wonder. Good directors who know which questions to ask, and ask them, and good boards that encourage questions defend against corruption.

Patronage by the machine results in price-fixing and removal of competition to the detriment of the taxpayer. Knudson suggested that in Arroyo Grande it would be interesting to consider how many applicants who did not get planning or building permission were those who did not use the recommended contractors. As time goes by that becomes increasingly difficult to ascertain because of statutes of limitation, but also because the new mayor, having ousted the honorable Jim Hill, who swept out her friend, the mayor that ruled for 13 years, has now completely removed anyone at the city who would have any institutional memory of these matters. She has also now disavowed her friendship with Adam Hill, the friend she most likely quoted to justify her stance that there was no problem at the sewer district. She has even gone as far as to say she is changing political parties. As the axe comes down, that is a very shrewd move.

Birthday Parties

The corrupt cannabis businesses in my county had a great scam going. They hosted lavish "birthday parties" and "campaign launches" on their private premises or other private venues or homes of well-heeled "friend-lies," extending extravagant invitations. Party favors—women, money, alcohol, and other drugs, were freely offered, and of course, at a birthday party guests have to bring gifts. I am told you could not get in the door unless you brought a gift—an envelope with money in it. A private birthday party is the perfect cover. All the council or board members and staff of any agency can attend without it being a Brown Act violation or without giving the appearance of one, because who could fault anyone for going to a birthday party? Who would fault someone going to a birthday party or campaign launch bearing a gift; even if money in an envelope?

The same applies to political campaign launches. All members of an agency or board can attend without questions of Brown Act violations because it is a political event, not a government event. Even easier, they are expected to ask for and donate money, and if cash was left lying around, although illegal, who would know whether or not it was all reported? Donations that campaign treasurers reported having received at these events came from subsidiaries or related businesses and employees, associates, and partners of the applicants seeking permits for cannabis businesses or real estate developments. An example of how that works is explained in a mailer (below) that I delivered to every house in my city when I campaigned against our current mayor.

LLCs: the Darkest of the Dark Money Alliances

WHO PAID FOR THE MAYOR'S [LEE] CAMPAIGN?

Grover Beach—When the donor or source of a political donation does not disclose the source of the donation, the money is Dark Money. Recipients and donors of Dark Money often use Limited Liability and Shell Companies to launder ill-gotten receipts, because LLCs obscure the donor's identity and the real source of money. Anyone can form an LLC with no more than the name, address, and registered agent/founding member and some states do not even require the name of the registered agent.

In 2006, the Department of Treasury condemned these lax requirements, saying LLCs are "inherently vulnerable to abuse," and can be used to move billions of dollars for everything from credit card fraud to terrorist financing. These loopholes make LLCs attractive vehicles to move political money to candidates while disguising the identity of the donor and the source of the money. This complete lack of transparency and accountability makes LLCs the darkest of the dark money groups.

Below are dark money practices of mayoral candidate Jeff Lee. They include donating through LLCs and organizations controlled by the same person, using PO Boxes instead of street addresses, and donating through companies with names that do not reveal that the donors are cannabis permit applicants. Donating on October 19, 2017, Sunny Coast Properties, LLC, solely owned by Cory Black, is registered at a home owned by the (successful) Monarch Dispensary applicant and CEO, Sunny Mullineaux's husband, and shows the same PO Box address as the Cannabis Tax measure 'Yes on L' Campaign. State records show Principal Officer and Treasurer Cory Black as the sole decision-maker of both Sunny Coast Properties, LLC and the 'Yes on L' campaign.

Two of the other successful dispensary applicants are also dark donors; i.e., the donations are not made in the name of the applicant or the dispensary—they are The Milkman and 805 Beach Breaks. The Fair Political Practices Commission fined Black in 2016 for hiding the source of donations to San Luis Obispo Mayor Jan Marx. At other times, Mayor Shoals and Supervisor Hill also donated to Lee. They have also been fined by the FPPC for unfair political practices.

When researched online the campaign statement by Mayor Jeff Lee for the period ended 12.31.17 reveals that 29 of the 46 largest donorations were cannabis related. Of the 29, 17 were employees, owners, or consultants for the city's seven selected dispensaries. Those 17 donors and the other 12 cannabis related donors had planning applications on file with the city. Nineteen of the 29 canabis-related donors were colleagues, employees, or clients of the 'Yes on Grover Beach Measure L16' campaign. Eight of the cannabis related donors were employed by or subsidiaries of Cory Black.

The cabal also held fundraisers and charitable events, and even set up The Grover Beach Foundation for the stated purpose of funding deserving causes in Grover Beach. Shoals and Adam Hill stacked the Foundation board with their friendlies. Of course, all the councilmembers and city staff could attend these events and of course the cash could flow at children's Easter egg hunts and Christmas and Easter turkey handouts.

Political Ideology is Nothing More than a Means to an End

Its dogma is the magic spell that unlocks the treasure chest. SLO County's Supervisor Hill knew how to spread a thin veneer of leftist philosophy and a sprinkling of Dem-speak to woo those higher up in the political system who, not knowing his true colors, would support him based on party and name recognition, or party voters who would cast their vote based on well-placed inferences.

People reported having informal conversations with Hill when he was first elected in 2008 in which he laughed about the assumption many of his supporters made that he would be a slow-growth advocate, when in reality he never met a development he didn't like, and analysis reveals that he had no legitimate discernible ideological political differences between his chosen party and the opposing political party. In fact, he was more pro-growth and more tied in with developers than any of his right-wing opponents. Hill had close ties with the PG&E nuclear power plant and took more money from developers and big business than any of his Republican counterparts. His activities bore little resemblance to that of his professed party, and like the Pendergast political machine, while loudly claiming adherence to Democratic values with state political higher-ups and his pet newspaper, he acted in ways more traditionally associated with those of conservative values. He knew where the money was and headed straight to it.

White Collar Crime Methodologies

Frustrated with the seeming lack of interest of any higher authorities or outside press, I began to question how much crime goes unaddressed. In a CBS *Moneywatch* news report on May 11, 2015, Bruce Kennedy wrote:

> "White collar crime is not as dramatic and clear-cut as violent crime, but its financial impact is much greater. The federal Financial Crisis Inquiry Commission, which investigated the causes of the 2008 Great Recession, concluded that along with financial regulation failures and breakdowns in corporate governance, "systemic breaches in accountability and ethics at all levels" played a large part in the crisis. Fraud, con jobs, theft, and embezzlement reportedly cost U.S. taxpayers between $300 billion and $600 billion annually—compared to the $100 billion generated by the illegal drug trade. The best deterrent for white collar crime is … to have strong internal financial integrity practices "reviewed by external independent auditors who are properly educated, skilled, trained and experienced." Sam Antar, a former CPA and convicted white-collar criminal, writes on his White Collar Fraud web site. 'Strong internal controls create barriers to crime and result in the increased integrity of financial information.'"

These same sound practices protect the people from the enemies within their government. White collar punishment does not fit the crime—while the financial value of white collar crime is as much as six times greater than the illegal drug trade, the penalties are much lower. In my county, white collar crime and illegal drug dealing often go together. It is one thing to be an old-time vigilante as described in Gregory's book. It is quite another to fight the good fight against white collar crime. It requires that you get one step ahead when, as Carl Knudson says, you are already ten steps behind. This white collar crime, dubbed by the FBI "Paper Terrorism", steals far more from us and is punished far less severely than other categories of crime.

As I sought to understand what was happening around me, I discovered that many of the methods used to divert government funds span centuries, and once proven to work fraudsters repeat them over and over, often with increasingly less caution and broader application as they succeed time and again. Modern day gangsters not only control their subservients and local government; they have the tools to manipulate public opinion with powerful effect through instant social media, thus influencing voters earlier than ever before. Examination of the historical role of machines illuminates the situation in our county today.

Diversion

In SLO County, the social services that kept the machines in power last century are still significantly underfunded this century. The huge need then and now enabled machine operatives to bolster their credibility by claiming a concern for the needy, when in reality their skimming of tax dollars was then, and remains now, the source of the inability to fund critically-needed rehab and mental health services, not just for the transient, not just to help reduce homeless numbers by treating addiction and mental health, but for families and seniors across the economic spectrum.

Rehab and mental health beds are critically low in our county; so low they can be counted on less than two hands. Our own supervisor had to go two counties south, more than a hundred miles, to a rehab facility for a mental health stay. Picture the toll it takes on a family when a parent or child needs overnight mental health services that are available only hundreds of miles away, or alternately, in the absence of mental health bed facilities, end up transported to the county jail. It is a vicious circle—we can't afford to provide the services and so the machine steps in, crowing about their good works as they fund Easter egg hunts and Christmas turkeys and donate to the homeless, a perpetual turkey and egg cycle.

Nearly all of the cannabis dispensary applicants claimed that their charitable works were donations to the homeless. And in many cases they really did make sizeable donations. Who better to help than the helpless who can't afford to refuse a handout and who don't have the resources or capacity to catch or call you out when you cheat?

Compliance

The SLO machine does not serve the poor; it merely claims concern for them. It serves those who can make them rich and those who seek enrichment by associating with the machine. Samuel Johnson said it best, "A Patron is one who looks with unconcern on a man struggling for life in the water, and, when he has reached ground encumbers him with help."

The boss may give you a job, but he will leave you in fear of losing your job. Michael Johnston observes that bosses remain bosses by "maintaining an imbalance of obligation in their favor."

Simply put, most of a boss's followers feel they owe the boss something, or at least they are obliged to support the boss actively if they are to win future benefits. For the majority of voters who continue to vote a party line, their future benefit is a candidate who "votes their way," rationalizing, "well, he's of the right party regardless of his behavior," or "he votes the way I want him to vote," meaning 'along party lines.'

A councilmember may reap the benefit by voting as requested when the county supervisor lobbies to remove your mayor from a committee because she dares to disagree with him. The supervisor sweetens the extortion when speaking at the lectern in public comment at the mayor's city council meeting, as Adam Hill did when he proclaimed, "I gave this much to your charities and struggling organizations, without which they could not carry out their missions. I can keep giving if you remove her from positions of authority."

Adam Hill, who had "owned" the city council since 2012, bestowed the county funds he was allocated to distribute depending on whether or not the locals followed his wishes, as he explained when lobbying the city council to remove me from the APCD where I was getting in his way, or when he refused funding to a highly effective, compassionate, creative housing charity because one of their workers had volunteered for my campaign when I ran against him for his supervisor seat.

For the average Joe, it's "Adam Hill or John Shoals did this for me." The boss gains compliance with his wishes because he offers to continue to fund local organizations, or to withhold funding, and does favors for constituents. Those who receive the benefit or avoid the punishment are complicit and perpetuate machine dependency. Machine bosses need to corrupt weaker beings to achieve their ends.

Favors

At the upper levels of the machine there is an opulent modus vivendi, whether it's expensive gambling habits, ambition, power, parties and drugs with developers, cocaine, sex, or wine. Like Pendergast, our SLO operatives have been careful not to leave a paper trail and careful not to live too high on the hog, but credible reports exist of vacations in suppliers' private planes to hunting lodges and tropical locations.

It is a legitimate business practice for a shareholder to hold shares as nominee for a principal unless the principal is seeking to evade tax or engage in an illegality. Pendergast hid his identity in corporations related to city business by allocating shares to family members or in company shares to loyal employees. Sometimes the favors are small infractions, as when our mayor's wife, overheard by one of my campaign volunteers in our local hardware store, asked for a discount and when clerks refused, responded with a coy, "But I'm the mayor's wife."

Logrolling is a term for a politician accepting promotion in exchange for agreeing to a policy may have been deemed corrupt, yet the political practice of representative A agreeing to vote for representative B's policies in exchange for B agreeing to vote for A's policies remains an acceptable part of American political life. Favors for votes. When does it cross the line?

The money flow is hard to identify because it is well camouflaged, and the power flow is harder still. In SLO County there was no outward obscenely high living but both Hill and Shoals had reputations as party animals, politically and socially. Think of the benefit for such individuals if they could bring cannabis interests to town…they could contract with unscrupulous dealers to set up legally approved cash businesses to supply narcotics.

Spin it Out

Another tactic that could keep the funds flowing was to spin out new projects. I found that the SSLOCSD administrator/engineer was a master at taking much more than the usual time to bring a new piece of equipment on, then working and reworking it, even to the point of legal action for which he was also paid, but I didn't realize how else it played out in my city until a few times people asked me, "How come nothing ever gets finished in Grover Beach?"

My theory? The longer it takes to complete public works, the more opportunity there is to keep collecting from the contractors, and the easier it is to make the excuse that prices just keep going up, thus raising prices, and getting more by way of annual kickbacks in exchange for keeping the projects on the books.

Contamination

Those at city level who were in a position to prosecute Pendergast's machine personnel did not do so because they owed their jobs and livelihoods to Pendergast. While this is true in cases in SLO today, there is a more subtle deterrent to whistleblowing. Take the case of the former government employee who sets up an engineering company. In his job as a government employee, he would have worked closely with county departments and staffers and would have prepared many staff reports and proposals to the board of supervisors over the 12 years during which he served as the county engineer. He would have interacted with hundreds of permit applicants—developers, contractors, architects, engineers.

Then, upon leaving the county and going into business on his own behalf, those relationships would remain and many more would develop as he came to administer dozens of additional government agencies, contracting as the engineer for numerous municipalities in three counties, bidding for government, commercial, and private infrastructure projects, chairing the regional engineers' association, and joining the prestigious city Rotary club. He would have worked with or had proposals approved by thousands of employees, elected representatives, and colleagues over the years.

There would be no advantage to anyone who ever worked with or associated with him to report questionable behavior because they and the whole county system and structure of engineers, administrators, politicians, and staff might come under public accusation of contamination by association. Once touched by the machine there is no safe way out. The yoke is strong and permanent. Complicity becomes the default position. Matlin argues that colleagues could overcome wrongdoing by exposing it, but when inert, are complicit.

If those associating with the machine are not just blinkered, but actual instigators, there is advantage in sticking together and necessity to continue to place people in positions of power to cover for their sins and the sins of predecessors. In the case of our sewer plant, the chairman's wife took his place on the city council and was the appointee to the board. In the neighboring city of Arroyo Grande, Adam Hill cabal favor seekers fought hard to discredit the honorable Mayor Jim Hill and to eliminate any city staffers who might have told the true story of city corruption if questioned by the authorities. To protect its position, the machine seeks to destroy the social credibility and financial or career stability of opponents so they have no platform to speak upon, or if they do, they will lack social standing and be too short of time and financial resources to launch a serious threat.

Loyalty is Everything

A fanatical spirit of personal loyalty marked the old-time machine, similar to the SLO machine's reverence for "collegiality." SLO machine opponents were exiled and told, "it would be best if you just left town."

If not driven out of town, the machine and its acolytes treated them as untouchables. My own party banished me while felons went unremarked and ethical violations of the FPPC Statement of Ethics (a signed pledge to operate fairly in politics) went unnoticed. 'Going along to get along' is the insurance that ensures job protection and the support of the SLO cabal for political advancement and appointments.

What's the Harm?

PATRONAGE IS POLITICAL PARTY LOSS

Thomas Dagger argues that "patronage interferes with the uninhibited, robust and wide-open discussion of public affairs."

Going along to get along takes precedence over discussion of public policy and party activity is subjugated to the advantages the machine offers.

Bossism violates the code of fair elections based on appraisal of candidates and issues, rather than loyalty to a leader; both bossism and patronage further the cause of bad leaders because they are based on blind loyalty to a leader or a party rather than selection based on skill, training, experience, education, and track record.

Morale Loss is a loss of confidence in the sanctity of constitutional values, which causes the public to lose trust in their government leading to widespread apathy, which further destroys the fabric of democracy.

The renowned American politician and sociologist Daniel Patrick Moynihan had this insight into the link between politics and crime: "An immobilized government is one where policy discussion is frozen and where response to demand by citizens for change is met with silence. If voters return that government to power time and again, democracy itself is threatened."

Obstruction of Free and Open Speech hinders best outcomes. Repeatedly, boards blocked operational audits of the administrator/engineer of our sewer district, and countless other public agencies in the region using the weasel words, "Let's just all move on. We're all good people here." They silenced and bamboozled citizens and the press who believed Supervisor Hill's "I'm the best friend you will ever have" and Wallace's "I am saving you so much money," even as these claims conflicted wildly with the facts. The greater the disparity between the truth of these claims and the facts, the more the citizens take the claims to heart.

Without a true operational audit, honest practitioners and the community lose an opportunity to learn how to do it better; how to hold elected and appointed representatives accountable to best practices on behalf of those they promise to serve. In blocking discussion of an audit and reorganization, the boards blocked the substantial financial benefits and good outcomes that public demand finally achieved.

Lack of Polical Will to take any retributive action is the outcome of patronage. There is no law allowing the removal of an elected board or councilmember. The stronger the machine becomes the less benefit there is for politicians and those exposed to the machine to change; thus thwarting any political will they might have had to ensure honest dealing.

Role Models

"All good citizens should observe and respect the law. It is impossible for parents to instill in their children right principles of citizenship when prominent citizens who have disregarded the law are received with public acclaim." Kansas City, Missouri Parent Teacher Council 1932

The challenge of the Kansas City PTA in 1932 protesting celebrating a Chamber president who had self-dealt millions of charity dollars resonated with me, because I had wrestled with the message we send to our young people by awarding an abusive colleague with a chairmanship of the board. Their words echoed throughout Kansas City for the next months. What are we teaching our future leaders? We are teaching them how to bully, how to coerce, how to steal from the public trust, and how to eradicate free thinkers or those who question the hierarchy. We are modeling that it is okay to do so; that we do not really care.

As Matlin said, "There are degrees of honesty, and very few people who can rightfully claim to be totally honest. Government, too, may not always act with perfect honesty, but democratic societies require that there should be no corruption in government, failing which, citizens can have no confidence that their political rulers have not been bought."

Economic Impact

Wallace was convicted of misdemeanors and repaid relatively small sums, and Hill was under investigation by the FBI at the time of his death, but the collateral damage in addition to the millions of dollars of reserves that disappeared under Wallace's "stewardship" was what could have been achieved had the sewer plant operated as it should have and for how much less. Where would the district be had it been run efficiently by high standards, or even reasonable standards?

Matlin argues that you cannot assess what the cost savings would have been if Kansas City had been operated ethically. I disagree. A municipal expert consultant or auditor certainly could come close, in the same way that agency managers and their teams estimate budget costs based on established municipal "industry" norms, or an economic impact study which estimates the effect of various influences.

Under a $40 million bond program, Kansas City constructed many civic buildings during the Depression. They kept people in jobs, building splendid public amenities: city hall, plazas, boulevards, museums, art centers, and inner-city high schools. They got good works done, addressing the needs of the poor when the government safety net was limited.

In San Luis Obispo County we also complete public works projects. But the question is not "did the Kansas City machine get some lasting good done?" It's, "how much more lasting good in the form of public works or social services would have been completed had the money flowed into the public treasury rather than out to the public self-servants?" If the $11m misappropriated by the machine had been available? If taxes had been paid on those earnings and added to the public till? If contracts and jobs had been filled based on merit and fair competition? Yes, the machine created jobs, but in the absence of the machine, greater stability and quality of life will flow from the economic impact generated by legitimate unfettered commerce.

The End

The demise of bosses usually arises out of their arrogance; when they self-destruct as victims of their excesses, whereby the justice system catches up with them, or their addictions destroy their health, mental or physical, or they must have more money than even their ill-gotten gains can support.

Pendergast's health declined, and in his later years his gambling addiction escalated, requiring extreme sums of money. The Fresno developers finally got caught when a whistle-blower of the "right" stature showed up. The duplicitous nature of the dispensary businesses approved by my city council—only those with felonies in the background reports of principals or spouses won dispensary permits—created a symbiotic relationship with political consultant Cory Black, Supervisor Adam Hill, Mayor Shoals and Mayor Pro Tem Lee. With dubious backgrounds, applicants for cannabis business licenses and permits needed Shoals and Black to create ordinances with loopholes that would allow them to operate and ensure they would be granted the necessary permits and licenses. Black, Hill, Shoals, and Lee in turn needed them, because those with clean backgrounds did not need "fixers" like Shoals and Black to establish credibility and were much less likely to pay to play. Shoals became even more valuable when, after being laid off as the PG&E government affairs representative, Santa Barbara County hired him as a planning supervisor. But the fixers were only valuable so long as they kept their government posts.

One thing they all had in common was that they couldn't take criticism and they were cowards. When someone disagreed, Hill would lash out with, "why is everybody picking on me?"

Shoals became self-righteous, even tearful, scolding anyone who spoke 'unkindly.' Their loyal supporters bought into both responses. When scheduled for a media interview shortly after sexually harassing three city staffers, Shoals called the host in tears, saying he had cheated on his wife and he was afraid someone would call in about it and he couldn't do the interview. It wasn't until he was promised that those calls would be screened that he agreed to appear.

When the FBI raided his home and his county office Supervisor Hill became a problem to those who had paid to play with him. A high public profile proved valuable to Supervisor Hill and cronies. That same public profile left them exposed. If they lost their elected or staff positions of power, or were prosecuted, they would not just lose their usefulness to the machine, they would become liabilities. Their felonious associates would know that they were cowards and would "talk" to save themselves. Overnight they could move from being indispensable to being dispensable to criminals whose reputations extended far beyond bullying and white collar crime, and whose networks and finances far exceeded those of small-town politicians. Furthermore, the devil these politicians were dancing with was their source of cocaine, and without government jobs and influence, their expensive supply dried up along with their income, leaving them at the mercy of drug dealers with increasingly more motive to lace their products with the lethal opiates that are now killing people at a far higher rate in San Luis Obispo County than the state or the nation.

Shoals, after years of showing up at government conferences with buxom beauties on his arm, and reputed sexual harassment, must have come to believe his indiscretions would always be protected, forgiven, and allowed. But just as his wife left him, his luck seemed to fail and he had his own #MeToo moment. Perhaps he had become too cocky for the 21st century, because the County of Santa Barbara and its female staffers were not willing to give him a pass or to run interference when he harassed female staff members. Claims of sexual harassment were found credible, and Shoals resigned. With no government position, and exposure of his behaviors, Shoals not only lost his value to the cabal but became a threat, attracting unwanted attention. Three years after my request that the council publicly eschew support for those who sexually harass staff or the public, the mayor got his comeuppance from a more evolved county government than ours.

KSBY TV reported that Shoals had resigned after a year on the job as a supervising planner for Santa Barbara County. County documents confirm that a woman working in his department complained that Shoals often asked her out for drinks after work, asked her to stand up and looked her up and down, shared inappropriate stories with her, and leered at her and an attractive customer. Shoals denied the claims, saying he did not believe he had harassed her.

If they could no longer function as government favor brokers, Shoals as the Santa Barbara County cannabis plant or Hill as the SLO purveyor of favorable votes on permits, their personal power would lay in squealing and dealing with the feds, betraying former beneficiaries and acolytes to protect themselves.

Supervisor Hill's collection of abuses were catching up with him, too. He was under investigation by the FBI, he was losing his political power base, and his assistant had accused him of sexual exploitation. He stopped attending board of supervisor and committee meetings, claiming depression. His publicly-funded health plan would cover a stay in a mental health facility for a period of time during which he could hide while questioned by investigators, but that would run out in weeks or months. Who would protect him when he returned home? On hearing that he was back in town, I commented to friends that I hoped the authorities were providing him somewhere safe, because in Shell Beach he would not live long. Within just hours of my conversations with friends, the news came out that he was dead. His only hope for survival would have been witness protection.

To the oblivious who think, "Oh well, now that Adam Hill is gone this whole business of the FBI raid of Hill's home and county office is over," or those who snipe, "Get over it, Debbie, he's dead," I say, "Adam was in way over his head. This is only the beginning."

Is his death not, in itself, a red flag? Adam was not the kingpin; he was merely a signpost to something much, much bigger.

JULY 28, 2021
Department of Justice: Cannabis King Confesses to Bribing Supervisor Hill and Mayor Shoals

The plea bargain outlined in court documents in which Dayspring confessed to bribing Hill and attempting to bribe Shoals indicated that Dayspring had confessed to the FBI in June 2020, just three months after the March raids, in the hope of securing a more lenient sentence than the possible thirteen years he faced. Together with his attorney, Dayspring agreed to cooperate with any government agency anywhere in the United States or abroad. The public were unaware of the results of the raids until thirteen months later in July 2021 when the plea bargain was filed.

The announcement that follows is downloaded from the Department of Justice (DOJ) website. It comes two and a half years after I resigned, citing what is now coming out in news reports. It takes years and years for the judicial system to bring down criminal enterprises. The DOJ must have a strong case before even requesting a warrant, and then afterward must cross every 't' and dot every 'i,' pulling in as many provable crimes and criminals as possible, especially the kingpin, before pressing charges.

Operatives do not share information outside of their immediate partnership or team to protect the security of the investigation, and the district attorney's office cannot discuss investigations lest a case be thrown out of court. In Fresno, it was more than twelve years from the first complaint to the final lawsuit. In Kansas City, it was eleven years. Along the way it seems as if nothing is happening. What gets it started are the complaints of brave citizens who want their communities to be the best that they can be. As incredibly frustrating as it is—in my case, I resigned when I could do no more and started to write this book—I am glad that the authorities are thorough. I am glad because I know that what is coming out in dribs and drabs through court filings and press releases is just the tip of the iceberg. I know there is so much more that even in ten years they will not get, just as there is more that I cannot write.

United States Department of Justice
THE UNITED STATES ATTORNEY'S OFFICE
CENTRAL DISTRICT of CALIFORNIA

FOR IMMEDIATE RELEASE
Wednesday, July 28, 2021

San Luis Obispo Man Agrees to Plead Guilty to Bribing County Supervisor to Vote on Issues Affecting His Cannabis Businesses

LOS ANGELES—Federal prosecutors today filed a criminal information charging a San Luis Obispo man with bribery for paying a county supervisor approximately $32,000—most of that in cash—in exchange for the supervisor's votes and influence on other votes affecting his cannabis business interests.

Helios Raphael Dayspring, a.k.a. "Bobby Dayspring," 35, was charged in federal court with one count of bribery and one count of subscribing to a false 2018 income tax return that deliberately failed to report millions of dollars in income to the IRS.

Federal Prosecutors today also filed a plea agreement in which Dayspring agreed to plead guilty to both felony offenses, pay $3-4 million in restitution to the IRS, and cooperate in the government's ongoing investigation.

According to the court documents, Dayspring owned, operated, and/or had a controlling interest in multiple farms that grew cannabis in San Luis Obispo County. He also had ownership interests in businesses that sold marijuana to the public, including in Grover Beach. To further his interests in the farms that grew cannabis in San Luis Obispo County, Dayspring began paying bribes to a San Luis Obispo County supervisor in the fall of 2016 and continued doing so through November 2019.

In total, Dayspring paid the late Third District supervisor multiple bribes in cash and money orders totaling $32,000. In exchange, the supervisor voted on matters affecting Dayspring's farms, including voting multiple times in favor of legislation that permitted Dayspring's farms to operate before it had obtained final permitting approvals.

In addition to bribing the San Luis Obispo County supervisor, Dayspring admitted in his plea agreement that he and his business associate attempted to bribe the then-mayor of Grover Beach in exchange for two dispensary licenses in that city. The attempted $100,000 bribe took place during a dinner meeting in September 2017. The mayor did not respond to the offer and Dayspring did not pay the bribe.

Dayspring also admitted that he substantially underreported his personal income on his federal tax return for the years 2014 through 2018, which resulted in the IRS losing more than $3-4 million in tax revenue.

Dayspring has agreed to surrender in this case and make his first appearance in United States District Court in Los Angeles on August 25. Once he pleads guilty to the bribery and tax charges, Dayspring will face a statutory maximum penalty of 13 years in federal prison.

The FBI and IRS Criminal Investigation investigated this matter, which is part of an ongoing public corruption investigation in San Luis Obispo County.

Any member of the public who has information related to this case or any other public corruption matter in San Luis Obispo County is encouraged to send information to the FBI's email tip line at pctips-losangeles@fbi.gov or to contact the FBI's Los Angeles Field Office at (310) 477-6565.

Assistant United States Attorney Thomas F. Rybarczyk of the Public Corruption and Civil Rights Section is prosecuting this case.

People ask why someone would sell out for $32,000, as indicated in the FBI press release. What's not being considered is that this is just one instance. This is what was confessed to by one man for a few transactions. This is the one that got caught. There have been many people bribing and many accepting bribes in many situations for many years. The sellout is not just $32,000. I want the Justice Department to have as much time as it needs to gather as much information as it can. I also want the people to do their part, as requested by the FBI. If you have firsthand knowledge of a crime, please report it. If you don't, it will most likely continue and get worse.

Once the Justice Department has reached the stage of asking for tips, as in the story below, they are certain there is a problem. It's up to us to help them to clean it up.

What gets it finished is the ongoing combined efforts of citizens, law enforcement, and the judicial system. If they can root out or prevent crime in local government, we all reap the rewards of a safer, more positive community.

Where is SLO County in this timeline? We are at the stage of our biggest opportunity. The opportunity to provide more information to the justice system if we have it, and the opportunity to work together to create something better that will stay better. The next four chapters suggest how we can do that.

Based on everything I have experienced and observed, I believe that these Justice Department releases are carefully crafted with a purpose. Assuming I am right, five phrases stand out to me.

The first is, "part of an ongoing public corruption investigation in San Luis Obispo County," i.e., it's not just about narcotics now, as it was in the 2019 DOJ podcast in a previous chapter. It's about ongoing public (government) corruption in San Luis Obispo County.

Second, Shoals was bribed but didn't take the bribe. Unless they have good reason to believe that Shoals was in on it and are seeking more information there is no reason to mention him.

Third is, "any member of the public who has information related to this case or any other public corruption matter in San Luis Obispo County." This is important. If you know of public corruption in San Luis Obispo County, this is how to report it.

Fourth, tips go to the Los Angeles field office. This is big; bigger than just our little county.

Fifth, the federal department of Public Corruption and Civil Rights are prosecuting the release. Indeed, it should be a civil right to be free of public corruption.

I will argue in the chapters that follow that because our government has grown so large and complex, we need additional checks and balances; in effect, social recognition of more estates committed to exercising oversight, more so when power is decentralized. I am not making a case for bigger government but for a reboot of how we think about government and its role today.

NOV 19, 2020
Hill's Assistant Paid off by County

KSBY News reported that San Luis Obispo County settled with Hill's assistant. Her redacted complaint was dated July 27th, ten days before Hill's demise. The complaint stated that she met Hill in October 2017 and entered into a sexual relationship before going to work for him. She said she broke off the relationship in October 2019, but remained friends with Hill, who continued to touch her inappropriately, and that she feared retaliation for ending their relationship. While the county does not admit liability, it did pay her six months' salary (more than $39,000) plus vacation pay, and covered six months of COBRA insurance payments.

"Al Capone would not have existed if decent men in Chicago had not for decades handed government over to the least desirable class of citizenship."

-Florence Allen

PART 4

THE SEVEN UNITED ESTATES

"The beauty of the American political system rests upon the fact that the citizen-voter is not required to place trust in the politicians for whom he or she votes. …the separation of powers paradigm provides checks and balances on the three estates of government. In theory, each estate can prevent the other two estates from abusing power. However, at a local government level if one estate abuses power and the other two estates are unwilling or unable to stop such abuse, the citizen is left unprotected."

—John Matlin, Ph.D.

CHAPTER 11 THE FOURTH ESTATE
Lapdog or Watchdog?

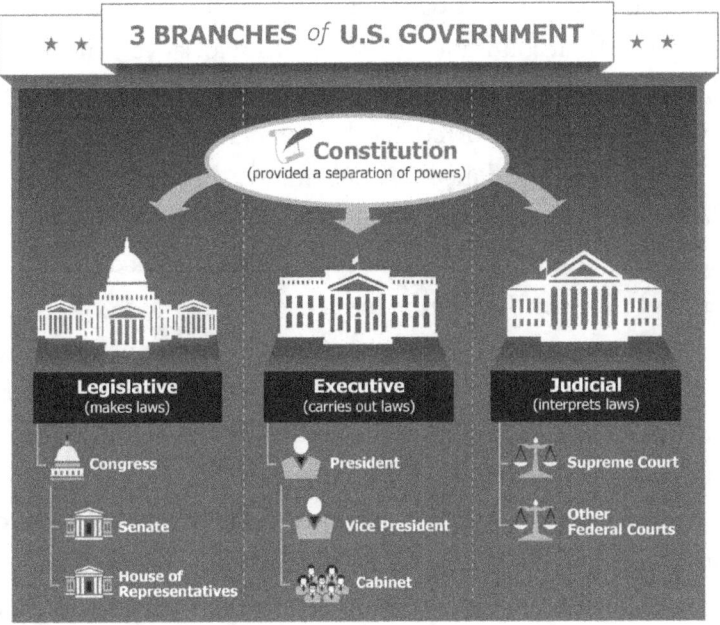

3 BRANCHES *of* **U.S. GOVERNMENT**

Constitution
(provided a separation of powers)

Legislative (makes laws)	Executive (carries out laws)	Judicial (interprets laws)
Congress	President	Supreme Court
Senate	Vice President	Other Federal Courts
House of Representatives	Cabinet	

While it is flattering to think, as expressed in the quote at the beginning of this Part 4, that our system of government is so beautifully constructed that citizens need not worry about trusting their representatives because systemic checks and balances are in place; the American voter DOES rely on elected representatives to serve his or her best interest. The American citizen has always been an essential part of government, without whom we founder. We have grown so much larger, both geographically and in population, that we need checks and balances that go much deeper and wider than those we needed when our Constitution was written. We need fourth, fifth, sixth, and even seventh estates in addition to the three estates set out in the constitution: the Legislative—Congress (Senate and House of Representatives) makes laws, Executive—(President, Vice President, Cabinet) carries out laws, and Judicial (Supreme Court and other Federal Courts) interprets the laws.

The three branches of government are referred to as the "Three Estates," established so that no one estate can take the others over. The press is referred to as the Fourth Estate because it has the capacity to hold government accountable. Media scrutiny of government is needed to preserve the sanctity of the separation of the Estates, and all the more so if that separation of powers has been violated. A look at the origins and meaning of the word 'media' is informative. From Latin, its meanings include 'form of transmission, intermediary, and more far-fetched, but illustrative that almost clairvoyance is sometimes needed to fact check— the plural of 'medium' in the psychic sense.

In cases of corruption the, press and media are often either accused of turning a blind eye/complicit or accused of sensationalizing or muckraking in the pejorative sense. The press and media, especially smaller local publications, are vulnerable to the same social coercion, tunnel vision, and economic or physical retribution as their fellow business owners and citizens. The beleaguered press can't afford not to cooperate with bad actors—they need sources, good stories, and advertising income in order to survive.

A quick internet review of the history and culture of journalism provides articles describing up to twenty-one different journalistic styles, but for the purposes of this chapter I will discuss the three that most affect fourth estatehood.

Propagandist journalists are those who report from a government perspective. While this is often considered a style used in non-democratic countries, it is not difficult to find propagandist journalists and media in the United States. When a news source aligns its editorial political platform too closely with those in political power, the paper may be nothing more than a mouthpiece for the political allies who feed reporters easy stories and provide copy. This is particularly odious because failure to fact check when informants pass on opinions enable the smear campaigns that, when printed and reprinted often enough, become "fact" in the minds of readers.

The journalistic style my professors taught me in high school and college was that of reporter—simply reporting the news without bias. Although it was considered legitimate to write human interest feature stories, the bias being that they were stories that, while newsworthy, were written to evoke positive 'feel good' emotions or empathy and draw in readers as light relief from hard news stories.

When my grandmother was in journalism school in 1920, I expect she would have been familiar with the tradition of "muckraking journalism." It is not something I recall hearing about from instructors in the seventies as a journalism student. Muckraking journalism had its heyday from 1890 until about 1915, and asserted that 'air is the best disinfectant.' The term muckraker was used in the turn of the 19th century Progressive Era to characterize reform-minded American journalists who took on corporate monopolies and political machines to raise public awareness and umbrage at urban poverty, unsafe working conditions, prostitution, and child labor. While most muckrakers followed a journalistic tradition, some, such as Upton Sinclair, have had lasting influence through their fictional accounts of the times.

Lincoln Steffen's series of muckraking articles on city politics and government in 1904 drew national attention to corrupt political machine bosses. However, then, as now, unless the muckraking tradition was the niche sector of the publication, there was usually too much for the proprietors to lose to do in-depth investigative reporting. Newspapers face the same ethical dilemma as the city manager and the city attorney—their financial survival depends on keeping the majority in power sweet, not on unbiased reporting. Muckraking is differentiated from "sensationalism," the use of salacious eye-popping headlines and stories to capture reader interest—the print version of digital "clickbait," with little regard for accuracy or serious news reporting.

Muckraking was the forerunner of investigative journalism as we know it today. Woodward and Bernstein of the *Washington Post* generated a revival of investigative reporting in the 1970s with their Watergate exposé. Investigative reporting takes months of research and puts the proprietor at risk of defamation lawsuits and litigation or even awards for damages, and for the individual journalist, it also takes courage. Depending on the subject matter, advertisers might jump ship if linked to an investigation.

The 'detached watchdog' journalism style is closest to the straight reporting style I was taught in journalism classes. The watchdog journalist covers issues and events, keeping the public informed. The watchdog is the journalistic version of the whistleblower—carefully fact-checking and alerting the public to matters that affect it and that citizens would not countenance if they knew about them. It is the investigative Washington Post watchdog reporters Woodward and Bernstein whose reporting led to the resignation of President Nixon.

The objective of the watchdog journalist is to write without bias, reporting the facts that the public otherwise might not have ready access to, but that could also prevent the abuse of power. Just as elected representatives must be free from outside financial influence, journalists must be free from the financial control of advertisers in order to perform as watchdogs completely and credibly. Journalists must distance themselves from ruling powers and challenge them, unlike "propagandist" journalists, whose loyalty is to those in power.

Woodward's 2018 book *Fear* opens with a note to readers defining 'deep background' as "the person being interviewed said it could be used but that they could not be named." Woodward encourages investigative journalists to use even more deep-background sources.

Woodward told *Business Insider's* Alan Smith on October 12, 2018, that he and Bernstein turned to using unnamed sources because otherwise "you can't get the truth." *The Daily* quotes Woodward, "Without allowing anonymity we wouldn't have got the most important stories about Watergate."

Woodward describes unnamed sources as "people who are willing to talk are people of conscience, people of courage, people who said, 'Look, the world needs to know this.'" On NBC's *Today* show, Woodward explained, "When information is highly sensitive or could get someone in trouble, people just aren't going to provide it on the record."

By way of example, Woodward noted that officials who decried the book's contents in public have privately told him it's accurate. "After the information in *Fear* started breaking, one key person in office called me and said, 'Everyone knows what you said here is true, it's a thousand percent correct.' And then this person had said some public things that contradict that. And I am not happy, but I have a smile on my face because the truth in all of this is going to emerge. There's too much evidence, too many witnesses."

The editor of the *Kansas City Star* for 20 years, William M. Reddig, tells the story of my first hometown in his book, *Tom's Town—Kansas City and the Pendergast Legend*, published by the University of Missouri in 1947.

Pendergast was able to hang on to power at the highest levels because he could hide from public exposure by the local press. This was apparent over the eighteen years in which he and cronies and the Missouri insurance companies re-appropriated their customers' money. Newspapers should have been broadcasting alarm at the massive fraud in which Pendergast was implicated and demanding restitution of substantial funds for citizens—their readers. Although *The Star* had called for an end to the litigation in a forceful editorial on October 9, 1934, it then failed to follow the story with further editorials or even an article. This raises the question as to whether it was simply an oversight that the press failed to cover the settlement when legal precedent was against the insurers, having lost in court in 1929. There is nothing to corroborate that the press colluded with the machine to avoid the issue. Neither is there evidence that the paper did not collude with Pendergast.

While *The Star* was not so unprofessional as to be a propogandist newspaper for the Pendergast machine, as was the smaller newspaper, *The Democrat*, it was often more lapdog than watchdog when it came to reporting crime.

How Do You Fact Check When There are No Facts?

In the 1930s, Kansas City's local newspapers as a whole often failed to inform their readership. It is arguable that even the most inquisitive of investigative journalists might not have uncovered the evidence of Pendergast's insurance payouts or civic manipulation. Historians and even the best U.S. Treasury investigator of his day, R. Hartman, point out that due to lack of paper trails, they had only hearsay of suspected and alleged Pendergast criminal activities and of his corporate ownerships, although they managed to compile the equivalent of a small telephone directory of Pendergast-controlled corporations.

Further complicating any investigation of the insurance scandal was that two of the bagmen for Pendergast had died by the time the settlement came to trial. The length of time that these cases dragged through the courts is also a failing, but one of the legal system. As time passes people forget, move on, pass away, and statutes of limitation kick in, illustrating the truth of the proverb, "Justice delayed is justice denied."

The conundrum? If the Pendergast business was suspect or corrupt, who would provide the evidence? Those involved certainly wouldn't talk. Those not involved would fear reprisals. Pendergast had no real competitors who would dish the dirt and he kept people happy, which would have been a further disincentive for speaking against him. Difficulty in verifying information made Pendergast "bulletproof." The press couldn't fact check, and so were stymied in their reporting.

This is why, as Woodward advocates, investigative reporting even when writers cannot disclose the source is critical in holding government accountable. It also speaks to the disingenuousness of my city hall exclaiming, when I resigned, that I never told them about the corruption (which, in fact, I did repeatedly, as documented in videos of council meetings at the time and recounted in previous chapters) and that I didn't provide any names or examples.

They knew I couldn't betray my informants by publicly providing names, dates, and events. Whether or not I provided names or examples was irrelevant because they knew very well what corruption I was referring to and knew exactly the names they claimed I didn't give, and more to which I didn't allude. In addition to their weak attempt at discrediting me, by appearing to be in the dark they may have been hoping to goad me into giving away what I knew so they would know what I had on them.

There is another deterrent today. Whistleblowers remain unprotected when speaking to the press and media. They may be willing to provide testimony to law enforcement with the knowledge that protection could be available and that the offender may be taken away. They have no protection if speaking to the press. Neither do journalists or publishers in that role.

Following the violent 1934 city election, *The Kansas City Star* launched extensive reporting on election fraud and abuses by the Democratic machine, which led to reforms enacted by the 1938 state legislature. This reporting, since it wasn't aimed at an individual, but at a process, was slightly less dangerous than reporting on Pendergast's corrupt activities.

"Make nice with Adam Hill"

Matlin surmised that not only could Pendergast have influenced advertisers to withdraw their support, thereby damaging a small newspaper financially and beyond the point of remaining in business, but Mafia henchmen like Lazio could have threatened and perpetrated personal violence as well as vandalism of the newspaper's building and fixtures, in the knowledge that the machine-controlled Kansas City Police Department would do little or nothing. It is little wonder that none of the small news outlets mounted any kind of challenge to Pendergast's power and that criticisms of the machine rarely condemned a machine member by name.

I have sympathy for the people in fear. It doesn't seem right to me that business owners should be punished for doing what they must do to survive in a corrupt system. I want them to be able to report corruption without being harmed. While they may have played along, the alternative was financial ruin, or worse.

Local online news source *CalCoastNews* is controversial, in part because Hill and those Velie exposéd have attacked it with poisonous lies that others have repeated and many have believed, while believing that the criminals exposed are either the victims or upstanding citizens. One of *CalCoastNews's* missions has been "to shine a light on the conduct of government officials which would have otherwise remained secret to the public."

CalCoastNews reporting has led to the exposure of more than a half dozen government employees for financial wrongdoing. The publication powerfully influenced the eventual turnaround of my sewer district and of several other districts previously and currently under investigation. Its reporting has led to the conviction of several real estate developer conmen who bilked locals for millions of dollars, draining their retirement accounts, and has been instrumental in exposing the illegal exploits in the cannabis industry.

In a court case filed in March 2019, two weeks after the FBI raided Hill's home and county office, Velie tells the story of the treatment that she and advertisers in her publication faced. Velie had been printing stories of misappropriation of donations for the homeless by Hill's fiancée, reported by her employees and colleagues. A businessman told Velie he was having trouble with a planning permit. A county employee told him to "make nice with Adam Hill" and the process would go smoother. The businessman took it as a threat to stop advertising with *CalCoastNews* or he would continue have difficulties with the County. The businessman showed three texts to Velie. In one text, Hill said he was working "to destroy CCN through a lawsuit," and if the businessman "did not stop advertising, he would go down with Velie."

The businessman later called Velie and asked her to stop writing about county government and SLO homeless issues. He told her that he had spoken with Hill about the permit issues and that Hill told him that if he agreed to call Velie and ask her to stop writing about homeless services, Hill would get King's issue resolved.

The businessman wrote in his declaration that Hill's intent was malicious, "It is one thing to be fairly exercising the First Amendment right by commenting on news-related matters and the persons involved in delivering the news, such as Karen Velie, and another to make statements that are intended to induce a person to take another course of action or face the threat or possibility of adverse governmental action for failing to do so."

He was one of many significant advertisers who ceased advertising due to harassment by Hill and his trolls.

Hill's next move was to have his troll claim that Velie had made a post on *Reddit* about anal sex and cocaine, using an apparently photoshopped *Reddit* post with her email address. This incited the editor of the local weekly, the *New Times*, to write on social media that Velie needed to be run out of town. Velie was threatened by a respondent to that post who then accosted her in person in front of a witness who reported the incident to the DA. The DA did not act, allowing 12 months to pass until the statute of limitations ran out. Not long after, a drowned cat was left on her front porch, and then the family dog was left on the front porch, having died, bleeding from every orifice, apparently poisoned. Velie faithfully reported these and other incidents to the sheriff's department, but no action was ever taken.

Although Hill denied that he paid and said he hardly knew troll, Aaron Ochs, Ochs in a later deposition reported regular conversations in which Hill advised him of Velie's "mental illnesses." Ochs also became an apparent sudden friend of Adam Hill's, appearing with him in photographs taken at Hill parties and political functions. Ochs returned the denial, decrying Hill postmortem when the FBI reported Hill's extortion.

Meanwhile, for twelve months Velie had been receiving emails from a County IP address from a "Kevin 99." Although government agencies are required by law to have email policies and protocols, when Velie reported it to a county supervisor, the supervisor was told that the County did not keep track of email users. After receiving nearly fifty such emails, in October 2015, Velie informed County Counsel Rita Neal that someone was utilizing a county IP address to attack her and her family, her business, and candidates for office. Neal said there was nothing she could do because the County cannot track IP addresses. When Velie then sent in a records request asking for all information regarding the emails, Neal responded, stating that the Internet Protocol address came from the social services building, but that there was no way to track who has used the IP address.

Another advertiser, a former elected representative, told her that Hill had asked him to stop advertising. When he refused, the trolls began to post that he was only advertising because Velie was blackmailing him. Eventually the ongoing harassment made it necessary for him to cease advertising for a year.

Velie rarely backed down on a story, but even Velie's tolerance for abuse had a limit. Several confidential sources told her during interviews that Hill was consulting for PB Companies and its owners, developer Ryan Petetit and attorney John Belsher, who were paying Hill $20,000 a month. Her sources included a former employee, two investors, two of Petetit's ex-girlfriends, and Petetit's former roommate. Hill denied that he consulted for developers, but the attacks on her advertisers and children escalated. People parked at the end of her driveway, following her and her family and blocking their entry.

After interviewing one of Petetit's ex-girlfriends, Velie received this warning in an email: "One last thing, please be careful as well. He has told me a couple of times he wants you gone, and he would pay someone off to get rid of you! Just be careful and watch your back!"

When Velie called the informant, she was told that Petetit was looking to hire a hit man to have Velie killed because of the documents she had obtained showing fraud and the connection between Petetit and Hill, which "could ruin everything."

Because of the threats, intimidation, harassment, and fear of harm to her family, Velie did not write the story.

I know of no agony greater than losing a child. In early 2016, Velie's 19-year-old daughter died in a tragic accident caused by a seizure. The trolls posted a photo of Velie and her daughter when she was born, calling her 'Satan's Spawn,' and posted photos of her deceased stepfather, also with demeaning comments. The troll went on to claim that Velie and Kevin Rice had murdered her daughter. There are other tragic instances of Velie's family being horribly abused by the machine, but I will not write about events affecting any of Hill's targets' children. They deserve privacy and protection. That is their story to tell.

Reporter Dan Blackburn's account of machine damage to both he and Velie, *A Failed Try to Kill CalCoastNews*, follows at the end of the chapter.

Symbiosis

At the end of the day, *The Star*'s owners and Pendergast needed to rely on each other to protect their respective business interests. The interests of Pendergast and the proprietors of *The Star* dovetailed, and both were likely to be materially adversely affected if they reported machine corruption. To this extent, even *The Star* would have been compromised. In the case of SLO County newspapers, cannabis companies place regular ads ranging from full page to classifieds. The question that the papers don't discuss is how much money they make from confessed felon Helios Dayspring's cannabis businesses. Nevertheless, members of the press have a choice: to enable the machines by not reporting or to "see something and say something." But as we so often find in SLO County, the machine had power over the first, second, third, and also the fourth estate.

Using the Press and Media to Humiliate Opponents

The Star's rival, *The Democrat*, with a propagandist approach to journalism, consistently favored Pendergast and denigrated Mayerberg, never addressing his platform, going so far as to accuse him of being a communist and having KKK and terrorist connections. By making untrue extreme claims, they deflected Mayerberg's inflammatory tactics (although true claims) with their own fabrications. These attacks and deprecation were reminiscent of the kind of scorn Hill and his cronies heaped on me in every way they could think of. People believe and repeat allegations and accusations when published by the media. Such tactics stifled "naysayers" who knew that to stand up to Adam Hill would be to suffer a beating in the local paper and threats to their children. This is the treatment SLO County senators, mayors, supervisors, and businesspeople got for attending a meeting the machine doesn't like, or speaking against a favored project of the boss, or for advertising. This is the threat that moved political opponents out of races and silenced opposing views, even more fiercely when it included exposing rumors about minor children or health issues of children. Trolls set up Facebook pages alleging fraud, then posted stories on *Topix* or fake posts on *Reddit*, and then reposted the libels on Facebook. Hill then posted on his Facebook page asking his thousands of followers to re-post and "like" the slurs.

Bad Players Make Good Copy

I suspect, with even more cynicism perhaps than a seasoned reporter, that to shut down these bad actors would be to shut down the drama that feeds the media story line and attracts readers. I suspect the same of my local newspaper, the *Tribune*—the "boss" controlled much of what they will and won't publish. A newspaper might continue the relationship to survive, or to create colorful copy or as the only means of staying afloat.

The New No News—Catch & Kill

The recent book and subsequent series by Ronan Farrow, *Catch and Kill*, reveals another way in which the press colludes to keep stories out of the mainstream media, by catching a story and then killing it. Is that why the media did not report that Shoals resigned following verified claims of sexual harassment on August 1, 2019, until December 2019?

County Garbage

The following article by Dan Blackburn illustrates the power of the modern-day SLO County machine to harm its enemies, in this case attempting to bankrupt an online media outlet and the families of the proprietors. In 2014, Velie received an offer of between $6 million and $8 million to acquire *CalCoastNews*, but when she disclosed the ongoing harassment and problems with interference with advertisers, the prospective buyers cancelled the offer.

Blackburn has a powerful journalistic and government pedigree. In his own words from his deposition in the March 2019 case filed against Hill, "I have been a professional journalist for my entire 55-year career, except for a seven-year stint with the Metropolitan Water District of Southern California and the California State Senate. I was a state capitol bureau chief for one of the nation's largest newspapers, the *Orange County Register*, and authored a best-selling account of an infamous serial murderess. I mention these facts because I can say—without the slightest exaggeration—that I have never witnessed, much less been embroiled in, such a chain of purposely-destructive activities as those aimed at Ms. Velie by Adam Hill and other officials of the County of San Luis Obispo."

A failed try to kill *CalCoastNews*
November 14, 2018
OPINION by DANIEL BLACKBURN
Courtesy of *CalCoastNews*

Six years ago, today, an article was published on *CalCoastNews* that would forever reshape the lives of its authors and their families—and ultimately those of the article's subjects.

The article discussed questionable practices by the county's garbage agency, the Integrated Waste Management Authority (IWMA), its 20-year manager William Worrell, and a favored contractor, Charles K. Tenborg. The article bore the bylines of Karen Velie and me.

A few weeks later, Worrell and Tenborg sent a demand for retraction. It would be declined. Then Tenborg filed the lawsuit; Worrell did not join. Now it is apparent why.

At the time, we were puzzled by Tenborg's choice of lawyers in filing the lawsuit, Kerr & Wagstaffe, a San Francisco law firm with a perceived reputation for representing First Amendment issues.

It was only much later that it was learned that Kerr & Wagstaffe has an ongoing 30-year-plus professional affiliation with local attorneys Adamski Moreski Madden Cumberland & Green LLP. Raymond Biering is a partner. He's also been counsel to the IWMA for the past 20 years, the guy whose legal opinions to Worrell and the IWMA board have led to the agency's current disarray and ongoing criminal investigation.

"Please be aware that my law firm has a close professional relationship with Mr. Tenborg's counsel, Jim Wagstaffe," Biering wrote in an email following the trial, in which he said he was declining to provide public information regarding issues at trial because of his relationship with Tenborg.

This relationship was never divulged by Wagstaffe. Instead, Wagstaffe told attorney James Duenow, a prominent patriarch in the San Luis Obispo County legal community, that the firms were not affiliated. It is a conflict for an attorney for a government agency to serve as counsel for consultants to the agency.

There's one place to look for overall culpability in the legal morass the IWMA currently finds itself in, and that's at Biering.

Nevertheless, the IWMA board today will consider assigning a contract for Adamski Moreski Madden Cumberland & Green to serve as the agency's counsel, simply demonstrating that some lessons are damned hard for some people to learn.

Wagstaffe, a dapper bantam rooster, was joined in Tenborg's representation by partner Ivo Labar, a hulking presence whose primary task seemed to be intimidation. One who was not intimidated was Duenow. He approached Wagstaffe during a break in the trial, asking if Wagstaffe knew he was "representing a polluter."

The comment was overheard by *New Times* reporter Chris McGuinness, who noted it in a brief article. McGuinness sat through the whole trial, to his credit, but as it turned out he didn't seem to absorb much of it. McGuinness was given government codes, rules, and laws covering issues disputed during trial, but nothing came of that.

The *New Times* was too busy attempting to discredit a competitor. These efforts continue to this very day.

It was an armchair turkey shoot for local media to determine the validity of the litigated report. They chose instead to dance upon what they prematurely thought would be our graves and that of *CalCoastNews*.

Introduction of much of our evidence was subsequently denied by Judge Barry LaBarbera on a series of technicalities. In the end, LaBarbera rejected 11 of 13 witnesses we planned to present.

We were the proverbial lambs led to slaughter. While our lawyers diddled, Wagstaffe and Labar trotted out a dog-and-pony show worthy of Perry Mason. The jury found, 11-1, that we had embarrassed and hurt Tenborg's feelings in defaming him and awarded him $1.1 million. This, despite testimony that made clear that neither Velie nor I had two nickels to rub together.

The lone juror siding with us approached us immediately following the verdict, introduced himself, and said he was a recent naturalized citizen of the United States of America. He said none of his fellow jurors "understood the First Amendment."

The *New York Times, Los Angeles Times* and other major publications reported on the trial result, receiving the tip compliments of county supervisor Adam Hill and one of his blogging buddies.

Hill has boasted often and publicly that he is the juice behind the lawsuit; he was incoming president of the IWMA board when the lawsuit was filed.

Hill long has nurtured a grudge against *CalCoastNews*, the only news entity to report on his unethical behavior and exploitation of his public office. A long series of articles in 2010-11 focused on the activities of Dee Torres, who ran the homeless division of Community Action Partnership of San Luis Obispo (CAPSLO).

She was placed on leave and left the agency following *CalCoastNews* reports of her abuse of gift cards intended for the homeless at Christmas.

We didn't know it at the time, but Torres and Hill were in a relationship. They have since married. And Hill went off.

Hill and his sycophant blogger fed a steady stream of lies throughout the local community with obvious intent to poison the jury pool. They insulted Velie's grandchildren and even helped facilitate the kids' kidnapping by the county's Child Protective Services. And they unleashed an unholy band of forked-tongue online assailants whose sole objective was trashing Velie.

There was a very specific reason things went awry at our trial. It's called perjury.

For example, two weeks before the trial's start, Tenborg admitted guilt in 17 separate incidences of fraudulent invoice submittals to the California Department of Toxic Substances Control (DTSC) and agreed to repay the state the full amount of money he had unlawfully obtained. Each of those deceitful invoices was for more than $2,000.

However, Tenborg testified before and during trial that he had always complied with all environmental regulations and that he had never been the subject of any enforcement action by the DTSC, a false claim that several government officials also parroted in court. Prior to our trial, DTSC officials declined to share that information because of the agency's ongoing investigation into Tenborg's allegedly illegal practices.

In the aftermath of the trial, Velie and I learned that we have many friends in this county and beyond. A group of them banded together to hire Carl Knudson, a prominent private investigator with a background as an IRS forensic sleuth whose work is credited with bringing down the Colombia cartels and unraveling the Oliver North fiasco in the late 1980s.

Knudson's assignment was to verify the facts contained in the offending article. He would discover much more beyond that scope.

The investigator's insertion into the equation had an almost immediate impact. Just months after the citizens' group retained Knudson, Wagstaffe proposed settlement offers to Velie and me.

As previously reported, Velie's offer stipulated that Tenborg would abandon his entire financial claim in exchange for her agreement to never again report on him or his companies. (Yes, this is just as suspicious as it sounds.)

Wagstaffe attorneys sought the same pledge from me, but my situation was different. Tenborg already had forced me into Chapter 7 bankruptcy, and I nearly lost the home I've owned with my wife for 22 years.

A trust fund had been established by the bankruptcy trustee and funded by a $100,000 second on my home, thanks to the generosity of one of my wife's sisters. Tenborg offered to divide his "share" of that fund's money.

And in what was described as a "non-negotiable" provision, a similar gag order was proposed to cover Worrell and the IWMA, also. Neither the IWMA nor Worrell was party to Tenborg's libel complaint against *CalCoastNews*.

The offer also would have required termination of Knudson's investigation, a matter over which neither Velie nor I had any control. We both rejected Tenborg's demands.

While these negotiations dragged on, Hill and his blogger buddy wondered online if Velie and I would choose suicide or simply leave town. The blogger buddy threatened to throw bleach in Velie daughter's eyes, earning him a temporary restraining order.

Now, however, armed with facts that Worrell, Tenborg, and Hill hoped we'd never possess, it is time to return serve. It is likely that all three men may have thought more than once that this is a fight they wish they'd never started.

Worrell, faced with evidence of his history of fiscal mismanagement and astounding abuse of an IWMA credit card, was forced to resign a year before he planned while county officials determine the status of his tax-supported retirement. And now he, Tenborg, Hill, and others are under a criminal investigation by the San Luis Obispo County District Attorney for their unchecked plunder of county taxpayers. The IWMA has been a piggy bank for its employees and favored contractors.

These bullies thought we were fatally wounded by their spurious lawsuit, and frankly, they came close. Hill and Tenborg boasted openly about "getting Blackburn's house." And Velie gets hassled into court every three months to explain, again, that she has no resources because of the lawsuit.

But we remain standing and continue publishing, unwilling to bend to this malicious attempt to muzzle this news agency. We continue to hold government accountable and to inform the public. Why? Because we care about our community, and we care about the truth.

It's been one hell of a ride, but the finish line is in sight—and that should be very, very disconcerting to Worrell, Tenborg, Hill, and their lying, scheming associates.

Daniel Blackburn can be harassed at blackburn.danielj@gmail.com

Using Unnamed Sources—"the Only Way to Address Corruption"

When someone tells me about corruption I cannot name them because doing so puts them and their families at risk of injury to reputation, property, and finances. When necessary for their safety, or my own, I do not name sources without their permission. In some cases I cannot name sources because they may be involved in ongoing investigations.

Woodward describes how he corroborates information from unnamed sources, "The sources are not anonymous; I know exactly who they are. With deep background, my rule is, I'm tape-recording it, I'm not going to say who gave me the information, but I'm going to use it, and I'm going to check it within an inch of its life, as much as I can, with multiple sources and documents and notes."

John Matlin, my initial source for the Kansas City chapter, says, "It is simplicity itself for an accusation of corruption to be made against any individual in power," so I carefully back up my assertions. I use my "3 Times" test to validate tips. If I receive the same unsolicited information from three unrelated sources, I research it. I "add down and across" in a similar manner to the way I check figures, by using three forms of calculating, to be sure the numbers, or facts, are congruent. I do not repeat information unless I can corroborate it.

Keepers of the Culture-a Historical Record

In addition to their role as the Fourth Estate, broadcasting current events, the press and media are keepers of our culture and social history. I have gleaned or corroborated much of the information in this book from press reports that chronicle both the historical events and the highlights of the 16 years I have served my community.

CHAPTER 12

THE FIFTH ESTATE
Who Does the Attorney Serve?

Another difference, also transparency-inspired and even more removed from private company boards, is that government boards must deliberate and vote in agendized meetings open to the public, making no decision until they have received public input in a public meeting. Members of private boards often reach consensus before board meetings and approve motions in a quick vote. Essentially, there is every legal privacy in private company business and no legal privacy in government business.

A third area of difference between private and government business is the protection of leadership. In private companies, silence clauses to protect company secrets are wise. Not so in government. In private companies, attorneys represent principles and the company against legal action. In the people's business, it is the people's interest that the attorney must protect, rather than covering for the slipups of city hall or elected officials. Government agencies should never use silence clauses to protect the agency or to protect government officials who misbehave except in legitimate cases of security or human relations. Payouts by insurance companies to employees for misconduct of government officials should be public information and the offender should pay if convicted. More on this in Chapter 12.

"The most noble of causes"–Jefferson Davis– "the defense of the rights of man."

"Debbie, who does the city attorney work for?" asked my friend, the constitutional attorney, days after I was elected.

Thinking back to the contracts I had seen between agency and city attorneys, I replied, "The City of Grover Beach."

Stew asked again, "Who does the city attorney work for?"

Digging deeper, I replied, "Well, he is employed by the city council, but he doesn't represent individual councilmembers."

Stew asked again. I was stumped. He replied, "The city attorney works for the people. His job is to interpret the law to be sure that the people are protected. Your city is their institution."

Over the years, I became increasingly aware of how often this is misunderstood and/or misrepresented or interpreted differently by agency attorneys and boards. This is in part because insurance companies and legal firms do not differentiate between the practice of corporate, criminal, and government law, even though the ownership and "product" of each is so uniquely different that one cannot apply to the other. This is a chicken and egg problem. It is not entirely the fault of the insurance companies or the attorneys. They would not need to work so hard to protect the agencies they serve on behalf of the people if the people's elected representatives behaved better, but before we get into that, let us talk about the attorney him or herself.

Agency attorneys are different from county or big city district attorneys or state or federal attorney generals who work within the court system. Agency attorneys sit in the meetings of the agency to advise as needed and draft the contracts and ordinances of the government agency, and occasionally act on behalf of the agency if sued or if the agency must sue or to line up the right experts to manage the legal matters they cannot handle themselves. Unlike the district attorney or attorney general, agency attorneys do not prosecute and they do not press charges. They act more in the role of corporate attorneys, working on the day-to-day business of the agency.

If you accept that the one who pays the attorney is the client, then the client in a criminal case would be a criminal or a victim. The client in a corporate case would be a company. With a government agency it is the people. The people pay the attorney. The agency attorney is there to serve the interest of the ratepayers; to make sure that in the work the attorney does for the agency the laws created to serve the people also protect the people. In the words of the Brown Act:

> The Legislature finds and declares that the public commissions, boards and councils and the other public agencies in this State exist to aid in the conduct of the people's business. ... The people of this State do not yield their sovereignty to the agencies which serve them. The people, in delegating authority, do not give their public servants the right to decide what is good for the people to know and what is not good for them to know. The people insist on remaining informed so that they may retain control over the instruments they have created.

The law is unambiguous. The people merely delegate authority. They do not give it away. They do not yield sovereignty to their agencies. They do not give their public servants the right to decide what is good for them to know and what is not good for them to know. We insist on remaining informed so that we retain control over the instruments we have created. The exceptions are few—negotiating contracts or lawsuits where the outcome might be compromised if not kept confidential, and employee relations where the privacy of the employee is the priority. Furthermore, and this is one that journalists rely on, agencies must make public records available on request, or provide an explanation within 10 days as to why they cannot be made available.

The First Attorney

Once a month, The Grange in Grover Beach sponsors a $5 Sunday morning pancake breakfast. People come from twenty-five miles away to the old Grange building, complete with stage and institutional kitchen and dining room, for this homemade meal cooked and served by cheery local volunteers. It is a wonderful opportunity to catch up on the history of the community.

Shortly after I was elected, a former city attorney came up to congratulate me at the monthly pancake breakfast. An unassuming character, his generosity and vision always eclipsed his means. He said something I wasn't expecting. Perhaps he had been following the news or was aware of my approach to governance, or perhaps it was because I am a woman, but he assumed that I had heard the accounts of young women being assaulted by members of the city council, as indeed I had. "You know, there were some things I didn't do right. Those girls were right. They deserved to be protected, and instead, I protected the councilmember who should have been in jail," he told me.

This went back much farther than the 2008 events I referenced in Chapter One. He was referring to earlier assaults.

I think the lights went on for him as he reflected on his decades of service to the city, years before the #MeToo movement.

I believe the attorney shared because he wanted me to do it differently. His epiphany and the disturbing stories, both old and recent, later moved me to relay my frightening experience of being locked in the county courthouse alone with a supervisor who told me he had a gun. At the time, I sensed that the DA and sheriff believed my account when I made it public, but I now wonder why the DA and sheriff didn't investigate when they heard about it. One would think that a mayor locked in a building by a supervisor might merit action. Not in SLO County.

As the #Me Too movement was beginning, my membership in the California League of Cities Women's Caucus gave me an opening to speak on the issue of public agencies funding and hiding the defense of senior staff or politician sexual harassment of employees or community members. The Women's Caucus asked each of us to publicly ask our councils to take a stand against this behavior. I raised the issue in a council meeting during council committee comments. A female council colleague with a law degree reported to members of the public that I was going to get the council sued. She was thinking like a lawyer, not like a representative of the people, making the same mistake made by agency lawyers—the person who would get the agency sued is the perpetrator, not the person who calls for justice. If the representatives behave they are unlikely to get their agency sued!

To sue in a case such as this is the very essence of our democracy; the very reason for our courts—to ensure justice and to give the minority a voice. Furthermore, the target of a lawsuit SHOULD be the agency if it is in collusion with the perpetrator. The perpetrator should pay the agency costs and the perpetrator should pay the victim damages. The institution put in place to SERVE the public is not there to serve the interests of the elected or their appointed, nor is it there to hide the crimes they commit and cover under color of authority.

This is akin to the abuse of power that was exhibited at the sanitation district. The district indemnified the administrator and his engineering firm. When his infractions became too many for the insurance company to continue to insure him, he didn't tell the public their sewer agency was uninsured, he just left them on the hook. The district's attorney wrote the indemnity into the administrator's contact. The board backed him. For whom were they working? Certainly not for the people who pay their salaries and employ them to protect their health and safety.

Things have changed; mostly because of the #MeToo movement, but they haven't changed enough.

I don't know of the details of the three Grover Beach employees allegedly sexually harassed by the mayor. I have been told they all lost their jobs while he kept his. I know that the city swears everyone to silence because it is a human relations matter. I know one whistleblower was told it would be best if she just left town; and she did.

Corporate lawyers can legitimately buy silence. Corporations deal in trade secrets and information that could hurt their ability to remain competitive, or even stay in business, if released. The government does not have trade secrets to protect. Government is a monopoly. Transparency will not put it out of business. Government must be a good steward of the funds allocated to it, not squander those funds or risk higher insurance costs, or worse, lose insurance cover altogether, to cover the misdeeds of the elected or their appointees or staff. The Brown Act tells us they cannot decide what we may know and not know.

Government agencies and their attorneys have applied the silence clause of "trade secrets" to cover human relations travesties, to gag and buy off the victims of staff or elected officials in cases of sexual harassment, racism, and whistle blowing. Even RICO doesn't fully address government misfeasance, because while it incentivizes and makes it possible for the people to sue their government, the payout is paid by taxpayer funds. The #MeToo movement has promulgated laws and lawsuits to protect victims of sexual crimes, but these protections do not go far enough. To fully honor the value of open government, these protections need to apply equally to any kind of harassment, racism, and whistle blowing, exposing and punishing the perpetrators rather than doling out large sums of taxpayer funds or campaign donations, covering up to avoid embarrassment, protect officeholders, and silence victims.

Government, like the Catholic church, has covered up leaders' transgressions and bought off those transgressed against to avoid bad publicity, leaving a trail of destruction along the way. But in the case of government, it affects the entire population, not just the membership of one organization. At least in the church, parishioners can stop giving. If we are unhappy with government, we cannot stop paying our taxes.

The good news of late is that new laws no longer allow government agencies to hide the sexual misbehavior of their elected officials. States are banning nondisclosure agreements that cover sexual harassment. In September 2018, California banned the agreements in cases involving sexual assault, harassment, or sex discrimination. New York and New

Jersey enacted similar laws. New York went farther, expanding its sexual harassment law to cover independent contractors in 2018 and improved protections for domestic workers in 2019. California went so far as to protect certain working relationships, including those with film producers.

Congress has reformed its process for staffers reporting sexual harassment. Allegations against legislators on both sides of the aisle have drawn attention to the issue of sexual misconduct by members of Congress, and Congress has taken steps to reform itself as a workplace. Last year, Congress passed legislation addressing issues advocates had raised with its process for congressional employees to report harassment or assault. The law eliminated a mandatory three-month waiting period for people reporting misconduct, requiring the accuser to go through counseling and mediation before filing a lawsuit. It also barred legislators from using taxpayer money to cover harassment settlements—last year, a report revealed that nearly $300,000 of taxpayer funds had been used for that purpose since 2003.

There remain gaps in these laws. Whistleblowers are still subject to silence clauses. Those suffering harassment not of a sexual nature are not yet covered by law. Our county cabal's hired gun fulfilled his job of firing our sewer plant's whistle blowing superintendent Clemons at a cost of over $200,000 to the agency. The hired gun was more richly rewarded, retiring at the age of fifty on full salary with full health care for his family of four for life, at a far, far higher cost to the ratepayers he was supposed to have served.

The tactics against Clemons were familiar, sounding much the same as the stories from the first three who claimed that Shoals sexually harassed them and the three whistle blowers at the sewer plant. The bosses played the same carrot and stick game—telling Clemons it would be best if he and his fiancé's family left town, buying him off with threats of releasing things about him that would make it tough for him to work again, and offering outrageous sums of money if he kept quiet, agreeing to do so themselves. Within days of the settlement in which they agreed to confidentiality, they blacklisted him. For the next year, he would be on the brink of a job offer and then it would fizzle at the last minute. Finally, after a year, he landed a consulting job in the next county and then a second in a different neighboring county.

Honest Fixes

Former Kansas City Mayor Kay Barnes, in her article *Civic Housekeepers: Women's Organizations, Civic Reform, And The 1940 Elections* Published by Park University, says, "In retrospect, 'telling the truth' may be one of the most significant contributions made by women in Kansas City politics."

It is this truth telling that brings the positive changes we seek in our government. It is time for us to demand that our agency attorneys stand on the side of truth.

The role of agency attorneys should be a neutral role at the very minimum, advising on the law surrounding charges brought by employees, which should be investigated by an outside third party, rather than the attorney.

Government silencing of whistleblowers should be banned. Compensation should compensate, not censor, censure, suppress, or silence to keep the truth concealed and sanitize public records. When agencies swear staff to silence and swear the victims to silence, the perpetrators go free to offend again. It is a tried-and-true method. The Sewer District bought Mascolo and Douglas off in a strategy used in the corporate world and incorrectly applied—buy them off and buy their silence, threatening severe legal penalties if they break silence. Here government and corporate practice must reach a critical fork in the road. While large payouts may compensate the victims for their suffering, they also buy their silence, preclude the embarrassment of exposure, and make it less likely they will be blacklisted for future jobs.

Joint Powers Insurance Authorities formed by government agencies do not act for the people whose tax dollars fund their agencies. Paid by tax dollars, they act for corrupt, negligent, and incompetent government officials.

Corporate legal practice has also migrated to government agencies in a way that serves the bureaucracy rather than the people the bureaucracy serves. Government agency lawyers are now practicing law not of the people and for the people to protect the PEOPLE from bad government as initially intended,, but to hide crimes committed under the color (power) of office while in office, and often even before taking office. Agency attorneys wrongly often see themselves as the city attorney, or the council attorney, or the "hush it up guy" who makes sure no one at the city is ever embarrassed, rather than the attorney who protects the people from their government.

Just as we need to teach best boardsmanship practice for elected officials, we need to raise up lawyers who champion good governance and recognize that business and criminal law practices must not be applied across the board to government agencies. The people's money belongs to the people, not to the lawyers who profit by protecting self-serving representatives.

I see two other problems with agency attorneys. Just as in criminal law, if elected representatives make a mistake that could result in prosecution, agency attorneys counsel them to deny everything; never admit guilt and buy silence. In institutions predicated on transparency, they threaten the victims that if they are paid off, in what may be legitimate damages, they may never speak about their experience, as if bullying and harassment were trade secrets to be protected. These aren't competitive advantages that threaten the survival of the shareholders if divulged, these are practices that threaten the shareholders if NOT divulged. These cover-ups run counter to open government. The cover up is possible because there is a loophole in the Brown Act that our representatives often seek to apply too liberally. Lawsuits, potential lawsuits, and employee matters may be discussed in closed session hearings. The other obstacle to transparency is "attorney privilege," which gives politicians and lawyers the cover of secrecy, and other parties to the communication the requirement of confidentiality.

This approach is a violation of the oath we take to protect the people we serve from attacks within and without. When a representative of the people attacks or assaults one of the people or misuses authority or position, that is an attack from within that we are sworn to root out. Hush money payouts are hidden from the public if they are covered by insurance. They are "off budget items." If not, they are hidden by being thrown in with related budget items where they won't show, such as salaries or employee benefits. Payouts should be a separate line item, and if the insurance company won't cover it, further investigation is needed to find out why.

Second, government agencies have very deep pockets. They are a perpetual piggy bank fed by taxes. The ability to increase their income by pursuing legal action is a very real conflict of interest for agency lawyers. Inasmuch as it is a conflict for agency lawyers, it is a conflict for politicians. They know that there will always be more. Taxpayer funds are the fountain that never runs dry. There is no incentive to be as careful or as accountable as they would if it was finite. As for agency attorneys, the more they can play on the egos or inexperience of the politicians they work with to get them involved in lawsuits, the more money they earn. Just as a good politician acts not in his or her own interests, but in the interests of those governed, a good lawyer keeps his clients out of court. While this conflict is regulated by private clients' reluctance to overspend, it is much less carefully monitored by members of the public, their institutions, and elected officials.

The courts are the legitimate resource for solving disputes that cannot otherwise be determined. They are the wrong place for the spats, whims, and egos of government agencies whose very existence is to address the problems of the electorate. They are especially the wrong place for spats between government agencies. Where government agencies are at odds, let the legislators sort it out. Or tell them to figure it out themselves without wasting taxpayer dollars. When public agencies use the legal system to do battle with one another, the taxpayers pay twice. As my parents said when they divorced, "only the lawyers got rich." The public cost multiplies when one public agency sues another.

Consider the ongoing saga of the Air Pollution Control District Officer who wants to fine a State Park because sand blows downwind from the dunes in the park, claiming it is because vehicles are in the dunes. When the Park tells them that even with no vehicles the wind will continue to blow and create sand dunes downwind, they and public groups end up suing one another. The APCD has legal fees. State Parks has legal fees. There is the expense of the courts paid for by the taxpayers. Individuals pay taxes and on top of that donate to sue—and win—the damages, fines, and costs awarded coming yet again from their taxes and their fellow taxpayers. The private group wins every case and is awarded $350,000 in costs, which they reinvest in more lawsuits against the APCD because it continues to try to enforce a ruling that was indefensible at the time it was made.

Meanwhile, the park is paying half a million tax dollars a year installing frivolous wind blocks and unsightly orange screens to mollify the APCD in a futile attempt to stop the wind from blowing the sand. But like a big bad wolf, the wind just keeps blowing and the waves just keep rolling that fine particulate off their crests and into the housing development that was built in the dunes, and the taxpayers keep paying for the lawsuits between their institutions.

At the same time, the APCD is monitoring the particulate and charging the cost back to the park, which is also monitoring the same particulate that Scripps Institute determines is actually blowing off the crashing waves, not the dunes, and not caused by the vehicles. The APCD continues to charge the (public) Park to monitor the particulate that blows across the dunes and demands that the Park pay for a permit to pollute (for sand to blow) and to spend upwards of $500,000 a year to mitigate the blowing sand and shutting down part of the access to vehicles and camping, thus reducing the income of the Park that produces more income than any other Park in the state system due to its unique opportunities to get out in the dunes in the only way possible—by vehicle. I would add, the Air Pollution Control Officer and agency attorney (now retired because he was also the attorney for the unscrupulous IWMA of a previous chapter) gets rich because they keep creating work for themselves and the agency, fanning the egos of the board as the work of this nonsense piles up almost as quickly as the APCO's pension fund and the dunes themselves!

Agency attorneys are in the same tenuous position as staff and all government contractors, there at the whim of the ruling body, so it is risky not to go along to get along. It would be more appropriate if their tenure was at the whim of the voters and they were able to act independent of the agency if necessary. This is a strong argument for electing agency attorneys rather than having them appointed by board majority. The counterargument by staff and councils will be that it is expensive to add another position to the ballot. Indeed, it is, but much less expensive than hiring attorneys who are working for the council majority rather than the people who elect them. It is much less expensive than the money spent on unnecessary lawsuits and hush money payouts.

The other protection against conflicts of interest would be to mandate that outside counsel be used for government agency lawsuits. This is often the case, but not always and a mandate would remove some of the bias, or worse, temptation to bolster personal income by egging agencies into lawsuits.

Justice Delayed is Justice Denied

Rabbi Mayerberg's KC Star opinion piece expressed it well:

> "Even in an imperfect social order I believe crime can be held in check, not by severity of the penalty, but by the speed and certainty with which justice is rendered. Let society rid itself of corrupt police departments, public officials, and conniving politicians; let men of courage and ability be elected to our benches; let the legal procedure be rid of all the technicalities by which testimony is hidden or perverted or delays are manufactured; in brief, establish a swiftly moving machinery of justice in America."

If it continues to be the case that the statutes of limitation pass as defendants stall for that very purpose, it should conversely be the case that there is no statute of limitation for crimes against the people. That takes away at least some of the incentive to stall. It is unethical to use the people's money to delay with arduous information requests; to either sicken or bankrupt a whistleblower or public agency out of the game in order to block a lawsuit. These tactics should be restricted. The People deserve quick efficacious solutions. Failures of the public trust should be redressed immediately. No errant public servant should ever be aided by a public agency attorney.

Delivering efficient and speedy justice is one of the fundamental duties of any government. If the government fails to do so, it fails in its duty to protect its citizens against further criminal activities. It also fails to issue a warning to potential criminals, thereby becoming less capable of checking unlawful activities.

When the judicial system takes too long to investigate a case and mete out proper justice evidence gets less and less reliable. Documents are lost, witnesses die, and prosecuting parties run out of money. There is also more scope for tampering with or losing evidence, and further stress for and threat of harm to witnesses and prosecutors.

If You Don't Have Discovery, You Won't Get Recovery

Finally, justice is slim because the evidence cannot be found, which has been the main finding of the DA in the story of the attempts to kill a small-town paper at the end of the previous chapter. The essence of this argument is expressed by an attorney involved in the breaking Pandora case in which wealthy trusts were able to hide works of art due to laws designed to make any discovery of assets difficult, according to Brooke Harrington, a Dartmouth College professor who explains it best, "If you don't have discovery, you won't get recovery."

In the case of the SLO County IWMA, files were shredded, and laws were so weak, or responsibility in dispute such that that clear evidence simply could not be produced.

GAG or GAGA

It seems that municipal authorities operate a Playbook 101 "Go Along to Get Along." In government acronym-speak it is GAG or GAGA, because there's nothing agency administrators hate worse than a brouhaha! It could mean they get fired by their agency board or they could be held accountable for their actions by the public.

Working with government administrators, agency lawyers will do just about anything to keep things quiet. They act for city hall, protecting the board or staff, or even themselves, rather than protecting the people of the community who have funded and established the agency to serve the community.

Think how much we would have been spared if Cal Poly (yes, another government agency hating a brouhaha) had done the right thing and been honest about why Adam Hill was let go. I expect their attorneys said to let it go. And in so doing, the result was that they looked after the interests of the corrupt, rather than the interests of the people who pay them. This is an instance where the people's money is well spent in stopping those who steal from their agencies.

What if, Instead, We had a "No Tolerance" Rule?

There are times when government must prosecute to protect the people. When someone defrauds the people, failing to prosecute the offender rewards their behavior and sends them off to steal again, costing far more in the long term than prosecuting immediately. Any crime against the people should be immediately prosecuted both as a deterrent to the offender and to would-be offenders and as a protection to the people.

CHAPTER 13

THE SIXTH ESTATE
GOVERNMENT CULTURE

"POST OF HONOR, PLACE OF PROFIT"

In local government the executive branch (city hall) is not elected, which leads to conflicts of interest in upholding its role as one of the three estates. To redress that imbalance, it is critical that we place more emphasis on the role of the city manager, in league with the city attorney, as an executive estate, reframing our thinking so as to honor them as a sixth estate tasked with guarding the balance of estates so critical to the citizens to whom city hall belongs.

Ben Franklin, as one of the authors of the United States Constitution, delivered the following speech in Philadelphia at the Constitutional Convention of 1787. Franklin's visionary message of 250 years ago is disconcertingly valid today.

> In this particular of salaries to the executive branch it is only from a persuasion that it is right, and from a sense of duty, that I hazard it. I see inconveniences in the appointment of salaries; I see none in refusing them, but, on the contrary, great advantages.
>
> There are two passions which have a powerful influence in the affairs of men. These are ambition and avarice—the love of power

and the love of money. Separately, each of these has great force in prompting men to action; but, when united in view of the same object, they have ... the most violent effects. Place before the eyes of such men a post of honor, that shall, at the same time, be a place of profit, and they will move heaven and earth to obtain it.

And of what kind are the men that will strive for this profitable preeminence, through all the bustle of cabal, the heat of contention, the infinite mutual abuse of parties, tearing to pieces the best of characters? It will not be the wise and moderate, the lovers of peace and good order, the men fittest for the trust. It will be the bold and the violent, the men of strong passions and indefatigable activity in their selfish pursuits. These will thrust themselves into your government and be your rulers. And these, too, will be mistaken in the expected happiness of their situation, for their vanquished competitors, of the same spirit, and from the same motives, will perpetually be endeavoring to distress their administration, thwart their measures, and render them odious to the people.

Besides these evils, ... though we may set out in the beginning with moderate salaries, we shall find that such will not be of long continuance. Reasons will never be wanting for proposed augmentations; and there will always be a party for giving more to the rulers, that the rulers may be able, in return, to give more to them. Hence, as all history informs us, there has been in every state and kingdom a constant kind of warfare between the governing and the governed; the one striving to obtain more for its support, and the other to pay less.

The saving of the salaries, that may at first be proposed, is not an object with me. The subsequent mischiefs of proposing them are what I apprehend.

I have great respect for each of the city managers I have known. They have been the professionals who understand how to run the business of the city and who must also manage large and diverse employee groups. It was city managers who often informed and inspired me as to the potential of their communities. They have carried and inspired the vision of their cities and driven it forward. The same goes for the employees in my city and in other government agencies I worked with. They are dedicated, conscientious, and kind. Their wellbeing matters to me. I think that came through when I was in office, and I hope it continues to. My exposition here is in no way meant to demean or undermine their work or their positions. They are not responsible for the situation we face with the Public Employees Retirement System (PERS), but they will be the ones who help us to fix it, and for that, I say again as I have so many times in the past for their excellent service, a heart-felt "thank you."

My message is and always has been "we can do better." We can all do better.

"What every bureaucracy counts on is the limited attention span most citizens have."

-Tacker

The Iroquois Seventh-Generation principle that the decisions we make today should be sustainable seven generations into the future applies not just to environmental issues, but to all decisions. If it formed the base of our representative expression of values, we would be less prone to kick the can down the road. Similarly, the Old Testament declares that the sins of the fathers will carry through to the third and fourth generations. In other words, the choices we make today, for better and for worse, may have effects that carry through centuries. It is far too common for our representatives to think only of the time in which they serve, and not of how their decisions affect even the next session, much less next generations. PERS is an example of this, having racked up millions of dollars of debt for cities and the state of California to the extent that it has bankrupted cities, including Providence, Rhode Island, and Stockton, California.

The Administrators

Around the turn of the century, as the country's population grew the need for greater administrative assistance and professional management in its municipalities grew with it. Professional government administrators evolved to meet the need. However, as employees rather than elected representatives they are beholden to the council majority, and more recently have become too powerful because they are a power behind the scenes. Along with this growth, two serious accountability issues arise. The first is that government employees are not intended to be in post for profit motives. They are intended to be in post for service. However, they have grown powerful as the population and tax revenues have increased.

Now they seek the income of private industry AND the security net of socialism, and in too many cases they get both. This means that huge percentages of the tax dollars meant to go to the service of the people go to provide full private-industry level paychecks and full family health benefits for life following early retirement. Consider a small town of 45,000 like San Luis Obispo, with a chief executive paid upwards of $300,000 a year. The financial burden is exacerbated because public servants can retire as early as the age of 55 and may live to the age of 90. The city could be paying full salary and benefits to their retired manager for as long as 45 years, while at the same time paying the current city manager who will retire on full benefits and salary for 45 years. Consider that successive managers retire after an average of five years at their highest salary. Even if the average job tenure was 10 years, at any given time taxpayers could be paying full salary and benefits for up to five city managers to do the job of one city manager for 10 years. But it doesn't stop there, because there are probably a hundred or more employees with similar benefits, if not as high a salary. It is reasonable for personnel costs to consume a portion of a city's budget. However, if salaries are to align with corporate remuneration, the percentage of revenue consumed by salaries should also align with corporate norms, in the thirty to forty percent range. While it takes people to administer services and infrastructure, it is unsustainable when 10% of a budget goes to retirees alone. Estimates by policy reviewers and watchdogs are that city and state personnel costs range from 55 to 80 percent of most city revenues. It goes one step worse than the tail wagging the dog. The wag is tailing the dog.

Private Profit for Public Servants at Public Expense

The Kansas City turnaround is a good example of the advantages of professional city management done right. The professionals have a duty as an agent of the people to bring this to us. Let me explain. An excellent manager will act in the best interests of his client, just as a good agent is legally bound to do. For instance, as a real estate agent the law demands that my first duty is to act in the best interest of my client. The best professionals do that. For the professional city manager, that means sorting out PERS for his or her clients, the public. That means helping us to move past the overloaded ratio of retirement outgoings to agency income, to find the solutions that our larger and more complex institutions now demand. It means regular department audits and evaluations of the efficacy of programs.

During my boomer lifetime, 'socialism' has been bandied about as a great evil. And yet, we are very much socialized. Not so much so as the more civilized European nations, but more so for an elite group—government employees who reap benefits at our expense. It may not be cradle to grave for the employee, but it is employment to grave and then cradle to the employee's grave for health care of their families. At any given time, an agency will be paying current employees full pay plus their pensions plus the PERS backlogs, PLUS all retirees until such time as they die. An agency could be supporting twice its actual number of employees—check it out! And you can be sure that it's not clearly detailed in the budget. As my son would have said as a teenager, "Mom, that's really messed up."

What is most insidious is that the same beneficiaries of this system that covers them cradle to grave have direct control in the case of congress and direct influence in the case of staff. In the case of the military, it is a fair system. If even some of the funds going toward local government and congress were shifted to military staff and their families and back to the people, it would be fair. It is not fair now. We must find a way to use government funds for the people—the shareholders—who fund it.

Sour Grapes

As a businessperson and single parent, always reliant on my own resourcefulness to provide for my retirement, my healthcare, maternity pay, and sick pay, I admit to sour grapes that such a sizable proportion of the taxes I pay goes to providing what I have never had for free whilst self-employed and never had as an elected volunteer. I willingly served 20-40 hours a week for $300 a month, that barely covered vehicle expenses, reducing my earning power for 15 years. That is the Ben Franklin model—that citizens take time out to serve.

I understand the argument that senior level government employment is "at will;" at the whim of political outcomes. So is mine. So is everyone's. I do not advocate denying them the same benefits available in the open market, but we must sort out the PERS imbalance and address a system that allows local and state retirees to start work again while still collecting full-time retirement pay plus benefits. We must address the system that provides both the benefits of total safety net and market salaries. It can be one or the other. We can't fund both. Employees could be given a choice—**security or high pay**, but like most of us, not both. Along with high pay should come the responsibility of self-funding retirement.

Culture Vulture

Several practices in agency culture thwart best community service.

My two biggest pet peeves are **budget line items and acronyms**. Line items should reflect rather than obscure, especially with regard to pensions, retirees, and current staff. If it's too difficult to understand it doesn't pass the smell test.

Everyone found it amusing when I declared acronyms cusswords and said there would be no cussing from staff or the council. The penalty for getting caught for using an acronym was the embarrassment of being asked to provide the real words it represents and discovering that often we aren't sure! How can the public participate if they don't know what an acronym means and while those who use it regularly know what it represents no one can tell them what words the letters represent?

The **"go along to get along" practice of kowtowing** to the council majority is the easy out for high level government executives, but it deprives councils of the experience and perspective that experienced municipal staff can provide. The city manager and city attorney are employed at will; the will of the council majority, specifically. Their risk is that if they do not please the council majority, which can change with every two-year election cycle, they can find themselves out of a job. But if they are to govern well, the council must be provided with options, straight talk, and straight facts; not just what they want to hear, and not just what agrees with their agendas.

On the other hand, when staff attempt to control outcomes the **tail begins wagging the dog**. Because administrators will usually be in post long after elected officials have moved on, they learn how to game the elected officials. They do the training of the officials, thereby controlling everything behind the scenes and sometimes much more openly participating in deliberations. It is the elected who have been elected to make the tough decisions. Staff are there to provide the information to help them make good decisions.

Aversion to controversy is the enemy of open government. There is a proclivity among administrators to sidle away from or gloss over anything that might cause eyebrows to raise. This is coupled with the view that the public are to be avoided when possible and the bad actions of a council are to be kept hidden.

City staff trains new government agency board members. The only training my colleagues and I received about our roles was our role in relationship to city staff. The message was that staff members run the city, and if we had questions as councilmembers we were to ask questions of staff through the city manager and give direction via board majority. We also received basic Brown Act and Ethics training. The general attitude was that the Brown Act was useful if the council wished to discuss sensitive matters, but that otherwise it was a pain in the backside because we could only talk with a minority of the council outside meetings. In addition to training at city hall, councilmembers need training in their roles and responsibilities as board members from independent outside sources.

This **lack of respect for the process of open meetings** was apparent across city boundaries and even statewide. The culture of city halls was a fear of controversy and a desire to quell or avoid anything that might lead to uncomfortable exchanges. It is understandably the best practice to protect the public image of an institution and its leaders. However, this has gone far awry in government agencies, and not only just with #MeToo cases. It extends to any situation with whistleblowers or councilmember misdeeds. It is particularly heinous when it occurs to protect a racket.

When it is government staff who train new councilmembers, and staff who supply the reports that guide council decisions, new councilmembers, whether intentionally or not, are indoctrinated to think the way staff thinks. As rookies, new councilmembers depend on staff to introduce them to their roles and the process of governance. Being thrown in at the deep end, they tend to adopt the prevailing culture of the organization. They can easily fall into the trap of thinking of themselves as city hall employees and guardians of city hall rather than guardians of the people.

Conversely, in the larger context of the county, it is easy for the county administrator to think of the elected officers who operate out of the county building and on behalf of the county, such as the auditor, the county clerk recorder, and the assessor as department heads, which they are not. They are the choice of the electorate as their representatives in these important roles of trust. They must remain independent of the bureaucracy even as they work within it.

Government agencies, like computer platforms of days past, don't

"talk to one another." That can be a convenient short-term way to preserve resources, as when the county auditor says it's not their job to ride herd on agencies that report to them, and the agencies say the auditor is supposed to keep their records. Or when the district attorney doesn't prosecute negligence because "it's the job of the board to exercise oversight." Or when massacres occur because reporting agencies didn't or couldn't pass on information about gun owners posing a risk. Long term there would be financial economies of scale and reduced social suffering if government agencies used the same software or if at least the programs were compatible. A culture in which agencies shift blame or do not work in tandem to problem-solve is not a healthy culture.

Finally, oftentimes **government agencies don't play well together.** One government agency sues another or many others, all on our dime. What other organization would allow its divisions to sue one another to the harm of the shareholders? And yet, we, the people, allow our government to continue internal spats and build fiefdoms without batting an eye, all at the expense of our best interest, stealing from ourselves by doing so. Sure, like a whispering campaign, it makes good reading, has entertainment value, and keeps the presses flowing while everyone wins except the shareholders caught in a perpetual lose-lose cycle that they fund. The lawyers make out. The agencies ask for more money from us to cover their legal costs, therefore not impacting their operating budgets, but creating work for themselves to the detriment of our quality of life when taxes increase to fund their spats.

CHAPTER 14 THE SEVENTH ESTATE— ILLUMINATION
Integrity Nation

NOVEMBER 2020

Voter turnout in SLO County was 88.35% of registered voters. Historically, my campaign teams considered 67% to be a reasonable local turnout, with about the same percentage voting by mail. According to SLO County Clerk Recorder Tommy Gong, the voter turnout was "one for the ages," breaking the 83.14% turnout in the 2008 presidential election; higher even than in 1960 when John F. Kennedy defeated Richard Nixon. I am encouraged. Voters in my county believe their votes matter.

Sanjoseinsider.com posed the question, "Did mailing each registered voter a ballot increase voter turnout?"

"Probably," said Lisa Bryant, a political science professor at California State University, Fresno, who specializes in election administration. "If we look at the data nationally, states that conduct all-mail or nearly all-mail elections have among the highest turnout rates in the country."

Turnout increases because it is easier for people to vote.

"They don't have to set aside time, try to estimate how long lines will be, or worry about transportation when they vote by mail," she said. "Voters also report … that they like being able to research information … while completing their ballot, which is hard to do in the voting booth."

Following the 2020 election, Tom McCarthy of the UK's *Guardian Newspaper* weighed in on American democracy:

Structural Features Make National Elections in the U.S. Hard To Steal...

MON 30 NOV 2020

"... While the election exposed key areas where American democracy is failing, it also highlighted structural features that make elections hard to steal."

McCarthy provides the following insights, the first being an argument in favor of decentralization if it is closely monitored. It works in elections because there is such a high level of citizen involvement and because registrars are elected and therefore directly accountable to the electorate. They are also attached to the country rather than being small, isolated units. The same citizen oversight and closer county association would protect against the temptation toward corruption that too easily arises with special districts.

1 Decentralization

National elections are broken down by fifty states and the District of Columbia. Elections within each state are run in turn by counties and by precincts within counties. People vote locally, in thousands of jurisdictions; ballots are tallied locally; and the results are reported locally, and then added up in the public eye. The sheer number of people involved defies both coordination and conspiracy.

On election night, the tributaries of local results become streams, and then flow together to form rivers, and then become a flood. No president or any other figure has the power to stop the result. While every national election is stained by voter suppression measures and strained by human error and voting irregularities, the totality of the vote, and the transparency of its accumulation, constitutes an overwhelming force.

2 Turnout

A persistent symptom of weakness in US democracy has been low voter turnout. Less voter participation means less representative government.

But turnout was a bright spot in 2020. As a uniquely polarizing and inescapable figure in politics, Trump appears to have been a huge driver of turnout, both for and against.

3 Integrity and transparency

US presidential elections are not subject to widespread fraud, miscounts, or other significant irregularities. This is in part thanks to the tireless work of activists and no thanks to routine attempts at voter suppression. No significant instances of fraud emerged from the 2020 election, conducted over more than a month with an unprecedented number of mail-in ballots cast amid a pandemic.

4 The courts

Trump's legal team has been much derided. But in key states, the campaign hired top-flight lawyers. On the whole, these lawyers have fared miserably, winning only one minor case out of 43 in six states, while losing 35 cases so far, according to a running tally maintained by the Democratic lawyer Marc Elias.

The judges who threw out Trump campaign cases include Trump appointees. Judge Steven Grimberg in the northern district of Georgia booted a complaint by a Trump elector seeking to block certification of the state's vote. "I didn't hear any justification for why the plaintiff delayed bringing this claim until two weeks after this election and on the cusp of these election results being certified," Grimberg wrote.

...Another Trump appointee, Judge J Nicholas Ranjan, threw out a Trump complaint in Pennsylvania challenging mail-in ballots. And district judge Matthew Brann of Pennsylvania, a former Republican party official and Federalist Society member, sternly jettisoned a separate Trump campaign challenge filed after the election.

"This court has been presented with strained legal arguments without merit and speculative accusations, unpled in the operative complaint and unsupported by evidence," Brann wrote. "In the United States of America, this cannot justify the disenfranchisement of a single voter, let alone all the voters of its sixth most populated state. Our people, laws, and institutions demand more."

5 The media

… American media has been terribly crippled by the loss over the last decade of countless local outlets that offered irreplaceable, knowledgeable coverage of local events…Strong and independent media, afforded powerful protections by the first amendment, remain a vital feature of US democracy. With no central authority over US elections, it falls to the media to project a winner.

Trump grew enraged when Fox News called the state of Arizona for Biden early on Wednesday after the election. But in doing so, the network—in its election-calling operations, at least—demonstrated its independence and investment in the truth.

The Associated Press worked for years to maintain and upgrade its elections operations while committing to unprecedented transparency in 2020 in explaining how its elections reporting worked. Other media outlets demonstrated similar will and resolve in waiting to call states until the result was plain but then calling them definitively when it was.

This commentary supports the importance of the Fourth Estate and leads into Seventh Estate—You, Me, Them. The People are the single most important Estate. Perhaps this record high voter turnout indicates that we are ready to step into the most vital role of all, the Seventh Estate.

I haven't directly addressed the question of *why* there is so much corruption in my little county. That's partly because I'm not sure I know the answer beyond what I have already written, and partly because, like the rest of us, I'd still rather not deal with it. I love my little county. I don't want to offend or upset. But having come this far, I will call it as I see it. The question is not the question posed by our local newspaper referring to our corrupt supervisor, "How do we leave it behind us," because we have been doing that for two hundred years. The question haunting many now, as it haunted me when I discovered widespread corruption, is, "How did it happen?"

A large part of the answer is in the misguided platitude that we must leave it behind us. That approach is about as effective as the child who covers his eyes and says, "You can't see me."

How Do We Not See What is in Our Faces?

We see what we look for. A highly intelligent friend explained it to me. He oversees safety-checking equipment in a nuclear plant. He has discovered that people see what they are looking for and miss most everything else. Even the most conscientious of nuclear engineers have to be taught to see what they are NOT looking for. I have seen it my family. We come from long lines of British, Swedish, Norwegian, Viking, and German stock. So, we didn't see my grandmother as any different, although others seeing family photos identify her as African American. Perhaps that's why when people ask me if I have Black, or Mexican, or Asian friends I can't immediately reply. I don't see race. I have to stop and think about it for a while. Like everyone else, I learned to see what I expected to see. I recall conversations not too long ago with an African American friend who grew up in Cleveland, Ohio. He said he just never really encountered or thought about racism. I'm sure many will be incredulous when they read this, but he said his family just taught him to ignore it. He said it served him well and enabled him to be gracious when he later encountered it. I treated discrimination against me as a woman much the same. I just kept on as if it wasn't there. Sometimes, denial serves us well. And sometimes it doesn't.

In our little county, we see the incredible span of the Pacific Ocean as we come around the bend of the 101 Highway north of Pismo Beach. We see the majestic dunes and the kite surfers and dune buggies. We see vineyards and craggy cliffs and row upon row of specialty Asian vegetables, and strawberry fields forever. We see centuries-old coastal oaks and owls and whales up close.

We Just Don't See that We are Being Fleeced

In our county, where the Pacific Gas & Electric nuclear power plant has such prominence, citizens and their levels of awareness can be described using terms that describe power outages, from Dimout to Brownout to Blackout to Lights Out with my guesstimate of the percentage of the population that each represents.

LIGHTS ON—TRANSPARENCY—The Vigilant, the Watchers, The Straight Talkers, The Guardians 1%

The greater good outweighs fear of the machine—they know all too well what is going on and are independent of the machine. They are the watchers with eyes to see and ears to hear. They can be the press. They can be the people. They can be our elected representatives. They can be the clergy. They can even be agency attorneys. They are the people who observe; who see what is happening and say something, who work to reach solutions. They are brave people who see with the eyes of their souls and hear with the ears of their hearts.

DIMOUT—The Oblivious 85%

Lack of public interest—no idea of what's going on with local politics. Many of us, as described above by my friend, are unaware of what is staring us in the face. Or, as in Proverbs, we have eyes to see and do not see and ears to hear but do not hear.

BROWN OUT—The Scared 13%

Fear of the machine outweighs the public interest—the powerful surge of the machine power causes any light they may have to flicker, flicker, flicker. Some DO see and DO hear, and they are scared. The scared know all too well what is going on and hide, pay protection money, and go along to get along.

BLACKOUT—The Corrupt 1%

Disregard for the public interest—the failure of power. Even a generator will eventually be unable to create light. To blackout is to stifle; to censor conflicting views. In a blackout, even with eyes wide open you cannot see. It causes tripping and falling. Medically, it is defined as a temporary loss of vision and momentary unconsciousness. It is blind loyalty—described by old-time Kansas City Star editor Reddig, "This myopic condition was combined in many cases with the deafness and dumbness which partisanship and sycophancy customarily produce."

It is the increasing opacity that the corrupt know and use well. And finally, there is the outcome—total loss of power by the people, succinctly put by the *Washington Post* in its tagline:

THE OUTCOME—LIGHTS OUT 100%. *"Democracy Dies in Darkness."*

How do we move this body of people who are voting, which is a crucial step in being represented, to being well represented? How do we turn on the lights, how do we create the transparency that makes the cockroaches scatter? How do we make it intolerable for the cockroaches to exist here at all?

As a woman in the business and political world, I have too much self-respect and self-control to cry or act out emotionally in public, but what makes me cry tears of frustration in private is the cost of corruption that I see and cannot fix. Here is the crunch: public funds are a cash cow—they are constant and can be increased. For crooks, such easy pickings are easily co-opted. Do you want to pay fewer taxes? Then start paying attention to where your money is going and demand that the graft be stopped. I believe that in our county we could find as much as 30% more available to serve us by doing so. There are other benefits, as well. Corruption is the single most fixable drain of public funds. Remove the crime money and unnecessary legal fees and increased insurance costs that go to defend public servants who commit crimes and our taxes will serve us rather than the thieves.

But We are Getting By OK, So Why Rock the Boat?

Matlin explains that the major hazard of patronage as practiced by the likes of Pendergast was not that it created and maintained a political empire but that it blurred illegality issues whilst ensuring vast personal fortunes for machine leaders at the public's expense. Equally seriously, it encouraged public officials to compromise public interest for private gain.

It's easy to rationalize that when there is so much money in the hands of government a little will go astray, can go astray. But ask yourself about the possibilities. What would be possible if, in our case, as much as a third of our (2021) county income of $633 million didn't go astray? How could our quality of life be better with $211 million? How could our health care be better? What are the glaring gaps in the services our government provides for us—the ones most of us agree are the remit of government? What if we cut out the go-between? What if some of the time and energy spent in providing charitable social support could be redirected to making sure our taxes do that instead? Let's dream for a minute about how it could be different.

"Protection Money" or bribes or extortion paid by developers and business owners to get projects approved or avoid damage to their businesses or reputations could stay with the companies to be reinvested in legitimate economic drivers. If not going to corrupt officials, it might make its way back to consumers in the form of reduced prices or in a more vibrant economy, more creativity, and more job creation.

Projects—development, and one-time infrastructure projects would be completed more quickly and at less cost if there were no delays caused by corrupt officials seeking to wring every last penny from contractors year after year and by artificially increasing the price tag as years go by in order to increase their 'take'.

Public Works costs would stop exceeding the rate of inflation if the cost of paying corrupt "middlemen" was not ratcheting up prices at rates outpacing inflation. This would allow citizens to get more works for their tax dollars rather than increasingly fewer works for their tax dollars, as their un-inflated tax dollars fail to keep up with zooming project costs.

If there was no incentive for "dark" money donations, those funds might be channeled to charity to create good publicity or at least steer the criminally inclined away from government employment. Campaign donations are considered "dark" when multiple donations come from the same person using different LLCs or employees; everything but the names and address of the applicants for the project awaiting government approval. Darker still is the cash that arrives in paper bags. When the intermediaries steal business this way, honest contractors lose jobs and the public loses tax income on undeclared booty.

Campaign reform advocate *Bill Ostrander speaking on 920 KVEC Hometown Radio in* August, 2021 noted that less than .6% of people give more than $200 in campaign donations, which means that the billions invested in campaigns comes from a very small group of people who establish the political discourse, determine the viable candidates by virtue of their financing, and skew legislative decisions to favor subjective interests. Our system of elections requires that candidates who run for election to be public representatives source their election funding from private sources. This is an enormous conflict of interest. He suggests that we can improve legislative decisions that support the "community interest" (democracy) over the "subjective interests" (pay to play, oligarchy, fascism), encourage more participation across minorities, the middle class, and women, and reduce the opportunity for corruption in government, generally, by publicly financing elections. Presently, in Congress, our elected representatives are spending between 30%—70% of their time—not working for constituents, but on the phone fundraising. Public funding of elections refocuses candidates' time on the community issues rather than on seeking donations. He points out that Adam Hill's extortion is an illegal example of Pay to Play, but Hill's admonition, "I'm doing important work for you guys, you need to pony up and support my campaign," is legal (if the funds were disclosed and deposited into his campaign account). It is illegal corruption because it is a form of extortion—he was strong-arming people to make a decision that benefitted their own financial interests.

Pay to play is about donors greasing the wheels so that what they want will come to pass; making an investment in an attempt to get the attention of their elected representative. The temptation and risk for corruption is great when you ask a person who is seeking public office to seek private contributions. The political machine, in exchange for favors, asks for a vote. A campaign contributor, in exchange for a donation, asks for consideration. At a grass-roots level, these trade-offs remain an acceptable political approach.

Ostrander suggests that's the crossover that we really need to discuss, while hoping that Adam Hill was an outlier. While pay to play exists in our government now and goes from top to bottom, Ostrander argues that we can't pillory politicians for chasing money because that's the system we have set up and agreed to and continue to accept. We all say, 'oh, corrupt politicians,' but it's the system that corrupts. He explains that we are biologically wired to be grateful when someone helps us. While polls show that as high as 92% of the population thinks money is negatively impacting our politics, the Supreme Court continues to protect our present system of financing campaigns under the premise of our First Amendment rights of free speech—that giving donations is your right to support a candidate. The only reason to abridge individual rights afforded us by the constitution and Bill of Rights is if the community, or governmental, interest is negatively affected by the rights of the individual. And, of course, corruption and pay to play schemes do have a very negative impact on all of us. Presently, conservative members of the court refuse to consider the community or governmental interest above our individual rights. The 2010 Citizens United decision reversed over 100 years of judicial rulings and turned on the spigot for money in our elections.

We have a love/hate relationship with our politicians. On the one hand we love our politicians. We want them to represent us and to make our world better. On the other hand, we revile them and say they are corrupt. The system we have of campaign donations contributes to our perception that politicians are corrupt. As the Supreme Court has opined, the appearance of corruption is equal to corruption itself because it undermines our faith in our institutions. It leads to voter apathy and perpetuates a system that invites people to be corrupt.

Finally, we could do what I set out to do when I was elected. We could direct our energy to problem solving and improving government service, improving our quality of life. Yes, we would need all of our estates to provide oversight, but we wouldn't have our most insightful minds, law enforcement, and the judiciary tied up in expensive investigations and prosecutions if our representatives were exercising appropriate oversight and our citizens were demanding it. We could do what our constitution intended and fulfill the promise that we have been taught to believe of our nation.

Public Administration expert James Q. Wilson argues that American government is so constituted through separation of powers that it cannot operate without corruption: "The boss, the machine, the political party, the leaders, the lobbyists, and the bagmen all operate to concert the actions of legally independent branches of government, facilitated through exchange of favors. The line which divides political corruption from acceptable practice is difficult to discern. This ambiguity works to the advantage of a machine."

Ostrander suggests that when we remove private money from elections we remove a significant component of the candidates' self-interest—the primal desire to succeed, that in our present system, facilitates the extortion to promote the subjective interests of a donor over the community interests which is a competition of ideas, rather than who is the best fundraiser. I argue that this competition of ideas could result in concrete time well spent on crafting solutions—that which politicians are well equipped to do—if they weren't spending at least half their day fundraising.

Who pays the corrupt official? It's not city hall. It's not the Public Works Department. It's you and me. The go-between is paid from our income, and the money that goes astray steals services, safety, health care, safe streets, repayment of PERS, and modern infrastructure. It demands higher and higher taxes and utility rates to fund both payola and essential services and projects. Or, as Ostrander suggests, the perverting demand for private money out of elections and we will see much more honest and responsive government.

Electing competent honest representatives would bring our money home to us. But so long as we make excuses for the lowest of standards, we will suffer, our neighbors will suffer, our friends and families will suffer, and just as we are still a corrupt county 170 years after our corrupt beginnings in the 1850s, in 2190 we will still be a corrupt county. The Chumash knew it, the Jews knew it—the sins of the fathers extend unto the generations to come. We all know it if we care to. Where there is smoke there is fire. We know that all too well. There's smoke. We must put out this fire.

REALTORS Go Vigilante

I end with two recent local how-to examples of ethical businesspeople-as-vigilantes. The first is a group of REALTORs who moved the dial on loan fraud in one short year. According to the FBI, in 2012 San Luis Obispo County ranked number one in California and number two in the nation for real estate loan embezzlement. Referring to real estate loan predators as "paper terrorists," Steve Van Dohlen, SLO County Deputy DA and Casey Nelson, Santa Barbara County DA Real Estate Specialist, working together with the FBI, transformed the county by 2013-14 from second to seventh position in the nation because REALTORS got together to recruit these experts to clean up the county and educate their real estate colleagues. "Those who perpetrate loan fraud are predators," said Casey. His advice? "If you see something wrong, report it." He even provided his email address to enable reporting: svondohlen@slo.co.ca.us.

Or, as requested by the Assistant US Attorney, *if you have information related to Cannabis, Bribery, or Unreported Income associated with Adam Hill or Shoals, or of any public corruption matter in SLO County, please send information to the FBI's email tip line at pctips-losangeles@fbi.gov or contact the FBI's Los Angeles Field -Office at (310) 477-6565.*

The *CalCoastTimes* story that follows is an example of one way to make sure your government honors your vote. These two attorneys have taken on the county seat, the county, and now the state, winning every time they tackle government gone awry, backed in this case by a SLO County judge who put the vote of the people first.

SLO County judge nixes marijuana billboards on interstate highways

November 22, 2020, By KAREN VELIE

A San Luis Obispo County judge ruled Friday that marijuana billboards on California's interstate highways and some state highways are prohibited by Proposition 64, a voter initiative approved in 2016.

California's Business and Professions Code bars marijuana businesses from advertising on "state or interstate highways which cross the California border." But the California Bureau of Cannabis Control interpreted the law to mean that billboards could be used to advertise marijuana businesses on interstate highways as long as they were not within fifteen miles of the border.

"The bureau determined that a 15-mile radius was a necessary and appropriate distance from the California border because it satisfies the intent of section 26152(d) of the Business and Professions Code, while assuring that bureau licensees have an opportunity to advertise and market along Interstate and State Highways if they satisfy the identified radius limitations," state regulators said in defense of their decision.

That 2019 interpretation led to cannabis billboards sprouting up along highways from San Diego to Crescent City.

Concerned with the impact cannabis advertising could have on children, Matthew Farmer filed a lawsuit challenging the state's interpretation. His attorneys Saro Rizzo and Stewart Jenkins battled the bureau and its interpretation...

SLO County Court Judge Ginger Garrett found that the bureau and Director Lori Ajax "*exceeded their authority in promulgating the advertisement placement regulation. The advertising placement regulation is clearly inconsistent with the advertising placement statute, expanding the scope of permissible advertising to most of California's state and interstate highway system, in direct contravention of the statute,*" Judge Garrett said in her ruling.

After it became apparent the state would likely lose the suit, Ajax announced plans to resign from the bureau.

"*This ruling is a major triumph on several fronts,*" Rizzo said. "*First, it's a victory for all Californians over the desires of unelected Sacramento bureaucrats who illegally tried to put corporate profits ahead of children's health. Second, it's a vindication of the doctrine of separation of powers in that an agency under the control of the Governor's Office was basically told that it cannot subvert the voters' will by adopting a regulation that clearly conflicted with a statute.*"

In addition to the violations of state law, Rizzo and Jenkins discovered that the Lady Bird Johnson Highway Beautification Act forbids the advertising of substances illegal under federal law on interstate highways. Federal law still criminalizes marijuana, and the placement of the cannabis billboards puts California in danger of losing 10 percent of its federal highway funding.

"*The most significant thing about this case is that one person, with a couple of good country lawyers, can compel a state agency through the court to obey the law,*" Jenkins said.

It takes an exceptionally long time to root out corruption, whether the healing happens organically, unto the seventh generation, or through the justice system and citizen activism. It took a decade of surveillance and research initiated by the state governor and the president and his cabinet before the department of the treasury and the justice department could bring down Kansas City machine boss, Tom Pendergast. The effort of crusaders, often seeming to lose the battle to win the war, brought honest government to Kansas City, and maintained it.

It should now be clear that we must act immediately when we see graft. To turn a blind eye to seek to avoid exposure buys time for the crooked to organize and gain power. The longer we give them the more power they amass; the more we stand to lose. The more ingrained and powerful graft becomes the more the resources needed to bring it down. I am just one of many who have worked for two decades to root out this corruption in our county. This book is one effort of hundreds of heart-felt and time-consuming efforts. It's not about me. It's not about you. It's about all of us.

It has been 55 years since Mario Savio, the leader of the 1960s Berkeley Free Speech Movement, gave his famous speech. I wonder, did he know that machines had controlled cities all over the country fifty to a hundred years before he was born? I didn't. As a child of the sixties, I thought "the machine" was a brilliant new construct. I have a sense of connection with Mario. A book commemorating the 50th year of his famous speech was given to every student enrolling on the Berkeley campus in 2014, one of them being my son, who worked as a student IT assistant for the campus police department in the basement of the Sproul Building that had been taken over by students demanding free speech in the 1960s; a time when my own father told me if I went to Berkeley he would disown me.

Campus police now have a better handle on how to work with kids and protesters, and our culture has evolved to realize that it is not only right but critical that young people be allowed a voice. It is our responsibility to teach and train our children to participate in their government. Savio's fight was for students to be allowed to have political tables and meetings at the University. He was right and we are doing better now. Kids who can be drafted and die at the age of eighteen can now also vote. In 2021, the University of California Berkeley was ranked the number one public university in the world and the best in America, outranking even private universities Harvard, Princeton, Yale, and Stanford. Nothing is more important than equipping our young people to participate in the political process because they are the authors of our future and the stewards of our inheritance.

I include Savio because he eloquently described 'the machine.' The machine, the cogs and wheels that Mario railed against, had the traits of censorship of the old school machine and our current machine, with its view that all opposition is revolution. Although claiming to be liberal, neither the press nor the chancellors of the California University system liked Savio, even as they occasionally unwillingly agreed he had a point.

Savio said of the machine:

> "There is a time when the operation of the machine becomes so odious, makes you so sick at heart, that you can't take part; you can't even passively take part, and you've got to put your bodies upon the gears and upon the wheels, upon the levers, upon all the apparatus, and you've got to make it stop. And you've got to indicate to the people who run it, to the people who own it, that unless you're free, the machine will be prevented from working at all!"

Savio was right about the machine. "We must put our bodies upon the gears and upon the wheels, upon the levers, upon all the apparatus, and make it stop."

Here again, the issue is freedom. Freedom from corruption that steals our public services, that censors diversity of opinion, that thwarts spirited discourse.

What Fuels the Machine? Fear Fuels it and Greed Runs it.

+ Complicit press and media whose existence depends on advertising from the machine and machine-controlled businesses.

+ Government employees whose employment depends on cooperation with machine politicians.

+ A business community controlled by fear, dependent on the machine for financial survival and the survival of their reputations.

+ Candidates for office who cannot be elected without the backing of the machine or whose aspirations have been fulfilled by the machine, thus generating an obligation to serve machine interests.

+ A frightened, misinformed, or non-participatory general populace.

+ Voters whose commitment to partisanship is stronger than their commitment to public integrity.

+ Political bosses driven to acquire increasingly more of what they need to feed an addiction, whether sex, money, substance abuse, or gambling.

+ Rationalizing machine behavior so we can then overlook it.

+ Would-be whistle blowers who are more concerned about the appearance of association with wrongdoers than they are about ethics.

Association with the machine is like a venereal disease—no one wants anyone to know they've got it or how they got it.

What has to be Present to Fix it?

- A public that has had enough and has the courage and generates enough people to stand and fight.

- A public willing to set aside gender, political, race, religious, and party divisions to fight together for honest representation.

- Engagement of outside legal, judicial, spiritual, and enforcement authorities.

- Engagement of the press and media on a state and national level.

- Engagement of political representatives up the line at the state and national level.

- Mobilization of individual groups and factions working together with a common goal—to replace the corruption with good government.

To sum up, people who are willing, as Mario Savio said … "to make it stop," who will "indicate to the people who run it, to the people who own it, that unless you're free, the machine will be prevented from working at all!"

What Does Your Responsibility as a Voter Look Like?

Good men and women do exist. Don't vote for someone because they 'vote your way' or vote your partisan preference. Ten former U.S. Secretaries of Defense said it best in a joint opinion article in the *Washington Post* on January 3, 2020:

> ## "Each of us swore an oath to support and defend the Constitution against all enemies, foreign and domestic. We did not swear it to an individual or a party."
>
> -Ashton Carter, Dick Cheney, William Cohen, Mark Esper, Robert Gates, Chuck Hagel, James Mattis, Leon Panetta, William Perry, and Donald Rumsfeld

Vote for bright independent thinkers whose motivation is the public good. Vote for representatives who you would choose as your children's role models…or your own; who inspire you to be better. Unless, of course, you want to be Kansas City or Fresno or SLO County. Vote for representatives with reformist zeal stronger than political ambition.

Not long ago, I heard a caller on a local radio talk show bemoaning the fact that we have no beds in our county for the mentally ill and no rehab beds. The caller blamed a political party. I wanted to call in to say, "The blame does not lie with the other political party, sir. The blame lies with all of us. We who continue to turn a blind eye, who continue to vote a party line, who continue to say, 'that's just how it is.' The blame lies with you and me. If we elected honest intelligent, brave, and true public servants, the 30% of the money we pay to the government that is squandered or siphoned to evil-doers would come back to our county and would fund those mental health and addiction facilities we so desperately need and deserve."

How does the machine meet its end; the boss be removed? As Machiavelli wrote—by the time everyone recognizes the corruption it is too late. This is the rule, but there are exceptions to the rule—battles won against corruption. Of course, it would be best ended before it takes hold—by sound accounting practices, good management, oversight, and prosecution of wrong-doing that stop it before it starts. But what if it is already well-established?

It must be a combined intervention of authorities—death or incarceration can stop it if there is no successor, but someone will always want to step in and grab the profit. It is the combined effort of all the estates. The Fourth Estate, the press, must do their job as the voice of the people. The Fifth Estate, the legal fraternity, must refuse to cover for corrupt politicians and represent the people instead. The Sixth Estate, the administrative branch of government, must have a culture that recognizes that city hall mustn't beat the people. The Seventh Estate, the people, must participate and insist that their institutions serve them.

The failures of the 15th Amendment to make voting possible for African Americans illustrate that if activists stop their work after a movement succeeds and do not follow up to be sure the changes they have fought for are implemented, the vacuum left by the change may lead to a worse situation than before.

When any of the estates are usurped and cannot function as watchdogs over the others, the state and federal judiciary must step in. Finally, the Legislative estate must continue to draft law that protects the people from their government. And, as I said so many times as I watched the corrupt grow more powerful when they faced no opposition, it may take more than earthly powers.

Rabbi Mayerberg and four organizations claim or have been given credit for bringing down the Pendergast machine—The Citizen's Association, *The Kansas City Star*, US Treasury Agent Rudolph Hartman under the direction of Henry Morgenthau, Maurice Milligan, and the FBI. In any takedown of a longstanding criminal machine, it is not just one man of courage and principle who re-establishes justice and order, but many courageous men and women and their families who inspire change with principle and tenacity; some who call it out, some who try and fail, some who pave the way, some who wind it up, and those behind the scenes who stand with them.

The one strong truth is that only the many can succeed. No one person can do it alone, because when the graft has been allowed to continue over the course of decades it becomes so strong that most of the locals are pawns in the game. Berkeley University became number one with an economically, racially, and socially diverse student body. It works. It takes a village to raise a government. We must be united estates.

The talk show host wondered, "But Debbie, what is the ending? You don't have the ending." Is there a happy ending? In my story that's a question that only the people of San Luis Obispo County can answer.

"What people want is very simple. They want an America as good as its promise."

–Congresswoman Barbara Jordan

APPENDIX 1 CAST OF CHARACTERS

Adam Hill—San Luis Obispo County Supervisor, Deceased

Barbara Nicolls—Former Grover Beach Councilmember, Member SSLOCSD Board

Bill Nicolls—Former Grover Beach Councilmember/Mayor Pro Tem, Chair SSLOCSD

Bruce Gibson—SLO County Supervisor

Caren Ray Ruesom—Former Appointed SLO County Supervisor, Mayor/Councilmember Arroyo Grande

Carl Knudson—Government Fraud Investigator

Cory Black—Political Consultant, Manager Grover Beach 'Yes on Measure L'

Dan Carpenter—Former SLO City Councilmember, Candidate SLO County Supervisor

Dave Congalton—Hometown News Radio Show Host, Author

Ed Waage—Mayor/Councilmember Pismo Beach, Candidate SLO County Supervisor

Jeff Lee—Mayor/Councilmember Grover Beach, SLO County Public Works Engineer

Jim Hill—Former Mayor Arroyo Grande, Former President OCSD, SSLOCSD Board

John Clemens—Former Superintendent, SSLOCSD

John Shoals—Former Grover Beach Mayor/Councilmember, PG&E Govt Affairs Rep, Santa Barbara County Planning Supervisor, Land Use Consultant

John L Wallace—Former Administrator, Engineer SSLOCSD and other agencies, Founder, John L. Wallace and Associates

Julie Tacker—Activist, Former Board Member Los Osos Community Services District

Karen Bright—Grover Beach Councilmember/Former Mayor Pro Tem

Karen Velie—Journalist, CalCoastNews.com

Kevin Rice—Activist, firefighter

Mariam Shah—Former Grover Beach Councilmember/Former Mayor Pro Tem

Mark & Julie London—Activists

Mary Lucey—Oceano Community Services District Board Member/ Former President, Former SSLOCSD Board Member

Matt Guererro—Former Oceano Community Services District President, Former SSLOCSD Chair, SLO County Judge

Michael Byrd—Former Candidate SLO County Supervisor, Real Estate Broker

Michael Seitz—Agency Attorney, SSLOCSD, Retired

Patty Welsh—Arroyo Grande resident/vandal

Peter Keith—Former Mayor/Councilmember Grover Beach, Investor, Philanthropist

Ray Biering—Former Agency Attorney APCD, IWMA, Retired

Steve Lieberman—Former Mayor/Councilmember Grover Beach, Fire Chief

Stew Jenkins—Attorney, Former Harbor Commissioner, Candidate SLO County Clerk Recorder

Tony Ferrara—Former Mayor/Councilmember Arroyo Grande, SSLOCSD Chair

APPENDIX 2 DEFINITIONS OF CORRUPTION

Bribery—Offering, promising, giving, accepting, or soliciting something of value to prompt an illegal or unethical action, or a breach of trust. Also referred to as Payola. Example: County Supervisor Adam Hill is paid by Cannabis Mogul Helios Dayspring for favorable decisions by the Board of Supervisors. (Chapter 3)

Coercion—Exploiting a position of authority to pressure on another to do something which he or she would not otherwise do, abuse of a relationship, the threat of taking away from another something he possesses. Example: Employees must do as the political machine boss wishes or lose their jobs. (Chapter 9)

Collusion—A secret agreement between parties to commit actions to deceive or defraud. Example: Agency officials covering up for staff members who steal or sexually harass staff rather than reporting them to law enforcement. (Chapter 12)

Dark Money—Donating money in the name of a company, ally, or employee not identifiable as the source, thus hiding the source. A form of money laundering—it is sneaky, but it looks innocuous. Example: Multiple campaign donations from applicants for city permits under different names rather than the name on the application. (Chapter 10)

Embezzlement—Dishonest and illegal appropriation, use, or trafficking of the funds, goods, or office by an officeholder for personal enrichment. Example: Demanding payouts for favorable land-use votes. (Chapter 6)

Extortion—Using coercive threats, directly or indirectly, under color of authority to demand unmerited cooperation or compensation. Example: Threats from a county supervisor to withhold support of charitable organizations if the mayor is not removed from a committee. (Chapter 5)

Fraud—Deceiving someone to gain an unfair or illegal advantage: financial, political, or otherwise. Example: Hiding last minute donations in order to win an election. (Chapter 2)

Malfeasance—An act by a public official that is legally unjustified, harmful, or contrary to law, wrongdoing. Example: An agency official hiring his own firm to do work for the agency. (Chapter 4)

Misfeasance—Performance of an official duty in an improper or unlawful manner or with an improper or corrupt motive. Example: Sexual harassment of members of staff. (Chapter 1)

Money Laundering—Moving illicitly obtained money through multiple entities to conceal its identity, source, and destination. Example: Using a chain of Limited Liability Companies (LLC) to hide payouts to public officials. (Chapter 7)

Nonfeasance—Failure to act when under an obligation to do so; a refusal (without sufficient excuse) to do that which it is your legal duty to do. Example: Upon finding that a vote will not go their way, the day before a vote, six directors and their alternates announce they cannot attend a board meeting, thus causing a cancelation of the meeting. (Chapter 5)

Pay the Piper—Overpaying because failing to pay the price may result in dire consequences, as in the Pied Piper story—when townsfolk didn't pay him for ridding the town of rats the piper kidnapped the town's children. Or, an idiom coming from the proverb "he who pays the piper calls the tune," implying that the person paying gets to call the shots. Example: Drug lords expect to be in charge of the outcome of their dispensary application if they pay $100,000 to the mayor. (Chapter 3)

Racketeering Influenced Corrupt Organizations Act (RICO)— Originally passed to prosecute the mafia, the RICO Act is now being applied to government organizations that undermine the rule of law, violate rights, and are opaque institutions, leading to lost public resources and weakened national integrity. Example: An unelected administrative agency overriding a vote of the people. (Chapter 14)

CONCERNS ABOUT SSLOCSD OPERATIONS

High costs, low accountability, best practice not implemented or followed

Presented by:
Debbie Peterson, Director SSLOCSD
February 6, 2013

1. Public perception of conflict of interest because District Administrator has a conflict of interest because of his dual simultaneous roles with the District and the Wallace Group. Grand Jury, Local Press, and Media

2. Culture of Secrecy. Resistant to suggestions and defensive response. Difficulty obtaining information. Audited accounts not provided by the district. Had to retrieve them County Auditor-Controller. DP, District correspondence

3. Constant repairs and breakdowns and multiple items out of service at the plant. Agendas, Factory Tour

4. Expenditure on chlorine ($500/day). Reported saving $500/day, but what were they losing annually before? +/- $182,500. Peer Review

5. Almost no checks and balances built into the system until outside reviews were demanded by the public. No separate financial officer. Administrator delegates work to the company under his control. No separate HR department. Peer Review, Grand Jury, County Auditor

6. Original contract (1984-2010) district indemnifies engineer/administrator. Not changed until 2011. The district still indemnifies

Administrator. All legal costs and fines are the responsibility of the district. Administrator and Engineer Contracts

7. Although district pays for insurance cover for administrator and engineer, it was unaware of a change whereby the district was not covered for negligence on the part of the administrator/engineer

8. No annual review of contractors or attorney for 15 years of service for attorney and +/- 25 years for administrator and engineer. Grand Jury, Peer Review

9. Board allowed Wallace to assign Centrifuge Project to his company with no going out to bid. $336,000 expended as of November 2010 and it was not complete at that time. Grand Jury

10. Ongoing high staff turnover (+/- 33% of total employees). Since 2009 +/-. DP

11. Multiple incidences of being over baseline coliforms in past 12 months. Water Board

12. Notice of Violation 12.19.12. Water Board

13. Excess legal fees of +/-$420,000 since 2007, assuming a baseline of

14. +/- $35,000 in legal fees. No documentation showing legal fees expended, fees in the pipeline, and projected fees. Legal fees due to multiple employee lawsuits, 2010 spill, non-working equipment. DP

15. 2006 onward losses of $400,000 to 1,000,000 +/- EVERY YEAR. Audited Accounts

16. Reserves dropped from $7.5m to $3m. Audited Accounts 2006 onward expenses exceed revenues 120—180% +/- every year since 2007. Audited Accounts

17. $1.1m fine. Water Board

18. Amended lawsuit filed 12.18.12 by six neighboring residents. Court Documents

19. Unable to track projects and expenses through budgets from year to year

to determine whether projects are within budget, what expenditures have been made, and which are paid to Wallace or Wallace Group. Grand Jury, DP

20. Periodic budget reviews and adjustment requests provide little if any information about Wallace Group cost overages within any account or capital project. Grand Jury

21. There are dollar amounts scattered throughout the budget that the District Administrator, at his discretion, assigns to the Wallace Group. Grand Jury

22. There is no budget or expense summary report that informs the Board how many budget dollars have been allocated to Wallace Group work. Grand Jury

23. Adversarial relationship with regulators.

24. Administrator is not providing the documentation required by 2011 contract detailing John Wallace and Wallace Group costs prior to payment of John Wallace or Wallace Group fees.

25. Administrator and engineering costs appear far higher than employee cost or other sanitary district costs for the same services.

26. 200+ Pages of Grand Jury, Auditor, Peer Review and Water Board Reviews & Lawsuits, all with similar concerns. 2009-2012.

27. Under the Brown Act, board members can only discuss amongst themselves District activities at Board meetings.

No 'not to exceed' clauses. No year-end final variances. Budget overruns and no evidence of attempts to cut costs. No multi-year comparisons. No month-end reconciliation of accounts. Auditor

SSLOCSD PAST MANAGEMENT
PRACTICES-KNUDSON REPORT
JANUARY 14, 2016

The Honorable District Board South San Luis Obispo County Sanitation
District P.O. Box 339 Oceano, CA 93475

Mr. John Clemons III, CPO, and Acting District Administrator South
San Luis Obispo County Sanitation District (DISTRICT) 1600 Aloha
Place Oceano, CA 93475

EXECUTIVE SUMMARY

Our goal as we conducted our investigative review of the Past Management
Practices of the "Wallace Years," was to be fair and objective and let the
evidence gathered speak for itself. This approach was endorsed by District
Management and the current Board of Directors. We are mindful that
there are different viewpoints about the success or failure of the operation
of the District during the "Wallace Years." However, we have strived to
represent all viewpoints that were relevant to the goals of our review.

At the beginning of our Past Management Practices review, we
sought out all the available South San Luis Obispo County Sanitation
District ("District") accounting/financial records for the periods 2004
to 2013, which were stored at the Oceano Wastewater Treatment Plant
("WWTP") or available through other witnesses or government agencies.
However, we believe that to fairly evaluate the management practices
during the 27-year career of John Wallace, we sought to also include
in our review, the District's accounting/financial records for the period
1986 to 2004, which were unorganized and found in different areas of

the District. In piecing the historical financial records together, we were able to gain a broader and a more balanced historical perspective.

The accounting/financial records of the District were unorganized and had suffered from years of mismanagement by the previous District Administrator. But, because Mr. Wallace insisted on being present during our interviews with his employees, current and former, we did not conduct the interview with others from the Wallace Group that were involved in the finances of the District. We did send and receive emails related to the billings of the Wallace Group.

During the years 1986 to 2004, John Wallace performed without incident as the District Administrator of the District in executing the financial and managerial duties of his office. There were no documented employee issues at the District and the Audited Financial Statement for the Fiscal Year Ending in 2004 showed $8.9 million in cash and cash equivalents on the Balance Sheet. The financial statements of the District at this point were simple and easy to follow. The monthly payments to Wallace & Associates were in the $3,000 to $5,000 range.

We noted in the District's Audited Financial Statements that the year 2000 was the end of the "Chuck Ellison Era".

However, 2004 to 2013 there were growing operational, financial and personnel issues at the District that culminated in 2011 with the investigations by the San Luis Obispo Grand Jury, the Central Coast Regional Water Quality Control Board ("Water Board") and legal proceedings against the District and John Wallace by at least three former District employees.

As early as 1986, there were institutional weaknesses in the District that would disrupt continuity in the process of evaluating and monitoring the performance of the District Administrator and the financial affairs of the District as follows:

There was a designed turnover of District Board Members on a yearly basis who are all elected officials from Arroyo Grande, Grover Beach and OCSD (participating agencies).

The three-page 1986 Contract between the District and John L.

Wallace and Associates had no performance standards or provisions for accountability, and renewed until July 2011, twenty-five years later. When Wallace and Associates changed its name and company structure in 2004, the District did not amend the 1986 contract to reflect the change. Written performance evaluations of the District Administrator/ District Engineer by the Board of Directors were not performed yearly and there was no transparency as to the Board's evaluations of Wallace to the Rate Payers.

There was no Purchasing and Construction Policy related to expenditures in place at the District and it wasn't until 1999 that the Board passed a resolution setting forth the policies and procedures for the Expenditure of District funds. The Board approved projects related to Administrative and Operational work at the District (mostly by the Wallace group), which could have been accomplished by qualified employees at the WWTP at no cost to the District.

However, the rationale, as expressed by one long-serving Board member was that the Plant Superintendent and the part-time secretary were not competent to perform the administrative duties such as: Staff Reports, Board Packets and Budget Reports, so this work was directed to the Wallace Group by the Board from 2001 until 2012 just before John Wallace retired. The fact that the Board deemed the Plant Superintendent to be incompetent is one thing, it is another to keep him on for over 10-years when the appropriate business decision would have been to bring in a qualified Superintendent and a full-time secretary.

There was no "contract" between the participating agencies and the District regarding the collection and payment of fees by the participating agencies. This was the only source of operating "revenue" for the District operating budget and expansion fund. A former Board Member said the local business practices were "rural" and business in the area was often done on a "handshake."

There was an apparent conflict of interest where the wife of the District's long serving legal counsel was employed by the Wallace Group in their HR Department and was involved in the sensitive personnel issues that were ongoing at the District between John Wallace and the employees of the District.

By 2001 the jobs traditionally performed by the Chief Plant Operator and the District Bookkeeper/Secretary had been taken over by John Wallace and assigned to the Wallace Group. Many of the administrative projects such as: Board Packets, Staff Reports, Yearly Budget Reports traditionally performed by the CPO-Plant Superintendent and the in-house secretary/bookkeeper were taken over by the Wallace Group and charged in their billings to the District (Thus double-paying for this work.) with the approval of the Board of Directors.

Wallace assumed control over all aspects of the financial affairs of the District including the approval of the Wallace Group invoices presented to the District for payment. Billings by the Wallace Group grew steadily from $3,600 and 81 hours per month in 1999 to over 600 hours and $70,000 per month by the end of 2010. During this time, the Wallace Group received over $6 million dollars for Administrative Fees, Engineering Fees, and Major Budget Item projects. during this same period of time, exceeded Revenue by a substantial amount every year.

The number of Major Budget Item Projects for which the Wallace Group received fees (MBI) grew from seven (7) MBI projects in 2003 grew to twenty-eight (28) MBI projects in 2011. There was also an increase in the number of Wallace Group employees charging time to Administrative, Engineering, and MBI Projects to the District.

Staff Reports were included in the "Board Packets" and were prepared by John Wallace acting as the District Administrator. The Staff Reports provided an explanation of Major Budget Item projects proposed at that time. There was a constant reference in the Staff Reports to "District Staff" performing work on MBI projects. These "District Staff" were actually Wallace Group employees.

The Board approved MBI Projects for the Wallace Group without the proscribed bidding process for projects that exceeded the $25,000 thresholds for MBI project(s).

Over fifty-six (56) boxes of the operating, personnel and business records of the District were stored at the Wallace Group offices, and at the time of Wallace's retirement, and thereafter there were missing or unaccounted for assets, such as the CAD drawings and GIS analysis paid for by the District. There was no formal inventory of the District's records at the District as required in the District's Operating Manual (O&M).

There was a steady depletion of the District's "Reserves," which were critical to the longevity of the plant. The use of "Reserve" funds for Operational expenses was contrary to District guidelines in Resolution 24 enacted in 1966 and confirmed by the District's outside auditor in their 2011-2012 Audit report to the Board of Directors.

The critical issue of back up precautions [redundancy] detailed in a 2005 Kennedy Jenks Report were not adequately addressed by the Wallace administration or the Board of Directors and the cost of the construction increased from $4-6 million in 2005 to $12 million (present dollars 2015). [$40 million 2020]

There were conflicts of interest in assigning administrative, engineering, and MBI work by Wallace as the District Administrator to the Wallace Group thereby bypassing or duplicating the duties of the CPO, bookkeeper, and the Operators at the plant. The fact that the Board of Directors sanctioned all or some of these actions, in our opinion does not eliminate the conflict. In our opinion, the obvious resolution to the lack of confidence that the Board of Directors had regarding the District Superintendent would have been to replace him with a person who had their confidence.

Finally, there was potential Malfeasance in office in the solicitation of payments by Wallace for the Wallace Group while acting in the capacity as the District Administrator for the District. Malfeasance is a public official's performance of an act that is contrary to law. Because potential violations of law are investigated and processed by law enforcement officials, we suggest that this report be provided to law enforcement officials for their determination.

In conclusion, the ending of the "Wallace Era" certainly distracted from his early successes, but as Wallace retired as the District Administrator/

Engineer at the beginning of 2013, the District reserves had been depleted to the level where the critical "redundancy" issues, outstanding since at least 2005, cannot be resolved without seeking outside funding. In the meantime, if the WWTP experiences a failure of the main operating components of the WWTP and there is a resulting sewage spill into the area, as in December 2010, the fines and penalties will be severe.

In evaluating the Past Management Practices, the question to be answered is; Is the District better off today after 27 years under the administration of John Wallace? The fact is that the WWTP is 27 years older, but the critical issues regarding "redundancy" still remain even after several reports issued by Kennedy Jenks Consulting beginning in 2005. The other question to ask is Did the Board of Directors manage the District Administrator? Did complacency or personal relations set in even though there were warning signs of increasing payments to the Wallace Group, decreasing reserves, increasing personnel issues with plant employees, and increasing plant violations?

The findings and conclusions in our report are not inconsistent with the findings of the 2011 San Luis Obispo County Grand Jury, the 2011 Water Quality Control Board's investigation, and the 2012 Audit by the San Luis Obispo County Auditor/Controller. Having said that, our findings were determined independently and are substantially different in depth of analysis and investigative efforts.

I did not redact the identities from the report of those individuals that I interviewed, and I did not promise or suggest to those individuals that their conversations would be held in confidence. However, there may be other legal concerns or information that we are not privy to or aware of, so it is our suggestion that the District's legal counsel consider this issue.

Respectfully submitted,

Carl R. Knudson, Knudson & Associates

NOTES

ACRONYMS

APCO: Air Pollution Control Officer
DA: District Attorney
EIR: Environmental Impact Report
FBI: Federal Bureau of Investigation
FPPC: Fair Political Practices Commission
IWMA: Integrated Waste Management Authority
LAFCO: Local Agency Formation Commission
LLC: Limited Liability Company
OCSD: Oceano Community Services District
OHMVRA: Off Highway Motor Vehicle Recreation Area
OHV: Off Highway Vehicle
PM: Particulate Matter
RWQCB Regional Water Quality Control Board
SLOAPCD (APCD): San Luis Obispo County (Air Pollution Control District)
SLOCOG (COG): San Luis Obispo County (Council of Governments)
SSLOCSD: South San Luis Obispo County Sanitation District
SWRCB: State Water Resources Control Board

INTRODUCTION TO NOTES

Documentation for this book is supported by federal court records (Central California District Court) (the production of documents through the discovery process); the personal files of the author; FBI archived case notes, published newspaper, television, and radio accounts, transcriptions of government video and audio tapes (SLO-SPAN.org Morro Bay, Ca. 93443 (805) 772-2715 agpvideo@agpvideo.com, Site pioneered by Roscoe Mathieu, Dave Husk and Steve Mathieu), staff reports, agendas, and minutes of public meetings. References to FBI information come from the full text of "Operation Rezone" https://archive.org/stream/OperationRezone/Operation Rezone_djvu.txt, unless otherwise noted from news reports.

Links to information on the internet were accurate at the time of publication; however, information on the internet is sometimes moved or deleted. The author has retained hard copies of references. If links no longer function, try deleting details at the end of the link and searching the website or publication indicated at the beginning of the link.

FOREWORD

"The FBI showed up at [Mayor] Jeff Lee's house one morning"
CalCoastNews https://*calcoastnews*.com/2020/11/fbi-raids-on-3-public-officials-target-cannabis-corruption/ November 9, 2020

INTRODUCTION

"It goes way back"
Author Jim Gregory details nefarious activities lost to time. History Press 2017 p.33 San Luis Obispo County Outlaws: Desperados, Vigilantes and Bootleggers by Jim Gregory | The History Press Books (arcadiapublishing.com)

PART I: CAN IT BE TRUE?

1. SUPERVISOR HILL IS DEAD

"the *LA Times* article, 'One Giant French Kiss Wrapped in Money,' quoted court filings."
https://www.latimes.com/california/story/2021-07-29/cannabis-businessman-bribe-san-luis-obispo-county-supervisor

The FBI had also raided Mayor Lee's home twice.
CalCoastNews https://calcoastnews.com/2020/11/fbi-raids-on-3-public-officials-target-cannabis-corruption July 9, 2020

"Oprah Winfrey"
http://www.oprah.com/own-oprahshow/happiest-city-in-america-san-luis-obispo-video. (Aired 1/26/11)

"Woodward, *Business Insider*"
10/12/18 interview with Alan Smith

"John Stossel"
Give Me a Break: How I Exposed Hucksters, Cheats, and Scam Artists and Became the Scourge of the Liberal Media. Harper Perennial https://www.amazon.com/Give-Me-Break-Exposed-Hucksters/dp/0060529156

"Many of the harassing emails"
2019 Declaration of Karen Velie, SLO County Superior Court Velie vs. Hill and County of SLO

"Adam Hill threatens Pismo Beach Council"
CalCoastNews https://calcoastnews.com/2012/10/supervisor-threatens-pismo-beach-council/ October 2, 2012

"Supervisor campaigns to shut down CalCoastNews"
CalCoastNews https://calcoastnews.com/2012/07/supervisor-campaigns-to-shut-down-

cal... July 16, 2012 by *CalCoastNews* staff

"June 2012"
2019 Declaration of Karen Velie, SLO County Superior Court Velie vs. Hill and County of SLO, Exhibits 1-67

"Hill then began contacting *CalCoastNews* advertisers"
2019 Declaration of Karen Velie, SLO County Superior Court Velie vs. Hill and County of SLO, Exhibits 1-67

2. LOCAL GOVERNMENT 101 TO 911

"Swearing In"
California Constitution SEC. 3. (Article 20 adopted 1879) (Sec. 3 amended Nov. 4, 1952, by Prop. 6. Res.Ch. 69, 1951)

"'The *Tribune* was right'"
CalCoastNews Apology from Supervisor Adam Hill—
https://calcoastnews.com/2012/12/apology-from-supervisor-adam-hill OPINION by SAN LUIS OBISPO SUPERVISOR ADAM HILL 22/12/2012

"San Luis Obispo Council of Governments Board Meeting."
Agenda Item 4A—http://www.slo-span.org/media.php?slo=1—These comments are found 1 hour 22 minutes and 55 seconds into the videotape of the meeting.

"City Council Committee Assignments"
20:14 Public Comment Adam Hill

"Hill had walked out of a supervisor's board meeting"
SLO County Board of Supervisors Board Meeting December 8, 2015

"confessed felon, Helios "Bobby" Dayspring"
The United States Attorney's Office Central District of California Department of Justice Wednesday July 28, 2021

"For the next few months Hill"
This reference and references to follow regarding Adam Hill's treatment of Karen Velie are taken from the Declaration of Karen Velie and Exhibits 1-67—KAREN VELIE, an individual, Plaintiff, vs. ADAM HILL, an individual, COUNTY OF SAN LUIS OBISPO; and DOES 1 through 50, Defendants, United States District Court, Central District of California, Case No.: 2:16CV-07839 DSF (Ex), September 11, 2014

"Meanwhile, over the previous twelve months"
Declaration of Karen Velie, Exhibit 29

"August 13, 2020, SLO County supervisor accused of sexual misconduct"
CalCoastTimes https://calcoasttimes. com/2020/11/19/slo-county-settles-adam-hill-sexual-harassment-lawsuit/ November 19, 2020 by Karen Velie

3. TREPIDATION 2015 -2020

"But it hasn't worked out this way in SLO County"
Centers for Disease Control and Prevention, National Center for
Health Statistics
https://www.washingtonpost.com/health/2021/11/17/overdose-deaths-pandemic-fentanyl/

"Mayor Shoals waved a glossy flyer"
https://slo-span.org/static/meetings-GBCC. php city council meeting 2.21.17 at 3 hours, 50 minutes

"Council member Mariam Shah"
https://www.ksby.com/news/local-news/2019/02/21/former-grover-beach-city-council-member-details-alleged-corruption-by-other-members

"February 4, 2018"
https://slocounty.granicus.com/MediaPlayer. php?view_id=2&clip_id=2834 (At 19:08 minutes into the meeting)

"FBI Seeks Tips on Corruption"
https://www.fbi.gov/audio-repository/ftw-podcast-marijuana-industry-corruption-081519.mp3/view

"*CalCoastNews* reported that the FBI"
CalCoastTimes https://calcoastnews. com/2020/05/fbi-agents-interviewing-san-luis-obispo-county-officials/ May 15, 2020 by Karen Velie

"SLO County remains a safe place to live." https://247wallst.com/special-report/2022/01/10/the-metro-where-your-car-is-least-likely-to-be-stolen-in-every-state/

PART II: THE DEVIL IS IN THE DISTRICT

4. SEWER TOUR

"John Oliver–Special "Ghost" Districts"
March 6, 2016, *Last Week Tonight* show https://www.youtube.com/watch?v=3saU5racsGE

"Ferrara's resume"
https://transparentcalifornia.com/pensions/search/?q=tony+ferrara&y= www.calema.ca.gov/...California Governor's Office of Emergency Services

"even lawmen felt they were being threatened"
Knudson Report, 2016. Interview with State Parks

"SSLOCSD Budget Graph"
Screen shot of the SSLOCSD Bylaws approved March 2, 2011, p.6; Fiscal Year Budget 2010-2011, Exhibit A, p. 97

"April 2011, Grand Jury"
https://slo.surfrider.org/wp-content/uploads/SSLOCSD-Report-FINAL.pdf

"Councilmember Ed Arnold"
Santa Maria Times https://santamariatimes. com/news/local/crime-and-courts/

d5e13466-ad14-11e0-ae0f-001cc4c002e0.
html Jul 13, 2011 by April Charlton/Senior
Staff Writer

"CC/IA-1. Appointments to Various Boards, Commissions, and Committees 2:37:12"

John Wallace Presentation & Council
Questions Item 3 on the Agenda Update
regarding the Overall South San Luis Obispo
Sanitation District, https://cal-span.org/
radio.php?site=slo-span&filename=https://
slo-span.org/media/Audio_Files/GBCC/
GBCC_12-07-16/GBCC_12-07-16.MP3

https://cal-span.org/radio.php?site=slo-
span&filename=https://slo-span.org/
media/Audio_Files/GBCC/GBCC_12-01-03/
GBCC_12-01-03.mp3 2 h

"January 26, 2011 See no evil, smell no evil: Is a South County sanitation district corking whistleblowers?"

BY COLIN RIGLEY New Times https://
www.newtimesslo.com/sanluisobispo/
IssueArchives?issue=2890670https://www.
newtimesslo.com/sanluisobispo/see-no-evil-
smell-no-evil/Content?oid=2941553

"Two Oceano leaders suddenly resign"

New Times San Luis Obispo https://
www.newtimesslo.com/sanluisobispo/
two-oceano-leaders-suddenly-resign/
Content?oid=2943403Show me BY ROBERT
A. MCDONALD staff writer March 28, 2011

"Show me the money"

New Times San Luis Obispo, https://www.
newtimesslo.com/sanluisobispo/show-me-
the-money/Content?oid=2941146

"The Regional Water Quality Control Board's public hearing was damning"

SEPTEMBER 7, 2012, PUBLIC HEARING TO
CONSIDER ADMINISTRATIVE CIVIL LIABILITY
COMPLAINT NO. R3-2012-0030 SOUTH
SAN LUIS OBISPO COUNTY SANITATION
DISTRICT TRANSCRIPT OF HEARING BEFORE

THE REGIONAL WATER QUALITY CONTROL
BOARD, CENTRAL COAST REGION

"The San Luis Obispo County District Attorney's office has filed felony"

CalCoastNews calcoastnews.com/2017/01/
john-wallace-arrested-on-felony-conflict-of-
interest-charges/#:~:text=The%20San%20
Luis%20Obispo%20County%20District%20
Attorney%E2%80%99s%20office, Obispo%20
County%20Sanitation%20District. %20
The%20announcement%20came%20
Tuesday by Karen Velie

"Release the sanitation district audit"

CalCoastNews Release the sanitation
district audit without interference, https://
calcoastnews.com/2015/12/release-
the-sanitation-district-audit-without-
interference/ December 16, 2015 Opinion by
Debbie Peterson

"January 10, 2018, Wallace case moved to Santa Maria after Guerrero appointed judge"

CalCoastNews https://*calcoastnews*.
com/2018/01/wallace-case-moved-santa-
maria-guerrero-appointed-judge/ January
10, 2018

"Fleeced residents deserve restitution from John Wallace"

CalCoastTimes https://*calcoasttimes*.
com/2018/03/27/fleeced-residents-deserve-
restitution-john-wallace/ Opinion by Julie
Tacker March 27, 2018

"March 6, 2018"

https://www.slocounty.ca.gov/Departments/
District-Attorney/Latest-News/2018/March/
Former-District-Administrator-of-South-San-
Luis-Ob.aspx

"Patty Welsh, the accuser"

3/11/2019 Judge Van Rooyen
Arroyo Grande City Council Meeting
1/24/17

"In 2020 the Agency referenced by Nicolls"
CalCoastNews San Simeon loses grant money, conflicts of interest exposed https://calcoastnews.com/2020/11/san-simeon-loses-grant-money-conflicts-of-interest-exposed/November 3, 2020 by Karen Velie

"*Cal CoastTimes* reported in November 2020"
https://calcoasttimes.com/?s=two+san+simeon+grants+re-scinded November 3, 2020 Karen Velie

"Since 2016 the agency has been in trouble"
CalCoastNews November 13, 2021 OPINION by HANK KRZCIUK

"Sept. 28, 2021, DA's Special Prosecution Division"
https://www.slocounty.ca.gov/Departments/District-Attorney/Latest-News/2021/September/District-Attorney%E2%80%99s-Office-files-unfair-competitio.aspxClick here to view a copy of the full complaint

"Political Reform Act of 1974"
California Government Code section 81001, subpart (b)

"The District serves as"
https://www.fppc.ca.gov/content/dam/fppc/documents/Stipulations/2021/november/6-Charles-Grace-Stip.pdf

"Meanwhile the FPPC was making its own history"
FPPC Case No. 2020-00416 STIPULATION, DECISION AND ORDER

"The Brown Act requires all meetings"
Gov. Code § 54953(a)

"a "meeting" occurs""
Gov. Code § 54952.2

"prejudice the position of the agency"
Gov. Code § 54956.9(a)

"pending litigation"
54956.9(d)(4)

"November 10, 2021"
CalCoastTimes https://calcoasttimes.com/2021/11/10/northern-slo-county-water-district-officials-violate-the-brown-act/ November 10, 2021 by Karen Velie

7. AIR POLLUTION TROLL DISTRICT

"Weakness"
Inspired by Star Wars: The Last Jedi (2015)

"State Geological Survey Senior Engineering Geologist and Hydrologist, Will Harris"
LICENSE_NUMBER=2222&P_LTE_ID=887

"As a contributor to the 2010 Dust Study [Harris]"
slocleanair.org PM2 final report.pdf (at page 2)

"trees that had historically functioned as wind blocks"
Historic Santa Maria Valley by Lucinda K. Ransick Chapter 1

"The Petition"
http://www.ipetitions.com/petition/repeal-the-dust-rule

"I wrote the West Mesa Dust Report"
www.DebbiePeterson.com

"Straight out of the staff report"
San Luis Obispo APCD Proposed Revisions to Rule 302 5/29/13 "As required by Section 40727 of the California Health & Safety Code, the District Board shall make findings of necessity, authority, clarity, consistency, on-duplication, and reference"

"January 23, 2013, APCD Board Meeting: Hill Promises Not to Send any More Letters on the Board's Behalf Without Board Agreement"
Agenda Item A1 Election of Officers—http://slocounty.granicus.com/MediaPlayer.php?view_id=7&clip_id=1425

"May 6, 2013, Grover Beach City Council Meeting"
Public Comment http://www.slospan.org/media.php?agency=gbcc
54:00, Supervisor Hill

"Hill was quick to respond"
Public Comment (audio at http://www.slo-span.org/media.php?slo=3) 1:42:11
SUPERVISOR ADAM HILL

"Harris, had the audacity to stand up during public comment"
https://www.youtube.com/watch?v=qMcST-Lihzw

"June 17, 2015, SLO County APCD Board Meeting"
http://slocounty.granicus.com/MediaPlayer.php?view_id=7&clip_id=2083 3:04:41 Mr. Will Harris starts his public comment on Item C-3

"Nipomo Ranch, Wednesday, April 10, 1861"
Up and Down California in 1860 to 1864, the journal of William H. Brewer, Professor of Agriculture in the Sheffield Scientific School from 1864 to 1903. Forgotten Books (August 24, 2018)

"October 1, 2020, Scripps study on dust at Oceano Dunes"
https://ohv.parks.ca.gov/pages/1140/files/Scripps%20response%20to%20APCD%20comments_110821.pdf

New Times, "we're just interested in getting the right science out there"
SLO New Times https://www.newtimesslo.com/sanluisobispo/news/Section?oid=2896479

"November 15, 2021, Court Ruling"
https://www.oceanodunes.org/category/legal/rulings/

"November 21, 2021"
CalCoastTimes https://calcoasttimes.com/2021/11/30/air-district-accused-again-of-misinformation-regarding-oceano-dunes/ November 21, 2021 Karen Velie

7. WHO OWNS THE WATER

"county website"
https://www.slocounty.ca.gov/

"Mark Arax, Author of West of the West"
West of the West: Dreamers, Believers, Builders, and Killers in the Golden State by Mark Arax P. 182

"Marijuana News"
http://420intel.com

"Postscript"
CalCoastNews San Simeon loses grant money, conflicts of interest exposed https://calcoastnews.com/2020/11/san-simeon-loses-grant-money-conflict-of-interest-exposed/ November 3, 2020 by Karen Velie

"Since 2016 SSCSD had been in trouble"
https://calcoastnews.com/2021/11/san-simeon-csd-refuses-to-apologize-to-owners-of-hearst-ranch/ November 13, 2021 by Henry Krzciuk

PART III PANTOMIMES, KINGS, AND MACHINES

8. THE FRESNO PANTOMIME

"Whether a function of its detached geography…"
LA Times August 7, 1994 Federal Probe Focuses on Fresno Land deals, LATimes.com

"Pismo Beach City Website"
https://www.pismobeach.org/319/ Department-History

"Agents Weddick and Moline"
Unless otherwise noted, references to and their case notes come from the Full text of Operation Rezone https://archive. org/stream/OperationRezone/Operation Rezone_djvu.txt

"Proposition 112"
http://www.fppc.ca.gov/about-fppc/about-the-political-reform-act.html

"Planning Commissioner:"
Federal Probe Focuses on Fresno Land Deals: Government: A hometown hero turns whistle-blower as an inquiry looks into the close ties between a handful of elected officials and local developers. August 07, 1994 Mark Arax Times Staff Writer

"A wide-ranging…"
Fresno Corruption Probe Snares Lobbyist : Ethics: He …, https://www.latimes.com/ archives/la-xpm-1995-07-07-mn-21063-story.html

"Stevens, an appointee," and "What flabbergasts me,"and "media reports noted"
Trouble in California's Heartland : U.S …, https://www.latimes.com/archives/la-xpm-1995-12-06-mn-10860-story.html

"Investigators say they have uncovered"
https://www.latimes.com/archives/la-xpm-1995-12-06-mn-10860-story.html

"Roberts pleaded guilty"
Fresno Corruption Probe Snares Lobbyist : Ethics: He …, https://www.latimes.com/ archives/la-xpm-1995-07-07-mn-21063-story.html

"Tom Bohigian"
Fresno Corruption Probe Snares Lobbyist : Ethics: He …, https://www.latimes.com/ archives/la-xpm-1995-07-07-mn-21063-story.html

"Jeffrey Harris"
Trouble in California's Heartland—L.A. Times, https://www.latimes.com/archives/la-xpm-1995-12-06-mn-10860-story.html

"SF Gate" 10/3/99 SF
https://www.sfgate.com/

"Former Assembly Speaker Charged with Taking Bribe"
November 7, 1998, | From Associated Press

9. THE KING OF KANSAS CITY MEETS THE MAYOR FOR THE AGES

"You have turned your city"
239 "To Council on McElroy". The Kansas City Star, 25th May, 1932, p. 1

"the words of former mayor"
Civic Housekeepers: Women's Organizations, Civic Reform …. https://www.pendergastkc. org/article/civic-housekeepers-women%E2%80%99s-organizations-civic-reform-and-1940-elections

"Impartial and fair elections"
FBI Involvement in Early Election Fraud Case in Kansas City. https://www.fbi.gov/news/ stories/fbi-involvement-in-early-election-fraud-case-in-kansas-city

"lack of accountability"
John B. Gage | The Pendergast Years. https://pendergastkc.org/article/biography/john-b-gage

"Mayerberg writes in his autobiography"
Chronicle of an American Crusader by Samuel S Mayerberg, copyright 1944 by SSSM, published by the Block Publishing Company

"Nixon's diary records the meeting, if not the content"
From online sources—President Nixon's daily diary. https://www.nixonlibrary.gov/sites/default/files/2018-07/1974%20Presidential%20Daily%20Diary.pdf

"Ancestry website"
www.Ancestry.com

"Hourly reports of an Armenia genocide"
Morgenthau, Henry Sr. Ambassador Morgenthau's Story—A Personal Account of the Aermenian Genocide

The "Armenian Question"
Audio recording of Chapter 24, "The Murder of a Nation," from Ambassador Morgenthau's Story.
raoulwallenberg.net. https://www.raoulwallenberg.net/wp-content/files_mf/1439907848HenryMorgenthauAmbassador.pdf

"A public fundraising committee to assist the Armenians"
Henry Morgenthau Sr.—Wikipedia. https://en.wikipedia.org/wiki/Henry_Morgenthau_Sr.

"The Progressive Party Waned"
The Kansas City Library

"Activism among women's clubs"
Women's Political Activism in the Interwar Period in Kansas City Author: David Hanzlick

Park University, Rockhurst University, https://www.pendergastkc.org/article/morally-and-legally-entitled-women%E2%80%99s-political-activism-interwar-period-kansas-city

"gangsta"
Frank Nash—Wikipedia. https://en.wikipedia.org/wiki/Frank_Nash

"FBI agents"
Nash, Frank "Jelly"—Encyclopedia of Arkansas. https://encyclopediaofarkansas.net/entries/frank-jelly-nash-4067/

"To control the city legislature"
John S. Matlin's. thesis Political Machines of the 1920s & 30's Tom Pendergast and the Kansas City Democratic Machine, 2009 p.82 (Hereafter Matlin will be referenced only as 'John S. Matlin')

"In the midst of the Great Depression"
John S. Matlin

"They were not disposed to let him off for they knew him as a confirmed free thinker."
Chronicle of an American Crusader by Samuel S Mayerberg, copyright 1944 by SSSM, published by the Block Publishing Company

"Researchers found Hartmann's treatise"
Rudolph H. Hartman, The Kansas City Investigation: Pendergast's Downfall, 1938–1939. University of Missouri Press. LCCN 99018273

"the dapper and personable Frank Nash"
Wikipedia—Frank Nash

"the oldest law firm west of the Mississippi River"
Wikipedia—John Gage

"A Kansas City Star cub reporter"
Reddig, pp. 195-199 and 220. "To Council on McElroy." The Kansas City Star

"In week three of his assault"
Star, 25th May 1932, p. 1. Annotated Charter of Kansas City, 1925

"A skulking hyena"
Larsen, Lawrence H. and Hulston, Nancy J. Pendergast. (Columbia, Missouri. 1997. University of Press.) pp. 105-6

"According to the Star's interpretation of the city charter"
Star continued reporting on Mayerberg, writing on 7th June 1932, that the latter would "The Mayerberg Charges."
The Kansas City Star, 1st June 1932

"On his return Mayerberg tried again to get police records."

"The Rabbi Home Eager."
The Kansas City Star, 21st July 1932, p.1.

"After just over three months, Mayerberg's campaign came to a sudden end"

"Rabbi Quits Politics."
The Missouri Democrat, 30th September 1932

"soreheads"
Larsen, Lawrence H. and Hulston, Nancy J. Pendergast. (Columbia, Missouri. 1997. University of Press.) p. 111

"multiply amounts quoted by 18 to arrive at 2021 values."
https://www.in2013dollars.com/us/inflation website to calculate values. (Values will change with time)

"The Union Station Massacre"
Frank "Jelly" Nash (1887–1933)—
Encyclopedia of Arkansas

"Who were these 20th century progressives?"
John S. Matlin p.63

"The Archives at Western"
Larsen and Hulston, op cit, p.38

"Although a machine was not averse to using mafia-style tactics"
John S. Matlin, p.102

"Beneficiaries of patronage would know that if they were disloyal, their jobs would be in danger."
John S. Matlin, p. 132

"There are degrees of honesty"
John S. Matlin p.219

Pendergast had just pleaded guilty to income tax evasion for not paying taxes on the insurance bribe received that had paid off his gambling debt.
Wikipedia—Pendergast

"The Wizard of Oz"
L. Frank Baum, *The Wonderful Wizard of Oz* (1900) Metro-Goldwyn-Mayer. A Musical adaptation of L. Frank Baum's 1900 children's fantasy novel

"Mugshot of Tom Pendergast"
National Archives at College Park. https://catalog.archives.gov/id/580698

"Here's how the Citizens Association Facebook page describes Gage."
https://www.facebook.com/pg/CitizensAssociationKansasCity/about/?ref=page_

"The city auditor found"
David McCullough. Truman. (New York. 1992. Simon & Schuster.) p. 239

"John B. Gage died today"
Associated Press, January 15, 1970

"The Chamber of Commerce formed the Nonpartisan"
David McCullough. Truman. (New York. 1992. Simon & Schuster.) p.239

10. THE MACHINE ISN'T DEAD HERE

"You can't trade on your office"
Press Release: Department of Justice, U.S. Attorney's Office
District of Massachusetts, Former Fall River Mayor Convicted of Extorting Marijuana Vendors and Defrauding Investors Friday, May 14, 2021

"It was not until the Great Society years of Lyndon Johnson"
John S. Matlin, p. 271

"Characteristics"
Michael Johnston. "Patrons and Clients, Jobs and Machines: A Case Study of the Uses of Patronage." The American Political Science Review. Vol. 73, No. 2. (Jun., 1979) p. 385

"Debts of influence owed to a boss"
Banfield, Edward C. and Wilson, James Q. City Politics. (Cambridge, Massachusetts. 1967. Harvard University Press.) p.115

"The boss may give you a job, but he will leave you in fear of losing your job."
Michael Johnston. "Patrons and Clients, Jobs pp. 385-398

"Patronage is Political Party Loss"
Dagger, Thomas G. "Political Patronage in Public Contracting." The University of Chicago Law Review, Vol. 51, No. 2. (Spring, 1984) pp. 518-558

"Strong Internal Controls"
https://www.cbsnews.com/news/getting-away-with-white-collar-crime/

"This complete lack of transparency"
White Collar Crimes and the Effects on Consumers and ..., https://ezinearticles.com/?White-Collar-Crimes-and-the-Effects-on-Consumers-and-Globalization&id=8803583

"State records show"
California Secretary of State Registrar of Companies, and 'Yes on L' campaign statements at Grover.org

"Mayor Lee"
Campaign disclosures are available at Grover.org

"$11m misappropriated by the machine"
Reddig, op cit, p.185.

"Former Grover Beach mayor resigns from Santa Barbara County job after harassment allegation"
By: KSBY Staff Posted at 6:05 PM, Dec 20, 2019

PART IV THE SEVEN UNITED ESTATES

"at local government level"
John S. Matlin p. 23"

11. THE FOURTH ESTATE

"The term muckraker"
Wikipedia—Muckraker

"filled a small telephone book"
Larsen and Hulston. op cit p.86

"Watchdog journalism informs"
Wikipedia—Watchdog Journalism

"and then this person has said"
'The Daily' Transcript New York Times
https://www.nytimes.com/2018/09/11/
podcasts/the-daily/woodward-interview-
daily-transcript.html

"On NBC's Today Show"
Bob Woodward's third Trump trilogy book
uses 'secret ..., https://news.yahoo.com/bob-
woodwards-third-trump-trilogy-012200354.
html

"After the information in Fear"
https://www.businessinsider.com/
woodward-white-house-official-said-book-
1000-true-opposite-in-public-2018-9

"John Matlin, my initial source"
John S. Matlin P. 229

"Hill's troll went on to post"
This reference and references to follow
regarding Adam Hill's treatment of Karen
Velie are taken from the Declaration of
Karen Velie and Exhibits 1-47—KAREN VELIE,
an individual, Plaintiff, vs. ADAM HILL, an
individual, COUNTY OF SAN LUIS OBISPO;
and DOES 1 through 50, Defendants, United
States District Court, Central District of
California, Case No.: 2:16CV-07839 DSF (Ex),
September 11, 2014

"Neal Responded"
Velie vs. Hill, Exhibit 29

**"After interviewing one of Petitit's
ex-girlfriends"**
Velie vs. Hill, Exhibit 30

"In early 2016"
Velie vs. Hill, Exhibit 38

"Dan Blackburn"
Case 2:16-cv-07839-DSF-E Document 32
Filed 01/09/17 Page 2 of 12 Page ID #:286

"advertisers to withdraw their support"
Matlin p.270

"A Failed Try to Kill CalCoastNews"
https://calcoasttimes.com/2018/11/14/a-
failed-attempt-to-kill-calcoastnews/

12. THE FIFTH ESTATE

"Congress has reformed its process"
https://www.vox.com/
identities/2019/10/4/20852639/me-too-
movement-sexual-harassment-law-2019

"Honest Fixes"
For more inspiration go to https://www.
pendergastkc.org/article/civic-housekeepers-
women%E2%80%99s-organizations-civic-
reform-and-1940-elections

13. THE SIXTH ESTATE

**"The Iroquois Seventh-Generation
principle"**
https://www.pbs.org/native-america/blogs/
native-voices/how-the-iroquois-great-law-of-
peace-shaped-us-democracy/

14. THE SEVENTH ESTATE ILLUMINATION

sanjoseinside.com
https://www.sanjoseinside.com/news/
election-2020-how-california-reached-
historic-voter-turnout-despite-pandemic-
distrust/

**"Structural Features Make National
Elections in the U.S. Hard To Steal"**
https://www.theguardian.com/us-
news/2020/nov/30/how-us-democracy-
survived-trump-election-lies-misinformation

"Public Administration expert, James Q. Wilson" Banfield, Edward C. and Wilson, James Q. City Politics. p. 344. 1967. Cambridge, Massachusetts. Harvard University Press

"But we are getting by"
Matlin p. 141

"SLO County judge nixes marijuana billboards"
https://calcoastnews.com/2020/11/slo-county-judge-nixes-marijuana-billboards-on-interstate-highways/ by Karen Velie

"Savio said of the Machine"
https://en.wikipedia.org/wiki/Mario_Savio

"What does your responsibility as a voter look like?"
https://abcnews.go.com/Politics/defense-secretaries-letter-warning-trump-signed-days/story?id=75036788

"SLO County remains a safe place to live."
SLO area ranks number one in California for low car theft https://calcoastnews.com/2022/01/slo-area-ranks-number-one-in-california-for-low-car-theft-rates/

"bringing down the machine"
Maurice M. Milligan. Missouri Waltz: The Inside Story of the Pendergast Machine by the Man Who Smashed It. (New York. 1948 Charles Scribner's Sons)

BIBLIOGRAPHY

Altman, Robert's 1996 film, *KANSAS CITY*

Annual Report of the City Comptroller for the Fiscal Year 1910, Beginning April 18, 1910, and Ending April 17, 1911. (1911. Kansas City, Missouri.)

Annual Report of the Director of Finance for the Fiscal Year 1930 (May 1st, 1930 to April 30th, 1931. Fratcher Printing Co.)

Arax, Mark & Wartzman, Rick. *The King of California.* (New York. 2003 Public Affairs.)

Arax, Mark. *In My Father's Name A Family, a Town, a Murder.* (1997. Simon & Schuster.)

Arax, Mark. *The Dreamt Land Chasing Water and Dust Across California.* (2019. Knopf.)

Arax, Mark. *West of the West Dreamers, Believers, Builders, And Killers In The Golden State.* (New York. 2011. Public Affairs.)

Baker, John Henry. *Urban Politics in America.* (New York. 1971. Charles Scribner & Sons.)

Banfield, Edward C. *"Corruption as a Feature of Governmental Organization.." Journal of Law and Economics, Vol. 18, No 3, Economic Analysis of Political Behaviour:* Universities-National Bureau Conference Series Number 29. (Dec., 1975.)

Banfield, Edward C. *A New Theory of Urban Politics.* (New York. 1961. The Free Press.)

Banfield, Edward C. and Wilson, James Q. *City Politics.* (1967. Cambridge, Massachusetts. Harvard University Press.)

Banfield, Edward C. *Political Influence.* (New York. 1961. The Free Press.)

Brewer, William H. *Up and Down California in 1860 to 1864, the journal of William H. Brewer*, Professor of Agriculture in the Sheffield Scientific School from 1864 to 1903. (August 24, 2018. Forgotten Books)

Burke, Edmond. *Select Works of Edmund Burke.* (ed. 1999. Liberty Fund.)

Cline & Emerick, Printers. *Semi-Annual Report of the City Comptroller for the Last Six and One-Half Months of the Fiscal Year*, 1900, Ending April 15, 1901. (Kansas City, Missouri. 1901. Cline Printing. Co.)

Cline Printing Co. *Annual Report of the City Comptroller*, Kansas City, Mo., for the Fiscal Year 1920, Beginning April 20, 1920 and Ending April 18, 1921. (Kansas City, Missouri. 1921. Cline Printing Co.)

Dagger, Thomas G. "Political Patronage in Public Contracting." *The University of Chicago Law Review*, Vol. 51, No. 2. (Spring, 1984.) "Discussion of the City Charter." Proceedings of the Academy of Political Science in the City of New York, Vol. 5, No. 3. The Government of the City of New York. (Apr., 1915.)

Darby, A.L. Director of Finance, Kansas City, Missouri. "Semi-Annual Report of the City Comptroller for the First Five and Two-Fifths Months of the Fiscal Year, 1900, Ending September

30, 1900." (Kansas City, Missouri. 1901.)

Farrow, Ronan. *Catch and Kill: Lies, Spies, and a Conspiracy to Protect Predators.* (2019. New York, New York. Little, Brown and Company, Hatchette Book Group.)

Francke, Terry. *Open Meetings in California* (Carmichael, CA. 2015. Californians Aware.)

Goldstein, Michael. *Blessed Disillusionment: Letting Go of What Cannot Save Us, Turning to What Can* (Berkeley, California. 2021. Michael Goldstein.)

Gregory, Jim. *San Luis Obispo County Outlaws: Desperados, Vigilantes and Bootleggers* (Charleston, South Carolina. 2017. The History Press.)

Hair, William Ivy. *The Kingfish and His Realm: The Life and Times of Huey P. Long.* (Baton Rouge. 1991. Louisiana State University Press.)

Hanzlick, David *Women's Political Activism in the Interwar Period in Kansas City.* Park University, Rockhurst University Citizens Association. https://www.facebook.com/pg/CitizensAssociationKansasCity/about/?ref=page_

Hartmann, Rudolph H. *The Kansas City Investigation: Pendergast's Downfall, 1938-1939.* (Columbia, Missouri. 1999. University of Missouri Press.)

Holzrichter Sr., James H. *A Just Cause: A True Story of Courage, Hope, & the Integrity of the American Dream* (2013.Holzrichter Consultancy)

Johnston, Michael. "Patrons and Clients, Jobs and Machines: A Case Study of the Uses of Patronage." *The American Political Science Review.* Vol. 73, No. 2. (June, 1979)

Johnston, Michael. *Political Corruption and Public Policy in America.* (Monterey, California. 1982. Brooks/Cola Publishing Co.)

Kucinich, Dennis J. *The Division of Light and Power.* (Cleveland, Ohio. 2007. Finney Avenue Books.)

Larsen, Lawrence H. and Hulston, Nancy J. Pendergast. (Columbia, Missouri. 1997. University of Press.)

Levy, Herbert. Henry Morgenthau, Jr. *The Remarkable Life of FDR's Secretary of the Treasury.* (New York, New York. 2010. Skyhorse Publishing.)

Leys, Colin. "What is the Problem about Corruption?" *The Journal of Modern African Studies, Vol. 3, No. 2.* (Aug., 1965.)

Long, Huey. *Every Man a King but No Man Wears a Crown.* (Chicago. 1964. Quadrangle Books.)

Mayerberg, Samuel S. *Chronicles of an American Crusader.* (New York. 1944. Bloch Publishing Co.)

McCullough, David. *Truman.* (1992. New York. Simon & Schuster.)

Milligan, Maurice. *Missouri Waltz.* (1948. New York. Charles Schreibner's Sons)

Missouri Valley Special Collections. Samuel S. Mayerberg Rabbi 1892-1964

Moreira, Peter. *The Jew Who Defeated Hitler Henry Morgenthau Jr., For, and How We Won the War* (Amherst, New York. Prometheus Books)

Morgenthau, Henry III. *Mostly Morgenthaus, A Family History.* (New York. 1991. Ticknor & Fields)

Morgenthau, Henry Sr. *The Murder of a Nation, Ambassador Morgenthau's Story—A Personal Account of the Aermenian Genocide.* (First Published by Doubleday, Page & Company in 1918. This edition published in 2017.)

Reddig, William W. Tom's Town. *Kansas City and the Pendergast Legend.* (Philadelphia.1947. J. B. Lippincott Company.)

Robert, Henry M. III. *Robert's Rules of Order, Newly Revised 11th Edition.* (Sarasota, Florida. 2011. Da Capo Press.)

Signer, Michael. *Cry Havoc: Charlottesville and American Democracy Under Siege.* (New York, New York. 2020. Public Affairs.)

Steffens, Joseph Lincoln. *The Struggle for Self-Government.* (New York. 1968. Johnson Reprint Corporation.)

Steffens, Lincoln. *The Shame of the Cities.* (New York. 1904. Phillips.)

Steffens, Lincoln. *The Autobiography of Lincoln Steffens.* (New York. 1931. Harcourt Brace & Co.)

Stossel, John. *Give Me a Break: How I exposed Hucksters, Cheaters, And Scam Artists and Became the Scourge of the Liberal Media...* (New York. 2004.Harper Perennial.) https://www.amazon.com/Give-Me-Break-Exposed-Hucksters/dp/0060529156

The FBI History Page. *Lawless Years, 1921-1944.* www.fbi/libref/history. The People's Chronology Page.

Wolfinger, Raymond. *The Politics of Progress.* (Englewood Cliffs. 1974. Prentice Hall.)

Woodward, Bob and Costa, Robert. *The Woodward Trilogy Fear, Rage, and Peril.* (New York, New York. 2021. Simon and Schuster.)

Woolner, Ann. *Washed in Gold: The Story Behind the Biggest Money-Laundering Investigation in U.S. History* (New York. 1994. Simon and Schuster.)

Articles and editorials have been quoted from *The San Luis Obispo New Times, CalCoastNews, CalCoastTimes, The Guardian (London), The Kansas City Star, The Missouri Democrat, The Kansas City Call, The Kansas City American (Kansas City, Missouri), The Independence Examiner (Independence, Missouri), The LA Times, The Washington Post, KSBY, WallSt.com, SFGate, Associated Press, CBS News, The New York Times, Vox.com, Business Insider, SanJoseInside.com, ABC News, Santa Maria Times*

ABOUT THE AUTHOR

A former mayor, council member, and planning commissioner, Debbie Peterson advocates for good government.

Prior to her work in government, Peterson helped her mother launch The Brownie Baker, baking handmade family recipe cakes and cookies, and expanded her mother's concept into a successful wholesale bakery, retail cafes, specialist bakeries, and a trucking and distribution outlet in Scotland and London. By 1992 the company had annual sales of $7 million and nearly one hundred employees.

The Scottish Association of Master Bakers named her an honorary Scottish Master Baker and she received the Scottish Young Business Personality of the Year award in 1992. After selling her companies she consulted for development agencies, advising business startups and manufacturers in business planning, marketing, and restructuring. The Scottish Development Agency commissioned her to write Great Scotswomen in Business.

The owner of a residential real estate company, Peterson continues to write, advocate for good government, travel and ski with friends and family.

She studied journalism and radio-TV at California State University, Fresno, before completing an undergraduate degree in communications and public relations at the University of Idaho.

Please visit DebbiePeterson.com to listen to Debbie's podcast Corruption Chronicles, sign up for her online course, read her blog, invite her to speak, for an interview, and learn about other books she has written.

Explore:

FOR MORE ON HOW TO BE A TRUE LOCAL
REPRESENTATIVE, PUBLIC SERVANT, OR CAPABLE
CITIZEN—GO TO DEBBIEPETERSON.COM:

- To invite Debbie to speak to your organization

- To listen to the *Corruption Chronicles* podcasts

- To sign up for *Double Dias,* the online course for elected
  representatives and concerned citizens

- To purchase other books by the author: *City Council 101, How
  to Beat City Hall, 365 Ways of Good Govern-ers*